THE FORMATION OF TURKEY

A History of the Near East
General Editor: Professor P.M. Holt

The Prophet and the Age of the Caliphates: the Islamic Near East from the sixth to the eleventh century
Hugh Kennedy

The Age of the Crusades: the Near East from the eleventh century to 1517
P.M. Holt

The Making of the Modern Near East 1792–1923
M.E. Yapp

The Near East since the First World War: A History to 1995.
Second Edition
M.E. Yapp

Medieval Persia 1040–1797
D.O. Morgan

THE FORMATION OF TURKEY

The Seljukid Sultanate of Rūm: Eleventh to Fourteenth Century

CLAUDE CAHEN

Translated and edited by P.M. Holt

Longman

An imprint of Pearson Education

Harlow, England · London · New York · Reading, Massachusetts · San Francisco
Toronto · Don Mills, Ontario · Sydney · Tokyo · Singapore · Hong Kong · Seoul
Taipei · Cape Town · Madrid · Mexico City · Amsterdam · Munich · Paris · Milan

Pearson Education Limited
Edinburgh Gate
Harlow
Essex CM20 2JE

and Associated Companies throughout the world.

Visit us on the World Wide Web at:
www.pearsoneduc.com

First published 2001

ISBN 0582 41491 1

British Library Cataloguing-in-Publication Data
A catalogue record for this book is available from the British Library

Library of Congress Cataloging-in-Publication Data
Cahen, Claude.
[Turquie pré-ottomane. English]
The formation of Turkey: the Seljukid Sultanate of Rum: eleventh to fourteenth century / Claude Cahen; translated and edited by P.M. Holt.
p. cm. — (A history of the Near East)
Includes bibliographical references and index.
ISBN 0-582-41491-1 (limp)
1. Turkey—History—To 1453. I. Holt, P.M. (Peter Malcolm). II. Title. III. Series.

DR481.C3313 2001
956.1′015—dc21 00-069015

10 9 8 7 6 5 4 3 2 1
05 04 03 02 01

Typeset in 11/13pt Baskerville MT by 35
Produced by Pearson Education Malaysia Sdn Bhd
Printed in Malaysia, VVP

CONTENTS

EDITOR'S NOTE

In essence, although not in title, this volume is the successor to Claude Cahen's *Pre-Ottoman Turkey*, London: Sidgwick and Jackson, 1968, an English translation by J. Jones-Williams from an unpublished draft of the work subsequently developed and published by Cahen as *La Turquie Pré-Ottomane*, Istanbul-Paris: IFEA, 1988. As there are substantial differences between Cahen's earlier draft and his book of 1988, as he indicates in his Preface (below, p. xi), the time seemed opportune for a new and independent English translation. For enabling me to produce this, my thanks are due in the first place to Dr Michel Cahen (son of the late Professor Claude Cahen, who died in 1991, and representative of the family), to the Institut Français d'Études Anatoliennes d'Istanbul (IFEA, holders of the copyright of the French-language version), to Messrs Macmillan (as successors to the legal rights of Sidgwick and Jackson), and to the staff of Pearson Education, notably Heather McCallum and Lorna Sharrock as Senior Editors. My particular gratitude is due to Andrew MacLennan, who as the Editorial Director of the Academic Department of Addison Wesley Longman successfully handled the long and arduous preliminary negotiations.

In my translation I have endeavoured to do justice to Claude Cahen's erudite and magisterial exposition of his subject. At the same time I have taken a number of editorial decisions with the intention of making his work more accessible to a wider readership. A few very specialized passages have been omitted, as have names of persons and places which do not play a significant part in the narrative. From Cahen's footnotes, which are mainly bibliographical, some are selected which supplement the text, and a few passages of the text have been converted into footnotes. I have added the appendices, while for Cahen's very detailed and comprehensive bibliography I have substituted a briefer bibliographical guide to generally accessible works. Cahen's own primary sources are given in its first section.

To attempt in the present work a uniform system of transliteration of Turkish, Persian and Arabic would probably be unhelpful to readers. Since modern Turkish has an established orthography, I have normally adopted this system for names of places, persons and tribal groups within roughly the bounds of the Republic of Turkey, corresponding approximately to

Seljukid Rūm. Purely Arabic and Persian names and terms are however transliterated following the system of *The Encyclopaedia of Islam*, but with *j* for *jīm,* and *q* for *qāf.* Certain anomalies will appear; notably, I have used the forms Mehmed and Süleyman in Turkish names instead of the Arabic original forms, Muḥammad and Sulaymān. For Byzantine names, I have normally followed the usages in *The Cambridge Medieval History*, Vol. IV, *The Byzantine Empire*; and for Mongol names (even where these are obviously Turkish), the forms in *The Cambridge History of Iran*, Vol. 5, *The Saljuq and Mongol Periods*. Where there are established conventional forms of personal and place names, these have usually been preferred. There is a special problem regarding place names as a result of the gradual transformation of Greek-speaking Byzantine Anatolia into Turkish-speaking Seljukid Rūm. Generally I have retained the Byzantine names of places until they were conquered by the Turks, while however showing both the Byzantine and Turkish names initially.

Throughout his book, Cahen almost invariably uses the AD/CE system of dating, although in a few instances he gives the Muslim *Hijrī* (AH) date. In this I have followed him, making here (as in a few other details) some silent corrections.

P.M. Holt
Kirtlington
April 2000

NAMES AND DATES

A full traditional Arabic name consists of four elements:

1. The personal name (Arabic, *ism*), e.g. Aḥmad.
2. The formal name (*kunya*), e.g. Abu'l-Qāsim, meaning 'Father of al-Qāsim'.
3. The patronymic (*nasab*), e.g. ibn 'Abdallāhi (abbreviated b. 'Abdallāhi), meaning 'son of 'Abdallāhi'.
4. The group-name (*nisba*) indicating the tribal, ethnic, religious or other group to which the individual belonged, e.g. al-Shāmī, meaning 'the Syrian'.

This was not usually applied to Turkish or Persian names. Cahen normally identifies individuals by their personal or group names, and I have usually followed his practice. See also the note prefixed to the List of the sultans (p. 277).

Cahen usually gives dates according to the Western solar calendar (AD). Where he uses the Islamic lunar calendar (AH=Anno Hegirae), I have supplied the Western equivalents.

AUTHOR'S PREFACE

In 1968 I published a book, *Pre-Ottoman Turkey*, requested by the English publishers, Sidgwick and Jackson of London, while reserving my right to give a more thorough and annotated French version. This existed in a certain way, at least for the chapters dealing with events, in a draft of 1949 which I used in 1968, but it was a little too juvenile; and detailed as were all the notes made for the other chapters, and also very useful in 1968, they yet did not completely correspond to the project I had conceived of the thorough French version. Unfortunately, as I had allowed myself to be carried into entirely different subjects of research, my work on pre-Ottoman Turkey has been considerably delayed, so that in the meantime it has naturally been further complicated by the appearance of a certain number of new works. At my age I think that it is better to give straightforwardly what I am now capable of, rather than to promise a 'definitive' volume which might never appear. What I am now publishing does not entirely correspond to the English version of 1968. I have practically almost suppressed the introduction relating to the Turks of Central Asia and the Great Seljuks, even though it means reintroducing some passages in the account of the Turks of Asia Minor which are needful for the understanding of their history. On the other hand, I have annotated, checked and developed the rest, particularly the parts on social and institutional history, and I have of course brought the bibliography up to date. The chapters concerning artistic life will probably be relegated to an appended fascicule, which will have as contributors one or two younger colleagues more capable than myself in this field. I do not know if I shall be granted time to produce the long-prepared but still unfinished fascicule on the fourteenth century. As to what I offer, I should say that I feel less certain than in 1968. It may serve as a basis for discussion, but I hope that it will not be taken for anything more.

The Turks have played a considerable part in the history of the Middle Ages and modern times. However, the developments of their history have, in the most recent period, set them in confrontation with most of the peoples of Europe, and indeed the other Muslim peoples, both Arabs and Iranians. In consequence Western historians have mostly approached Turkish history with hostile prejudices, and have tended to minimize or denigrate all that the Turks have done. In a quite understandable reaction as the modern Turkish nation-state came into being, Turkish historians have often exaggerated the positive aspects of this history. Whatever our sentiments in other respects, objectivity requires us to scrap these prejudices on both sides, and to attempt to accomplish our task as historians in a rigorously scientific spirit and with the fullest possible documentation.

In this respect a great step forward was taken in the middle of this century, when the Ottoman archives, hardly less rich than the European archives, became available to scholars. They become extensive only from the sixteenth century, but for all that they are not negligible for the last centuries of our Middle Ages. Whatever progress has latterly been made in other countries, the Turks are now particularly well placed for us – on condition however that those who have not grown up with the languages in which the documents and contemporary works are written must needs learn them. It is somewhat astonishing to see that works long held to be authoritative have been written by scholars with no idea of Turkish.

It is fashionable today to despise the history of events. Neither Oriental nor Western history can return to it in the spirit of the past. Yet nevertheless it remains the fact that the different aspects of history, whether Oriental or Western, cannot be rent asunder; and however it may be, we are obliged to start from the sources as they are, and not as we might wish them to be. Through them we should try to see what they do not tell us explicitly, but it is not for us to cast them aside. I hope the reader will see how I have tried to present my findings in a spirit of interconnection.

When Turks are mentioned in history, it usually means the Ottoman Empire because of the significant part it has played in the past of the Muslim peoples and of Christian south-eastern Europe, so much that the name of Turks is often given to peoples who are only partly such, while little thought is given to those Turks who were not Ottomans. Those of Central Asia and eastern Europe are hardly known except to specialists, while those who preceded the Ottomans in western Asia and the Mediterranean are only known to the extent that they were involved with the Iranians, the Byzantines and the Crusaders. Very often Ottomanists begin their research on the origins of the Ottoman dynasty, modest as they were, as if from that moment they played an essential part in the world around them, and many seem to believe that there were no Turks of greater importance in their vicinity. Some scholars have indeed begun to react to this, but very few have emphasized that the other Turks had their originality, and that they were not necessarily inclined to be incorporated in the Ottoman Empire, even if this did occur in the end. The existence of modern Turkey calls attention to the most Turkish part of the territories concerned in this period, but authors have not always placed our Turks of Asia Minor in the world around them with sufficient precision and the necessary links and breaks. To aid in this work is the aim of the present book, which needless to say does not form its conclusion.

The territory studied corresponds broadly to that of Byzantine Anatolia, thus excluding the regions of Upper Mesopotamia which were subsequently integrated into Turkish territory but which formed for centuries part of the Arab world, and which even under Turkish domination continued to live in the traditions of those countries and in other principalities than those of Asia Minor.

Before beginning this account, it is my pleasant duty to thank all who have helped me, not forgetting those mentioned in the English edition, several of whom are now deceased. The French version has been made possible through the joint agreement of the Institut Français d'Études Anatoliennes d'Istanbul and its Director, my friend Jean-Louis Bacqué-Grammont. Finally, the appearance of this work could not have been brought about without the devotion and competence of Thérèse Naud.

PUBLISHER'S ACKNOWLEDGEMENTS

We are grateful to the following for permission to reproduce copyright material:

Map from C.F. Beckingham (ed.), *Atlas of the Arab World and the Middle East*, Macmillan, 1960.

Whilst every effort has been made to trace the owners of copyright material, in a few cases this has proved impossible and we take this opportunity to offer our apologies to any copyright holders whose rights we may have unwittingly infringed.

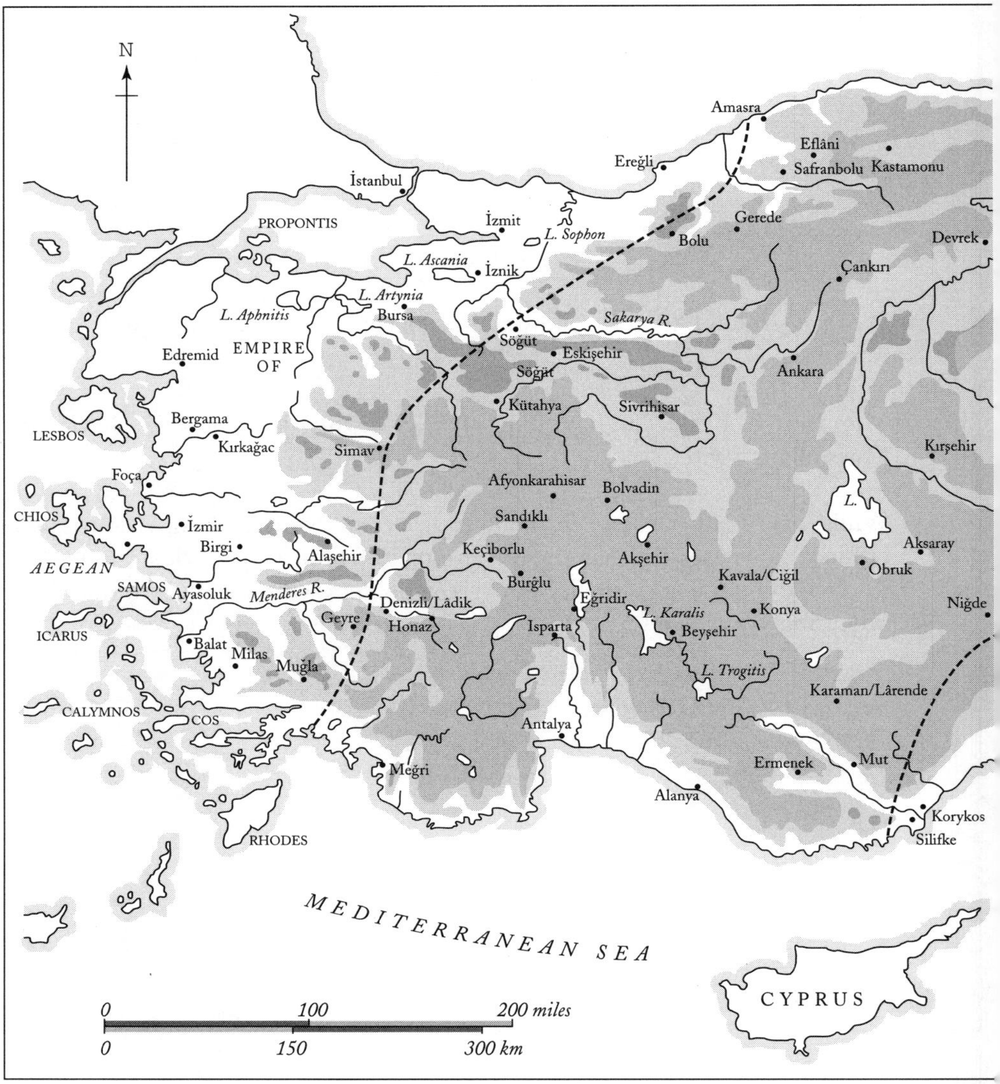

The Seljukid Sultanate of Rūm.

Source: Adapted from C.F. Beckingham (ed.), *Atlas of the Arab World and the Middle East*, Macmillan, 1960.

BLACK SEA
Sinop
Bafra
Kızılırmak R.
Samsun
Yeşilırmak
Ünye
Fatsa
Trabzon
EMPIRE OF TREBIZOND
Giresun
Kars
Amasya
Niksar
Gümüşhane
Kuğuniya/Şebinkarahisar
Bayburt
Zile
Tokat
Kösedağ (1243)
Erzurum
Sivas
Erzincan
Kemah
Malazgirt
(1071)
Divriği
Ahlat
Pınarbaşı
Kayseri
Khartpert
Yenişehir
Develikarahisar
Yeşilhisar
Euphrates R.
Malatya
Ergani
Mayyāfāriqīn
Sarus R.
Elbistan
Kâhta
Tigris R.
Adiyaman
Suwayda
Āmid
Sis
Keysun
KINGDOM OF
Maraş
Besni
Samsat
Seyhan R.
Viranşehir
Mardin
Misis
Birecik
Nuseybin
Tarsus
Toprakkale
Sarūj
Āyās
(Yumurtalik)
İskenderun
Ayyubid
Orontes
Tilbaşar
Antioch
R. Orontes
0–500 metres
500–1000 metres
over 1000 metres

INTRODUCTION

Summary history of the Turks before Turkey

The Turks who have given their name to present-day Turkey are one branch of a group of peoples who, under this name or others, have spread extensively over a large part of central and western Asia, as well as eastern Europe. Those who are to be studied here originated from the Oghuz complex, nomadic pastoralists and horsemen, who in the tenth century CE were occupying the steppes extending from the western slopes of the Altai to the lower Volga south of the Siberian forests. In contrast to some of their kinsmen further east or further west, who had been in contact with Romano-Byzantine and Chinese civilization respectively, the Oghuz remained relatively apart from these, but for two or three centuries they had been in touch to the south with soldiers, merchants or men of religion coming from the world of Islam. Towards the end of the tenth century the principal groups of these Oghuz underwent at least superficial conversion to Islam. Known henceforward as Turcomans, they extended by degrees to the borders of Iran, which was under the Samanids, then the Ghaznavids. In 1040 under the leadership of the Seljukids, they inflicted on the Ghaznavids the decisive defeat of Dandānqān, which at a stroke opened up all the steppes of the Iranian plateau to the victors. In Iran religious conflicts had been raging for several generations between Sunnī and Shī'ī Muslims, and some Sunnī aristocratic groups complained of the laxity of the regime under which they were living. It was probably under the influence of religious scholars from these circles that the Seljukids, if not all the Turks, embraced Islam. No doubt these circles thought that it was to their interest to reach an understanding with the newcomers, and this might also help them to escape pillage. It is also certain that the nomadic Turkish horsemen had throughout their history shown themselves superior to the regular armies opposing them. Arriving at the gates of Iraq, the Turks were in a country which had not less been torn by religious conflicts. The Sunnīs around the Caliphate 'protected' by the Shī'ī Buyids thought of calling in the Turks, who were also Sunnīs. In 1055 the Seljukid chief, Ṭughril Beg, entered Baghdad without striking a blow. There he officially received the title of 'sultan', and was commissioned to regain Arab western Asia and beyond it Egypt, where the Ismā'īlī Fatimid caliph was reigning.

Such at least was the caliphal policy, and such was that of Ṭughril Beg, inasmuch as he wished to appear the redresser of the traditions of orthodox Islam, and thus the legitimate holder of authority over all Muslims. There were however other elements in his position which he wished to have, or were appropriate to it. Among the old Muslims was that of the Holy War (*jihād*) against the Christian Empire of Byzantium. In the eleventh century it had almost entirely faded, but it was not forgotten. To reawaken it would increase the new sultan's prestige, especially among the peoples of the Syro-Mesopotamian borders. This attitude was connected in a way with the traditions of the forays of the islamized Turks of Central Asia as heirs of the Muslim *ghāzīs* against Turks when they were heathen – even if this heritage was more explicitly expressed in the language of the religious intellectuals than in the Turcoman masses. They in any case had no difficulty in turning their forays to another front, and Ṭughril himself would not find this spirit completely alien. However it may be, he well knew that his strength for any policy whatsoever lay in his Turcomans. They did not easily adapt to fighting in countries that were too hot for their animals, and where it was forbidden to pillage Muslims, or to take their families with them. They massed in Ādharbāyjān, on the traditional route of invasions which crossed Armenia to end up in Asia Minor. They quickily discovered that they could penetrate beyond the Armeno-Byzantine frontier, and take booty before the heavy troops of the fortresses could intercept them. Sometimes however Ṭughril could only let them be, but this presented him with the danger that these bands might become increasingly habituated to autonomy, and indeed to accepting fugitive rebels in opposition to him. Ṭughril however had no intention of annexing any territory of the eternal Empire of Rūm; but he had to show himself beside his Turcomans, and anyhow he could go on campaign to reannex former Muslim territory recently conquered by the Byzantines. Hence the diversity of the attacks on Armenia and beyond, on the hinterland of Trebizond and the upper courses of the two Euphrates rivers. Hence finally a campaign by Ṭughril himself against Manzikert (Malazgirt), in which, it must be said, he did not show much persistence. The internal discords of Byzantium progressively opened the way to new bands of Turcomans, on whom the parties called against their rivals.

Ṭughril died in 1063. His successor, his nephew Alp Arslan, accentuated the Turcoman orientation of his policy to confirm his authority, by going personally on campaign against the Armenian metropolis of Ani and the marches of Georgia, attacked again four years later. During this time deep westward thrusts continued, although the Byzantine government, lacking comprehension, always endeavoured to ward them off by diplomacy. Bands led by officially recognized chiefs preferred to move along the Syro-Mesopotamian frontier of the Byzantine Empire, but others penetrated right into Greek territory, devastated Cappadocia and even reached Amorium on the Anatolian plateau before joining with other Turks, who had meanwhile been engaged by the Arab ruler of Aleppo.

However, at Constantinople the civilian party, which had held power for some twenty years, was forced to give place to the general Romanus Diogenes (the Emperor Romanus IV), who decided to organize a vigorous military reaction to get rid of the invader. The affair was complicated by the actual state of the regions to be crossed, and the composite character of an army particularly of mercenaries. It appears however to have been facilitated for him by the fact that Alp Arslan, following the caliph's instructions, turned at the same time towards Syria, probably intending to go on to Egypt. He was however warned in time to regroup especially his light troops, to confront the army of Romanus Diogenes in eastern Anatolia. They met at Manzikert in August 1071, and a crushing defeat for Byzantium ensued. For the first time in history a Byzantine emperor was made prisoner by a Muslim army.

PART ONE

General History of Turkey before the Mongols

CHAPTER ONE

Settlement of the Turks in Asia Minor to 1107

The battle of Manzikert may be regarded as the act which gave birth to Turkey. Not that Alp Arslan wished to conquer Byzantine Asia Minor: he set his august captive free for a ransom, a promise of alliance and some rectification of the frontiers. He did not think it possible to bring the Empire of Rūm to an end, and no doubt it was not an unfavourable prospect that the Greeks, left free to fight the Turcomans on their territory, would thereby limit the danger that they presented to himself. Nevertheless the conquest of Anatolia ensued. No administrative or military structure was in a condition to oppose it, even if the Turcomans themselves had no precise political aim at that time. Nothing obliged them to return their accumulated booty to the East. The Byzantines themselves caused them to penetrate further than they would have wished, and opened places to them that they might not have taken on account of their partisan struggles. Moreover the greater part of the population in the eastern half of Anatolia was not Greek but Armenian or Monophysite, little attached to the Byzantine Empire, and sometimes, in view of the weakness of the Christian armies, preferring to submit to the invader for better or worse.

The disorganization of Byzantine Anatolia, and the yet primitive organization of the Turcomans, explain the incapacity of the chroniclers of this period to report even the major facts. Those of the year 1073, of which something is known, give a good idea of it. In this year Roussel of Bailleul, the leader of the Norman mercenaries, sent to Caesarea (Kayseri) with Isaac Comnenus, abandoned his chief, who was then captured by the Turks, while his brother, Alexius, had great difficulty in bringing the army back west of Ancyra (Ankara). The Emperor Michael VII Ducas sent his uncle John Ducas against Roussel, who took him and proclaimed him emperor as a rival to Michael. John then called upon the Turkish band of Artuk. Near to Nicomedia (İzmit) Roussel and John Ducas were captured, but Roussel was liberated by Artuk (against the wishes of Byzantium), and withdrew to the east. Alexius Comnenus paid another Turkish chief to deliver Roussel to him at Amasea (Amasya). This did not signify that the way to the west was open, for in order to escape Alexius had with great difficulty to take ship at Heraclea (Ereğli). At the same time the presence of the Turks was noted near Miletus (Balat) and Trebizond (Trabzon).

Little is known of what happened in these regions in the five or six following years. It can be certain only that the Turkish bands remained there, sometimes mixed with Norman or Armenian contingents left from the Byzantine army but on terms with the Turks. On the other hand, it is in this period that the sons of Kutlumuş appeared on the southern flank of Anatolia. One of them was to be the ancestor of the entire Seljukid lineage of Rūm. Their father, Kutlumuş, had been the chief of a branch of the Seljukids, and often in revolt against his cousins, the Great Seljukids, by whom he had been put to death. What had happened to his four sons during Alp Arslan's sultanate is unknown, but a semi-legendary tradition, which seems to be confirmed by subsequent events, shows them in a condition approaching captivity on the middle Euphrates. When Alp Arslan died, they succeeded in escaping, unless indeed the young new ruler, Malik-Shāh, facilitated their escape in order to make peace with them. However this may be, a number of Turcomans now gathered around them so that they became a significant factor in regional politics. In 1075 the Turcoman Atsız, the master of Palestine in conflict with Egypt, had to deal with an alliance of a rival at Acre and the troops of two of the sons of Kutlumuş, on whom he had called for aid. Atsız defeated them and, proclaiming his loyalty to Malik-Shāh, he sent them to him as prisoners. The other two sons, who had stayed behind, withdrew to southern Anatolia, where their standing as Seljukids no doubt helped them to reconstitute an important, quasi-official force; but their attitude in 1075 and subsequent years proves that they were still adversaries of the Great Seljuks.

Once again Byzantine quarrels contributed to their fortune. In 1078 the general Nicephorus Botaneiates, in revolt against the Emperor Michael VII, denuded Asia Minor of its remaining Byzantine troops. Through the Comneni family he won for his cause Erisğen (alias Chrysosculos), a relative of Malik-Shāh, who had fled to Constantinople and become a Byzantine. Michael appealed to the sons of Kutlumuş against Nicephorus, who escaped them, and won them over through Erisğen's mediation. They declared fealty to him as their sovereign, so becoming full-blooded Byzantines. In fact they remained independent, with the tiresome circumstance for the Byzantines that they held all the territory around Nicaea (İznik) and the Asian shore of the Bosphorus. They were to stay, for their Emperor

Nicephorus III had to struggle against a pretender in Europe, Bryennius. Nicephorus obtained help to fight him from the sons of Kutlumuş, whom of course he had to pay. Shortly afterwards Nicephorus Melissenus, supported almost solely by the Turks, revolted in Asia and won over the sons of Kutlumuş in his turn. Their party was of little importance to them, since profit was to be made from either side. Melissenus opened to them the towns which they had been unable to occupy, and these became their bases of operations henceforth. The arrival of another pretender, Alexius Comnenus, changed nothing for the moment, for he had to deal with a Norman attack in Europe, against which he called the same Turks to aid.

Naturally nothing of all this was by Malik-Shāh's instructions. He had no interest in seeing his dangerous cousins obtaining power of any kind. On the contrary, he sent to Constantinople to demand the capture and return of the two surviving sons of Kutlumuş, Manṣūr and Süleyman – a demand backed by an army under the command of his general, Bursuq (Porsuk), who killed Manṣūr but failed against Süleyman and his men. About this time the usage appeared, entirely unofficially, of styling Süleyman 'sultan'. In brief, the Greeks had created a Turkish sultan within the Byzantine Empire.

Süleyman must nevertheless have realized that to keep his new-found power he was too much at risk in the west, and must maintain his relations with the Turcomans of eastern Anatolia. So he turned back to the east, there also aided by his more or less clear new position as deputy for the Byzantines. Alexius Comnenus, since 1081 the Emperor Alexius I, was not unhappy to encourage him in order to keep him at a distance, and to dispose of the Armenian principality in the Taurus region and northern Syria held by Philaretus, who had aided his rivals. Süleyman passed into Cilicia, then took Antioch (Antakya) in December 1094. Here two significant facts occur: for the appointment of a *qāḍī* in Cilicia, he turned to the ruler of Tripoli, a Shīʿī hostile to the Great Seljuks; and in Antioch he favoured the native Christians against the unpopular Byzantine Church. Unfortunately for him, he could not avoid involvement in the quarrels of Syria, where he met his death in 1086. Malik-Shāh had no difficulty in occupying almost the whole of Syria–Palestine.

So after a long period of apparent lack of interest, Malik-Shāh was able to concern himself with Asia Minor, where Süleyman's ever-hostile power could only have given him offence. When Süleyman had moved away from western Anatolia, he left lieutenants there such as Abu'l-Qāsim on the Straits and Hasan Buldacı in the central Taurus and Cappadocia. Playing off one of these Turks against the other, Alexius Comnenus tried to control their activities on the Straits and the Aegean coast.[1] Without hazarding himself in Asia Minor Malik-Shāh applied himself to the establishment of a solid base extending from Ādharbāyjān to the middle Euphrates for the incursions of his lieutenants, *Sarhang*-Savtekin, then Buzan and others. About 1090 he sent an army, again commanded by Bursuq, preceded by an ambassador who was commissioned to offer to Alexius the withdrawal of the Turks from all the coastal regions in return for an alliance. Alexius was mistrustful, and perhaps he did not clearly distinguish the Turks dependent on Malik-Shāh from the others. He won over the ambassador, whom he created a Byzantine *dux*, an equivocal position which enabled him to regain Sinope (Sinop) in the sultan's name. But when Bursuq arrived, Alexius considered him a more dangerous invader than Abu'l-Q̧āsim, whose demand for reconciliation he accepted. He received him at Constantinople, and sent him to Nicaea against Bursuq, who had to withdraw.

Malik-Shāh did not however give up hope of bringing about the submission of the Turks of Asia Minor with the help of Alexius, the sole means of obtaining it at that distance. He did not covet any Byzantine territory, but he considered himself the chief of all the Turks wherever they were. In 1092 he sent Buzan to Anatolia with the twofold mission of reducing Abu'l-Q̧āsim, and of offering Alexius an alliance sealed by the marriage of a son of the sultan to a daughter of the emperor: Byzantium would recover all the territories left to Süleyman, and the military help he might need. Abu'l-Q̧āsim decided to go and make his peace with Malik-Shāh, but was taken on the way and strangled. Alexius could not as a Christian accept the marriage proposal, but he responded politely to the sultan by sending an embassy in return. Unfortunately Malik-Shāh had died before it reached him, and the sultan's army left Anatolia. In fact the situation in the country hardly changed. Hasan Buldacı inherited İznik, Süleyman's young son, Kılıc Arslan, lately captured at Antioch, escaped, and gathered around himself the Turks who had once been his father's subjects. While he himself seemed to be occupied above all with securing his links with the east, his lieutenants such as particularly Çaka, with the more or less freely rendered help of the native sailors, occupied the great ports and the Aegean isles – Clazomenae, Phocaea (Eskifoca), Smyrna (İzmir), Chios, Mitylene and Samos. Alexius succeeded in retaking these places from him, but not in curtailing his piratical activities in the Dardanelles, which were all the more redoubtable in that they enabled Çaka to enter into relations with the Petcheneg Turks of Europe, who encircled Constantinople. Alexius then resorted to trickery: he made peace with Kılıc Arslan, and led him to fear the ambitions of Buldacı, who had become his father-in-law. Kılıc Arslan invited Buldacı to a banquet where he was killed, without on the whole any great change ensuing. If it had not been for the imminent arrival of the crusaders, the Turks might perhaps have established principalities along the coasts similar to those which came into existence in the fourteenth century;

the attachment which was shown to the retention of Nicaea also shows the role which the Turks intended to play in Byzantine affairs. At the same time, the quarrels which faced Malik-Shāh's successors made risky their intervention in Asia Minor.

It was probably in the same period that on the fringes of the possessions of the Seljukids of Iran, zones commanded briefly by the Seljukid Yāqūtī, then by his son Ismā'īl, other principalities took shape; perhaps not just at this point those of the Saltukids of Erzurum or the Menguçekids of Erzincan (although family legend made them present at the battle of Manzikert), but certainly the principality of Danişmend.

It is not known when or how the principality of Danişmend began to be formed. There is an explicit reference to the family only *c.* 1095 on the eve of the First Crusade, the narrators of which tell of a certain Danişmend. The name, Persian by etymology (*dānishmand,* wise, learned), conjures up a kind of social and religious chief, and in spite of later legends it is difficult to believe that a chief of Turcomans could be other then a Turcoman himself. But there is no clear knowledge of the family's first activities. It is likely that Danişmend, properly named Tailu, is the one who must have died in 1104. His successor is sometimes called Gümüştekin, a Turkish name, or Muḥammad, an Arab name, or Amīr Gazi, which evokes his martial qualities. They were established in central Asia Minor from Sivas (Gk. Sebastea) to Cappadocia, perhaps at Ankara; for even if the Turcomans were but little sedentarized as yet, they nevertheless tended to group themselves regionally under one or two chiefs. Danişmendid opposition to Kılıc Arslan had less to do with the nature of their troops, at this time Turcomans on both sides, than with the fact that Kılıc Arslan based his pretensions, which were moreover often recognized, upon his being a Seljukid. In spite of his hostility to the other Seljukids, this gave him the idea of creating for himself a political structure of the Irano-Turkish type like that of the sultanate of his kinsmen. Their relative opposition did not prevent marriage-links between the Danişmendids and the Seljukids of Rūm.[2] Apart from the Seljukid ruler, Danişmend was the only great Turkish chief known to the chroniclers of the Crusades, who call Kılıc Arslan 'Soliman' like his father, although this double name is unknown in the Arabic sources.

The central Taurus region was where the men of Kılıc Arslan and Danişmend lived side by side, freely interpenetrating without the possibility of the tracing of a frontier between them. Both rulers aspired to the possession of Malatya (Gk. Melitene), the principal route-centre and strategic keypoint of eastern Anatolia on the way to Upper Mesopotamia. Kılıc Arslan directed his activity in this direction, for now he could attach only a reduced importance to the Straits and the Aegean region, and he did not seek to become involved with Alexius Comnenus; hence the way he held to south-west Anatolia. Certainly he left wife, children and treasure at Nicaea, but as a secure base as much as a capital. In these conditions he heard of the arrival of the crusaders, to whom however he had at first no reason to attach more importance than to the Norman contingents with whom the Turks had long been acquainted in the country, sometimes as enemies, sometimes as accomplices. It is well known how the impatience of Peter the Hermit's men resulted in their massacre by the Turks of Nicaea in 1096, an event which contributed to their idea that the crusade was a trivial affair. The crusade proper was thus able to cross the Bosphorus and reach Nicaea without Kılıc Arslan receiving notice in time to save the town or his family, which was however well treated by the Byzantines, who knew that they might need them in the future as in the past. Kılıc Arslan then tried to intercept the crusaders on their entry upon the Anatolian plateau near Dorylaeum (Eskişehir), having obtained help from Danişmend. It was a very hard-fought battle, but in the end Kılıc Arslan was beaten, and gave up the defence of western Anatolia. The Turks were after all still semi-nomads, and to be driven back or dispersed did not signify their destruction, any more than the Franks' march across the plateau signified their wish to occupy the country. Even the Greeks in the rear could only regain possession of the western valleys. The skirmishes which took place when the Franks reached the Taurus, where the Turks were trying to destroy some Armenian lordships, did not modify the course of events. The crusaders made for Edessa and Antioch, which they were to conquer. These cities did indeed belong to Turks, but to dependants of Malik-Shāh's heirs; the Turks of Anatolia made no attempt to help them.

Danişmend had been much less affected than Kılıc Arslan by the passage of the crusaders, and he remained in a position to renew the attack on Malatya, where perhaps for a moment under the very vague suzerainty of Süleyman or Kılıc Arslan, the Armenian Byzantine governor, Gabriel, had maintained himself in power, or been reinstalled. He appealed for help to one of the chief crusaders, Bohemond, who had become prince of Antioch, and had ventured in the direction of Maraş (Ar. Marʿash) to reduce some local Armenian lords, as Danişmend was doing a little further north. Bohemond imprudently took the road to Malatya, and was surprised by a contingent of Danişmend's Turcomans, who sent him off to captivity in Niksar (Neocaesarea), while two Armenian bishops were killed. Malatya was however saved by reinforcements from Baldwin of Edessa, but was finally to yield to Danişmend in 1102.

In the meantime Danişmend had been recalled to the west by the approach of a new crusade, which had chosen this time to penetrate into the heart of Anatolia by the northern route. There the crusaders were annihilated. Other crusaders had however taken the route of the crusaders of

1097, but Kılıc Arslan, taught by experience, laid the country waste before them without really confronting them. They also in the end were decimated near Ereğli.

Danişmend however was not unaware that Bohemond had long been the enemy of Alexius Comnenus, and that he had secured possession of Antioch in violation of the promise he had made to the emperor. Henceforward Alexius regarded the struggle against Bohemond as more important than the struggle against the Turks, who held only the interior of the country without having yet organized a real power there. He made an offer to pay Bohemond's ransom if he would hand him over. Kılıc Arslan, who no doubt regarded Danişmend as his subordinate, claimed a part of the ransom. Bohemond was then able to persuade Danişmend to prefer the ransom offered by Baldwin of Edessa, and an alliance with the Franks against Kılıc Arslan. Kılıc Arslan had drawn closer to Alexius Comnenus, whom he had allowed to destroy the last Turkish nest on the Aegean, held by Tangripermes (Tanrıvermiş) at Smyrna and Ayasoluk (now Selçuk) away from the crusaders. Moreover he promised him help against any enemy who might arise. Bohemond returned to Europe to organize an expedition against the Byzantines, and in fact landed in Epirus in 1107; Kılıc Arslan sent Alexius the promised Turkish contingent.

In 1104 Danişmend died. There were difficulties over the succession, and in 1106 Kılıc Arslan occupied Malatya. It was then that he was tempted by appeals from Upper Mesopotamia, where there had been a revolt of Sultan Muḥammad's amirs. The proximity of Kılıc Arslan, whom they knew to be the hereditary enemy of the Great Seljuks, seemed to them an opportunity to be seized. Kılıc Arslan was evidently aware of the old rivalry between the two branches of the family. Unlike the Turcomans established in Asia Minor, he had no doubt not given up the idea of maintaining contact with the bases of his people in Iran, and of intervening in the quarrels of his kinsmen. He advanced to Mosul. Muḥammad had however rallied his partisans, while Kılıc Arslan was weakened by the absence of the contingent sent to Alexius Comnenus. A battle took place on the Khābūr, a tributary on the left bank of the Euphrates. Kılıc Arslan was killed, and his son, Shāhānshāh, made prisoner (June 1107).

This date marks a turning-point in the history of Asia Minor, and we must stop for a moment to see the balance-sheet of this first phase.

One point is that we have reached the end of the first wave of the peopling of Asia Minor by Turks. Apart from small exceptions, there will be no more until the Mongol invasion in the thirteenth century. The Turcomans installed in Anatolia were henceforward to some extent divided among three or four powers, above all the Seljukids and the Danişmendids, but without there being very precisely organized links between them and their rulers. Although their pasture-grounds were limited, the great majority of them were semi-nomadic pastoralists and, except for some garrisons in towns of importance to their rulers, they were still predominantly people of the plains. Agriculture was in the hands of the indigenous inhabitants, but had suffered greatly as a result of the depredations of the invaders and the flight of a great number of the peasants, especially from western Anatolia, whence at least those in the easiest circumstances could reach Byzantine territory. Once the time of disorder was past, attempts were made to hold or bring back the peasants, but this process was only just beginning. The Turcomans were attracted to the frontier-zones, which they could pillage. Scholars gave this activity a colour of Holy War by calling them *ghāzīs* (T. sing. *gazi*), but they designated themselves in these zones as men of the frontier (T. *uc*), corresponding to the Greek *akritai*. It is obviously impossible to suggest a figure for the number of the immigrants, and consequently the proportion of the new Turkish population; it is equally impossible to determine the extent of the damage or the activity continuing in the country at this time. It must only be said that the trend in the Byzantine Empire towards great estates, exploited for the breeding of cattle, must somewhat have facilitated the establishment of the newcomers. Also one must consider eastern Asia as having on the whole been less disturbed. The Armenians continued to be numerous there, and after the first phase seem to have come tolerably to terms with the new masters. At a later stage the documentation will allow a somewhat more precise treatment.

A fundamental distinction must be made between these Turks of Asia Minor and those further to the south, who occupied the traditional Arab territories. Vague as the frontier was, it corresponded approximately to that of the Byzantine Empire previously and that of modern Turkey. Whatever the indigenous elements in Asia Minor to the north, there was a complete peopling by Turks; in the south, a military occupation without a true peopling.[3] Upper Mesopotamia was an intermediate zone, occupied by Turcomans subject for the most part to the Artukid dynasty; but these had been faithful servants of the Great Seljuks, and essentially left in being the structures of a province which was among the richest of the traditional Arab Muslim world. The Turks of the north, by contrast, knew that they were in the territory of Rūm, the Roman Byzantine Empire, even if that was less and less to signify dependence. The word *Rūm*, after having signified the Byzantine Christians or Christian foreigners in general, was soon to designate the land of the Turks of Asia Minor.

CHAPTER TWO

Turkish activity in the West under Shāhānshāh

The events following the death of Kılıc Arslan set in a clear light the various factors which have been specified. It brought about a temporary weakening of the dynasty, on the one hand enabling the Turcomans to resume their raids on the frontiers, and on the other enabling Sultan Muḥammad to make the last intervention in Asia Minor by a Seljukid of Iran. These two phenomena were able exactly then to combine for a moment because Muḥammad was organizing a huge enterprise against the Christians of Syria, which, launched in the name of the Holy War, could be extended to the struggle against the Byzantines. At the same time it furnished the best opportunity to both sides of reducing the ungovernable chiefs to obedience.

There were Turcoman raids at the end of 1107 and in 1108 against the Armenians of Cilicia, of Pertous near Maraş and Ḥiṣn Manṣūr (T. Adiyaman), where the Armenian lord of Upper Syria, Kogh Vasil, captured a 'Sultan of Armenia', who was no doubt 'Alī, the Saltukid of Erzurum. There were more raids in 1109–10, this time against the western Byzantines at Lampe (south of the Hellespont), Smyrna, Pergamum (Bergama) and Kelbianos. Sent out by Ḥasan of Cappadocia, perhaps the regent, who himself attacked Philadelphia (Alaşehir), these were isolated bands, which were destroyed or repulsed by the Byzantine general Philokales.

Sultan Muḥammad's intervention was itself facilitated by the circumstances of the succession to Kılıc Arslan. At Malatya power was exercised by the mother of his young son, Toğrıl Arslan. She married several chiefs in succession, who were promoted to be the child's *atabegs*, and finally in 1113 the Artukid Balak, who was in the course of conquering Khanzīt, i.e. the Armenian territory lying in the great bend of the Euphrates, north-northwest of Malatya. She had previously sent his predecessor to Muḥammad accused of having intrigued with enemies, and had despatched his Turks together with those from Muḥammad on expeditions against the Armenians of the Jahān (a region east of Maraş, west of the Euphrates and north of Edessa) and Upper Cilicia.

As for the principal Seljukid domain around Konya: since Kılıc Arslan's eldest son had died in battle against Gümüştekin the Danişmendid, the heir was deemed to be the second son, Shāhānshāh alias Malik-Shāh, who however had been made prisoner in the Mesopotamian disaster, and power was exercised by one of his cousins. Nevertheless one party sent a Ḥanafī *faqīh* to negotiate with Sultan Muḥammad for his liberation, on the grounds that his presence would be useful in the war against the infidels. Set free (rather than having escaped according to another account), Shāhānshāh returned in any case in 1109 and put his cousin to death.

The course of events suggests that on this occasion Sultan Muḥammad obliged Shāhānshāh to recognize some kind of suzerainty. It was at this moment that Muḥammad sent an army to attack the Franks in Syria. Another of his contingents joined the Anatolian Turks to resume the expected war against the Byzantines. Philadelphia was attacked, but the Byzantine, Constantine Gavras, beat the Turks near Kalbianos. In fact, as both Muḥammad and Alexius Comnenus were at war with the Franks, warfare between them was paradoxical. As early as 1110 the Byzantine emperor sent an ambassador to Muḥammad to encourage him to fight the Franks; in 1112 peace negotiations were held in Anatolia between the two rulers. Muḥammad was to die in 1118 without intervening again after his check in Syria, and his successor was in no position to concern himself with Anatolian affairs.

A peace concluded in these conditions naturally did not signify any interruption in the war between Shāhānshāh's Turks and the Greeks. In 1113 Lopadion, Poimanenon, Parion and Abydos on the Dardanelles, and Adramyttium on the Aegean, were attacked by the Emir Koutogmes (perhaps Kutlumuş or Kutduğmuş), the archisatrap (*beglerbegi*) Mehmed (formerly Kılıc Arslan's governor of İznik, where he had known Eumathios Kamytzes, now Alexius's governor), and the archisatrap Monolykes (Manaluğ, later described as an old and wise counsellor of Shāhānshāh). They captured Kamytzes. According to Anna Comnena, Muslims from Karme fought beside their Turcomans. This did not prevent Monolykes from reappearing before Nicaea and Poimanenon, and Shāhānshāh himself resumed the campaign with troops mustered from all sides. In these circumstances Alexius was convinced of the necessity of giving up his fruitless distant warfare in Cilicia and Syria, and of attacking the enemy at hand. Wishing to strike at his heart, he led an expedition by Dorylaeum, Kedrea, Polybotos and finally Philomelium (Akşehir), where one Poucheas was in command, while the Turks stole away in classical fashion to ravage the country. Lacking the power to occupy it permanently, Alexius evacuated the Christian population. Shāhānshāh and Monolykes pursued them, but were beaten.

Here a typical event occurred. Shāhānshāh asked for peace, and had an audience with Alexius in which, to believe Anna Comnena, not only did his 'satraps' and Monolykes 'worship' the emperor, but also Shāhānshāh himself leapt from his steed as a sign of respect, and was raised by Alexius according to custom. He is reported to have agreed to leave to the Roman Empire its limits as in the time of Romanus Diogenes, beyond which his Turks would retire, promising no longer to disturb the frontiers. These terms are evidently impossible, but in them and in accordance with Byzantine traditions, there can at least be seen a recognition by Shāhānshāh of Byzantine suzerainty over Anatolia, and in practice an alliance reviving his father's policy. This, no doubt, is just what the Turcomans did not want. During Shāhānshāh's absence a revolt brought his brother Mas'ūd to power. In vain did Alexius warn his guest, and offer him reinforcements. Despite a favourable welcome he received from the Christians of Tyragion (a small place quite near Philomelium), Shāhānshāh was taken by Poucheas's treason, blinded and then strangled.

So peace with Byzantium was not restored. Soon after Alexius Comnenus's death in 1118, the Turks can be found infiltrating the upper Maeander (Menderes), masters of Laodicea ad Lycum (Lâdik) and Sozopolis (Burğlu, now Uluborlu), and intercepting the route to Antalya, and consequently Byzantine communications with Cilicia and Syria. In 1119 John II Comnenus retook Laodicea, and in 1120 Sozopolis and Hierakoryphites, fortifying his conquests in order to secure them. There was no reaction from Mas'ūd, who, like his predecessors, avoided clashes with armed forces.

Nor was peace restored in the east between Malatya and the Armenians, who had profited from Mas'ūd's revolt to lay their hands again on the Jahān. Toğril Arslan, working in liaison with Balak on the Euphrates, drove them out for the last time in spite of reprisal operations aimed at Malatya. Another Seljukid, Dolab, met his death on the Syrian border in battle with the Frank, William of 'Azāz, in alliance with the Artukid chief, Ilgazi.

CHAPTER THREE

The rise of the Danişmendids and the Byzantine recovery

The overthrow of Shāhānshāh was followed by the rise of the Danişmendids. Their activity at this time turned particularly towards the east. Toğrıl Arslan and Balak had invaded Mengüçek's territory in reprisal for a raid he had made in 1118, and he went to Trebizond to seek aid of the Byzantine *dux* Constantine Gavras. Thereupon Balak called upon Gümüştekin. Gavras and Mengüçek were taken prisoner; the latter, the son-in-law of the Danişmendid, was perhaps immediately set free, the former ransomed for 30,000 dinars (see below, p. 36). Then on Balak's death in 1124 a quarrel broke out over the sharing of the succession between Toğrıl Arslan and Balak's cousin, Süleyman of Mayyāfāriqīn, son of the Artukid Ilgazi who was Balak's uncle, and later Temürtaş, Süleyman's brother and successor at Mayyāfāriqīn. Toğrıl Arslan occupied Gargar and Masara on the Euphrates in the region of Maraş. Gümüştekin profited from this situation. Backed by the agreement of Mas'ūd, whose father-in-law and protector he was, he attacked Malatya. Toğrıl Arslan's mother vainly sent him to appeal to the Franks, who were held back by the siege of Aleppo, and tried to augment her resources by pressure on the notables. In December 1124 Malatya again became part of the Danişmendid state. As Khanzīt had in the meantime fallen to a cousin of Temürtaş named Dāwūd, hostilities broke out between him and Gümüştekin, who retained Masara. Toğrıl Arslan's mother retired there, while her son tried to stir up the region.

A time of troubles ensued for the Turks of Anatolia, whose various chiefs intrigued with the neighbouring Christians. Mas'ūd's brother, 'Arab, accused him of treason to their family, and revolted against him. Mas'ūd was forced to flee to Constantinople, where John II Comnenus gave him the means to build up an army, thanks to which he, in alliance with Gümüştekin, forced 'Arab to seek refuge with Toros I, the Armenian ruler of Upper

Cilicia, in 1125 or 1126. Returning the next year at the head of Turks and Armenians, 'Arab captured in succession Mehmed of Masara, the son of Gümüştekin, and his son, the emir Yūnus. Gümüştekin however retook Comana, and freed his son, while 'Arab may have put to death Yeğen, another of Gümüştekin's sons. After a series of heavy combats 'Arab had in his turn to flee to the Greeks, where he died. Mas'ūd accordingly regained his throne, but Gümüştekin was the most powerful person in Anatolia.

These troubles created anew for the Byzantines, albeit with other partners, the situation of Kılıc Arslan's time, and the internal dissensions of the Turks sheltered Greek territory from serious incursions. Soon the reverse was true: the Turks found themselves solicited by Greeks in revolt, as in the eleventh century. Already in 1129 or 1130 Gümüştekin invaded the Black Sea coast, perhaps in reprisal for assistance given to 'Arab. Kassianos, a Greek governor there, submitted to him without making much resistance. In the following year John Comnenus's own brother, Isaac, fled to Gümüştekin after the failure of a conspiracy. After going on to Trebizond, he returned to Gümüştekin. Then he went on to Leon I, who had just succeeded his brother Toros in Cilicia, and who gave him his daughter with Misis (Mamistra) and Adana as dowry. Isaac travelled to Jerusalem, quarrelled with his father-in-law, and only made his peace with John in 1140, after having incited all his Christian and Turkish enemies against him. A little later Isaac's son went in his turn to Mas'ūd, became a Muslim, and married a daughter of the Seljukid ruler. There was nevertheless no question of revolts within the Byzantine Empire, and these developments did not endanger John Comnenus's military forces.

Gümüştekin, who wished for vengeance on the Armenians who had been 'Arab's allies, profited from Toros's death in 1129 by invading Cilicia. There by chance he encountered near Misis the prince of Antioch, Bohemond II, who was also at odds with the Armenians. He inflicted on him a defeat in which the young prince died, and he sent his head to the caliph in February 1130. In a new campaign in 1131 he obliged Leon to promise to pay tribute, and to abstain from any act of hostility. Then he attacked the county of Edessa through the province of Maraş. He attacked various places, e.g. Synnada (south of Kütahya), and was frequently accompanied by Mas'ūd, his son-in-law, his pupil and the legitimator of his power. At the beginning of 1135 the caliph and the Great Seljuk sultan sent him the title and insignia of a king (*malik*), officially investing him with 'the northern country'.

Perhaps he asked for them because of John Comnenus's attacks. Long diverted from Asian affairs by threats in Europe, the emperor now decided to combat the new power. Starting in 1132 from a base he had fortified on the River Rhyndacus, he entered Paphlagonia, took Kastamonu, briefly crossed the Kızılırmak (Gk. Halys), and according to the Byzantine poet Theodore Prodromus obtained the submission of a number of emirs including Toğrıl of Amasya, Alp Arslan of Çankırı (Gk. Gangra) who appear to have Seljuk names, and İnal, perhaps a son of Gümüştekin who is known from a coin. As early as the winter of 1132–33 however, Gümüştekin had retaken Kastamonu.

At that point Gümüştekin died in the winter of 1134–35. In vain did his son Mehmed assume his father's royal insignia, and have his brothers put to death. One of them, 'Ayn al-Dawla, rebelled in the Jahān, from whence he was only driven out two years later, and took refuge with Count Joscelin of Edessa. At the same time Mehmed quarrelled with Mas'ūd the Seljukid, whom John Comnenus succeeded in drawing into an alliance. Thanks to this he was able to lead a Byzantine army to regain Çankırı, where a certain number of Muslims entered his service. He ran a serious risk during the expedition as Mehmed regained Mas'ūd by concessions, and his contingent thereupon abandoned the Greek army. Nevertheless Mehmed turned his operations towards Keysun, and John Comnenus judged the frontier to be sufficiently clear on this side to undertake a memorable expedition to Cilicia and Syria, which led Mehmed to break off his own expedition.

Naturally Mehmed and Mas'ūd, allies once more, made attacks on the Byzantine lines of communication in Cilicia in 1137–38. Mehmed profited from the absence of the Greeks to make a new attack on 'the country of Kassianos'. It was no doubt in this period also that he retook Çankırı, and again penetrated the region of the Sangarios (Sakarya) – events which were among the reasons for the return of John Comnenus to Constantinople. Then Mehmed conducted new raids in the direction of Keysun and the Taurus to the north of Cilicia. In the following years the Turks of Malatya were particularly aggressive in the northern marches of the county of Edessa. In the winter of 1139–40 John Comnenus, who had reasserted the direct control of Byzantium over Trebizond, proceeded by way of the Black Sea coast to attack Niksar, which Mehmed had just refortified. However he withdrew, embarrassed by the desertion of Isaac Comnenus's sons. The next year the emperor led another expedition, this time to relieve Sozopolis, which was under Turkish attack and, while on the way to Antalya, to reinforce the borders of Lake Karalis (now Beyşehir). At this point Mehmed died.[4]

CHAPTER FOUR

The break-up of the Danişmendids: the Seljukids between Byzantium and Nūr al-Dīn

Mehmed's death brought about a reversal of the power-relations in Asia Minor between Danişmendids and Seljukids as the unity of his realm did not survive him. His son, Dhu'l-Nūn, was confronted by a revolt of Mehmed's two brothers, Yağıbasan the governor of Sivas, who married Mehmed's widow, and ʿAyn al-Dawla. In spite of a force sent by Yağıbasan, the latter returned from his stay among the Franks, helped by Dhu'l-Nūn's brother Yūnus, the lord of Masara, and by the inhabitants of Malatya. He seized this town and Arka. Then the two brothers were reconciled, ʿAyn al-Dawla occupied the Jahan. Dhu'l-Nūn was reduced to taking flight to Synnada. Masʿūd sided with Dhu'l-Nūn, threatened Sivas and negotiated separately with ʿAyn al-Dawla through the mediation of his niece, ʿAyn al-Dawla's wife. Then, on not obtaining satisfaction, he besieged Malatya in the summer of 1143, and occupied the Jahān in 1144. He came to terms with Yağıbasan, with whom he again besieged Malatya, and received favourably a request for help from the Artukid, Kara Arslan, who was threatened by Zengī. At this time of uncertainty however Masʿūd took Ankara, Çankırı and the Byzantine frontiers of this province from Yağıbasan.

These conflicts naturally affected the situation on the Byzantine side. The Turks had an opportunity there when John Comnenus died in Cilicia in April 1143, a little while after Mehmed. His son, Manuel I Comnenus, returned to Constantinople, regaining from the Turks on the way Pracana above Seleucia (Silifke), and liberating his brother Andronicus and the latter's son-in-law, who had been captured during a hunting-party as they left Cilicia. In the following year he repulsed the Turks who had ventured into the region of Malangia and Pitheca on the Sangarios, south-east of Nicaea. Other Turks, perhaps loyal to the Seljukids, had retaken Pracana; yet others pillaged the region of the Maeander (Menderes) in the direction of Kelbianos. Good relations – a novelty – were temporarily established between Yağıbasan and Manuel Comnenus against their common enemy, Masʿūd. In 1146 Manuel set out for Konya in a new campaign. He reached Akşehir by the Menderes, then advanced on Konya. Masʿūd had left the city, dividing his troops into two corps between Konya and Kavala (now Çigil). He had effected a reconciliation with Yağıbasan, from whom he expected reinforcements. Scattered combats took place, in the course of which Masʿūd's cupbearer and Gavras, a chief of Greek origin who had been brought up among the Turks, and governed a province, were captured. Manuel was unable to destroy the enemy army, but scorned overtures for peace, in which perhaps a part was played by the Turkish wife of his cousin, John Comnenus, who had gone over to the Turks. So he withdrew, repulsing as he went the band of a certain 'Rama' from the Menderes region. He was perhaps preparing for a new campaign when the Second Crusade was announced. He then willingly accepted the peace offers, brought from Masʿūd by one of his generals.

As the Greeks did not aid the crusaders in any way, but rather incited the Turks against them, the Turks did not incur any grave risk from the crusade. Avoiding as always set battles, they harassed the Western armies. The forces of the Emperor Conrad III marched directly for Konya by the route of the First Crusade. Near to Eskişehir (Gk. Dorylaeum), a Turkish chief called Manplanes by the Greeks drew them into an ambush, from which they escaped with great difficulty. Arriving exhausted at Akşehir, they had to retrace their steps in the most difficult conditions, pursued by Turkish archers. A little later the army of Louis VII cut across to Antalya with greater prudence, but they were equally troubled by the Turks in the valley of Kelbianos (Decervion of the Franks), and then at the crossing of the Maeander. The Turks, more or less helped by the Greeks, harassed them until they embarked at Antalya.

The Turkish peace with the Greeks outlived the departure of the Franks; thus Masʿūd was now able to turn to the south-east. Perhaps he was even able to trouble Maraş before the crusade through his son, Kılıc Arslan. Immediately after the crusade, Prince Raymond of Antioch carried out a reprisal raid to the north. It was in these conditions that relations were established between Masʿūd and the lord of Aleppo, the illustrious Nūr al-Dīn. Each party readily accepted the help against the Franks that an operation by the other could provide, but sought to annex as quickly as possible from the resulting spoils the regions in the vicinity of the other's sphere of action, so as to prevent any encroachment on his own.

Nūr al-Dīn had carried out a first diversion in agreement with Masʿūd in 1148. In 1149 he inflicted a disastrous defeat on the Franks of Antioch in which Prince Raymond died. The action of the two rulers was now extended. Beyond the Jahān there appears for the first time a Seljukid policy of entry into Upper Syria which was to develop, and was to establish those contacts between the Muslim nomads of Asia Minor and of Syria which Süleyman b. Kutlumuş had begun seven years earlier, and which had been interrupted for half a century by the formation of the Crusader states. By the summer of 1149 Masʿūd was in occupation of Maraş, and its Frankish inhabitants, in spite of having obtained leave to retire to Antioch, were massacred on the way. He then occupied Sam and Duluk on the Syrian borders, and harassed Tall Bāshir (T. Tilbaşar; Frankish, Turbessel), the capital of what was left of the county of Edessa on the right bank of the Euphrates. A truce conditional on the payment of tribute was brought about by the arrival of Frankish reinforcements from Jerusalem and the mediation of Nūr al-Dīn, who, although he had sent the help requested by Masʿūd, sought to limit his action. In 1150 however, when Joscelin of Tall Bāshir was captured by the Turcomans of Syria, the attack was resumed. Masʿūd and Nūr al-Dīn undertook the siege together, agreeing that it should be given to Nūr al-Dīn as the dowry for one of Masʿūd's daughters whom the Syrian ruler was marrying to seal the bargain. Masʿūd in fact made a revolt the pretext for leaving his intended son-in-law to make the conquest which would solely profit him, so he gave it up. In reality Masʿūd occupied Keysun, Besni (Armenian, Behesni), Raban and Merzban further to the north, and marked the importance he attached to these new territories by constituting them as an apanage for his son and heir presumptive, Kılıc Arslan. The Franks, almost encircled, then decided to cede Tall Bāshir to Manuel Comnenus, who was happy at what he believed to be a chance to set his foot again in Syria. Its Franks then retired to Antioch, harassed by Seljukid and Aleppine troops. In 1151, however, while Nūr al-Dīn's troops forced the Greeks in Tall Bāshir to capitulate, Masʿūd occupied ʿAynṭāb (now Gaziantep). The partition of the Frankish possessions lying between the Euphrates and Syria was completed.

Thereupon on the death of ʿAyn al-Dawla of Malatya (who for his part had attacked the Armenians above Samosata (Samsat)), his son Dhu'l-Qarnayn acted on the advice of Yağıbasan, and refused to make the submission which Masʿūd demanded. Masʿūd's threats obtained the acquiescence of Yağıbasan, to whom he gave his daughter. Masʿūd then attacked Malatya, but, implored by Dhu'l-Qarnayn's mother (who was his stepsister), he contented himself with the ruler's personal act of homage (1152). Dhu'l-Qarnayn's mother however exerted pressure on the population. Incited by the female soothsayers who surrounded her, she quarrelled with her son, and was driven out by a rising of Turkish chiefs.

In Anatolia relations between the Byzantines and the Danişmendids had once again deteriorated. Yağıbasan attacked the Black Sea districts of

Oinaeum (Ünye) and Paurae (Bafra) near Samsun. As regards Masʿūd, however, it does not seem that the Tall Bāshir affair had permanently compromised his relations with Manuel. It was perhaps at his instigation that in 1153 Masʿūd had invaded Cilicia, where the Armenian Roupenid, Toros, was building up a principality at the expense of the Greeks. On this occasion he was won over to an agreement with Toros, and it may have been about this time that the Greeks lost (perhaps to Turcomans) Panura and Sybila, which lay on the route from Silifke to Lârende (now Karaman) by Mut. It was certainly on Manuel's demand that Masʿūd again invaded Cilicia with his son, Kılıc Arslan, in 1154. It was an unhappy campaign, for a contingent venturing in the direction of Alexandretta (İskenderun) was cut to pieces by Toros's brother, Sdefane, who was reinforced by Templars; and, while Masʿūd himself was besieging Tall Ḥamdūn (Toprakkale), mosquitoes and the climate launched an attack on his men and animals which forced him to retire. Ten months later, about April 1155, he died after a relatively long reign of twenty-nine years.

The accession of Kılıc Arslan II, who was to have a reign of almost the same length, opened with the usual family conflicts, which were prevented from becoming dangerous by a parallel division among the Danişmendids. The new sultan distrusted one of his brothers as well as the principal minister, the head *qāḍī*, and the chiefs who supported him. Another brother, Shāhānshāh, had taken refuge in his domain of Çankırı and Ankara, which he had received from Masʿūd, and he had married a Danişmendid princess. Yağıbasan became an active partisan of Shāhānshāh, and attacked the region of Yenişehir (Gk. Larissa), then the Jahān. At the same time he sought the intervention of Nūr al-Dīn, who, happy to dispose of a rival, took ʿAynṭāb, Duluk and Merzban. There was a lively ferment among the Christians of the recently annexed province of Keysun and, aided by this, Sdefane was able to take Pertous near Maraş briefly, and lead a raid to Besni. But Kılıc Arslan succeeded in making peace with Yağıbasan on conditions which are unknown. He secured himself against Manuel Comnenus's intervention by surrendering, on an ambassador's demand, the places he had occupied in Isauria. At the same time Yağıbasan promised for his part to respect the Byzantine alliance. In 1157 Kılıc Arslan was able to re-establish his authority over the province of Keysun, which he conciliated by a policy of tolerance after the blunders of the previous governors. He also proposed to Toros, Reynald of Antioch and Baldwin II of Jerusalem an alliance against Nūr al-Dīn.

But at this point Manuel Comnenus decided to lead an expedition, which should re-establish Byzantine domination or suzerainty in Cilicia or northern Syria on the further side of Anatolia. On his route, which went around the official Seljukid possessions, he only came up against feeble autonomous

Turcoman bands in Lesser Phrygia. While staying at Antioch at the beginning of 1159, he received among others an embassy from Yağıbasan. Although there were no hostilities with Kılıc Arslan, Manuel remained anxious to be forearmed against him. He gave up the expedition against Nūr al-Dīn that he had promised the Franks, in exchange for an alliance with him against Kılıc Arslan, which was welcomed by Nūr al-Dīn, ever anxious about Seljukid encroachment on his northern borders. On his return journey Manuel, hastening to regain Constantinople, where his absence might have given rise to intrigues, crossed Seljukid territory. Turks of Lârende on the frontier fled, thinking that he was going to attack Konya. Others, on ascertaining that he had no plans for hostilities, provided him with supplies, but, as he was about to re-enter Byzantine territory near Kütahya, frontier bands tried once more and vainly to attack his rear. So a few months later at the end of 1159, Manuel ordered his officers to conduct simultaneous operations against nearby bands, while he himself led a reprisal raid on the upper Rhyndacus and towards Eskişehir. In vain did Kılıc Arslan send an ambassador to him at Pylae in Bithynia, to which he had withdrawn, with instructions to deny responsibility for the attacks and to restore the agreement.

Having secured his positions in Cilicia and Syria, Manuel had in fact decided to resume an interventionist policy against Kılıc Arslan. His task was made easier by the resumption of the war between Kılıc Arslan and Yağıbasan in connection with the continued dissensions among the Danişmendids. Around 1158 there were hostilities of Kılıc Arslan in alliance with Dhu'l-Nun of Sivas and Kayseri against Yağıbasan. A temporary reconciliation seems to have been followed by renewed tension when Dhu'l-Qarnayn of Malatya died towards the end of 1160. Yağıbasan installed his young nephew Mehmed as his successor, while at the same time seeking (as Kılıc Arslan himself claimed) to dispose of him by murder, and replace him by his brother, Shāhānshāh. A new war broke out in which Kılıc Arslan was beaten, perhaps in the direction of the Jahān. At the same moment Nūr al-Dīn, whose brother Amīr-Amīrān, an unfortunate rebel, had taken refuge with Kılıc Arslan, took from him Besni, Keysun, Raban and Maraş, with the help of a governor who made terms to save his position. So it was in favourable conditions that Manuel Comnenus was able to resume an active policy in Anatolia.

In the winter of 1160–61 Manuel led an expedition by way of Philadelphia (Alaşehir) and the upper Menderes, where the Turkish chief Süleyman, while harrying him, sent a kinsman (who may once have served in the Byzantine army) to negotiate. But, when the emperor had gone, the Turks reappeared, took an unidentified place called Phileta, and ravaged the country of Lâdik and Lesser Phrygia. It was clear that local operations of this kind were insufficient to close a semi-desert frontier against autonomous bands. It was necessary to strike a heavier blow. To achieve this Manuel resumed his former relationship with Shāhānshāh of Ankara and Yağıbasan, whom he incited to re-enter the lists. There may well have been a connection between this and the hostilities between Yağıbasan and Kılıc Arslan. At the same time Manuel sent his general, Kontostephanos, to call out the contingents which the Cilician Armenians and the Syrian Franks had been required to promise him in 1159, and which fought a Seljukid force on their way. Then Kılıc Arslan negotiated. He recognized the acquisitions made by Nūr al-Dīn, whose wife, Kılıc Arslan's sister, restored peace between the two rulers. He recognized the Jahān as belonging to the Danişmendid who had just beaten him, and perhaps other places as belonging to Shāhānshāh. Manuel was offered the restitution of his prisoners; then after the check by Kontostephanos, Kılıc Arslan promised to respect the Greek frontiers, and to make his subjects respect them, to fight the enemies of the Empire and to furnish a contingent. In this alliance the last article might attract subsidies, and the first was necessarily a form of words. Then after sending his 'chancellor Christopher' to Constantinople to cut off his opponents' persistent intrigues with Manuel, Kılıc Arslan resolved upon a considerable gesture by going in person to the emperor in Constantinople.

The reception was organized with the splendour usual at Byzantium on solemn occasions of this kind – splendour aimed at impressing the barbarian, and at the same time bedazzling the subjects in the capital with the submission of a recent enemy and the triumph of imperial policy. The visit lasted for eighty days during which there were lavish feasts and games, in which the Muslims, including Amīr-Amīran, strove to win admiration of their exploits, and Manuel overwhelmed his guest with sumptuous presents. The treaty already negotiated was reinforced by the guarantees of Turkish chiefs who had accompanied their ruler to Constantinople, while others sought to be reconciled with him throught Manuel. According to the Byzantine historian Nicetas Choniates, Kılıc Arslan promised to surrender Sivas. If this is more than empty words, it should be understood in the sense of giving it to a chief who recognized himself likewise as a Byzantine vassal.

At the price of some contingents of reinforcements (e.g. against the Hungarians in 1167), and above all of giving satisfaction to that prestige of which, as Kılıc Arslan surely knew, Manuel and Byzantine political circles were so greedy, the Seljukid ruler had in fact obtained security on his western frontier as well as subsidies. Constantine Gavras, sent to receive the promised restitutions and parts of the conquered territories, obtained only evasive answers; but Manuel's activities in Europe over several years in fact guaranteed that, however the Turks behaved, Byzantine abstention would continue. Henceforward it became possible for Kılıc Arslan to engage wholeheartedly in the struggle against his rivals. Yağıbasan had recognized young Mehmed at Malatya, but had not given up the idea of extending his power eastwards, since it was becoming difficult towards the west. When called upon by the lord of Āmid (Diyarbakır), who was being threatened by the Artukid Kara Arslan of Khartpert, Kılıc Arslan, although he was Kara Arslan's father-in-law, proceeded to lay waste the region of Shamash-Kazak. This brought him into conflict also, in a fairly new fashion as it seems, with the Mengüçekid ruler of Kemah, who was killed in the war. He was also at war again with Dhu'l-Nūn, who perhaps had to join Yağıbasan's party on defeat, for we find Kılıc Arslan attacking him at the same time as Yağıbasan from the direction of Sivas. Kılıc Arslan had made an alliance against them with the Saltukid ruler of Erzurum, who has sent him his daughter. However, Yağıbasan had carried her off and married her to Dhu'l-Nūn, who was defeated and asked help of Manuel Comnenus on Yağıbasan's death.

Fate assisted Kılıc Arslan's attack on the Danişmendids. In 1164 Yağıbasan died when staying with his ally Shāhānshāh at Çankırı. His place was taken, whether or not directly, by Ismā'īl, the son of Yağıbasan's brother, Ibrāhīm, who married his widow. On the Jahān, however, a certain Maḥmūd, the son of an unknown Mahdī, had been proclaimed; he was perhaps unconnected with the Danişmendids. Kılıc Arslan profited from this new division. Reconciled with Dhu'l-Nūn, he annexed the Jahān with Elbistan, while the Armenian Toros laid waste the province of Maraş further south. Four years later, however, Kılıc Arslan again broke with Dhu'l-Nūn and seized all his territories. In 1169 he took Ankara and Çankırı from his brother Shāhānshāh, in spite of his probably being a Byzantine vassal, and banished him. He now faced only Ismā'īl, who was reduced to Sivas, and the outlying ruler of Malatya, the young Afrīdūn, who had succeeded his brother, Abu'l-Qāsim, on his accidental death in 1171. Abu'l-Qāsim himself had in 1169 taken the place of Mehmed, who had been driven out by a revolt of the military chiefs. Afrīdūn was only saved in 1171 from an attack by Kılıc Arslan through the traditional support of the Artukid lord of Ḥişn Kayfā (Hasankeyf), Nūr al-Dīn Mehmed, whose sister (originally intended for his brother) he had married. He sent the commandant of Khartpert to reinforce Afrīdūn.

Those rulers deprived of their possessions or threatened by Kılıc Arslan turned towards Nūr al-Dīn Maḥmūd b. Zengī, as they were unable to count on effective support from Byzantium. He had hitherto subordinated all his activities to the defence of Shīrkūh, his lieutenant in Egypt, against the Franks, avoiding complications in the north, and had even given up Maraş, Keysun and Besni to Kılıc Arslan *c.* 1166–67. But after 1171 Egypt was conquered, and firmly secured against Frankish attacks in the possession of Shīrkūh's nephew, Saladin. Nūr al-Dīn was now naturally displeased to see the growth of his northern neighbour's power, and Kılıc Arslan's recent victories had considerably increased his prestige and means of action. Shāhānshāh, who had solicited Manuel in vain, and Dhu'l-Nūn were close to Nūr al-Dīn, and Afrīdūn was asking his help. Nūr al-Dīn organized a vast coalition of his vassals: his nephew in Mosul, the Artukids of Ḥişn Kayfā and Mardin, the Armenian Mleh, who had just driven the Byzantines from Cilicia with his aid – all joined troops from Nūr al-Dīn's own territories, and were to rally around Ismā'īl at Sivas in the first, and for sixty years the only, intervention of the Syrians and Mesopotamians in the heart of Asia Minor. At the end of 1171 Kılıc Arslan in Kayseri succeeded in avoiding a fight. He agreed to negotiate, to liberate the prisoners of Malatya and to give Shāhānshāh a pension. He refused however to surrender the conquered territories and, when he was asked to set free Shāhānshāh's seven children whom he had captured, it is said that he had one killed and roasted, giving warning that the others would suffer the same fate if he did not withdraw. At that point winter compelled the allies to retire. Their stay had caused a famine at Sivas and the inhabitants revolted, massacring Ismā'īl, his wife, his children and five of his slaves. At the beginning of 1172 Dhu'l-Nūn, who was then at Damascus, was called upon to succeed him, and arrived with a new contingent provided by Nūr al-Dīn. At about the same time the widow of Yağıbasan (and also of Ismā'īl, if the date is possible) negotiated for the coming of Dhu'l-Nūn to Amasya, but she was butchered by the population, and Kılıc Arslan occupied the town. He then naturally endeavoured to attack Dhu'l-Nūn at Sivas. Nūr al-Dīn himself took the field in 1173, accompanied by an uncle of Kılıc Arslan, who had been deprived of his governorship of Keysun by his nephew. Nūr al-Dīn again occupied Maraş, Besni, Keysun and Merzban. He then crossed the Taurus, and encountered the Seljukid army on the upper Ceyhan (Aksu) in Cappadocia. He had obtained from the caliph official investiture with all Kılıc Arslan's territories. Kılıc Arslan started negotiations, as he always did when in serious danger, and Nūr al-Dīn, being unwilling to stay so far from his Syrian territories, was compliant. It was agreed that Kılıc Arslan should leave Sivas to Dhu'l-Nūn under the suzerainty of Nūr al-Dīn, who left in the city a garrison and an adminstrator of Christian origin named 'Abd al-Masīḥ, the former minister of his nephew in Mosul. Ankara was perhaps also restored to Shāhānshāh, and Kılıc Arslan had to make up his losses by resuming the war against the Byzantines.

Relations on this side did indeed gradually become more strained. Since Kılıc Arslan's visit to Constantinople they had been officially correct. Certainly he had not restored any of his conquests, but had that really been expected? The violations of the frontier by Turcoman bands had not ceased, e.g. in the Pentapolis near Sandıklı; in an uncertain year they had even sacked Laodicea ad Lycum (Lâdik), which remained unfortified, but this was not a matter of Seljukid policy. When a raid into the Pentapolis occasioned the arrival of Manuel, the neighbouring official Turkish chief, Süleyman (mentioned earlier in 1160), explained to the emperor that these were actions against the wishes of both Kılıc Arslan and himself, and he offered bloodstock in compensation. The problems were settled in a friendly fashion, and a courteous correspondence was maintained between the two rulers. To encourage Kılıc Arslan to continue in this way, even against his own subjects, Manuel lavished gifts on him. It is likely enough that Kılıc Arslan had lent an ear to Byzantine conspirators, and had shown little enthusiasm for taking action against the Turcomans. It is possible that, as Nicetas says, he may have asserted that the more harm his people did to the Greeks, the more presents he received from them. At least, when Byzantine troops carried out reprisals against Turcoman nomads in Greek territory, he did not protect them. Meanwhile, by constructing strongholds at Pergamum (Bergama), Chliara (Kırkağac) and Adramyttium (Edremid), Manuel was able little by little to restore some security to this country, as was shown by the renewed payment of taxes by the peasants, and by the fact that it was later a firm element in the little Empire of Nicaea. For another thing Kılıc Arslan sent Manuel the reinforcements against the Bulgarians which he had promised in 1167. There was reason for Nūr al-Dīn's reproaches that he did not fight the Greeks. All this had cost him little, had brought him an abundance of presents, and allowed him to begin the unification of Asia Minor to his own advantage with a success that was interrupted only by the intervention of Nūr al-Dīn. As for Byzantium, the bases for attack were certainly better organized.

The inter-Muslim agreement of 1173 gave Constantinople the impression of an anti-Byzantine alliance of Nūr al-Dīn, Kılıc Arslan, Shāhānshāh and Mleh. In fact, when Manuel first demanded an explanation, Kılıc Arslan replied, evidently alluding to Nūr al-Dīn's reproaches and the investiture which he had received from Baghdad, that his own pacific policy towards Byzantium had embroiled him with the caliph and the Muslims. However, as Manuel advanced towards Alaşehir with the clear intention of attacking if the treaty was not confirmed, Kılıc Arslan deferred to him for the moment.

At that point Nūr al-Dīn died in 1174. Kılıc Arslan's opponents, who had been sustained only by his prestige or his reinforcements, did not even attempt to resist. 'Abd al-Masīḥ fled to Mosul, Dhu'l-Nūn and Shāhānshāh to Constantinople. Kılıc Arslan proceeded to occupy their possessions without striking a blow.

At this moment Manuel, entreated by the evicted rulers, found himself for the first time in a position to intervene seriously. He saw Nūr al-Dīn's death less as that of an adversary than of a possible ally of Kılıc Arslan, and so as an encouragement to a bolder policy. In the winter of 1174–75 he demanded the return of the towns previously promised him. Kılıc Arslan, who had not yet occupied all the possessions of Shāhānshāh and Dhu'l-Nūn, thought of a profitable stratagem. He demanded that a Greek contingent should be sent to take delivery of the towns; then he promised help to the threatened towns, and caused them to recognize his authority. It was the same at Amasya, whither Shāhānshāh was summoned by his partisans, and whither Manuel sent at his request the troops of Paphlagonia and Trebizond under Michael Gavras. Shāhānshāh was to join them from the west, but was put to flight on the way by Kılıc Arslan, so that Gavras dared not enter Amasya, and Kılıc Arslan took possession of it. This time however Manuel was not disposed to be trifled with, and set great preparations in train. On the frontier he had Dorylaeum (Eskişehir) and Sublaeum (Keçiborlu) reconstructed and fortified as places of refuge for the people and military bases, having previously repulsed the Turkish nomads of the vicinity in a series of combats. In the winter of 1175–76 Kılıc Arslan was uneasy, and sent his adviser, another Gavras (perhaps the one who was in the service of Mas'ūd in 1146), to ask for the renewal of the treaties. It was in vain. Manuel assembled troops and provisions from the whole empire for a great campaign. He may well have seen it as only the first in a series of enterprises conducted in liaison with the Franks of Syria against Muslim rulers generally.

The attack was to be made on several fronts. A Paphlagonian army under Andronicus Vatatzes was to proceed with Dhu'l-Nūn to attack Niksar, where they hoped for help from his former subjects, but the besieged townspeople sowed dissension between Dhu'l-Nūn and Vatatzes, and inflicted a disaster on the Greeks in which Vatatzes lost his life. Meanwhile Manuel himself led the main army, which was intended to reach Konya by way of the upper Menderes. From Sublaeum he entered the pass of Myriocephalum.

Kılıc Arslan made fresh overtures of peace. In spite of the advice of his chief officers, aware as they were of the problems of moving a heavy army across such difficult and desolate country, Manuel replied that peace would be dictated at Konya. For his part Kılıc Arslan had had time to assemble troops from all his realm. The pass was narrow, and the Greek army was extended over a great distance. Kılıc Arslan posted his men in ambush on the heights of both sides, and attacked. He cut the enemy forces into two parts, which were prevented from joining up by the carcases of animals and remains of vehicles. The rearguard, from which Manuel fled, was massacred, and the rest of the army, which Manuel had rejoined, was encircled on a hill where it was entrenched. The Greeks and the Turcomans expected the resumption of hostilities at dawn, but Gavras offered peace on

Kılıc Arslan's behalf, subject to the payment of tribute and the destruction of the fortresses of Dorylaeum and Sublaeum. Overjoyed, Manuel accepted, and the wreck of the Byzantine army withdrew in the autumn of 1176.

In some respects the Turkish victory at Myriocephalum was a replica of that at Manzikert a century before. Certainly it did not immediately result in new territorial gains for the Turcomans, and one may ask why Kılıc Arslan did not exploit it more. At least the Turcoman bands could continue their nomadic way of life in the territories from which Manuel had sought to exclude them, occasionally pillaging them. In 1177 a group led by the *atabeg* (doubtless the *amīr ispahsālār atabeg* Badr al-Dīn Shāhānshāh b. Arslan Doğmuş, known from inscriptions in the Danişmendid town of Niksar), which had raided the Menderes valley down to the sea, was partly destroyed by John Vatatzes on its return. Another group surprised a Byzantine force which was seeking to re-establish peace in the area by the occupation of Charax to the east of Chonae (Honaz) and Laodicea ad Lycum. At the end of 1179 other Turcomans in the region of Claudiopolis in Bithynia were driven back by Manuel, who had hastened there in person. There is no doubt that in general the incursions continued. Above all Myriocephalum signified the loss of all hope that Byzantium would recover in fact the Asian territories which in theory she had never relinquished, and thus necessarily the hope of playing a large part in Syrian politics. It signified that henceforth there would be a permanent and completely independent Turkish state in Anatolia.

If Kılıc Arslan did not press his advantage further, it was because this war was forced on him by the Byzantine state, and did not harmonize with his real policy. He may well not have regarded as useful the conquest of devastated territories, or as easy the sustained attack on the Aegean littoral, which might have provoked Christian help. Facing the Turcomans, it was enough for him to be able to send them there. Being in the midst of Christian populations which, unlike those of Armenia and Cappadocia, were at least partly morally bound to Byzantium – did he feel that more conquests would enhance his power? For him as for his better known successors, the fundamental problem was to complete the internal unification of Asia Minor, and to play a growing role in Muslim policy in Armenia, Syria and Mesopotamia; all these were matters from which too great activity in the west would have distracted him.

Soon after Myriocephalum in fact he again turned his attention towards the east. In 1175 Afrīdūn of Malatya had been killed by his brother Mehmed, who had previously been driven out by a revolt. He had then lived with Nūr al-Dīn, with the Franks and with Kılıc Arslan, who had given him Ereğli in the Konya region. He had tried to retake Malatya, and had been captured by Nūr al-Dīn. Liberated by his captor's death, he had reoccupied the city, but, when a bad harvest made him unpopular once again at the end of 1177, he handed Malatya over to Kılıc Arslan, who thus at last realized the desire of holding the key to the upper Euphrates, always cherished by his father and himself. At the same time he was provided with a new opportunity for intervention within Syria by the struggle in northern Syria and Mesopotamia between the Zengids and the new master of Egypt, Saladin, with his lust for conquest. Thus for half a century the rulers of Aleppo, threatened from the south, were to enjoy Seljukid support. In 1179 Kılıc Arslan attacked Raban, which the ruler of Aleppo had been compelled to cede to Saladin. When in the following year Nūr al-Dīn Mehmed of Ḥiṣn Kayfā repudiated his wife, Kılıc Arslan's daughter, a conflict between the two rulers ensued. Nūr al-Dīn Mehmed appealed to Saladin, who duly invaded the Seljukid territories north of Besni in his support. Kılıc Arslan was obliged to accept a compromise, in return for which Saladin helped him to avenge the wrongs caused by the Armenian Roupen of Cilicia to the Turcomans of the Anatolian borders.

The death of Manuel Comnenus in 1180 and the troubles which followed it naturally reinforced the position of the Turks. Under Alexius II Comnenus (1180–83) and Andronicus I Comnenus (1183–85), Kılıc Arslan once more caused the Kütahya region to be devastated, and the city soon fell. Soon after the accession of Isaac II Angelus (1185–95) the region of Kelbianos to the north of the lower Menderes was devastated in its turn on Kılıc Arslan's order by a chief named Sami. Sozopolis, now a mere islet in Turcoman country, also fell in the time of Alexius or Andronicus; under the name of Burğlu (nowadays Uluborlu) it was to become the centre of Seljukid administration for south-western Anatolia. The Greeks themselves increased the audacity of the Turks; at Nicaea the townspeople called on the Turks for help against Andronicus – admittedly, when they were carried away in the fall of the town, they were impaled around its ramparts. At Philadelphia (Alaşehir) John Vatatzes was the enemy of Andronicus. Towards the beginning of the reign of Isaac Angelus, the town fell into the hands of a certain 'Mangaphas'. It is not clear if he was one of the 'three brothers' who, according to Michael the Syrian, seized this town about 1184 with the aid of Turkish troops. In a letter that Kılıc Arslan addressed to Michael the Syrian, apparently in 1185, he speaks of the homage that a ruler of Alaşehir came to pay him. Kılıc Arslan gave him massive assistance, which enabled him to crush the emperor. It is in connection with these deeds that Kılıc Arslan's letter places the vast conquests 'of country never occupied by the Turks' stretching 'to the sea' together with a place called Diadion, which he announces to Michael. Indeed Nicetas recounts that Kılıc Arslan long threatened Antalya, and Diadion is evidently Düden, known to Ibn Bībī as one stage from Antalya on the way to Konya. Finally, it is certain in this period that must be placed the beginning of the thrust, the details of which are not available, which led the Turcomans in south-western Anatolia to the flanks of Lycia, where they were at the beginning of the following century. In 1190 the Emperor Frederick Barbarossa found Laodicea ad Lycum to be Greek, but as the outpost in a country infested with Turcomans.

CHAPTER FIVE

Eastern Asia Minor in the twelfth century

In the preceding chapters it will have been noted that hardly anything has been said about eastern Anatolia. This is partly due to the state of documentation, which is itself linked to a local situation remote from the great political centres which had any culture. Indeed insofar as this is meaningful, it is difficult to know if the masters of Erzincan and Erzurum were theoretically within the sphere of influence of the sultan of Iran (more precisely of Ādharbāyjān); it is more likely that, with the development of the sultanate of Rūm, it was within its sphere that they placed themselves. However, we must say what we can of these two principalities, both because they were to be incorporated in the state of Rūm, just as previously their territories had been in the Byzantine Empire, and because the course of events until present-day Turkey was to show that this incorporation was to be firm. In any case neighbourhood implied relations, which the course of history was to show to be permanent.

Very little is known of the history of the principalities of Erzincan and Erzerum under the Mengüçekids and the Saltukids respectively before their incorporation into the Seljukid state. According to the genealogy claimed by the rulers of Erzurum in the twelfth century, they were descended from a certain Abu'l-Qāsim, whose very existence cannot be established. 'Alī, perhaps his son, is attested in 496/1103 as master of Erzurum, whence he went to Ahlat to enter the service of the Great Seljuk Sultan Muḥammad, who had taken refuge there after a defeat by his cousin Berk Yaruk. He seems also to have been mentioned about this time at the latest by the Armenian chronicler Mxit'ar of Arivank', who calls him 'Alī Armeni-Arslan. A little later the English chronicler Ordericus Vitalis knew of ''Alī, the king of the Medes', the ally of the Artukid Balak, who sent him Frankish prisoners as a gift. It is curious that at the time of Ilgazi's campaign against the Georgians, ʿAlī is not mentioned although it took place in Erzurum (1120 or 1121).

By contrast it is above all in connection with struggles against the Georgians that we hear of his son and successor, Saltuk. The latter had a daughter who married Shāh-i Arman Sökmen II of Ahlat about 1130; in 1143/1148–49 this princess made the Pilgrimage. In 1153 or 1154 Saltuk was at war with the Georgians because of revolts at Ani, which no doubt they had encouraged, and which threatened to end with the expulsion of its old Muslim ruling family. Saltuk was defeated and captured, but ransomed thanks to his daughter Shāhbānū. In 1164 Sultan Kılıc Arslan II, who wished to make an alliance with Saltuk against the Danişmendid Yağıbasan, sought the hand of one of his daughters, but she was captured on the way by Yağıbasan, and compelled to marry his son Dhu'l-Nūn (above, p. 27). In addition an inscription in the citadel of Erzurum mentions a certain Diyā' al-Dīn Inanc Yabğu Alp Toğrıl Beg, son of Muẓaffar Ghāzī, son of Abu'l-Qāsim.

Some copper coins dating from the reign of Saltuk, who died in Rajab 563/May 1168, and his son Abu'l-Fatḥ Mehmed are interesting like those of neighbouring principalities, not only because of their fidelity to Byzantine types in showing St George, but also because of the orthography, which is given in all the chronicles as Saltuk, but here as Salduk. They also bear the names of the Iranian sultans Masʿūd and Ṭughril, which signifies that the Saltukids of that period still considered themselves as being in some way in the Great Seljuk sphere of influence.

Of Saltuk's son, Mehmed, only his relations with the Georgians are known. His son Muẓaffar al-Dīn was one of the suitors of Tamar, the young queen of Georgia, but he had to be content with an illegitimate princess of the blood royal. Shortly afterwards David, the husband chosen by Tamar, sacked Erzurum, which was defended by a certain Nāṣir al-Dīn Kızıl Arslan, the same as Mehmed according to the coins mentioned above. He died before 593/1197, when we find his place taken by Abū Manṣūr, known to Ibn Bībī in 597/1201, when he was overthrown by Sultan Rukn al-Dīn Süleyman II. In a pompous inscription Mehmed and Abū Manṣūr designate themselves as the founders of the new Great Mosque of Erzurum. It is interesting to note that there as elsewhere the old Turkish titles are forgotten; they now give themselves only traditional Arabic titles.

The Mengüçekids of Erzincan, Kuğuniya (now Şebinkarahisar) and Divriği are no better known. The first mention of the eponym of the family Mengüçek, does not go back to shortly after Manzikert, as imagined by obsequious later authors, but only to 1118, when he was fighting from Kemah against Malatya. As the Seljukid ruler of this city, Toğrıl Arslan, and his *atabeg* Balak, took reprisals, he went, remarkably enough, to seek aid from the Byzantine *dux* of Trebizond, Constantine Gavras. But the two allies were beaten by Balak, who had called on the help of the Danişmendid Gümüştekin, and Mengüçek was made prisoner. As, however, he was Gümüştekin's son-in-law, he was set free unharmed (above, p. 20).

This lifting of the curtain does not seem, however, to have been followed by similar events; and the history of the principality of Erzincan is passed over in such silence by chroniclers from all parts that one must conclude that it cannot have comprised any very outstanding episodes. Mengüçek was succeeded by a son, Isḥāq, who is known only from the genealogy of later rulers as traced on their inscriptions and coins. According to the same sources Isḥāq left two sons, between whom he partitioned his possessions; the first, Süleyman, receiving Divriği, and the second, Dāwūd, keeping Erzincan. With about one late exception, inscriptions are extant only from the Divriği branch, which was more active in building (or at least in epigraphy) than the others. There are coins of the collateral branches. It is not known whether there was any bond of vassalship.

The first reappearance of the Erzincan principality occurs only about 1163, when its ruler was with the Danişmendid Yağıbasan, as an ally of a descendant of Balak whom Yağıbasan was attacking, and was killed in the fighting. This ruler was evidently Dāwūd, since his son, Bahrām-Shāh (who is well known) was to reign more than sixty years. The possibility of his being Isḥāq may be excluded since we know precisely that this was the length of Bahrām-Shāh's reign. We can also conclude from its duration that Dāwūd must have met his death when still young and after a short reign, and thus place Isḥāq roughly between about 1130 and 1150.

From the following generation onwards we begin to have some data. Shāhānshāh of Divriği, who reigned until at least 592/1196, entitled himself in his inscriptions *amir ispahsālār*, while in one he parades a series of titles which show him as being, like many other Muslim rulers, at least officially anxious to fight heretics within and infidels without. To this is linked another series of Turkish titles, carefully conserved in a period when they had been allowed to fall into desuetude in most of the other Turcoman families, including Erzurum. He appears as the builder of the citadel mosque, and of the tomb of his wife and himself. The first was completed in 576/1180–81, the other in 592/1195–96. In the latter year there was also completed the tomb of an emir who was his great chamberlain (*ḥājib*), and is shown by his title to have made the Pilgrimage. The architect of the mosque may have been the convert son of an Armenian of Ādharbāyjān, and this may also apply to the architect of the tomb. There would be nothing surprising about this. At Erzincan, as at Erzurum, the Armenian proportion of the population could be estimated from the drinkers of wine in public, and it could not have been very different at Divriği.

Shāhānshāh's cousin, Fakhr al-Dīn Bahrām-Shāh of Erzincan, does not appear to have been a builder; on the other hand, we have coins of his ranging from 563/1167–68 to 616/1219–20. On a 590s' coin he bears the title of *gazi*, which may suggest operations against Trebizond, or participation in the campaigns of his neighbours to the west or south against their Christian adversaries. It is ironical to note that this same coin is nevertheless struck on a Byzantine model. Bahrām-Shāh's principal title to glory however lies in the fact that to him is dedicated the *Makhzan al-asrār*, one of the chief works of the great Persian poet, Niẓāmī of Ganja, which, whether he understood it or not, does at least show that he had an interesting wish to encourage the expansion of Iranian culture around himself. His generosity is also eulogized.

After the disappearance of the Danişmendids and the principality of Malatya, and *a fortiori* with the passing of the Saltukids of Erzurum also, the attitude of Bahrām-Shāh towards the Seljukids was that of a great vassal. This would explain his intervention to reconcile the old Kılıc Arslan II and his son Quṭb al-Dīn, and the facilities later given to Rukn al-Dīn Süleyman II on his intervention in Erzurum. He was also Kılıc Arslan's brother-in-law, and the two families were again brought together later by the marriage of Kay Kāwūs with Bahrām-Shāh's daughter or grand-daughter. The Mengüçekid ruler of Divriği had even more reason to appear in the guise of a vassal; he owed to his insignificance his survival after his kinsmen's lands had been annexed. From this lineage Aḥmad-Shāh b. Süleyman b. Shāhānshāh is attested epigraphically from 626/1228–29 to 640/1242–43. One of his uncles, Isḥāq b. Shāhānshāh, signed the *waqfiyya* of the caravanserai of Karatay in 645/1248. He himself was responsible for the construction of a fine mosque, which still exists, and the completion of the citadel. His son, Ṣāliḥ, improved it in 650/1252–53. The family finally disappeared in obscure circumstances.

CHAPTER SIX

The crisis of growth

The Seljukid state at the date now reached was about to pass through a crisis. In 1185–87 there developed a vast but unfortunately ill-understood Turcoman movement. It originated outside Asia Minor in the strict sense of the word, since the first stages took place in Upper Mesopotamia and Diyār Bakr, in the form of quarrels such as inevitably occurred from time to time between Turcomans and Kurds as they moved in their seasonal search for pasture. Why were these of more serious import? Why did the resulting agitation extend over vast regions? These are questions to which one has difficulty in seeing an answer. Had some new influx of immigrants been the cause? There is nothing to suggest this, for the Oghuz invasions of Iran in the twelfth century do not appear to have had repercussions, at least directly, in the west. Had special economic conditions given rise to a social crisis? Had the movement, the material effects of which will be described, a religious aspect also, like others in the following century? There are so many apparently unanswerable questions.

The fact remains that combats took place in Diyār Bakr and Diyār Rabīʿa between transhumant Turcoman and Kurdish pastoralists, and the Turcomans, led by a certain Rustam, set about massacring the Kurds. Then, indifferent to the religion of the inhabitants, one finds them extending their devastations from the frontiers of Georgia to Cappadocia. Some of them, when returning from a raid into Upper Cilicia in the winter of 1186–87, were caught unawares by the Roupenid prince, Leon II, who in reprisal led a raid into Seljukid territory. Others regrouped on the northern borders of Aleppo and Antioch, gave a shock to Prince Bohemond III, thrust forwards as far as Latakia, and pillaged the lower Orontes and the Amanus. In the end they were destroyed, and Rustam probably killed, by Bohemond in a mountain pass. The echo of this success reached Constantinople, but apparently led to no change in the Turcoman movement based in Seljukid territory.

It was apparently about this time that Kılıc Arslan II, now in his seventies, decided to partition his territories among his sons. They were ten in number, and to them must be added a brother of the sultan with his son. One of the ten must however have disappeared, since the sources agree in mentioning only eleven portions. Tokat went to Rukn al-Dīn Sulaymān-Shāh (the future Sultan Süleyman II), Niksar to Nāṣir al-Dīn Berk Yaruk-Shāh, Elbistan to Mughīth al-Dīn Toğrıl-Shāh, Kayseri to Nūr al-Dīn Maḥmūd Sulṭān-Shāh, Sivas and Aksaray to Quṭb al-Dīn Malik-Shāh, Malatya to Mu'izz al-Dīn Qayṣar-Shāh, Niğde to Arslan-Shāh, Ankara to Muḥyī al-Dīn Mas'ūd-Shāh, Burğlu to Ghiyāth al-Dīn Kay Khusraw (the future Sultan Kay Khusraw I), and finally Ereğli at the entrance to the Taurus, and Amasya to Sancar-Shāh and Niẓām al-Dīn Argun-Shāh, Kılıc Arslan's brother and nephew, respectively. Their governments were registered in Kılıc Arslan's *divan*, and each had to bring him his troops annually. It seems that at first Kılıc Arslan had intended to keep only the capital, Konya, for himself.

Did Kılıc Arslan wish to appease his sons' impatience, to secure that none of them would be dispossessed on his death, or to ensure that the action rendered necessary by Turcoman disorder would be effective? However it might be, jealousy quickily developed among the brothers and even endangered their relations with Kılıc Arslan, as he seemed to support one or another against the demands of his opponent. So conflicts arose, and offered tempting opportunities of diverting Turcoman ardour by embroiling them against the enemy, so that the family disputes of the Seljukids had apparently the effect of enlarging the field of action and the power of the Turcoman bands.

The eldest son was Quṭb al-Dīn Malik-Shāh. Whether or not he was the intended heir, he meant to secure the reality of the succession without delay by seizing Konya and his father's administration. Probably in the first half of 1189 he made an unsuccessful attack on his father, which ended in a massacre of Turcomans but not a disaster. Quṭb al-Dīn first succeeded in getting rid of his opponent, his father's old adviser Ikhtiyār al-Dīn Ḥasan b. Gavras, by sowing mistrust between him and Kılıc Arslan. Ikhtiyār al-Dīn asked permission to retire to Bahrām-Shāh of Erzincan, Kılıc Arslan's son-in-law and the neighbour to Trebizond, whence perhaps he himself came. On the way he was slaughtered by Turcomans, perhaps with the complicity of Bahrām-Shāh, who inherited his wealth. Then in the winter of 1189–90, in conditions which are not clear, Quṭb al-Dīn succeeded in gaining a share in his father's government and in getting possession of Konya – all this, it would seem, with the aid of Rustam's Turcomans.

The crusade of Frederick Barbarossa impinged on this situation. Frederick had established relations with Kılıc Arslan before 1178 because of Manuel Comnenus's opposition to his Italian policy. Availing himself of these old contacts, Frederick sent a German lord, Gottfried von Wiesenbach, to Konya in 1188 to make diplomatic preparations for the passage of his troops through Asia Minor. He had been sent a first response while still at Nuremberg. A more solemn embassy accompanied by Gottfried was to greet him during the march, but because of the great tension between Frederick and the Greeks, it was detained in Constantinople for some weeks and relieved of the gifts intended for the German emperor. Liberated at the time of an agreement concluded between Isaac Angelus and Frederick, who was then at Adrianople, it met him on 14 February 1190 and promised the sultan's cooperation as he passed through Seljukid territory. It was to remain with him at the beginning of the campaign. A few days later another embassy arrived. This was sent by Quṭb al-Dīn to overtake his father's embassy, which he had not authorized. It made the same promises, but its object was certainly to prevent Frederick's being drawn into any Anatolian policy hostile to Quṭb al-Dīn.

If indeed Kılıc Arslan's sole wish was sincerely to arrange for the transit of the new crusaders as peaceably as possibly, this was not the attitude of all the Turks. Kılıc Arslan himself had to take into account the growing influence of Saladin. At the end of 1187 he sent Ḥasan b. Gavras to congratulate Saladin on the taking of Jerusalem, and to betroth Quṭb al-Dīn to his daughter. Saladin naturally encouraged the Seljukid rulers to resist the crusaders, and no doubt sent them subsidies to that end. It is moreover obvious that, apart from their ungovernable nature, the Turcomans had a natural inclination to attempt to pillage and destroy the crusading army; and Quṭb al-Dīn was apparently linked to them in 1190 as previously.

This serves to explain the varied reactions on the Turkish side towards the Germans, when they set out at the end of April from the Greek outposts of Philadelphia and Laodicea ad Lycum, which were already cut off by Turcoman bands. In any case these autonomous frontiersmen had no idea of respecting the peaceful instructions of any sultan. Lent by Kay Khusraw to a Byzantine rebel, Mancaphas, they pillaged Phrygia and Caria until Isaac Angelus won the rebel over from Kay Khusraw with the promise that his life should be spared. It was to be expected that the Turcomans would refuse to provision the crusaders, and would harass and try to ambush them. Kılıc Arslan's envoys explained this to Frederick Barbarossa, and rejoiced more or less wholeheartedly at the defeats which he inflicted on these bands in revolt against Seljukid authority. But it appeared furthermore that afterwards Quṭb al-Dīn himself intervened against the Germans with other Turcomans, 'those of Rustam' – so called as if he were still their leader. In these circumstances official Seljukid chiefs came more or less willingly from their provinces, such as Muḥyī al-Dīn, the ruler of Ankara, and the emir of 'Crazzara' or 'Gandra' (perhaps Çankırı), and directly on the crusaders' route, the emir of Akşehir. They were drawn into hostilities with Barbarossa. Kılıc Arslan's own ambassadors, who were no doubt anxious, were induced to leave the German army to go with the Seljukid governors, as they said, but they were never seen again. From all this there resulted a series of combats in which the Turkish bands were dispersed, and the Germans arrived before the walls of Konya. They no longer felt the favourable attitude towards a Kılıc Arslan whom they could rescue; on the contrary they were determined to take by force what had been refused to them by the seeming perfidy of their opponent. No doubt Kılıc Arslan tried in vain to negotiate; when the attack began, he could only take refuge in the citadel of Konya. The defeat of Quṭb al-Dīn's attempt to relieve the capital, and the beginning of pillage by the Germans, led to a decline in his influence. He had already been criticized by Muḥyī al-Dīn, and was now glad to leave his father to settle matters. Casting the blame on his son, Kılıc Arslan concluded an agreement with the German emperor, who was anxious to reach Syria. It was in the spirit of the promises made in February, except that it was now necessary to hand over hostages. He provisioned the crusading army, which was able to reach Cilicia without further trouble other than attacks by Turkish frontiersmen from Lârende. They were less serious than those at the start, but induced the Germans to hold on to their hostages. This was at the beginning of June 1190.

Quṭb al-Dīn's position was perhaps weakened by these events; in any case it was finally shaken in the following year. At Malatya, Mu'izz al-Dīn, whom he had wanted to dispossess, went to seek Saladin's help. Married by him to a daughter of al-'Ādil, Saladin's brother (then in the course of conquering Diyār Bakr), he felt himself henceforward to be firmly based. Then Quṭb al-Dīn, who had resolved to lay his hands on Nūr al-Dīn Sulṭān-Shāh's portion, took Kılıc Arslan to Kayseri; but Kılıc Arslan profited from the operations by making his escape. Then for some time the old man led a wandering life, going from son to son, which impressed the chroniclers, trying to restore a friendly understanding, and to obtain support against Quṭb al-Dīn, who remained master of Konya, Aksaray and the sultan's treasury. He finally reached an agreement with Ghiyāth al-Dīn Kay Khusraw, who, it is of some significance, was the son of a Christian mother, and was established, perhaps for that reason, in the frontier lands of the west. These had long been overrun by the Turcomans, but the principal places which had hitherto remained to the Byzantines had been acquired from them allowing their integration into Seljuk administration. Kay Khusraw could perhaps count on indigenous Christian support, and certainly on that of the frontier Turcomans, who, however little profit he could expect from them, were as ready to intervene in Anatolian quarrels as they once had been in those of the Greeks. There is in fact formal evidence that it was with their aid (no doubt in fighting the Turcomans of the east, those of Quṭb al-Dīn and Rustam) that Kay Khusraw restored his father to Konya, and then went on to Aksaray. At that point the aged Kılıc Arslan II died in 588/1192, some seventy-seven years of age, after a reign of thirty-eight years. He recognized Kay Khusraw as his heir.

The troubles to which the succession gave rise have been clearly established by Paul Wittek. Kay Khusraw naturally did not succeed in obtaining his brothers' recognition. They acted like independent sovereigns, each minting his own coinage, while some sought to enhance themselves at the expense of others. Quṭb al-Dīn, who had remained master of Sivas and Aksaray, attacked Kayseri in the winter of 1193–94, and put Nūr al-Dīn Maḥmūd and his minister Ḥasan to death. Then he attacked Elbistan, where the prince, Mughīth al-Dīn, escaped defeat in the winter of 1194–95 only with the help of the Armenian prince of Cilicia, Leon II, whose vassal he became. Quṭb al-Dīn died shortly afterwards, but the territorial regrouping which he had begun was continued by Süleyman II Rukn al-Dīn Sulaymān-Shah, who added all Quṭb al-Dīn's inheritance to his own portion of Tokat. In 1197 he took Konya from Kay Khusraw. Immediately afterwards he captured Niksar and Amasya; then in 1201 Malatya, whence his brother Muʿizz al-Dīn fled to al-ʿĀdil, the chief of the Ayyubids, who installed him in Edessa. Rukn al-Dīn then drove the Saltukids from Erzurum, where he installed his brother Mughīth al-Dīn in exchange for Elbistan. Finally after two years of pressure and hostility he occupied Ankara in 1204. There he put to death his brother Muḥyī al-Dīn Masʿūd, who had perhaps lately made approaches to the Byzantines against him. Kay Khusraw had not maintained himself in his former apanage of Burğlu, but had taken refuge in Constantinople.[6] Thus Seljukid unity was re-established. In fact Rukn al-Dīn Süleyman II, who died a few days after his victory at Ankara, did not profit from it, nor did his young son, Kılıc Arslan III, for at this moment the frontier Turcomans reappeared on the scene, discontented at the reign of a child – or profiting from it. Three descendants of the Danişmendid Yağıbasan, using an intermediary, sought out Kay Khusraw. He was with the Byzantine Mavrozomes, a member of the Greek military aristocracy, who was perhaps married to an illegitimate daughter of Manuel Comnenus. Kay Khusraw had taken refuge with him when Constantinople fell to the Latins in 1204. After some resistance organized by orthodox Muslim circles on the pretext that he was the son of an infidel, Kay Khusraw seized Konya in 1205. This latest crisis did not shake Seljukid unity, which was to last until the coming of the Mongols.

The nature of the Turcoman expansion explains why the quarrels among the Seljukid princes in no way hindered the development which had begun previously. During the same period there occurred the revolt of the first Pseudo-Alexius, a Byzantine rebel, who came from Harmala on the Maeander (Menderes) to the aged Kılıc Arslan before his dispossession by Quṭb al-Dīn and obtained a decree ordering the Turcomans to help him. He attracted numerous bands, and occupied part of the Menderes region. At Chonae (Honaz) he caused or permitted the destruction of the mosaic of Christ in the church of St Michael, which presumes a date before the exploits of Mancaphas; shortly afterwards he was killed. At an uncertain date John Vatatzes drove Mancaphas out of Philadelphia. He fled to Konya, and obtained authorization from the sultan to recruit what frontier Turcomans he pleased. With them he spread desolation in the countryside of Laodicea ad Lycum and Chonae (where he burnt the church of St Michael), which were therefore still Greek. If the Byzantine chronicler Nicetas may be believed, he reproached his bands for the humanity they showed towards their Christian neighbours. Finally, on his return to Konya, he was handed over to Isaac Angelus by Kay Khusraw (who had recently succeeded his father) on condition that he was punished only by imprisonment. There is however no indication that the Turcomans ever evacuated the districts to which Mancaphas had brought them. The course of events in fact makes it almost certain (as Wittek has shown) that Laodicea was conquered by the Turks in this period, perhaps without there being any real establishment of a new administration before Mavrozomes (see below). A few years later, towards the beginning of 1197, the Emperor Alexius III Angelus arrested the merchants from Konya in Constantinople, in consequence of Kay Khusraw's interception (perhaps for what he believed a friendly motive) of horses sent to the emperor from Egypt. The sultan made a surprise campaign against Geyre and the Dandalsu, a tributary of the lower Menderes, and alarmed Antioch on the Menderes before leaving for Lampe and Burğlu. Other raids on the lower Menderes are noted about the same time. In these circumstances it is surprising that a little later Alexius III gave a sympathetic welcome (but no help) to Kay Khusraw, when he was ousted by Rukn al-Dīn Süleyman. As will appear, however, relations with Süleyman became strained in their turn. As far as the Menderes region was concerned, he encouraged the depredations of the young Michael Comnenus in 1198 by granting him bands of Turcomans. After the fall of Laodicea (Lâdik), Antioch nevertheless remained the Greek frontier base on the Menderes until the time of the Palaeologi.

The provisional epilogue of these frontier struggles is placed in Kay Khusraw's second sultanate (601–8/1205–11). Mavrozomes, the Byzantine lord with whom he had found refuge on the Latin capture of Constantinople, and who had given him his daughter in marriage, was on bad terms with Theodore I Lascaris, the ruler of the Empire of Nicaea. Kay Khusraw took Mavrozomes with him on his return to Konya. To obtain free passage across Greek territory, Kay Khusraw promised to restore Chonae and Laodicea; but when he reached the frontier, his sons, whom he had left as hostages, fled, and any cession of territory to the Byzantines was out of the question. When Kay Khusraw was established in Konya, Mavrozomes went raiding the Menderes at the head of Turkish forces, and was defeated. Theodore Lascaris needed peace with Kay Khusraw in order to be able to fight the Latins. He formally recognized Kay Khusraw's possession of Laodicea and Chonae, which were given to Mavrozomes to hold as a transitional regime. When Mavrozomes fairly quickly disappeared, Lâdik remained incorporated in the Turkish domains as the principal base of Seljukid authority in the frontier territory.

Further to the north Dorylaeum (Eskişehir) had also fallen to the Turcomans, no doubt before Kılıc Arslan II's death, without perhaps being really incorporated in the Seljukid realm. In this direction also Byzantine dissension helped the progress of the Turks. Under Alexius III, about 1196, a second Pseudo-Alexius, who had at first found refuge in Cilicia, received help from the Seljukid prince of Ankara, Muḥyī al-Dīn Mas'ūd. Thanks to this he occupied Dadybra (Devrek), inland east of Ereğli on the Black Sea coast. Krateia (Gerede) and Claudiopolis (Bolu), which constituted the frontier bases in this region under Manuel, apparently fell at this time. It is remarkable that the Greek writer Nicetas, at the beginning of the thirteenth century, gives its Turkish name to the little mountain chain of the Babadağ near to Devrek, thus bearing witness to the degree to which the country was already turcicized. This Pseudo-Alexius was soon killed, but the territory was not recovered. Alexius III could barely ensure the security of the districts to the west of Dorylaeum. However, Alexius concluded an agreement with Muḥyī al-Dīn Mas'ūd, who was threatened by Rukn al-Dīn Süleyman, and who sent him reinforcements against the Wallachians.

It was above all to the eastern and northern frontiers of the Seljukid state that Rukn al-Dīn Süleyman, unlike Kay Khusraw, turned his attention. Did the reason lie in the interests of his original domains around Tokat, or in the habits of his Turcoman following, which differed from the Turcomans of the Byzantine border attached to Kay Khusraw? Did he judge it preferable to turn the activity of his warriors eastwards, in order to maintain a peace with Byzantium which was jeopardized by his attitude in regard to the Black Sea? Or as the heir of Quṭb al-Dīn, and himself originally the lord of an old Turcoman region, did he give priority to a policy of Muslim unification eastwards, such as had been begun by Kılıc Arslan II? Or did his experience of the disorders caused by Turcomans coming from Armenia make him wish to lay his hands on this reason also? Was he called upon by the Saltukid ruler of Erzurum because of the growing power of the Georgians in alliance with Trebizond, in regard to which he might himself have frontier grievances, or commercial rivalry if he attracted to Samsun the caravans which generally passed from Erzurum to Trebizond? The questions are unanswerable. In any case the known facts are that between 1201 and 1203 Rukn al-Dīn Süleyman entered the territory of Erzurum at the head of contingents led by his brother Mughīth Toğrıl-Shāh of Elbistan, the Mengüçekid Bahrām-Shāh of Erzincan, perhaps the Artukid ruler of Khartpert, and the frontier Turcomans. Whether the Saltukid Abū Manṣūr of Erzurum refused to take part in a war against the Georgians, according to the probably partial account of Ibn Bībī (and it is hard to see why Rukn al-Dīn Süleyman should undertake it on his own as he had no common frontier with them), or whether it was an act of pure treason since Abū Manṣūr received him as an ally, according to the Georgian chronicler and the Arabic historian Ibn al-Athīr – however it might be, Rukn al-Dīn Süleyman arrested Abū Manṣūr, occupied his principality and, as has been mentioned, installed his brother Mughīth al-Dīn there in exchange for Elbistan. He then attacked the Georgians, and was beaten; but Mughīth al-Dīn kept Erzurum.

On the Black Sea coast, Wittek has shown that the Turks of Tokat, who had long been traversing the districts of Oinaeum (Ünye) and Paurae (Bafra), had probably occupied Amisus (Samsun) a little before 1194, and it thus became the northern maritime outlet for Anatolia. At least, Alexius III *c.* 1200 fell on Turkish merchants from Samsun sailing on the Black Sea. The taking of Samsun could also explain the rupture between Alexius and Rukn al-Dīn Süleyman, at a time when a common hostility to Kay Khusraw should have drawn them together. However this may be, it was not the final Turkish occupation. In 1204 or 1205, David Comnenus, the joint ruler of Trebizond, on the march westwards to dispute with Theodore Lascaris the spoils of the Byzantine Empire after its overthrow by the Fourth Crusade, 'closed the sea', as Ibn al-Athīr says. The result was a great crisis among the merchants of Sivas, no doubt augmented by the uncertainties of Kılıc Arslan III's minority. There is moreover no evidence that a genuine Seljukid, not merely a Turcoman, administration and military occupation had been set up in this sector. Kay Khusraw, having regained the sultanate, tried and failed to liberate the coast by operations against Trebizond. Not until 1214 and under his successor did the conquest of Sinope (Sinop) reopen the Black Sea to the Seljukid state – this time for good.

In regard to al-ʿĀdil the Ayyubid (whom as had been seen Muʿizz al-Dīn of Malatya cultivated as an ally), Rukn al-Dīn Süleyman resumed his father's policy of watchfulness on the Euphrates by re-establishing the Seljukid protectorate over Khartpert, and by receiving as a vassal al-Afḍal, a son of Saladin, whom al-ʿĀdil had exiled to a little apanage at Samosata (Samsat). He was moreover allied to another of Saladin's sons, al-Ẓāhir of Aleppo, who feared al-ʿĀdil. At al-Ẓāhir's call, as well as that of Prince Bohemond IV of Antioch and Tripoli, Rukn al-Dīn Süleyman attacked through the Taurus King Leon I of Cilicia (formerly Prince Leon II), who was attempting to seize Antioch. It is evident that he thereby served his own interests also: the Armenians had taken advantage of simultaneous crises in the Frankish, Seljukid and Byzantine states to set up a vigorous little kingdom and, as the heirs of Byzantium, to lay their hands on various coastal places in Isauria previously held by the Greeks. To fight them formed part of the same general programme as the war against Trebizond and the Georgians.

CHAPTER SEVEN

The apogee of the Seljukid State (1205–43)

The second reign of Kay Khusraw I (1205–11)

The replacement of Rukn al-Dīn Süleyman II by Kay Khusraw did not bring about the complete change of policy in regard to the problems of the east that one might have imagined. The new sultan was not indifferent to them, and if he was more interested in his western territories, this was with the exception of the possessions of the Empire of Nicaea because of his agreement with Theodore I Lascaris at the time of his return to power. In the east, apart from the unsuccessful operations against Trebizond already mentioned, he intervened in his turn against the Armenians and, at least through an intermediary, against al-ʿĀdil. At Erzurum Mughīth al-Dīn recognized him as suzerain, as he had Rukn al-Dīn Süleyman previously, and in 604/1207–8 opposed, although vainly, Ayyubid ambition to take Ahlat. Al-Afḍal, also his vassal, had to proceed on his orders to relieve the Artukid of Khartpert when attacked by the Artukid of Āmid. From Leon of Cilicia, whose guest he had formerly been, he claimed the goods he had left which, he said, had not been returned to him; and at the same time in 1209 that he took Pertous (fifteen miles north-west of Maraş) from him, he required him to respect his allies at Aleppo and Antioch, who had called on his support against Leon.

It was however in the west that the great enterprise of Kay Khusraw's second sultanate took place; but there once again, because of his agreement with Theodore Lascaris, outside the Empire of Nicaea and indeed on the possessions of its enemies. In these territories, it will be admitted that the emperor of Nicaea had more or less explicitly recognized that the sultan had as full liberty to operate as against Trebizond and the Armenians of Cilicia. Under Kılıc Arslan III, and no doubt after long encirclement by the Turcomans, Isparta (Gk. Baris) had fallen into the hands of the Turks; Aldobrandini, the lord of Antalya, a Byzantine adventurer from Tuscany, had perhaps tried to save it. In 1207 Kay Khursraw attacked Antalya itself. He doubtless judged it necessary to establish a firm Seljukid base in a land which the Turcomans had long traversed and gone beyond, but there is also above all evidence of commercial relations as well. In the new conditions of the eastern Mediterranean, Antalya could not fail to fall increasingly under Cypriot influence. Merchants from Alexandria complained to Kay Khusraw of their sufferings at the hands of Franks in Antalya. It was in every way the normal southern outlet for Anatolia and Konya, the major port in relations with Egypt. To save themselves, the people of Antalya applied to the regent of Cyprus, Walter of Montbéliard, who brought 200 knights over and compelled the Turks to withdraw slightly. But the Franks were powerless to prevent the attacker devastating the countryside, where the people of Antalya had their estates and means of subsistence. Moreover struggles for power broke out between the local people and the Cypriots. According to Ibn al-Athīr (who lacks confirmation from any source from those directly involved) the Greeks finally called upon the Turks against the Franks; it is at least certain that the principal Frankish source considers that Walter conquered Antalya, while according to Ibn Bībī the Turks had only the Franks to fight. A three-day sack ensued in March 1207. The majority of the Franks fell; then Kay Khusraw constituted the city and its province into a new government for the benefit of his freedman, Mubāriz al-Dīn Ertöküş b. Abdallāh, of whom more will be heard.

The end of Kay Khusraw's reign was however marked by a new breach with the Greeks – the last to be recorded in Seljukid history. Its cause is given diversely by the chroniclers. According to George Acropolites it arose from the intrigues of the old Alexius III Angelus, who came to Kay Khusraw seeking aid to overthrow Theodore Lascaris in return for his former hospitality, and the sultan considered this a good opportunity to attempt the conquest of the whole of Asia Minor. Ibn Bībī does not mention Alexius, but suggests with greater probability the existence of differences between Theodore Lascaris and Kay Khusraw about the right of the Turcoman nomads to pass beyond the official Nicaean-Seljukid frontiers. The *Tārīkh-i Saljūq* contains among legendary details a possible allusion to a Byzantine group, scandalized by the helpless abandonment of Antalya, who demanded redress from the Turks. Finally, some part must evidently be allowed to the diplomacy of Henry of Hainault, the Latin emperor of Constantinople, because of his wars with Theodore Lascaris. Connected with this is the sultan's rapprochement with Venice, evidenced at the political level (at the same time as his interest in commerce) by the treaty they concluded some time after the conquest of Antalya, in which he conceded important privileges to the Venetians. A battle between Kay Khusraw and Theodore Lascaris took place near Antioch on the Menderes, which was under attack from the Turks. The sultan won, but was killed in pursuit of the enemy. This brought about the withdrawal of the Turks, and the capture of the *çaşnigir* Sayf al-Din İneh. The frontier remained stabilized in 1211 immediately to the east of Antioch.

The reign of Kay Kāwūs (1211–20)

The succession to Kay Khusraw I once more gave rise to some difficulties because he had three sons, but it seems there were no further general problems. He had installed his eldest son, 'Izz al-Dīn Kay Kāwūs, at Malatya; another, 'Alā' al-Dīn Kay Qubādh, at Tokat; a third, Kay Farīdūn Ibrāhīm, was, it seems, at Antalya. It appears that the final choice of the sultan lay with the great emirs. Most of them agreed on Kay Kāwūs, who moved first to Kayseri; but Kay Qubādh in Tokat in alliance with Mughīth al-Dīn of Erzurum, Leon of Cilicia and the Danişmendid Ẓāhir al-Dīn İli the *pervane*, refused to recognize him, and proceeded to besiege him. Kay Kāwūs was however supported by the *çaşnigir* Mubāriz al-Dīn Çavlı, the *amīr akhūr* Zayn al-Dīn Bashārā, the *amīr majlis* Mubāriz al-Dīn Bashārā and finally the governor of Kayseri, Jalāl al-Dīn Qayṣar. After thinking of fleeing in order to bring troops recruited among the frontier Turcomans from Konya, Kay Kāwuš succeeded in winning over Ẓāhir al-Dīn and Leon. Disagreement arose between Mughīth al-Dīn and Kay Qubādh, who withdrew to Ankara, while Ẓāhir al-Dīn judged it prudent to move to Cilicia. Kay Kāwūs then entered Konya, and went on to besiege Ankara, where Kay Qubādh was supported by the *beglerbegis* Sayf al-Dīn Kızıl and Ḥusām al-Dīn Amīr Çopan, Turcoman chiefs of the province of Kastamonu. Kay Kāwūs was however the winner. Sayf al-Dīn İneh the *çaşnigir*, liberated by Theodore Lascaris, occupied Ankara for him after its capitulation. Kay Qubādh was sent to honourable imprisonment at Minşar in the province of Malatya, or at Höyük near to Sivas.

There remained Kay Farīdūn. On Kay Khusraw's death there had been a rising of the people of Antalya supported by Frankish contingents. Kay Farīdūn had led the rising, and had himself sought the Cypriot troops. The city was retaken by Kay Kāwūs, and Kay Farīdūn was confined within an apanage of three districts, where he seems to have been secluded from 1212.

The situation could have been more dangerous for Kay Kāwūs if Theodore Lascaris had sought to profit from it, but he, sufficiently absorbed on his other frontiers, limited himself to concluding an agreement with the sultan through the mediation of Sayf al-Dīn İneh. This, it seems, stipulated mutual respect for the existing frontiers. Whether the parties regarded it so or not, this treaty does in fact mark the start of virtually a final peace between the two states. Henceforward the sultans of Konya were to carry out their military operations on other frontiers with other ideas, against the Christians of Cilicia or Trebizond, or the Muslims beyond the Euphrates or in Syria.

One may be amazed at this change of front, not so much at the sultans' expansion to the east as at their abstention in the west. There could be various reasons. The Asian state of Nicaea defended its eastern frontier better than had the former semi-European Empire of Constantinople. The Seljukids did not wish to eliminate this buffer state separating them from the Franks, who were judged to be more dangerous. They did not wish to reinforce the Christian population in their state, but rather the Muslim population. They did not judge conquest in the east, which appeared urgent in view of the turmoil there, to be compatible with parallel activity in the west. All these reasons are hypothetical and undocumented but may vie for acceptance. The resulting direction of effort is in any event patent.

Kay Kāwūs's policy had then as its aims to develop the maritime outlets, the acquisition of which had been begun by Kay Khusraw; to develop influence in the affairs of Syria and Upper Mesopotamia; and to consolidate the frontier on the Taurus, following a tradition which had been picked up by Rukn al-Dīn Süleyman and Kay Khusraw.

In the south with Antalya regained, Kay Kāwūs was concerned to allow the port to pursue and develop its precious activity. This he did by establishing a modus vivendi with the king of Cyprus, whose interests in this matter coincided with his own. The difficulty was that in Kay Kāwūs's policy in regard to Syria and Cilicia, he supported parties opposed to Cyprus, but an increasingly precise correspondence exchanged between the end of 1213 and the end of 1216, at the sultan's initiative as it would seem, allowed the conclusion of agreements. These assured to the merchants of the two states secure commercial conditions in each other's territory, while reserving the liberty to fight or to support respectively Leon of Cilicia and his nephew Raymond Roupen. The latter held Antioch from 1216 to 1219.

In the north the great success of Kay Kāwūs's reign was the acquisition of Sinop, which for the first time firmly opened a window on the Black Sea for the Seljukid state. The urgency of this was all the greater in that Theodore Lascaris had defeated Trebizond, and was extending his rule eastwards along the coast, so that without a difficult war with him, which would be contrary to his policy, Kay Kāwūs risked finding himself finally deprived of any access to the Black Sea. On the other hand by acting quickly and taking Sinop at the far western extremity of the Empire of Trebizond, he could stop further expansion without a breach with Nicaea. In his hands

Sinop would henceforward prevent all contact between the two Byzantine states without greatly dissatisfying Theodore Lascaris, who would thus be protected from further attacks by his rival, the Grand Comnenus of Trebizond. It is possible that David Comnenus, the brother of Alexius Comnenus of Trebizond and the real military chief of the family, was killed during the operations which then took place, or their preliminaries. The capture of Sinop was partly the result of the good fortune which allowed Kay Kāwūs to take Alexius by surprise when he was venturing into Turcoman country in the debatable land between the two states. The sight of their emperor led captive beneath their walls did not easily persuade the townspople of Sinop to obey his order, given under duress, to surrender their city. Ultimately however they capitulated on 1 November 1214, on a promise that their lives and possessions would be safe, and Alexius was set free. Furthermore he became Kay Kāwūs's vassal, promising the payment of an annual tribute and the sending of military contingents on demand. These terms were certainly not regularly carried out, but Sinop remained in Seljukid possession. The ramparts were restored and completed at the expense of fifteen emirs, whose names survive in the inscriptions commemorating their respective tasks. A governor was installed in the person of an Armenian, probably a convert, named Hetoum; a Turkish garrison was brought in, and the chief church was turned into a mosque. Sinop, a very strong place, was henceforward the Seljukid outlet and base on the Black Sea. Its importance will soon appear.

As regards Cilicia, Leon I's undertakings towards Kay Khusraw had certainly not survived that sultan's death. On the contrary, we have seen how the Armenian ruler tried to break out of the Taurus, and to intervene in Seljukid affairs. When Leon set out in 1216 to take Antioch for his nephew Raymond from Bohemond IV, Bohemond once again, like his ally al-Ẓāhir of Aleppo, appealed for a diversion by the sultan. Kay Kāwūs did not hesitate. At the end of 1216 he took the two fortresses of Ganchin or Shogagan and Janjin in northern Cilicia – the latter, if this information is correct, only temporarily, since Kay Qubādh had to retake it later. He defeated and captured the Armenian constable, Constantine, and in 1218 obtained the cession of the stronghold of Lu'lu'a as his ransom. This was a place of the first importance on the route from Sis to Kayseri, and was henceforward to be one of the most powerful Seljukid bases, at the same time controlling the profitable silver mines in its vicinity.

Beyond Cilicia, Kay Kāwūs's reign marks the active resumption of the policy of intervention in Syria. In his last years al-Ẓāhir had sought a reconciliation with al-ʿĀdil in order to secure the succession of his young son (al-ʿAzīz Muḥammad) to Aleppo, while at the same time he maintained contact with Kay Kāwūs as a means of reinsurance. This limited the help on which the sultan could count in Syria, or even against the Cilicians, whom al-'Ādil supported. When al-Ẓāhir died in the last days of 1216, Kay Kāwūs thought this a good opportunity to establish himself more firmly in Syria.

In order not to alienate opinion by an open wish to annex a country in which he seemed a foreigner, he put forward the candidature of his Ayyubid vassal, al-Afḍal, al-Ẓāhir's brother, to succeed to Aleppo. He thought that the arrival of the Fifth Crusade would prevent the Aleppines from receiving help from al-'Ādil or his sons. In the spring of 1218 Kay Kāwūs and al-Afḍal occupied the north of the province of Aleppo, which his ancestors had briefly possessed – Merzban, Raban and Tall Bāshir, where he exhumed and burnt the corpse of Ẓāhir al-Dīn İli. Beside the troops of the eastern Seljukid provinces and the frontier Turcomans, the essential role in the expedition was played by the emir of Maraş, Nuṣrat al-Dīn Ḥasan b. Ibrāhīm. In the face of this danger the regent of Aleppo, al-Ẓāhir's widow, appealed to her brother al-Ashraf Mūsā, al-'Ādil's son and lieutenant in the Jazīra, who had come to Syria to support him against the Franks. Unmindful of his former disagreements with al-Ẓāhir, he hastened and, whether by surprise or by intrigue with Kay Kāwūs's emirs, he inflicted a crushing defeat on the Seljukid army near to Buzā'a. It dispersed in the direction of Elbistan, abandoning all its conquests.

The enterprise was unfortunate and, depending as always on al-Afḍal, Kay Kāwūs sought revenge by an attack on the Jazīra. There Badr al-Dīn Lu'lu' (who, although he was the minister of the last Zengid, a minor, was seeking power for himself) and his supporter al-Ashraf were confronted by the child-ruler's uncle and the Artukid ruler of Ḥiṣn Kayfā and Āmid. In spite of the latter's previous conflict with the Seljukids, they appealed to Kay Kāwūs, who had reinforced his position on his eastern frontier by marriage with the daughter of his vassal or ally, Bahrām-Shāh of Erzincan. Kay Kāwūs had nothing to fear from Mughīth al-Dīn, whose policy in regard to al-Ashraf was parallel to his own. Beyond the Jazīra he had shown his good relations with the caliph by requesting the insignia of the *futuwwa*, which were brought by Shaykh Shihāb al-Dīn 'Umar al-Suhrawardī. He prepared an expedition beyond the Euphrates, but in 617/December 1220 he died. The coalition broke up. Lu'lu' and al-Ashraf won, and there also Seljukid influence suffered a check.

The reign of Kay Qubādh I (1220–37)

'Alā' al-Dīn Kay Qubādh I, who succeeded his brother Kay Kāwūs I, was to leave to posterity the memory of the most renowned ruler of the dynasty

– partly, it is true, because he was the last of them to be independent. His accession was comparatively easy in spite of the disaffection of some emirs who, having formerly opposed him to Kay Kāwūs's advantage, would now perhaps have preferred Kay Farīdūn or Mughīth al-Dīn of Erzurum. There again appeared the decisive role of some great emirs, even those who had earlier supported Kay Kāwūs at his accession against Kay Qubādh. There was as well Sharaf al-Dīn Mehmed the *pervane*, and those who now went to seek him in prison, and organized the journey and ceremonies of his return. With no precedent in the accounts of previous accessions, Shaykh 'Umar al-Suhrawardī came in especially solemn manner to bring the new ruler an official diploma from the caliph for the sultanate over the land of Rūm; it is not known who took the initiative in this.

The new sovereign was certainly a personality. Ibn Bībī, who knew his contemporaries and close relatives, describes him as being instructed in religion, history and chemistry, as knowing and practising several arts, a lover of sport and a chess-player. He was attached to the example and teachings of Maḥmūd of Ghazna, Qābūs b. Wushmgīr and Niẓām al-Mulk. He was moreover generous. Others found him haughty and mistrustful. It will be seen that he was always concerned to keep great and potentially dangerous emirs in obedience, and he strictly limited their means. It may be that his policy of conquest was a response at one and the same time to aims inherited from his predecessors, and to a desire for prestige among monarchs and for the redirection of the activities of such emirs towards external benefits.

The first conquests were realized at the expense of the Armenians of Cilicia or of the Greco-Armenian lords who were formerly dependants of Byzantium, and were now doubtless more or less clearly such of Leon I and his successors. The first was the conquest in 1221 of Kalonoros (Alaiye, later Alanya) on the eastern coast of the gulf of Antalya. Its Greek lord, Kir Farīd, capitulated after a vigorous siege of two months, and took in exchange the government of Akşehir in Seljukid territory. The place was renamed Alaiye after the sultan. Henceforward it was one of the principal strongholds of the Seljukid rulers, as well as a winter residence during the Anatolian cold season. The occupation of the coast between Antalya and Alanya was completed by the taking of Alara. Then in 1225, in consequence of operations conducted in Isauria facing Cyprus by Ertöküş, the governor of the province, other places including Anamur were acquired. The coastal frontier was pushed back eastwards to the district of Silifke (Gk. Seleucia), a possession of the Hospitallers under Armenian suzerainty. These conquests were rounded off by a corresponding penetration of the mountainous hinterland. In 1222 Bohemond IV of Antioch, formerly allied to the Seljukids but now protector of Cilicia (his son, Philip, having succeeded

Leon), repulsed a Turkish threat. In 1225 however Bohemond renewed the old alliance as Philip had been overthrown by the Armenian lord, Constantine of Lampron, for the benefit of his own son, Hetoum. Operations led by Çavlı the *çaşnigir* and the emir Comnenus ended in the final occupation of Janjin, and the establishment in the massif of Ermenek and Mut of a march-territory for a certain Qamar al-Dīn, who was to leave his name to it. This country into which Turcomans were to infiltrate, or to which they were attracted, was subsequently to become the centre of one of their most important groups, the cradle of the Karamanids. It seems that in 1231, thanks to reinforcements brought by the Emperor Frederick II and the Khwarazmian invasion of Seljukid territory, the Cypriots conspired with the governor of Alanya to retake the city. The plot, if it existed, was dis-covered, the governor put to death, and henceforward the integration of these important new regions in the Seljukid realm was undisturbed.

On the opposite coast Seljukid policy appears still bolder, inasmuch as it was not limited to attacks on the frontier of Trebizond, but disputed on the sea and as far as the Crimea the commercial preponderance and political supremacy which Trebizond had acquired since the fall of the Byzantine Empire. With the exception of the Crimean campaign, which is well documented from the Seljukid point of view, the facts here are difficult to put together. The hostilities, in which frontier peoples not well known to Ibn Bībī especially participated, appear only in a few incongruous, scattered and incomplete notices.

Relations had been established between the inhabitants of the northern coasts of the Black Sea and the subjects of the Seljukids. At the time of the first Mongol invasion of southern Russia, merchants from the great Crimean port of Sughdāq and other Russian peoples from further north took refuge in Seljukid Asia Minor, evidently by way of Sinop. However, since the break-up of the Byzantine Empire, the Crimean ports had been vassals of Trebizond, to which they were attached by their commercial interests more than to Nicaea, and perhaps even Constantinople since the Latin conquest. This dependence could not have pleased the merchants of Sinop, once it had become a Seljukid possession. There are a Muslim tale and a tale from Trebizond about an episode which illustrates this rivalry, albeit in irreconcilable terms. A ship of Russian refugees having been wrecked, the sultan's authorities seized all that could be saved, as was the general custom. So writes Ibn al-Athīr, while an author of Trebizond says that the ship was carrying the tribute due from Cherson to Trebizond. Hetoum of Sinop attacked it while knowing this, and furthermore pillaged the coasts of *Gothia* in 1223. Hostilities ensued between the Seljukids and Trebizond, where the new emperor, Andronicus Gidos, made a raid by sea on Sinop. In consequence Hetoum agreed to an exchange of captives. A Seljukid prince, named only Melik by the author from Trebizond, thereupon attacked Trebizond, but suffered a disaster at its gates (perhaps being made prisoner), in consequence of which he had to acknowledge himself a vassal or ally of the city. One is tempted to imagine that the attack came from Mughīth al-Dīn Toğrıl-Shāh of Erzurum or his successor. It is known that his relations with Kay Qubādh were very bad in the following years, and it is possible that the tension between them goes back to the quarrel of 1212. Nevertheless their policies perhaps remained parallel, and the real break may have been a consequence of the new alignment of Mughīth al-Dīn's policy following his defeat. In any case, it seems impossible that Melik can signify Kay Qubādh, as Ibn Bībī would not have failed to mention a campaign in that direction. Ibn al-Athīr knows only that five years later, Kay Qubādh's expedition against Erzurum was interrupted by the necessity of going to ward off an attack of Trebizond on Sinop, evidently a diversion to help Mughīth al-Dīn, now an ally.

Meanwhile the memorable Crimean campaign took place. Is it to this that the author from Trebizond alludes as mere pillaging, by slightly compressing the dates? Apart from this possible exception, only Ibn Bībī mentions this important expedition. After the Mongol retreat, Russian influence prevailed at Sughdāq. Merchants coming from Seljukid territory said that they had to suffer unjustifiable confiscations. Kay Qubādh carried out an operation against Sughdāq by the agency of the head of the province of Kastamonu, Ḥusām al-Dīn Amīr Çopan, his old friend of Ankara days. The people of Sughdāq asked the Kipchaks to intervene, but they were crushed. When the Russians sought to negotiate, the port had to capitulate and accept, as well as the indemnification of the merchants, the establishment of a Seljukid protectorate. This was marked by the founding of a mosque, the installation of a garrison, and the nomination of a *qāḍī* (? 1225). There is no information as to whether this protectorate remained in force until the final Mongol conquest in 1239.

Even more than his predecessors did Kay Qubādh practise an active policy of intervention in Armenia and the Mesopotamian frontier regions in accordance with his 'international' policy. The latent disharmony which opposed al-Ashraf to his brother, al-Muʿaẓẓam of Damascus, no doubt contributed to the entente which Kay Qubādh, contrary to his predecessors, concluded with him on his accession. In 1226–27 al-Masʿūd Mawdūd, the Artukid lord of Āmid and Ḥiṣn Kayfā, participated in a coalition of the Jazīra against al-Ashraf, who appealed to the sultan. Kay Qubādh was delighted to take from his unreliable neighbour, al-Masʿūd, his strongholds west of the Euphrates. There were two expeditions, one against Kâhta to the south, the other to the north. At the last moment al-Masʿūd won over al-Ashraf, who then vainly tried to save Kâhta. Al-Ashraf tried at the same time to effect a rapprochement with al-Muʿaẓẓam, and went to him in Damascus. Kay Qubādh tried to take part in the negotiations between the Ayyubids, since about this time he sent ambassadors to al-Ashraf, to the Artukid Ghāzī of Mayyāfāriqīn, to al-Muʿaẓẓam of Damascus, to al-Mujāhid of Ḥimṣ (who was influential at Aleppo, and an ally of al-Ashraf), and finally to al-Kāmil, the sultan of Egypt and head of the Ayyubids, and his representative at Damascus. The instructions of these ambassadors are however unknown.

It was partly in connection with these events that Kay Qubādh annexed the principality of Erzincan, and intervened in that of Erzurum. Very little is known of events in either. At Erzincan the aged Mengüçekid Bahrām-Shāh died in 622/1225. Some emirs complained to Kay Qubādh about his son and successor, Dāwūd-Shāh, and he distributed *iqṭāʿ*s to them. Dāwūd-Shāh became anxious and went to Kayseri. After an audience with the sultan, a treaty was drafted between them. Dāwūd-Shāh must however have obtained the impression that a rupture was imminent, for immediately on his return (at least according to the Seljukid version) he opened negotiations with the prince of Erzurum, with al-Ashraf, and with a certain ʿAlāʾ al-Dīn called *Naw-Musulmān* (i.e. New Muslim), the chief of the Assassins of Alamūt, who had obtained this name after concluding an agreement with the Caliph al-Nāṣir. Finally Dāwūd-Shāh negotiated with the Khwārazm-Shāh Jalāl al-Dīn Mengübirti when he appeared in western Iran, offering these potential allies the stronghold of Kemah in exchange for their help. Al-Ashraf came to Erzincan. The sultan however learnt of these intrigues, and sent an army to attack the city. The emirs vainly advised Dāwūd-Shāh to send his son to attempt to obtain a reconciliation with Kay Qubādh. At the last moment, perhaps no longer counting on help as not being ready in time, he had to agree to participate in the campaign which Kay Qubādh was preparing against Erzincan. Then when the Seljukid army was in his native city, he had to give up his principality in exchange for an important *iqṭāʿ*, and Kay Qubādh gave him Akşehir (which no longer belonged to Kir Farīd), lying deep in the heart of Anatolia. Another Mengüçekid, the lord of Kuğuniya, likewise accepted similar compensation for himself and his three sons on the approach of the Seljukid army. The grant included the city of Kırşehir, where he remained with marriage-links to the sultan until the reign of Kay Khusraw II.

The principality of Erzincan had never caused trouble to the Seljukids. It is evident that if Kay Qubādh now suppressed it, this was not because of the emirs' complaints, which furnished an additional classical pretext, but because the imminence of a final settlement with the ruler of Erzurum and the Ayyubids (behind whom loomed the Khwarazmian threat) caused the sultan to feel for the first time the necessity of the firm and direct possession of a particularly important strategic territory. Only at Divriği, which could only be docile, being more remote, less important and encircled by Seljukid territory, did Kay Qubādh allow a last Mengüçekid to survive to at least 650/1252, to judge from inscriptions and a *waqfiyya*. As for Erzincan, the government was given to Ertöküş. He had recently been promoted to be *atabeg* to Kay Khusraw, the sultan's eldest son, who was not regarded as the heir apparent, and no doubt was ultimately intended to receive Erzincan as an apanage.

The situation in Erzurum before Kay Qubādh's intervention is hardly better known. Like Rukn al-Dīn Süleyman and Kay Khusraw, Mughīth al-Dīn Toğrıl-Shāh had begun his reign in opposition to the sons of al-ʿĀdil, when in 604/1207–8 he came to the aid of Balaban, the lord of Ahlat, against al-Awḥad b. al-ʿĀdil of Mesopotamia, who sought to seize the city and the lordship. Mughīth al-Dīn was however unable to stop al-Awḥad, for, once established at Ahlat, he had treacherously done Balaban to death, and then was driven out by a rising of the townspeople, who had themselves called on al-Awḥad. Subsequently on al-Awḥad's death in 607/1210, Ahlat passed to his brother al-Ashraf, in whose affairs Mughīth al-Dīn does not seem to have meddled either as an ally or an enemy. It was also perhaps because he preferred to turn his attention to Trebizond and the Georgians – he was perhaps the author and the victim of the unfortunate expedition against Trebizond in 1223 mentioned above. The Georgians had been troublesome neighbours since their occupation of Kars about 1206, and at times Mughīth al-Dīn had to pay them tribute. Georgian offensives were however directed almost exclusively towards Arrān, Ādharbāyjān and Ahlat. In fact, around 1223 Mughīth al-Dīn yielded to the demand of the queen of Georgia, Rusudan, who had received one of his sons as a negotiator or a hostage. She now offered to marry him, if he would become a Christian – a serious matter, which Mughīth al-Dīn accepted. We are ignorant of his relations with his neighbours in Ādharbāyjān. Two inscriptions appear to indicate that in 610/1213 Bayburt was a dependency of Erzurum, and in 625/1227–28 of Erzincan – perhaps an effect of the defeat by Trebizond of the close alliance of Bahrām-Shāh with Kay Kāwūs and Kay Qubādh. As regards Kay Qubādh, it is not known if the quarrel of 1212, following the only known intervention of Mughīth al-Dīn in the affairs of Asia Minor, had any consequences. There is no proof that his few partisans at the time of Kay Kāwūs's death were incited by him. He died in 622/1225 at about the same time as Bahrām-Shāh.

It is no doubt with Mughīth al-Dīn's successor, Rukn al-Dīn Jahān-Shāh, that Dāwūd-Shāh of Erzincan tried to negotiate against Kay Qubādh. It is known that the sultan's attack on Erzincan was followed by another, probably preconceived, against Erzurum, which he was obliged to break off by a diversion from Trebizond. Jahān-Shāh had also obtained backing by offering his homage to al-Ashraf, which brought to him al-Ashraf's principal lieutenant in the far north-east of the Ayyubid realm, the *ḥājib* Ḥusām al-Dīn b. Abī ʿAlī. It was the moment when the brief alliance between Kay Qubādh and al-Ashraf slackened. Furthermore Jahān-Shāh and al-Ashraf found themselves drawn together by the common danger newly presented by the Khwarazmian advance. In 623/1226 a Khwarazmian detachment from Georgia pillaged the countryside of Erzurum up to the edge of Khartpert. At the same time Jalāl al-Dīn Mengübirti, allied to al-Ashraf's enemies in the Jazīra and Syria, reached Ahlat. In 624/1227, after he was forced to lift the siege, Jahān-Shāh aided the *ḥājib* to make a reprisal expedition into Ādharbāyjān. So it was normal for the *ḥājib* in turn to help him in the following year against Kay Qubādh, who they might also think was not hostile to Jalāl al-Dīn.

It was in fact at about this time that the Khwārazm-Shāh Jalāl al-Dīn Mengübirti began to intervene as an important factor in the politics of western Asia. The son of the Khwārazm-Shāh Muḥammad, whom the Mongols had driven out of his realm, he had reassembled around himself the bands of tough warriors who had formerly brought about the expansion of his father's possessions. Fleeing the Mongols, reduced to conquering in order to survive, profiting from the break-up of the Iranian powers, he carved out for himself an empire of which north-eastern Iran gradually appeared to become the central zone. With his fate constantly in the balance between power and death, and the terror caused by his men, while he awaited the obscure end which he was to find on the morrow of his very greatest successes – all this won him among his contemporaries a considerable reputation in which admiration and dread were mingled. It seems that the former feeling predominated among the Turks of Asia Minor, although he threatened and fought them. This was perhaps because of some feeling of ethnic kinship, which was clearer than in the neighbouring states, where the rulers, even when of Turkish origin, were too much detribalized. Or perhaps it was because of the country whence he came, that of their ancestors, the memory of which was revived by the numerous new refugees in flight before Jalāl al-Dīn himself or his Mongol adversaries.

For several years Jalāl al-Dīn's influence had been perceptible in the rivalries at work in Upper Mesopotamia among the Ayyubids, the Artukids and Lu'lu' of Mosul. However, as long as his expansion westwards was carried out at the expense of the Georgians, and indeed of al-Ashraf, Rukn al-Dīn Jahān-Shāh, or the Artukid of Khartpert, the impending danger clearly constituted by the Khwarazmian conquest of such places as Ahlat, the guardian of one of the invasion routes into Asia Minor, was compensated by the immediate advantage of the weakening of troublesome neighbours.

Since for his part Jalāl al-Dīn certainly did not intend for the time being to provoke intervention on behalf of his enemies by the powerful Seljukid sultan, the relations between the two rulers were at first correct. In 1225 the *qāḍī* Mujīr al-Dīn Ṭāhir b. Saʿd al-Khwārazmī was sent by Jalāl al-Dīn to make contact, somewhat haughtily, with both Kay Qubādh and the princes of Syria. The mission was perhaps insufficiently successful, since he was imprisoned for a while on his return. However, Kay Qubādh sent a friendly embassy in response to Jalāl al-Dīn, who was then at Ganja. In the following year an envoy from Kay Qubādh's vezir went for discussions with the vezir of Jalāl al-Dīn, who was demanding a subsidy from the Seljukid state towards the expenses of fighting the Mongols; he emphasized the burden on Kay Qubādh of his wars against the western infidels. In 1227 Jalāl al-Dīn, who had passed the previous year in southern Iran, returned to the north and without delay undertook the siege of Ahlat. This was at the time when a coolness developed in the relations between Kay Qubādh and al-Ashraf; an envoy who brought presents to Jalāl al-Dīn not only told him of the intrigues being carried on against him, but suggested the marriage of Kay Qubādh's son, Kay Khusraw, to a daughter of Jalāl al-Dīn and also proposed an alliance against al-Ashraf.

In 1229 however matters took a fresh turn. Jalāl al-Dīn had just captured Ahlat after a frightful siege, thanks to the absence of al-Ashraf, who was detained in Syria. The two Artukids of Diyār Bakr at once substituted his name in the *khuṭba* for that of Kay Qubādh, which they had used from the time of his alliance with al-Ashraf. Rukn al-Dīn Jahān-Shāh's actions were more serious. His collaboration with al-Ashraf's forces against Jalāl al-Dīn has been mentioned. He had imprisoned merchants on the way to Jalāl al-Dīn's country and had put to death one of his ambassadors returning from Kay Qubādh. But Jalāl al-Dīn had captured the son of Mughīth al-Dīn who was married to the queen of Georgia; admittedly he had fled, and she had not sought his return as she was in quest of new loves. Rukn al-Dīn Jahān-Shāh in fear offered his homage to Jalāl al-Dīn, and begged him for help against Kay Qubādh. Whether the conquest of Asia Minor was Jalāl al-Dīn's own idea, or whether it was suggested to him by Rukn al-Dīn Jahān-Shāh, it was on this that he decided and not on the continuation of negotiations with Kay Qubādh. Even before the siege of Ahlat an embassy from the sultan had set out for Jalāl al-Dīn, but it was delayed by Rukn al-Dīn, and perhaps hastened his decision to go to Jalāl al-Dīn's camp and offer his final submission. The sultan's embassy arrived only at the end of the siege, when the agreement between Jalāl al-Dīn and Jahān-Shāh had been firmly concluded. The presents brought by the ambassadors could neither change Jalāl al-Dīn's mind, nor save the embassy from an ignominious reception. When Kay Qubādh heard of his ambassadors' delay, it was in vain that he sent Kamyar, his personal *pervane*, to join them at Ahlat; he was not more fortunate. A Khwarazmian embassy to Kay Qubādh sent, according to Nasawī, in response to that from Kay Qubādh, but according to Ibn Bībī before it, had the same result. Kay Qubādh's ambassadors also vainly endeavoured to make Jahān-Shāh realize, as they passed through Erzurum, the dangers of his attitude. Kamyar could only hasten to warn his master that danger was imminent.

Kay Qubādh immediately came to a conclusion. At the same time as despatching 2,000 horsemen to Erzincan under Çavlı the *çaşnigir*, he sent Kamyar to explain to al-Kāmil (who was then at Ḥarrān) and al-Ashraf the impossibility of any agreement with Jalāl al-Dīn, and the immediate necessity of forming a coalition against the Khwarazmians. Al-Ashraf, as a victim of the Khwarazmians, was won over in advance; al-Kāmil, who wanted to be the protector of all the Ayyubid princes, might easily have been so, but because of the Emperor Frederick II's crusade he could only send to al-Ashraf reinforcements from Aleppines, from Ghāzī of Mayyāfāriqīn, and some other Ayyubids of the second rank. The entire Ayyubid army disposed of 5,000 elite troops including a Kurdish contingent from Aleppo and light Arab horsemen. Kay Qubādh himself is estimated to have had 12,000 to 20,000 men with urgently obtained contingents from his vassals or his forced allies of Cilicia and Franks. Çavlı came and rejoined him with the frontiersmen. It was said in Asia Minor that Jalāl al-Dīn had on his side 100,000 men – at any rate a certain superiority in numbers. The junction of the allied forces was effected at Sivas, whither the Syrian army had arrived by way of Elbistan, and it was marked by a ceremonious interview between Kay Qubādh and al-Ashraf. Rukn al-Dīn Jahān-Shāh had informed Jalāl al-Dīn of the combination hatched against him, and he besieged Manzikert (Malazgirt). He sent Rukn al-Dīn ahead to Khartpert to try to stop the junction of the enemy forces; but he fell ill, and without his backing Rukn al-Dīn's corps could not reach the place. Leaving his vezir to continue the siege, Jalāl al-Dīn decided there and then to invade Seljukid territory by the northern route. He marched on Erzincan, then passed it by, and chose a battlefield at Yasıçoman, a grassy basin west of the city on the route to Sivas. On the way he had almost destroyed a Seljukid vanguard on 24 Ramaḍān 628/28 July 1231. The main body of the allied army followed by way of Akşehir of Erzincan. The clash took place on 25 Ramaḍān/29 July. There were indecisive conflicts for three days; it was in a sense a success for the allies to have proved that their adversary was not invincible. They became accustomed to his way of fighting, and al-Ashraf noted his points of weakness. The final battle took place on 28 Ramaḍān/1 August. Later accounts by the participants betray the rivalry of their self-esteem. According to the Syrian versions, the Seljukid army was for a while in disarray, and it was al-Ashraf's troops who gained the victory. Their role was decisive in any event, and the impression that they gained partly explains al-Kāmil's enterprise (to be described shortly). Jalāl al-Dīn was beaten and, panic-stricken by an Ayyubid assault on his tent, he fled, abandoning his treasures. He raised the siege of Manzikert, evacuated Ahlat and halted only in Ādharbāyjān. The Khwarazmians were pushed back into ravines, river-beds and ruined houses, and were massacred en masse, apart from 3,000 who succeeded in finding refuge in the territory of Trebizond (no doubt an ally), together with others who were dispersed, and whom Jalāl al-Dīn could not hope to rally. An enormous quantity of booty was gathered, and numbers of prisoners filled the slave-markets. A considerable impression was created by such a disaster inflicted on a man and an army before whom Iran had trembled for ten years. Christians as well as Muslims gave Kay Qubādh a triumphant welcome.

For Kay Qubādh the principal gain for the Khwarazmian defeat was the annexation of the principality of Erzurum. Rukn al-Dīn Jahān-Shāh had been captured in the catastrophe. Accompanied by al-Ashraf, Kay Qubādh went on to invest the city. Deprived of any possibility of help and with their prince a prisoner, the magnates of Erzurum negotiated with the sultan, while al-Ashraf interceded for his former ally. In exchange for his principality, Jahān-Shāh obtained Aksaray and Ayyubhisar in the heart of his conqueror's territory. Erzurum was not given as an apanage this time, but kept under direct administration. Thus the Seljukid state, confronting the upheavals of the Iranian world and the approach of the Mongols, grew in western Armenia, as the Byzantine Empire had done two centuries before at the first news of the Turkish influx. It was to be equally vain, as the future was to show.

Al-Ashraf however took a Georgian place in revenge for their participation in the Khwarazmian attack – participation which in some respects was under duress but accorded with traditional Georgian ambitions. He then reconquered Manzikert and Ahlat with the cooperation of 5,000 Seljukid horsemen under the command of Mubāriz al-Din Çavlı the *çaşnigir*. It was just then that the alarm at Alanya (previously mentioned) occurred, and this obliged Kay Qubādh to make a precipitate departure. Doubtless profiting from the dispersal of Seljukid forces at the same time as the discomfiture of the Khwarazmians, Mongol forces which had reached Ādharbāyjān forced the Armenian frontier and carried out a raid into the hinterland as far as the province of Sivas and up to the gates of Khartpert and Malatya. The sultan hastily despatched Kamyar with slave troops of the Guard and the Bedchamber against them, but the enemy had disappeared. With Çavlı established at Erzurum in charge of the defence of the frontier, he studied future means of protection. It seemed to them that the Georgians, yesterday the allies of Rukn al-Dīn Jahān-Shāh, then the vassals of the Khwarazmians, were now perhaps accomplices of the Mongols or were incapable of stopping them. In any case it would be useful to extend the glacis protecting the sultanate at their expense, and no doubt Kay Qubādh and Çavlı did not view unfavourably the idea of compensating with Georgian booty the losses due to recent Khwarazmian and Mongol pillage in Armenia. Great numbers of foot-soldiers rallied. Georgia was invaded, thirty frontier places fell in a week. Queen Rusudan had no reason to wish to keep her unhappy country at war with the Seljukids, after its devastation by the Khwarazmians and the Mongols in succession. She resumed with this new partner the policy followed in the past with the prince of Erzurum; she asked for a rapprochement sanctioned by the marriage of the daughter she had had by Toğrıl-Shah's son with the son of Kay Qubādh, Kay Khusraw. The matter was agreed in principle, although the actual marriage was not to be celebrated until later. Thereupon the Seljukid army returned to Erzincan.

Seljukid Armenia had suffered profoundly from this succession of invasions and wars. Famine was raging. Moreover al-Ashraf appeared to abandon his remote and weaker provinces to their fate, and to concern himself only with Syria and Diyār Bakr. This situation could be prejudicial even to the defence of the Seljukid territories. For this reason, if Ibn Bībī may be credited, or simply because he found the occasion favourable to the resumption of his policy of eastward expansion, which had been interrupted only by the Khwarazmian danger, Kay Qubādh ordered Kamyar to take charge of the organization of all the country from Bitlis to Tiflis, and Kamyar occupied Ahlat. The organizational measures taken in all the eastern provinces proved that it was a final taking into possession. Kamyar had drawn the sultan's attention to the devastation of the country. Kay Qubādh sent commissioners to register the possessions of the dead or fugitive inhabitants, to redistribute land and provisions to the surviving landowners and cultivators, to reappoint commandants of fortresses and so forth. This brought the fugitives back from Arrān and Georgia. Sinān al-Dīn Kaymaz was nominated *serleşker* of all the eastern territories.

There was however a lack of sufficient military forces for permanent maintenance in this region, but no lack of roaming bands of Khwarazmians. They wandered about causing mischief, footloose among the belligerents, and were ready to hire themselves out to the first bidder to obtain a little security. Some under their principal chief, Qīrkhān, welcomed for the moment by Ghāzī of Mayyāfāriqīn and al-Ashraf, were to be found south of Ahlat on Lake Van. Kaymaz arranged with him for the entry of the Khwarazmians into Seljukid service. He went with other chiefs to a ceremonious session arranged by Kaymaz. There in front of the commissioners they took the oath in return for the distribution of the territory in *iqṭāʿ*

with title-deeds. Such as it was, the solution proved illusory. Mongols were still to be found in Mūghān. A contingent of them numbering 700 surprised Khwarazmians in the pastures of Dogodaph, and they fled panic-stricken. To keep them in territory which was constantly exposed to Mongol attack appeared impossible to the chief commissioner. He brought their chiefs to Kayseri. Kay Qubādh was there, and he distributed important lands to them in *iqṭāʿ*. They were dispersed in the interior of the realm at Amasya, Lârende and Niğde. He could thus count on their forces being mobilized in the event of future conflict.

As after the victory of Yasıçoman the Khwarazmian threat had ended in the unification of western Armenia under Seljukid rule, so too it had ended in the almost complete unification of Diyār Bakr under that of the Ayyubids, whose chief, al-Kāmil, had succeeded with al-Ashraf's help in taking Āmid and Ḥiṣn Kayfā from the Artukids. The two territories were allotted to al-Kāmil's son, al-Ṣāliḥ Ayyūb. Only Mardin further to the south remained to the Artukids, although it was closely encircled. Henceforward Seljukid and Ayyubid ambitions were directly at odds, and the taking of Ahlat from al-Ashraf could leave neither him nor al-Kāmil indifferent. The campaign of 1231 had perhaps given the Ayyubids the impression that an invasion of Asia Minor would not be very difficult, although none had been attempted since Nūr al-Dīn. Al-Kāmil made the attempt with contingents from all his kinsmen and vassals including al-ʿAzīz of Aleppo, and was joined for some unknown reason by the sons of al-Afḍal of Samosata. Preparations of this kind could naturally not have been carried out without the knowledge of Kay Qubādh, who took defensive measures. Kamyar with Ḥusām al-Dīn Qaymarī and the contingent of Sire Basri, who was perhaps a Frank from Cilicia, were to guard the pass protecting the route from Syria by way of al-Ḥadath to Elbistan. This left Kay Qubādh time to arrive three days later at the head of an important army including Qīrkhān's Khwarazmians and all the necessary supplies of arms. After several days of skirmishing, al-Kāmil gave up the attempt to force a way and withdrew to the Jazīra, passing by the source of the Aksu, Besni and Ḥiṣn Manṣūr. The last town was given up to fire and sword on his orders. Established at Suwayda, he no doubt prepared to resume the offensive, and sent his ally, the Artukid lord of Khartpert, a contingent which he had asked for, consisting of 3,000 men and 500 horsemen, commanded by his lieutenant in the Jazīra and al-Muẓaffar, the prince of Ḥamāh. Thereupon Kay Qubādh recalled all the detachments of troops which were guarding the passes, including a corps that Kamyar had just led to al-Bīra (Birecik) on the Euphrates in order to block a river crossing on which the Syrians were counting. A battle took place beneath the walls of Khartpert, which ended in the enemy being forced back into the fortress, and the capitulation of the place after a month's siege. Al-Kāmil's troops were liberated after the chiefs had been generously received. Of the Seljukid forces, only one soldier, it was said, had been killed – a Frank. Some of al-Kāmil's vassals had balked at following him in an enterprise in which they saw no profit for themselves, and they even feared that it would lead to their having to exchange their domains in Syria and the Jazīra for less fruitful estates in Asia Minor. Some of them had perhaps even negotiated with Kay Qubādh. Al-Kāmil had to withdraw to Egypt in 630/1233 without any hope of returning.

In the following year Kay Qubādh even sent Kamyar to take Ḥarrān, Sarūj, Edessa, Suwayda and ultimately al-Raqqa – in brief the whole of Diyār Muḍar. At Ḥarrān and Edessa difficult sieges were required, but these ended in their capitulation, thanks partly to Georgian and Frankish con-tingents. Treasures and shops were looted, and part of the population of Edessa deported. It is true that as the region was of vital importance for communications between the Ayyubid domains in Syria and the Jazīra, al-Kāmil came to recover it, taking the Seljukid garrison of Edessa prisoner in their turn. Instead of continuing the fight on this front, Kay Qubādh decided (against Kamyar's advice, but on that of the *pervane* Tāj al-Dīn) to attack Āmid itself. Tāj al-Dīn received an army, which was assisted by al-Manṣūr of Mardin, and the Khwarazmians went on to pillage the territories of Nuseybin (Nisibis), Sinjār and perhaps even Mardin a little, to avenge, as they said, their masters' old hostility towards Jalāl al-Dīn. The siege was however unsuccessful, and thereupon was raised through the caliph's intervention. Kay Qubādh nevertheless prepared to resume it in person, for an alliance was in process of formation against al-Kāmil, whose authoritarianism and eastern policy had alienated al-Ashraf, while at the same time in Aleppo, where al-ʿAzīz had just died (634/1236), his widow was acting as regent for the young al-Nāṣir Yūsuf. In the event it was Kay Qubādh's son, Kay Khusraw II, who was to realize his father's ambition several years later.

In spite of these little difficulties, Kay Qubādh was at that moment incontestably at the zenith of his power. He was the sole and uncontested master of the whole of Asia Minor from the coast facing Rhodes to the sources of the Tigris, and from Eskişehir to Mount Ararat. The neighbouring Christian princes had alliance agreements (tinged with certain forms of vassalage) with him. Some coins bore witness to this, as later under Kay Khusraw II, such as that of King Hetoum, unfortunately undated, which bears on the recto the name of Sultan ʿAlā' al-Dīn Kay Qubādh. It may be granted that Trebizond, later in some degree of vassalage to Kay Qubādh's son, was also to him since his taking of Erzurum or his agreement with the Georgians.

Behind the scenes however the Mongol threat was beginning to show itself. It was this which had driven Jalāl al-Dīn to invade Asia Minor, and which had transformed his defeat into final loss by attacking him in the rear. A little later, as has been mentioned, Mongol detachments had pressed raids up to the gates of Sivas and Malatya, without any idea of conquest but so much the more devastating. The influence that these facts had on relations between Kay Qubādh on the one hand, and the Georgians and Ayyubids on the other has been indicated. He had nonetheless paid tribute to the Mongols to turn them aside, but this had not stopped them from reappearing in the region of Dogodaph against the Khwarazmians, making necessary the incorporation in the Seljukid state. If there had not been greater encroachment, it was because the Mongols' object had then been the subjugation of Georgia, and their operations in Armenia had only been for cover or supply. In 1236 there arrived an embassy in which two Mongols were accompanied by a person who was in fact the leader, a former Iranian emir, now a merchant, Shams al-Dīn 'Umar Qazwīnī, who, after taking refuge from the Mongols at Erzurum, had afterwards decided to pay court to them. The Great Khan required the periodical sending of an ambassador bearing tribute. For several years in fact there were no further developments because of the internal dissensions of the Mongols of Iran. Kay Qubādh prepared a courteous answer, but it was sent by his successor as he died on 4 Shawwāl 634/31 May 1237. In the ensuing two or three centuries there were numerous petty chiefs who wished to link themselves to the Seljukid past, and took their titles and rights to the great sultan of the dynasty.

The reign of Kay Khusraw II to the Mongol invasion

On Kay Qubādh's death one sees how much power was held by the great emirs. The sultan had three sons, 'Izz al-Dīn, Rukn al-Dīn and Kay Khusraw. The first two were his sons by his Ayyubid wife, and the sultan had caused an oath to be taken to the elder, 'Izz al-Dīn, but Kay Khusraw was the oldest of the three. In spite of their oath, the emirs brought Kay Khusraw to power, some of them voluntarily such as Altınbeh, Tāj al-Dīn and Köpek. Others, such as Kamyar and Qīrkhān, went over to him as a result of 'Izz al-Dīn's weakness. Inaugurated in these conditions, the start of the new reign was marked by sanguinary rivalry in the ruler's entourage. In appearance however they did not jeopardize the continuation of Kay Qubādh's expansionist policies, at least in external relations.

The most influential person with Kay Khusraw was Köpek, an ambitious emir. It was easy to convince the fickle ruler that the emirs who had not been his partisans from the start remained hostile to him. The most dangerous, by reason of the forces he had at his back, was the chief of the Khwarazmians, Qīrkhān. Kay Khusraw had him arrested and imprisoned. The Khwarazmians naturally felt themselves threatened, and escaped beyond the Euphrates, taking the route coming from Arapkir, and pillaging all the way. The sultan, who had no intention of letting the force they represented pass to others, in vain sent Kamyar to catch them, and bring them back. The *serleşker* of Malatya, Ertöküş, sought to intercept them near to Khartpert, where he had the assistance of the *subaşı* of that place. He sent them an envoy, but in vain. A battle took place in which Ertöküş was captured, the *subaşı* killed and a mass of booty fell to the Khwarazmians. They nevertheless proceeded to the Jazīra, and installed themselves in Diyār Muḍar.

This was now a pretext for Köpek to cast suspicion on Kamyar and various emirs. Helped by Tāj al-Dīn, he first brought about the execution of Altınbeh, although he was Kay Khusraw's *atabeg* and strong supporter. This did not prevent Kamyar and another grandee, Shams al-Dīn al-Iṣfahānī, standing on their guard, or Tāj al-Dīn himself from deeming a withdrawal to his *iqṭāʿ* at Ankara the more prudent course. When he arrived at Akşehir, he was accused to Köpek of intriguing against the sultan, and a *fatwā* against him was obtained from the jurists. Köpek went to Ankara to arrest him, brought him to a tribunal of the sultan in session with his magnates at Konya, and took him back to Ankara, where he was publicly executed. Kay Khusraw, for his part, on returning from Antalya to Kayseri, incarcerated the mother of his two younger brothers at Ankara, where she was soon afterwards strangled; the two young princes were interned at Burğlu. When Kay Khusraw had had three sons by three different women, he ordered ʿIzz al-Dīn's *atabeg*, Mubāriz al-Dīn Armaghān-Shāh, to kill him and his brother. Others claim that Armaghān-Shāh was able to save them without the sultan's knowledge.

These tragedies were less harmful to Kay Khusraw's external policy than Köpek's need to justify publicly the elimination of his rivals by successes of his own. Al-Ashraf died in 635/1237, a few months after Kay Qubādh. Al-Kāmil had taken Damascus from his designated successor, while Aleppo felt increasingly threatened by him. Kay Khusraw promised his cooperation to the regent, the grandmother of the young ruler, al-Nāṣir Yūsuf, married Ghāziya Khātūn, one of his sisters, and offered al-Nāṣir one of his own sisters in fair exchange. Then al-Kāmil in his turn passed away on 21 Rajab 635/9 March 1238. An alliance was immediately formed against his son, al-Ṣāliḥ Ayyūb, the master of his possessions in the Jazīra, by all the other rulers of northern Syria and the Jazīra. In vain did al-Ṣāliḥ and his son, al-Mughīth ʿUmar, attempt a reconciliation with Kay Khusraw, either directly or through the mediation of Aleppo. On the contrary, an alliance was contracted between Aleppo and Kay Khusraw as well as al-Mujāhid Shīrkūh of Ḥimṣ, Shihāb al-Dīn Ghāzī of Mayyāfāriqīn and the Artukid al-Manṣūr of Mardin. As his part in the spoils, Kay Khusraw would take Samsat and Āmid the dispossessed former prince of which, the sultan's kinsman, had just visited him. He had been liberated when al-ʿĀdil II Abū Bakr went to Egypt as al-Kāmil's successor, and no doubt transferred his rights in Damascus to Kay Khusraw. Aleppo moreover would pronounce the *khuṭba* and strike coinage in Kay Khusraw's name, a stipulation confirmed in practice by extant coins. A Seljukid army was then led by Köpek himself against Samsat, where al-Afḍal's sons did not attempt to resist. They were allowed only to carry away the cross kept in the citadel, which as an object of veneration to Christians was a source of revenue to them. A further thrust was even projected to resume the attack on Āmid, but at this moment al-Ṣāliḥ Ayyūb had just won over the Khwarazmians after their initial hostility at the cost of ceding Muḍar, and the need to guard against them caused the campaign to be broken off.

Nevertheless Köpek considered the success sufficient to have Qaymarī arrested at Malatya. He had to ransom himself by the payment of vast sums both to the sultan and to Köpek. Kamyar was imprisoned at Konya by Köpek, and executed at Kayala. At this moment however Kay Khusraw, either of his own volition or at the suggestion of some disquieted emirs, decided that enough was enough. Köpek was drawn into a trap, contrived by the sultan, by the *amīr jāndār* Karaca, who had hurried from Sivas, the *amīr majlis*, and the *amīr ʿalam* Tuğan, and was butchered. The direction of the treasury was given to Jalāl al-Dīn Karatay, the *niyābat al-salṭana* to Shams al-Dīn Iṣfahānī, and lastly the vezirate to Muhadhdhab al-Dīn. This probably took place in 637/1239–40.

It was at this time that Kay Khusraw's Georgian marriage, agreed during his father's lifetime, took place, and soon resulted in the birth of a son. It might be of particular interest that at this moment there began to reappear the threat from the Mongols, with whom Rusudan had concluded an agreement of vassalage. The young princess, who was accompanied by a *catholicos*, at first remained a Christian; in the end however she was compelled to accept Islam. With her, Rusudan had sent her nephew David, against whom she subsequently perpetrated murky intrigues, causing him to be imprisoned by Kay Khusraw, to whom she denounced him as guilty of adultery with the queen.

Perhaps because of the Mongol danger, and in any case taking note of the obstacles presented by the Khwarazmians to the realization of his designs in the Jazīra, Kay Khusraw was aware of the harm caused by his break with them. He tried to make use of Köpek's fall to win them back. The interpreter Majd al-Dīn went to them, and asked them to return to the land of Rūm; they only offered to cease their depredations on the frontiers, and to transfer to Kay Khusraw the homage they paid to al-Ṣāliḥ, who at that time was involved in tragic complications in Syria. Kay Khusraw then concluded and completed the alliance of Aleppo, Ḥimṣ, Mardin, Mayyāfāriqīn and Mosul, negotiated some time previously between all the opponents of al-Ṣāliḥ and of the Khwarazmians. At the beginning of 638/summer 1240 a body of troops from Aleppo had answered his call for help against a Mongol attack on Erzurum; now the 3,000 horsemen sent by Kay Khusraw from his frontier regions of Khartpert, Malatya, Elbistan and Maraş under *malik al-umarā'* Ẓāhir al-Dīn the interpreter participated in the victory won by the allies over the Khwarazmians on 24 Rabi II 638/13 November 1240. Ḥarrān, the residence of their chief, Berke Khan, fell to the troops of Aleppo. The Seljukid army was reinforced by fresh contingents brought up by Çavlı the *çaşnigir*, Yutaş the *çaşnigir* and *subaşı* of Niksar, and other chiefs of 'the land of Danişmend' as well as Kurdish groups. Exploiting its success, it went on to invest Āmid, one of al-Ṣāliḥ Ayyūb's possessions. Nāṣir al-Dīn Arslan, Ẓāhir al-Dīn's lieutenant, succeeded in making contact with one of the townspeople and in the midst of the fighting the Kurdish corps was able to take possession of a tower. A capitulation was signed by al-Ṣāliḥ Ayyūb's son, al-Mu'aẓẓam Tūrān-Shāh, and al-Ṣāliḥ, who was now the master of Egypt, sent his agreement in return for an indemnity. The city which had resisted Kay Qubādh was annexed by Kay Khusraw, and the command as *serleşker* was given to Mūbariz al-Dīn 'Īsā the *jāndār*. Suwayda had at the same time been acquired on the way in 638/beginning of 1241. Reductions of taxes followed, as testified by an inscription of 639/1241–42. Two years later, after the crushing of a Turcoman revolt (to be discussed below), Kay Khusraw was to attempt the completion of this conquest by the taking of Mayyāfāriqīn, thanks to the cooperation of the same allies, this time against Shihāb al-Dīn Ghāzī the Artukid, who was trying to resume on his own account the policy of al-Ṣāliḥ Ayyūb and the Khwarazmians. The siege was raging when the approach of the Mongols became known. Peace was then hastily concluded through the mediation of al-Mu'aẓẓam Tūrān-Shāh (not al-Ṣāliḥ's son but a surviving son of Saladin) who had brought the allies reinforcements from Damascus. So in 641/the beginning of 1243 the enemy of yesterday sought to become tomorrow's ally.

To all appearance Kay Khusraw had then power superior to his father's, if measured by extent of territory. Simon of St Quentin, who is somewhat gullible but has nevertheless collected some excellent information (although sometimes confusing vassals and occasional allies), reports with some probability that the king of Armenia's due contribution was (or perhaps had once been) 1,400 lances for four months, apart from twenty-nine from the autonomous lord of Lampron. From John Vatatzes, the emperor of Nicaea, were due 400 without restriction of time or place; from Trebizond, 200; also 1,000 from Aleppo. The last however were perhaps at Kay Khusraw's own expense to judge from the recruitment for the campaign against the Mongols (to be discussed below). Simon of St Quentin says that the king of Armenia or his old father, Constantine, and the Emperor John Vatatzes came to Kayseri, which was one of the sultan's most frequent residences, but this is not confirmed by any other source. All this may refer to preparations for the war against the Mongols, and so may be somewhat exceptional. That Kay Khusraw, equally with al-Ṣāliḥ Ayyūb of Egypt, was considered the most powerful ruler in the Near East is indisputable.

As earlier mentioned, peace generally existed between the Greeks of Nicaea and the Turks from the accession of Kay Kāwūs onwards. However, the Syrian chronicler Ibn Naẓīf, an exact contemporary of Kay Qubādh, mentions two battles around 1230 between this sultan and 'Laskarī', i.e. John Vatatzes, the son of Theodore Lascaris. In the first the sultan was victorious, not so in the second. It is difficult to believe that these battles, which are not mentioned by either the chroniclers of Asia Minor or those of Nicaea, can have been more than inconsequential frontier engagements. It is nevertheless known that at the end of his reign, Kay Qubādh sent an embassy to Pope Gregory IX, and that Kay Khusraw, who gave a favourable reception to Latin missionaries, was negotiating about 1242 with Baldwin II of Constantinople about a marriage. Baldwin disclosed this to Blanche of Castile, the queen of France, and justified it by their common hostility to Vatatzes. The arrival of the Mongols was to change everything, for against this new enemy Kay Khusraw and his successors preferred the direct support of neighbouring Nicaea to alliance with the distant Franks. Vatatzes himself came to Konya then. But there can be little doubt that there was tension which might have had important results, had there not been the Mongol invasion.

When all is said, there were weaknesses in the Seljukid structure and in Kay Khusraw's policy that the Mongol irruption brought clearly into view, but which existed previously, and were already visible.

The Mongol advance across Iran to Ādharbāyjān pushed back simultaneously Iranians and Turcomans, who were forced to seek new pastures in Asia Minor, and disturbed the peace of their predecessors in these regions. It is difficult to know whether the events to be discussed resulted from these migrations, or from an independent movement among the Turcomans of Asia Minor itself. The so-called Bābā'ī movement deserves as close study as possible because of its further repercussions.

Its importance is also indirectly attested by the fact that it gained attention not only from Ibn Bībī but also from the Christian chronicler Bar

Hebraeus, the Syrian Muslim Sibṭ Ibn al-Jawzī, and above all the Dominican missionary Simon of St Quentin, through whom as an intermediary the paradox arises that the best account of the facts is to be found in the Western chronicler Vincent of Beauvais.

About the year 630/1233 there was living in the region of Kafarsud, in contact with the middle Taurus, northern Syria and the Euphrates, a certain Isḥāq, regarded by the local people as a charlatan or a prophet, and commonly called Baba Isḥāq. Around 638/1240 he had gathered enough disciples around himself to disturb all the territory between Malatya to the east, Amasya to the north and Maraş to the south-west; it is likely that somehow or other he had profited from the presence of the Khwarazmians. Against him was sent Muẓaffar al-Dīn b. ʿAlī Shīr, probably the chief of the Germiyan, who was twice defeated near Malatya. Then the *ikdişbaşı* Khurram-Shāh was crushed in his turn near Sivas. The sultan, who had withdrawn to the island of Qubādhābād, now despatched the commandant of Amasya, Armaghān-Shāh, against Baba Isḥāq. Aided by a contingent of Frankish mercenaries (to whom Simon of St Quentin ascribes all the merit), he succeeded in shutting the company of Baba Isḥāq in a cave, and their leader was put to death. But the rebels escaped westwards to Kırşehir, sowing terror everywhere, and it took two more years to eliminate them. Nothing is known of what Baba Isḥāq preached, except that he claimed to be the Apostle of God, Baba Rasul – rendered by Simon of St Quentin as *Paperoissole.* On the other hand, it is known that among the Turcomans recently arrived from Central Asia, there was the veneration of a certain Baba Ilyās belonging to the tradition of Aḥmad Yesevi. What connection there may be between Baba Isḥāq and Baba Ilyās will be considered.

At this juncture the Mongols arrived. Interrupted awhile by the succession struggle to the Great Khan Ögedei, they now returned, headed effectively by Baiju *noyan* under the nominal command of Chormaghun, who was sick, and the distant control of Batu in Russia. In the winter of 1242–43, while other Mongols penetrated Upper Mesopotamia, Baiju attacked Erzurum. The massive force and ardour of the Mongol thrust was as ever complemented by treason, and the so-called Tartars captured the city without the delay of a siege, which at that time of year at an altitude of over 1,000 metres would have been harsh. They now held the key to Asia Minor, which they invaded in the spring. At the news of the danger, which he does not seem to have realized was imminent, Kay Khusraw not only recalled the distant forces, but sent to demand (with abundance of money and gifts) the largest possible reinforcements from his vassals and allies, even from his enemies of yesterday now reconciled by the common danger. These included Ghāzī of Mayyāfāriqīn (a city recently taken by the Mongols but then evacuated), Aleppo, Trebizond, perhaps Nicaea, Armenians,

Franks and so forth. They were to assemble at Sivas, to which the sultan went. Around him the panic usual everywhere at the approach of the Mongols alternated with impatience to go forth and stop them before they had occupied or devastated half the realm. With an important but heterogeneous army, and not delaying for those who were long in coming (the Armenians were already treating with the Mongols), Kay Khusraw proceeded to take up his position at the pass of Kösedağ in the province of Erzincan. The position was inevitably difficult for Baiju, but he was able to throw his opponent into confusion by the well-tried tactic of a feigned flight followed by a sudden return. In the evening of 6 Muḥarram 641/26 June 1243 the Seljukid army had ceased to exist. The sultan picked up his treasure at Tokat and fled to Ankara, while his mother made her way to Cilicia. The Mongols occupied Sivas, and took revenge on Kayseri for its brief resistance by a terrible sack. If they made no further advance for the time being, it was perhaps because they did not wish to over-extend beyond their other fronts, and because Kay Khusraw's vezir opened a timely negotiation (see p. 173). But the defeat of Kösedağ was irredeemable. On that day the course of history was unalterably diverted for Asia Minor.

PART TWO

Society and Institutions before the Mongols

CHAPTER EIGHT

The birth of Turkey

The turcicization of Asia Minor, even though incomplete, has often appeared the object of an astonishment which is itself basically astonishing. During the course of history many other countries have changed their ethnic character, and in every case we have only to try to understand how that change has taken place and, if possible, to what extent and in what proportion.

It is clearly impossible to set a figure on Turkish immigration into Asia Minor. In general it is difficult to imagine that the movements of peoples at that period could at any one time have concerned more than a few tens of thousands of individuals, possibly two or three hundred thousand, even if the texts give the impression of enormous masses. Let us bear in mind that the regular armies in battle comprised at most some thousands of men. However there are various factors which in general, or in the particular case of Asia Minor, increase the relative significance of this order of magnitude, if not its absolute importance. First, as has been said, at the time of the Turkish penetration Asia Minor as a whole, in spite of regional exceptions, was thinly populated, and flight, massacre and subjugation during the conquest still further reduced this population. Second, the elements which composed it were disparate so that, if they were as a whole evidently superior in numbers to the new immigrants, the outcome was altogether less certain. In any case the disproportion is less if the Turks are compared with each of these elements separately, and so if one balances the power of penetration against the power of resistance. In any case Turks and Turks alone are everywhere to be found, while there are Greek regions, Armenian regions and so forth. Third, it is certain that the great majority of the Turks who came from Central Asia settled in Ādharbāyjān and Asia Minor, and finally more in the latter than in the former. There they found living conditions sufficiently close to their traditions to limit the need for adaptation, unlike in the Arab lands or central and southern Iran. Finally, and this is perhaps the essential point, one cannot, as has been said, regard the ethnic effect of an invasion as an instantaneous and static phenomenon. What counts is not only the number of the immigrants but the social and economic situation which they occupy, and also the way in which the interrelationships of the peoples are organized, particularly marriages and the birth rate. Furthermore it is certain that whether by abduction, or more ordinarily because the heads of indigenous families sought to be left in quiet by the conquerors, many of their daughters must have been mated in fact or legally with the immigrants; consequently their children, brought up as Turks, must have brought the advantage of their fecundity to the Turks, and withdrawn it from indigenous society. Statistics and exactitude cannot indeed be provided in these matters, which should perhaps be qualified, if possible, and even in some cases dismissed as doubtful; but these ideas and the general trend of developments appear likely enough. Of course there resulted from this racial mixture some alteration of the typical Turk, but this did not keep the children from regarding themselves, and being regarded, psychically as Turks. In some cases the ethnic superiority of the victor might quickly be put in jeopardy by his monopoly of warfare, whereby he was decimated. This is perhaps to some extent what happened to the Mongols later, as it had happened, for instance, to the Vandals in North Africa. It does not seem however that for the Turks of Asia Minor war was permanent or murderous enough to involve such a consequence either temporarily or locally without being counterbalanced by the other factors.

However this may be, it is certain that, while Muslim authors continue to give the name of *Rūm* (which no longer has a precise political significance) to Asia Minor, and then to the state which the Seljukids built up there, Westerners on the other hand, from Barbarossa's crusade at the latest, call this country *Turchia*, which is not their practice for the other lands under Turkish domination. So however we measure the Turkishness of Asia Minor, and however vague the frontiers of this *Turchia*, contemporaries felt the Turkish phenomenon as giving it as a whole a specific quality. It is true, as will appear from another point of view, that the Turkish Muslim people of Asia Minor were not really conscious of this Turkish phenomenon before the time of the Mongols, but this does not allow us to dismiss the overall impression of foreigners on the pretext that internally those concerned were more conscious of their differences than of their unity in regard to others.[7]

This said, we must now go into more detail, and attempt a more precise characterization of the phenomenon of turcicization.

First of all, from the geographical point of view it is probable that turcicization was not of equal density everywhere. Seen through the chronicles which predominantly report frontier incidents, turcicization appears especially important on all the fringes of the Turkish political domain; to the west and north confronting the Greeks, to the south the Armenians. The Georgians for their part were caused more anxiety by the frontier with Ādharbāyjān, which was fairly open, than by the difficult mountains which separated them from Asia Minor. There is no doubt, as scattered episodes remind us, that Turks also populated the interior. It remains the case however that the truly Turcoman element was massed above all on the frontiers, whether spontaneously or by the organized transfer of population. It sometimes happens that Byzantine writers give place names in their Turkish form, as if no one remembered the original form.

The distinction just made shows at once that the problem is as much social as ethnic. When the Westerners spoke of *Turchia*, it is certain that they were thinking above all of the open country held by the Turcomans, who had to be confronted in battle, and whom also they sometimes called 'bedouin', applying a term properly used of nomad Arabs. The problem of the towns is different, and will be considered later.

The turcicization of the open country was then essentially the work of the Turcomans. There remained, of course, an indigenous rural population, varying according to region, and generally very much in the majority. All its members had not been killed or fled; as freemen or in servitude, many remained in Cappadocia, in Armenia, on the borders of the Anatolian plateau and so forth. In the frontier zones of the west, the Byzantines, thanks to successful operations, had regained some territory, creating a sort of no man's land, and thereby increasing the importance of the Turcomans; but it happened also that the Seljukids acquired territory, and installed Turcomans in conditions which secured their stability. The principal question, which is difficult to solve, is the view to take of the Turcomans in the Seljukid period. Were they purely nomads or no longer such? It has already been said that this question is perhaps somewhat excessively close to the hearts of contemporary Turkish scholars, and that even in Central Asia there was some diminution of nomadism; but perhaps the sedentaries emigrated less than the others. In fact, and for this period, this is not the question. The Turcomans of Central Asia made use of the two-humped Bactrian camel, which in the Iranian borderlands was often crossed with the female Arabian dromedary to give a more adaptable stock for varied climates. However, it must be borne in mind that neither the Bactrian nor the Arabian camel is a fighting animal. It may be a source of milk or hair, but its principal function is as a baggage carrier. The two animals essential to the Turcoman were the horse and the sheep. For two millennia the horse had been the animal for warfare, and the Turks as heirs of the ancient Scythians were past masters in the art of its use, particularly for mounted archery of a kind which was known and practised neither by the Arabs nor the Byzantines. The sheep was the essential animal for nourishment and textiles. According to the region, transhumances over long distances might be necessary for climatic reasons, but in any case it could only travel slowly, and wherever possible the tent-dwelling pastoralists mostly remained attached to restricted areas. In this respect acclimatization in central and western Asia Minor would not pose any great problem for them. It was already a country of great estates, devoted, even when around villages of sedentaries, to the rearing of horses and sheep. Did the Turkish sheep and horses cross-breed with their native kin, or simply add to their number? It is certain only that the great majority of the new arrivals were nomadic pastoralists of limited range. It will be seen that there were also Turcomans who were foresters and woodcutters, which if not agriculture is also not stock-breeding. This was the case of many of the Turcomans of the Taurus mountains, which were still covered by vast forests, and perhaps of some of those called *Ağaceri*s. Pure nomadism was rare; there was almost always a symbiosis between nomadic elements and sedentary cultivators. That the latter were still on the whole the original population is certain, but that in certain regions there were many Turks among them cannot be excluded.

The *waqfiyya*s and other documents of the thirteenth century and the more numerous ones of the fourteenth (too few of which have been published) may give some indication of the progressive ethnical mixture of the populations, and perhaps in some fortunate cases it would be possible, thanks to them, to follow the chronological rhythm of islamization or turcicization. One must only be careful to differentiate among the regions. More particularly it must be noted that those villages and plots of land the owners or occupants of which are named are in the vicinity of towns, where the process of islamization or occupation by Muslims was likely to be more rapid than in the remote open country. This said, it may be remarked that a *waqf* on possessions near Konya in 598/1201 mentions explicitly the abundance of 'infidels'; the villages mentioned however have mixed names. The conclusions to be drawn from this remain imprecise; a village with an indigenous name might have inhabitants or an owner who are Turkish, while a village with a Turkish name, even if new or newly occupied, might have indigenous inhabitants who stayed or were brought back, as the name might be only that of an owner or an ethnic group; taken as a whole however the mixture is significant. The same impressions are drawn from the mid-century *waqf*s of Karatay to the south of Kayseri. More precise information comes from the cases where the name is not that of a village or an entire estate, but of an individual plot. The conclusion broadly speaking, and always in an urban area, is that there were Muslims beside Christians. On the whole there is no reason to doubt the impressions of travellers that in the open country the great majority of the people remained Christian. To this we shall return.

As has been said, mixed unions in their usual form did not really deturcicize the Turkish element. One would like to know to what extent there were cases of real mixtures of populations. It may be that the Kurds offer a case in point, and perhaps an example is provided by the Germiyan, of whom more will be said. Perhaps there were others in the Taurus mountains with the colonies of 'Bulgars' (who were perhaps Mardaites), and could hardly have totally disappeared. The problem can only be stated. It may just be noted that in literature written later to glorify Turcoman dynasties, far from hostility being shown to other rural Muslim elements especially the Kurds, a brotherhood in arms under Turcoman leadership appears the rule. On the whole, in the possible examples of ethnic mixture the final gain went to turcicization. The Turks cannot be seen as having been absorbed by the indigenous groups, and the fact of Turkish domination is a sufficient explanation of this; but there may have been a turcicization of some groups whose ancestry, even on the male side, have been indigenous.[8] In the towns there were the *ikdiş* (see below, pp. 114–15).

A closer approach to the history of the Turcomans of Rūm would be possible if we were certain both of the interpretation of the names of some Turcoman groups, and also of the land system of Seljukid Asia Minor. The second question will be discussed later. The first brings us back to the tribal organization and the identification of the groups. This is a point on which in methodology one must mistrust Yazicioğlu 'Alī. He wrote his adaptation of Ibn Bībī's history (*Selcukname*) in the fifteenth century, and introduced the names of tribes which were held to be the most important in the view of the Turcomans of the day, who evidently wished to discover their ancestors in the origins of Turkish Asia Minor. But none of these names appears in Ibn Bībī, and consequently it is impossible to think that they had in his time that importance which they had acquired in the days of Yazicioğlu. This being so, it is absolutely necessary to keep to contemporary, or at least relatively ancient sources. The Turks of Central Asia had no doubt, like other nomads, a certain form of tribal organization, but we must not let ourselves be carried away by legendary description. Tradition depicts the ancient Oghuz as divided into twenty-four tribes, and history does indeed know of a group of *Dokuz Oğuz*, the Nine Tribes. However, no text of the period shows us the tribal organization effective among the Oghuz. Some of the twenty-four names are attested here and there in the Seljukid period, but in Asia Minor the only one really so recorded is a group of Çepni on the Black Sea coast. Ethnic designations such as Afşar applied to certain individuals prove nothing about the organization of the groups to which they belonged. As regards the numerous tribal names of the sixteenth century, they are the fruit of an evolution which proves nothing about the Seljukid period; quite the contrary, the groupings which were constituted at that time were just that, assembled behind some chiefs, whose names they often retained, whereas the rulers, when they were able to do anything, appear rather to have worked to bring about dispersal and mixture.

In Asia Minor the question is complicated by the fact that, if the names of tribes are exceptional there (and in the thirteenth century they occur solely as designations of individuals), yet from the beginning of Turkish penetration in the middle of the twelfth century there is fairly frequent mention of a group of uncertain orthography: *(y)a(r)uki*, *yavuki* and other variants, of which no convincing explanation has yet been proposed. Eleventh-century Muslim authors often call the Turks *ghāzī*s (T. *gazi*s) of the frontiers (T. *uc*), meaning exactly frontiersmen, and thus an equivalent of the Byzantine *akritai*, or in the sense of the Arabic *ghāzī*, fighters in the Holy War. But it is difficult to discover any linguistic erosion which could turn *uc* into *ya(r)uk*. Attempts have been made by a slightly less ridiculous but equally unwarranted treatment to derive them from the Iva, a tribe known in Ādharbāyjān in the twelfth and thirteenth centuries, or from the *navakī*s, the casters of darts, a corps of which is attested although not in the Seljukid period, and finally from the *yürük*, a name for the nomadic Turks of Asia Minor to the present day. The last hypothesis, historically attractive but linguistically weak, remains in the end as shaky as the others, and the problem remains unsolved. What alone is almost certain is that this is not a tribal name, i.e. the penetration into Asia Minor like the whole Seljukid invasion was made by mixed bands outside the framework of the large tribal groupings. Moreover there is nothing to prove that tribal consciousness was as strong among the Turks of the Seljukid period as it was later to become as a factor in organization.

The only other name which certainly appears as a collective term in the ancient texts is that of the *Ağaceri*s (literally, men of the trees), which is not much clearer than the previous one. It is not the name of a traditional Oghuz tribe, nor is it (as seems to have been believed on the strength of a fortuitous phonetic comparison) a former Russian people transferred to Asia Minor, although the exclusively Turkish character of the *Ağaceri*s cannot be shown. They are noted only in the thirteenth century, on the whole in the central and eastern Taurus region up to the gates of Malatya, as essentially a troublesome element on whom the regular authorities made war. It was probably the same group who, flooding across the frontiers soon after the Mongol invasion, are noted north of Antioch and Aleppo as 'Turcomans of Syria', not to mention the partial dispersion which is met with at later periods. In Syria, a contemporary described them as follows:

> These Turcomans are a savage people, having neither towns nor castle, lodging always in tents of felt. They have beasts in great plenty, sheep and ewes, some goats, even cows and bulls. They live like shepherds, and do not undertake any cultivation; nor of all the Saracens is there any manner of people who are more given to feats of arms.

It is true that the place names of modern Asia Minor include many names of localities and villages which refer to those of most of the traditional Oghuz tribes. It is historically important to distinguish periods, and to regard as pre-Mongol only the rare place names which could have been found before the mid-thirteenth century. Both by pushing back the Turcomans and by bringing them in, the Mongols stirred up a new Turcoman influx, as well as a redistribution to some extent of those already there; and the new arrivals could not have been tribally and socially identical with their predecessors. Without going so far as to assert that the groups attested by later nomenclature could not have existed previously, it is prudent not to affirm that they did exist. When it is possible to determine the date of a place name, this can indicate the date of sedentarization of the group named. Conversely, the fact that the place name is that of a tribal group known to history at a certain period may, subject to other confirmation, perhaps justify a surmise as to the period when the village was established, and so of the sedentarization of its people there. It is possible that the period of sedentarization may not be the same in all cases for different regions and the various kinds of Turcomans. Among the names which occur, some are those of tribes attested in the Seljukid migration generally, either directly as groups or indirectly as designations of individuals. This is insufficient to prove that either their establishment or their sedentarization in Asia Minor preceded the Mongol conquest.

The Turks of Asia Minor were officially Muslims, whereas the native peoples were not. However, turcicization and islamization must not be entirely equated. At the time of the conquest or later Armenian or Georgian notables first, and Greeks later, were converted to Islam in order to keep their lands, to make a career, to contract a good marriage or for some other reason, so that after a time this must have resulted in a cultural and quasi-ethnic turcicization of their descendants. This does not imply that they themselves were really turcicized, or even that they understood Turkish rather than Arabic or Persian. Slaves brought back from frontier raids (and at the start of the invasion, from all the country) were generally quickly manumitted, and represent another islamized element. Persons of this description may often be recognized because their fathers' name is given simply as ʿAbdallāh. There were also Iranian immigrants (see below), precisely under whose growing influence new Muslims might be won for Islam under its less Turkish forms. Ethnic matters will be further considered in the subsequent study of culture and society.

Everything that has been said applies essentially to the open countryside, where such existed. However, Asia Minor had been, and after a time became again under the Turks, a land of towns, or at least a land in which towns played an essential role. At the start, naturally, the devastation of the countryside, which placed in jeopardy the provisioning of the towns and ruined the landowners, then the occupation of the towns themselves, instigated emigration, particularly of those who had means; while the Turcoman chiefs, who did not settle in the towns, and viewed them as nests of infidels, did not favour the townspeople. This situation might continue or be repeated over a long period in the special region of the frontiers, where the surrender of fortified towns generally took place after the devastation of their countryside. It was not perpetuated in the regions where there was real and stabilized occupation.

It is well known that in the East generally nomad chiefs turn more easily into townspeople than into peasants (even if their men are induced to become peasants), although they may go off from time to time for a spell in the desert or the steppe. Whether nomads or not, the Turkish chiefs quickly established themselves in the towns. The Seljukids knew from their past what a town was, and we saw that Süleyman endowed one of his first conquests with its official *qāḍī*; moreover where they might be slow in establishing themselves in a town, the Byzantines, as we saw, established them there themselves. Although the Danişmendids were more closely Turcomans, it does not seem that they acted very differently. In a more restricted area, they restored the fortifications, and settled there voluntarily, or installed provincial governors or holders of apanages with their garrisons. As states came into existence, whatever the degree of Byzantine and Islamic Iranian influences, the city was (apart from regional and perhaps indigenous exceptions) the political, social and cultural centre, as it was in all Muslim countries.

What is important for us at the moment is the population of the towns. It is certain that at the start their small number of inhabitants consisted, in addition to the Turkish garrison with its slaves and freedmen, of indigenous people who had stayed on or had been brought back, and with a more or less clear gap between the old occupants and the new ones. Gradually however there were added to them people of mixed race, as will appear. Then Iranians, particularly from the north-west, and indeed Khurasanians also, came in, to become important in the thirteenth century, perhaps numerically and always socially. Certainly there were elements of the Iranian civil and religious aristocracy, driven out by the Khwarazmians or the Mongols, before the Mongols sent them as their representatives. There were also more humble men of religion, officials, artisans and merchants. So it is certain that the population of the towns was not identical to that of the countryside. It cannot be denied that the Turkish element was important, but it was not exclusive, and in the organization of the new regime the other immigrants had considerable influence in every respect, and this affected the Turks themselves. We shall return to this in speaking of the cultural life, but must point out here that the Iranians exercised an iranianizing, and thus in a sense a de-turcicizing, influence on the Turks. At the end of the thirteenth century, the townsman of Konya who wrote the *Tārīkh-i āl-i Saljūq* and who, although he wrote in Persian, was certainly a Turk to judge by some of his pronunciations, reserved the name of 'Turks' for the Turcomans with a touch of contempt, while calling the townspeople simply 'Muslims'. If this is not the usage of all his contemporaries, it is at least symptomatic. While at the same time in Egypt, the Mamluks felt and called themselves Turks in distinction from the native population, in Asia Minor and in distinction from the Turcomans, even the townspeople of Turkish stock were not really conscious of it. They called themselves Muslims, and said so as often in Persian as in Turkish. Final turcicization, although incomplete, would take place under and after the Mongols.

It is not less certain that even in its Turkish elements, Asia Minor gave foreigners, and in particular foreign Muslims, the impression of a country that was really alien to them, in short a 'Turkey' distinct above all from the Arab world. In the eleventh century hardly anyone travelled there, and an envoy of Nūr al-Dīn spoke on his return about the country he had seen somewhat as a modern traveller would speak of an expedition into the heart of the remotest regions of Asia or Africa. Even in the thirteenth century, the travel impressions of the caliph's ambassador Ibn al-Jawzī are noteworthy. The dress is of course different from that of the Arabs, and in the countryside from that of the Iranians. But it was the women above all who struck the Europeans as much as the Muslims because of the freedom of their way of life (they were unveiled, at least the Turcoman women), and their sturdiness. Ricold of Monte Croce claimed that they gave birth without interrupting the advance of the caravan.

When all is said about the Turkish and Muslim element, it is quite certain that there remained natives of Asia Minor who were probably much more numerous than the Turks – as ten to one according to William of Rubruck in the thirteenth century. To establish the permanence of a population group, it is not enough to state that it has remained until the present day, for varying circumstances might favour the return to, and the recolonization of, partially abandoned areas. It is possible that this might have occurred under the Mongol protectorate, and it was certainly so in the last two centuries of the Ottoman Empire. Nevertheless, until the contrary is proved, the existence of an indigenous group until modern times is a presumption of its existence throughout history. That does not of course dispense us from searching in the ancient sources for direct proof and precise information about its existence. We shall come back to these ancient peoples in connection with the organization of inter-confessional relations and the systems of taxation and landed property. Here one or two words will be enough.

Western Armenia remained a largely Armenian country. Details are lacking for Erzurum, although it may be broadly asserted, but for Erzincan it is still more certain. Perhaps already at this date, and in any event under the Mongols and at the end of the Middle Ages, Erzincan was of greater importance than Erzurum; in spite of its Turkish Muslim establishment, it remained above all a great Armenian city. Southern Armenia had however suffered even then greater encroachments from Kurdish peoples. It has been seen that further west Cappadocia had been partially settled by Armenians through Byzantine policy. The Turkish conquest fell upon Cilicia, where an Armenian principality was gradually organized from the Armenians of Cappadocia; some however remained, particularly in the middle Taurus and its southern slopes, straddling the frontier between Asia Minor and Mesopotamia. It would be hard to explain how the Monophysites maintained the principal seat of their patriarch at the convent of Mar Bar Sauma in the mountain to the south of Malatya, if their important communities in Upper Mesopotamia had lacked extension in this direction. As for the Greeks, they or hellenized populations continued to be represented throughout the whole coastal and mountain fringe of Anatolia proper, of Trebizond and its hinterland in Isauria, passing by the Danişmendid country, the provinces of Kastamonu and even Ankara, the upper valleys of rivers flowing into the Sea of Marmara or the Aegean, and the Antalya region. They still remained numerous in the very heart of Cappadocia, and in the agricultural and urban parts of the Anatolian plateau itself.

The conclusion is therefore twofold and apparently contradictory. On the one hand it is certain that the majority of the population was not Turkish, not even Muslim, and was not unified. It is also certain, on the other hand, that a Turkey was coming into being because, as in the steppe of Asiatic Russia and differently from the other countries subjugated by the Turks, here a Turkish people made itself at home, its omnipresence in the Anatolian country as a whole in characteristic contrast to the divisions of the native peoples. At will appear, Turkishness does not characterize all the Muslims, not even all the Turks, but this orientation characterizes Asia Minor by contrast with the other Muslim countries.

As well as the Muslim Turks and the non-Muslims, about whom more will be said, a word should be said about the Kurds, however little may be known about them at this period. Apart from the Iranian mountains, they essentially occupied the south-eastern quarter of Anatolia up to the borders of Mesopotamia, perhaps having been driven from their classical home by the Turkish invasion. They were integrated into the Seljukid state at the time of its eastwards expansion. Also something will later be said about the special group of the Germiyan, who were on bad terms with the Turcomans as their rivals over pasturage.

CHAPTER NINE

Economic life

If the chronicles of the First Crusade and so forth leave a desolate impression of the interior of Asia Minor, the fact is that the travellers who saw it in the thirteenth century carried away, on the contrary, a memory of prosperity by the standards of their time. Evidently it was to a large extent a reconstructed prosperity, yet one should not ascribe to the first Turcoman invasion effects that perhaps it did not have. Certainly the Turcomans killed, hunted down or subjugated not a few, relative to the existing population, and the inevitable result was the abandonment of much cultivated land, failure to maintain works of art and so on. But it must be repeated that from the start of this period, in the first place, the economy of the interior of Asia Minor before the Turcomans was one of sparsely peopled *latifundia*; in the second place, the Turcomans did not behave in the same way everywhere; they had no reason to destroy plantations of trees, some of which would probably recover; it was no longer to their interest, or that of any nomad, to do away with the oases of sedentary cultivation. These are indeed unwarranted general suppositions, since there is practically no evidence of the beginnings of their occupation, but they are likely enough. The arrival of sheep-grazing on a large scale no doubt accentuated the steppe-like character of various central regions, but the sheep-nomads should not simply be represented as necessarily hostile to the vicinity of sedentary cultivators. The forests, which remained important in most of the zones of the mountain-fringe, must also be taken into consideration. In any case the picture changes completely after some generations. It must also be clearly understood that, independently of the merits or faults in the behaviour of the incoming Turcomans, there was in the structure of the Turkish principalities and then of the Turkish state in Asia Minor an inherent positive element. Byzantine Asia Minor of the late period, a detached margin of the West, was largely an external property of great absentee landlords, who were interested in its exploitation only insofar as it brought them in revenues which they could spend outside it, whereas the new centres, established or re-established by the Turks, created a profitable demand of whatever size on the spot.

From the mid-thirteenth century there are indications of the development of the new state of affairs. The frontier zones were evidently the most disadvantaged and, when they could, the Byzantines, on finding peasants still there, repatriated them to repeople their lands which lay more in the interior or the territories which they had somewhat securely reconquered. But the opposite also took place, and the sultans settled on their agricultural lands people captured or brought in from the frontiers. It is possible that some of these people preferred a regime of lighter taxation or the conditions offered for their settlement to their memories of the Byzantine tax-collectors or the *latifundia* proprietors. It is also possible that some had greater confidence in agreements with the Turks, even with occasional quarrels, than in Byzantine military protection, which was proving illusory or in any event insufficiently omnipresent. The example recorded of the settlement of Greek peasants around Lake Karalis has no reason to be entirely unique; and more conclusively the sultans had good cause to look to the development of their internal territories. The cities had to be the centres for the agricultural exploitation of fairly extensive peripheries. Here is not the place for a fresh discussion of the role some Turcomans may have had in the recolonization in parts of the frontier zones. Even if they had sometimes been settled there by the sultans for partly military reasons, their presence had nevertheless some economic significance. In any case, even when they remained nomads, it is clear from the scandalized statements of participants in the Second Crusade in particular that a normal barter economy arose between Greek peasants and Turcoman pastoralists, and this was accompanied by the development of peaceful relations.

When one can begin to redraw a picture of the economy of Asia Minor, particularly in the first half of the thirteenth century, it appears to be genuinely prosperous simultaneously for agriculture, industry and commerce, each supporting the others.

Simon of St Quentin, who spent some years in Asia Minor just before and just after the disaster of Kösedağ, was a little credulous and a little misleading; nevertheless he saw the country, and part of what he says about the Seljukid state gives a picture of wealth and power in town and countryside. He gives few details about agriculture, but dwells a little more on stockbreeding; he knows the value of a herd of sheep and its wool, and the distinctive features of the breeding of goats, which also provide useful hair. For matters of this kind, there is no reason not to use somewhat later descriptions also. Ibn Saʿīd, writing in Syria or Mesopotamia in the early days of Mongol dominance, and using the information of travellers who must have seen the country a little earlier, lays stress, when dealing with the country they knew well from Kayseri to Sivas or to Aksaray and Konya, on the abundance of almost uninterrupted cultivation along the roads – certainly the pastures also, but above all the gardens, the waters, the orchards of apricots, plums, pears, lemons, peaches, almonds and so forth. Around Konya the Qamar al-Dīn plum had a particularly high reputation. It took its name from an emir who created at Konya a garden which was already known to ʿAlī al-Harawī before 1200; it was perhaps he who governed the Isaurian Taurus under Kay Qubādh, and left it his name. Later Mustawfī Qazwīnī was to see (or imagine) grapes everywhere; and Ibn Baṭṭūṭa, when near Antalya, was to speak of apricots being dried and exported to Egypt. According to him too, cultivation also fringed the way from Erzincan to Erzurum. Abu'l-Fidā', who also reproduces Ibn Saʿīd's information in the fourteenth century, makes too few changes in it for his account to be rated as distinct and original evidence; nevertheless he also mentions the fruit trees of the Malatya region, and is astonished that property in them is not individual as in ordinary Muslim countries – in the classical Sharīʿa the peasant who cultivates on the land of a proprietor has a share in the property of the produce. Ibn Baṭṭūṭa also speaks of the timber of the southern mountains, which was exported to Egypt by Antalya and the gulf of Meğri,[9] and Ibn Saʿīd mentions the timber of the province of Kastamonu, which was used for the arsenals of Sinop.

On agriculture and stockbreeding, al-ʿUmarī gives us information which is doubtless of some value for the thirteenth century. Being naturally particularly sensitive to the special characteristics of the country, he also was struck in the first place by the fruits – oranges, perhaps dates and bananas, particularly on the southern coast. Attention was paid to the breeding of cattle and horses, but pre-eminently to sheep and goats, which last had hair like silk, much exported to neighbouring Muslim countries. The honey was exquisite, and there was also sugar. Everything was cheaper there than anywhere else – but it is true that this is not necessarily a sign of prosperity. Al-ʿUmarī repeatedly adds similar impressions to these generalities for each region that he describes, and mentions wheat and barley as cereals, as throughout the Mediterranean. Horses, mules and sheep appear also in the tribute paid to the Mongols, while *waqfiyyas* in the vicinity of towns call to mind the abundance of cultivators' villages.

It is difficult to feel enough confidence in the numbers of villages in some fourteenth-century principalities as given by al-ʿUmarī to reproduce them here, still less to sum them up. All the same, the impression is of a populated countryside, above all in western Anatolia. Ibn Saʿīd believed that in his time the Seljukid realm comprised 400,000 villages, 36,000 of which were in ruins. No doubt one would go too far either to accept these figures as valid, or to dismiss them as useless, since he did not make them up. If the percentage of ruined villages is worth anything, it is of slight value, given on the one hand the devastation at the outset of the conquest, and on the other the fact that in the soil and climates of the Near East generally, and at the technical levels of those days, it was frequently necessary to abandon a site and move to another nearby. Place names in Syria and Turkey recall these cases of 'ruins' which are mere changes of site, and are sometimes subsequently reoccupied or exploited anew.

Whatever may be the exact list of all the kinds of cultivation and their quantitative importance, one would like to know whether the cultivated plants and the animals raised were, regardless of their relative amounts, just the same as in Byzantine times. Was there, for instance, an introduction of Iranian fruits new to the gardens or estates of Anatolia, or was there an increase? The fat-tailed sheep were evidently largely the descendants of those driven before the invading Turcomans, but was there any cross-breeding with them or the special goats? The Muslims of the surrounding countries were surprised to see the means of transport, among themselves consisting of camels without vehicles, which in Anatolia was often by ox-carts – a tradition evidently connected with the land and not with the Turks. Was the relative abundance of horses inherited from Byzantium, which bred a large number of them, or from Central Asia, or the two? Perhaps it is impossible to answer these questions. Nevertheless they should be raised, and their answer would be of great significance for the wider problem of continuity or discontinuity in the history of rural Asia Minor.

There are similar problems in regard to industry and the exploitation of mineral resources. Simon of St Quentin mentions the existence of lapis lazuli quarries, of salt works, of alum quarries (perhaps near to Aksaray and Sivas), of iron mines and three silver mines. Alum and the metals particularly merit some remark. The alum is not rightly viewed in an Anatolian context. This substance, much employed in the medieval dyeing industry as well as having some secondary uses, had been known since ancient times, when its deposits had been exploited in Asia Minor and elsewhere. Some exploitation may have continued into Byzantine times, although this is not actually known, and in any case there does not seem to have been trade in it. In fact and somewhat paradoxically, it was principally the European textile industry which wanted alum, since the East used dyestuffs which did not require it as taste and fashion differed there from those of the Franks. It is well known that from the end of the thirteenth century to the middle of the fifteenth almost all the alum used in Europe came from quarries in Asia Minor, and that the trade was virtually a monopoly of the Genoese. It is less generally known that in the twelfth century the West sought its alum in Egypt. In any event the basis for the intensive exploitation of alum was not indigenous industry, which made little use of it, but purchase by the Franks. This is very clear for Egypt, and does not appear less so for Asia Minor, where, as will appear, in 1255 the alum trade was in the hands of two Italians. It is not easy to know when and how the exploitation began. When in 1236 the commune of Marseilles obtained a grant of commercial privileges from the king of Cyprus, the alum of Rūm was mentioned among the products for which the island was an entrepôt. It is possible that several years earlier it was concealed under the name of 'alum of Aleppo', mentioned in some documents, as the existence of alum near Aleppo is very unlikely, and Aleppo would only be the market for alum of Sivas. However that may be, there is no trace of exploitation in the twelfth century, while in the thirteenth exploitation was going on. As the deposits had not changed, one must conclude that the alum of Sivas was in reality from Kuğuniya, and that of Aksaray probably from Kütahya. It is not known if the Franks were directly interested in it already before 1243. The alum of Egypt had not disappeared but that of Asia Minor was as good, and as that of Egypt brought revenue to the state treasury, perhaps slightly better terms could be obtained from the Seljukid state.

The iron mines to which Simon alludes are unknown. A later text notes one in the Isaurian Taurus, but there must have been many others which were shallow and on a small scale. Silver was more important for the state as providing financial means. Since later al-ʿUmarī notes just three mines, those of Gümüşsaray, Lu'lu'a (taken from the Armenians by Kay Qubādh) and Baburt (possibly Gümüşhane), these must be exactly those of Simon's time. There is no mention of the copper mines, which in Marco Polo's time were to feed a celebrated industry of Erzincan. In general terms it is known that there were as today important copper mines at Ergani, to the north-west of Āmid in Diyār Bakr, and there is no reason why production should have ceased when the country passed into the power of the Seljukids. Various localities bear names in *maden* (Ar. *maʿdin*), i.e. mine, but the dates of exploitation cannot be ascertained. Metalworkers and goldsmiths were among the witnesses to *waqfiyya*s.

It is for the Mongol period in particular that there is information about the textile industries of Rūm. Only the question of continuity will be mentioned for the moment. There was of course a Byzantine textile industry, supplied by wool from the sheep of Asia Minor among other products. Simon states that red caps like those worn by the Turks themselves found sale as far away as France and England. Moreover luxury fabrics, by no means all imported, then appear among the sultans' treasures, and carpets of Sivas were sought after by a rich merchant of Baghdad from the beginning of the thirteenth century, according to the contemporary Ibn Saʿīd; while he states that in the middle of the century Aksaray was also famous for its carpets, which the frontier Turcomans made for export.[10] The word 'carpets' covers different commodities, and one must distinguish between luxury embroidered fabrics, the technique of which had been inherited by Byzantium as well as the Muslim states from a remoter past, and the knotted woollen carpets, which seem to have been devised in Central Asia around the first centuries of our era, and which are properly the 'Oriental carpets' of today. There is not space here for technical details. It is known that in the fourteenth century the Greeks at Denizli, and from the end of the thirteenth at the latest the Armenians at Erzincan, wove remarkable embroidered fabrics, which seem to have perpetuated or revived the ancient traditions of their peoples. As regards the Armenians (whose carpets are famous later in any case) some texts give the impression that their carpets may date from a century or two before the arrival of the Turks. However, with the exception of the products of a similar technique in Spain, the oldest surviving carpets from outside Central Asia come from the Konya region in the thirteenth century. One thus gains the impression, reinforced by the texts mentioned above, that the new technique was possibly imported by the Turks when they immigrated. At a more popular level, the Turcomans clearly did not ask the indigenous peoples to weave the cloth of their tents or their matting. The *waqfiyya*s mention dyers with Muslim names; however, in the fourteenth century Pegolotti recommends merchants who want to bring Western textiles to market at Antalya, to import them in a finished state because of the lack there of cloth-shearers and finishers.

Every country of the Near East has known pottery since ancient times, but artistic ceramics in the sense of ornamental wall-coverings and so forth was particularly developed in Iran. It is unquestionable that the ceramic art of Asia Minor is connected with that of Iran, but there is no doubt that in the thirteenth century the ceramics were made on the spot by artisans, whose diversity is shown by three surviving names – one Iranian, a second from Mosul, the third perhaps Greek. Sculpture in wood is also connected with a range of traditions spread throughout the Near East; it is not surprising to find the names of two sculptors, one Georgian, the other from the Taurus, connected with forest regions.

Trade

Byzantine Asia Minor was crossed by several caravan routes, which on one side converged on Constantinople, and on the other radiated out towards the Syrian frontier to Antioch and Aleppo, by Melitene (Malatya) to Upper Mesopotamia, and Armenia, Ādharbāyjān and Iran. From this last direction however caravans used most frequently to cut across eastern Asia Minor by Erzurum, and unload their merchandise at Trebizond, whence it continued on its way by sea. The importance of this trade in Asia Minor itself should not be overestimated. It crossed over the territory itself without any real involvement. At times war put the very passage of the merchants in jeopardy, while depopulation resulted in the more lasting exclusion of any large-scale trading. Perhaps some regional maritime trade united Attalia (Antalya) and Egypt, but maritime relations were more frequently conducted directly between Syria or Egypt and Constantinople. As regards the Black Sea, the trade of all its coastlands drained off to Constantinople; the relations between the Muslim world and the peoples of the steppe and the forest passed to a small extent by the edge of the Caucasus and above all Central Asia.

Of course the general disorganization accompanying the belligerent phase of the Turkish conquest must for a time have limited trading possibilities, although there is no explicit confirmation of this. However, by the beginning of the thirteenth century, particularly after the Latin conquest of Constantinople, it is apparent that on the contrary the Turkish occupation had brought profit to trade, partly because of its integration, however incomplete, with the Muslim world, and partly because of the presence of a court and centres valuable in themselves were henceforward to attract merchants to the markets of the country itself, and not to routes on which they did not make a stop.

It is extremely difficult to gauge the rate of this revival, or in other words to say whether there was already a significant amount of trade in twelfth-century Asia Minor. If an anecdote of Abū Ḥāmid al-Gharnāṭī is to be believed, merchants had been coming from Russia since the beginning of the century. The first caravanserais go back to the reign of Kılıc Arslan II, and their number increased in the following century to serve the route from Konya to Kayseri. Built partly in the open country, they bear witness to the lack of urban staging-posts, and at the same time to the attention paid to the revival of trade and to ensuring the security of traders, especially those on their way to the court. Michael the Syrian mentions the loss in 1135 of a caravan of 500 Persian merchants in a snowstorm, an indication of both the revival of attempts to attract trade, and of their inadequate organization.

From the very end of the century evidence increases of trade becoming active and its organization around new centres. In 1197 the Ayyubid ruler of Egypt, al-ʿAzīz ʿUthmān, sent presents to Alexius III Angelus by way of Anatolia and when these were intercepted for political reasons by Kay Khusraw I, all the Seljukid merchants in Constantinople were arrested in reprisal. A *waqfiyya* of 598/1201–2, which incidentally mentions a new marketplace beside the old one at Konya, cites among the witnesses two merchants from Tabrīz in Ādharbāyjān as well as a Turkish merchant of Konya. In the same period Samsun on the Black Sea had been a Seljukid possession for several years and, while investigating a shipwreck at Ceresonta (Giresun), Alexius Angelus fell upon some Seljukid subjects embarking there for Constantinople; to obtain compensation, they turned to the Sultan Rukn al-Dīn Süleyman II. According to the contemporary Ibn al-ʿAthīr, merchants from Syria and Mesopotamia were meeting at Sivas with Russians and Kipchaks (i.e. pagan Turks) from the countries north of the Black Sea before 602/1205–6. It is certain that at that time and long afterwards Sivas was the great market for trade in Asia Minor, the meeting-place of routes crossing from east to west, or coming from Syria, Mesopotamia and the Black Sea, where there was a clash of interests between Trebizond and the Seljukid state, some political consequences of which have been mentioned. Trebizond, backed by the principality of Erzurum, naturally wanted to keep exclusive control of the route from Iran to Erzurum and Trebizond itself, and at the same time to attract the Crimean and Russian merchants, who were temporarily diverted from Constantinople by the fall of the Empire to the Latins. Mention has been made of the crisis, decisive for Sivas, of the loss of Samsun, which was compensated a little later by the more firmly based conquest of Sinop.

In the same period the conquest of Antalya on the south coast was unquestionably due in part to commercial reasons. Alexandrian merchants had complained of confiscations committed by the Frankish lord of the city, the Tuscan Aldobrandini; and it is evident that many Franks, particularly those now established in Cyprus, had an interest in the port not closely coinciding with that of the Muslims. Once the Turkish conquest was irreversible, they came to terms for the same reasons. An agreement was reached in 1213 on reciprocal security for the subjects of the two states coming from one to trade in the other. In 1216 a more formal treaty detailed the mutual guarantees, in particular in regard to dues, the right to asylum if pursued by corsairs, and respect for property in the event of shipwreck in territorial waters. The last point was currently a matter of privilege but not automatic in the absence of a treaty. These texts imply the existence of a fleet, which, although apparently only the successor of that which Antalya had in Byzantine times, was nonetheless henceforth a Seljukid fleet.

The Venetians, masters of the trade of the Latin Empire and adversaries of the Greeks, were naturally most assiduous in seeking to establish direct and advantageous links with the Seljukid state. They did this in the Black Sea, but even before that at Antalya, since it must be to this port that a grant of privileges refers, which was made by Kay Khusraw I, and renewed with amendments by Kay Kāwūs I and then Kay Qubādh I. In the grant by the last, extant and dating form 1220, they are conceded a reduction of customs duties (normally at least 10 per cent) to 2 per cent *ad valorem*, and even duty-free trade in cereals, precious metals including goldsmiths' and silversmiths' work, precious stones and pearls. Their personal security was of course recognized, as of goods even in the event of shipwreck. As in other Muslim ports at this period, they obtained judicial autonomy in regard to their internal affairs, and a privilege respecting other Latins that, should there be dispute with one of them, the judges would be nominated by the Venetians. The duration of the treaty was for two years only, but there is no reason to suppose that it was not renewed more or less tacitly over a long period; the Venetian statutes of 1255 speak especially of the link established by Venice between Alexandria and Antalya. As for the other Latins mentioned in the treaty, only the Pisans are named, but other texts prove that at Antalya there were also Provençals and Genoese.

The Venetians were almost the only Latins in the Black Sea, since no one could enter it from the Mediterranean without their goodwill. Our documentation on their presence in the Turkish ports there is weak. A private document mentions their passage to Samsun in 1212, when the port was held by Trebizond, but evidently the commercial interest was only in its relations with the Seljukid hinterland. But in the Black Sea, the Venetians were above all interested in the Russian trade.

Here there was competition among three parties: Venice (and occasionally other Latins as well), Trebizond and (after the occupation of Sinop, for which this was the motive) the Seljukid state. Only the political events, to which allusion has been made, tell us this, but they are sufficiently eloquent. For the Turks the Russian trade was significant, on the one hand as obtaining for them the furs, honey and slaves for which it was normally the reason, on the other as vying with Trebizond for their transport to more distant Muslim lands. In 1223 a Mongol army had just taken the great Crimean port of Sughdāq, the chief point of this trade. Numerous merchants from Sughdāq and Russian merchants from elsewhere fled to Asia Minor, and were wrecked off the coast. This gave rise to conflict between the Seljukids and Trebizond, as the former confiscated their goods in accordance with the usage where there was no grant of privileges, while the latter asserted that the wrecked ship was carrying the tribute of *Gothia* to its suzerain, Trebizond, and that the seizure constituted an act of blatant political hostility. The allegiance of the Russian Black Sea ports to Trebizond in fact infuriated the Seljukids and, since the Mongols did not stay, this link would be restored, if there was no intervention. Pretexts were found. A merchant of Antalya, travelling by land from Syria to Cilicia, Antalya and Anatolia, claimed that he had complaints against Franks in Antalya,

Armenians in Cilicia and Russians in the Crimea. At Sughdāq, Seljukid subjects suffered confiscations. As previously noted, in 1232 an expedition led by the commandant of Kastamonu ended in the establishment of a Seljukid protectorate over Sughdāq, and this was to last until the final conquest of southern Russia by the Mongols in 1239.

These events show that, if foreign merchants frequented Turkey, Seljukid subjects also (and apparently of all faiths since a mosque was built at Sughdāq) shared in the external trade of the country. But the foreigners were not limited to the ports. Many Iranians came as far as Sivas and Konya to trade, and one of them was a spy in the service of the Mongols. There were also some Italians from Syria, or from Cyprus on their way to Damascus or Aleppo, meeting compatriots of other callings. This was to grow under the Mongols, but it must be emphasized as not enough attention has been paid to its previous existence.

The first decades of the thirteenth century were those in which the great sultans built the caravanserais, the ruins of which still mark the lines of the old major traffic routes. There were of course caravanserais (Ar. *khān*, T. *han*) in every Muslim country, especially Iran. In Central Asia, where the merchants had to cross vast spaces in climatic conditions that were often rigorous, the states had built little halting posts as far apart as possible, near to watering-places where feasible. The caravanserais no doubt derive from the two traditions. It is stressed that they were particularly useful in winter, when the caravans continued to move in spite of snow and there were no villages to provide adequate shelter especially in the mountainous zones, where settlements are few and far between. The catastrophe of the Iranian merchants, mentioned above, showed their utility. Even in the twelfth century Kılıc Arslan II had built an imposing caravanserai near Konya, while subsequently sultans and notables were rivals in their zeal in this matter. Before 1243 certainly thirty, and probably ten more, caravanserais can be counted by their existing ruins alone, while others were added under the Mongols. According to Ibn Saʿīd, on the single route from Kayseri to Sivas there were twenty in the mid-thirteenth century.[11] Furthermore some bridges, e.g. on the Kızılırmak, were made or reconstructed. The routes appear to have remained as they were.

Retail trade was carried on as everywhere for towns in markets, of which there is no special knowledge. Fairs have sometimes been spoken of, but without obvious evidence; in both Muslim and Byzantine lands, real fairs (except that of the Islamic Pilgrimage) are an abnormal phenomenon, playing little part in the economy for the very reason of the permanent and stable trade. Naturally there were seasons when foreign merchants arrived; and on a more local level there may have been as elsewhere periodical gatherings in the suburbs of some provincial capitals for the barter of goods between nomads and sedentaries. At the present time all this is speculative. Trade was naturally generally conducted according to the usages of Muslim law.

Weights and measures

It is improbable that the weights and measures noted by al-ʿUmarī and Pegolotti in the fourteenth century, which are invariably different from the Iranian Mongol equivalents, were drastically changed by the Mongol conquest. Until the contrary is proved, they may be considered valid for the preceding period. A general account is not possible here, but some examples may be given of data of historical interest. The two fundamental units of which al-ʿUmarī speaks are the *mudd*, measuring capacity, and the *raṭl*, measuring weight. These may be translations of local terms, since *raṭl* and *mudd* are fairly widely used. However this may be, the unit which he calls *raṭl* equals (according to him), 12 Egyptian (*Miṣrī*) *raṭls*, i.e. 1,680 *dirhams* of weight, but sometimes only 8, i.e. 1,120. At Sivas, however, according to Pegolotti, they used a *raṭl* which was double that of Acre, i.e. 1,140 *dirhams*. It is well known that no medieval country, even the most advanced, achieved unity in weights and measures and so this diversity is not surprising. What however is striking is that here on the whole the units are large, since for example the *raṭl Miṣrī* was the equivalent of 140 *dirhams* (437.5 grs), and heavier than what was called the *raṭl Rūmī* (i.e. the *Roman* pound, not that of Rūm), which was equivalent to 102 5/7 *dirhams* (321.43 grs). It is only in Iran that the term *raṭl* was used of a large unit, more closely corresponding to the *mann* of the Muslim legal system, equivalent to 2 *raṭls*, which is of the same order of size as the *raṭl* of Asia Minor. On the other hand, al-ʿUmarī fixes the *raṭl* in use among the Germiyan at a still greater weight, viz. 3,120 *dirhams*, and units of this order are still attested in eastern Asia Minor in the fifteenth and sixteenth centuries. But in the time of Ibn Bībī a *mann* of 260 *dirhams* was also known, and this was the legal Islamic *mann*. It is difficult to draw firm conclusions from these data; the system does not appear to relate to the Byzantine tradition and it differs from the usage in Arab lands, even if the Arabic word *raṭl* was actually used.

The impression changes, however, if one passes to other units. Under the Arabic word *mudd*, of which al-ʿUmarī speaks, and which, he says, was sometimes pronounced *mut*, there can be little doubt that here as in Syria the Byzantine *modios* lies half-concealed. He says that it was equivalent, in different places, from 0.75 to 1.5 *irdabb*s of Egypt, i.e. at about 90 litres to the *irdabb* from 72.5 to 135 litres. This is effectively of the same order of size as the Syro-Egyptian *modios* and would not correspond to any *mudd*. Here there is a possible relationship with the Byzantines. Otherwise several texts instance as a measure of area the *faddān*, an Egyptian term, but we are not told to what it corresponds. The Iranian unit *par excellence*, the *jarīb*, makes no appearance even in authors writing in Persian. On the contrary, land is measured by a unit of exploitation of variable area. The term used, *çift*, is borrowed from the Persian *juft* meaning a pair, but translating the Byzantine *zeugon* (Latin, *iugum*) and following the Byzantine usage.

Briefly and very hesitantly it may be suggested that there was a mixture of weights and measures of various provenance, and that there was perhaps a more marked continuity with Byzantium for matters connected with the land, and with the Iranian world for matters of trade.

In the fourteenth century, the impression given by al-ʿUmarī about prices is that they were clearly lower there than elsewhere, especially in the western principalities. The difference, although slight for agricultural products, is extremely large for livestock (except for thoroughbred horses) and their products. This is obviously too natural a characteristic for it to be questioned in the period of independence. Furthermore, low prices do not naturally indicate prosperity; they may be an element in wealth or poverty as the case may be. Precise data are too lacking to afford an answer, to seek in what relates to monetary circulation the national revenue or average income, which are doubtless for ever incalculable, or the ways of living. It would perhaps be a little easier to deduce the consequences for the history of international trade from the partial price-gap.

Coinage

Some difficult problems are posed by the coinage of the Turkish states of Asia Minor.

It is clearly evident that in the earliest period following the establishment of the Turks there the only money was what the occupiers found, which must have been fairly abundant, being on the one hand accumulated by them as tribute or booty, or on the other hidden when possible by the indigenous people. The first mintings appear only under the Danişmendid Gümüştekin Gazi, and probably a little later under the Seljukid Sultan Masʿūd I. Until the middle of the century at least they are solely of copper, that is to say, intended only for local trade. Silver was to appear under Kılıc Arslan II, gold only in the thirteenth century.

It is not surprising that some coins of Gümüştekin, of his successor Mehmed, of the latter's brother İnal, even again of Dhu'l-Nūn and

Dhu'l-Qarnayn, should bear Greek legends, as did a seal of the last-named, which is not known to have its like among other princes. Nevertheless there are no Greek legends on any of the old Seljukid coins, which were minted in no less hellenized regions. The Danişmendid coins bear no mention of their place of minting, those of the first Seljukids mention only Konya. What is most remarkable is that the Danişmendid coins bear frankly Christian images, e.g. the bust of the Saviour Christ laying his hand on the ruler's head; or semi-Christian, e.g. St George slaying the dragon; or again they may be religiously neutral but of a Byzantine character with a portrait of the ruler or the representation of a lion. The last alone appears on the earliest Seljukid coins.

The first idea which comes to mind as an explanation of these characteristics is that they were made by indigenous artists in the Byzantine tradition because there was nobody else, and because the principal users were the indigenous peoples, who would neither have accepted nor understood other coins. But the problem is a little more complicated than it seems, for these coins are not alone in this period in showing these characteristics, or at least in bearing images of a Byzantine character. Such are some of those of the truly Muslim Nūr al-Dīn Maḥmūd b. Zengi, and they are in any case abundant among the Artukids of Diyār Bakr. There, in an old Islamic country trading more with Mesopotamia than with Byzantium or Asia Minor, and copper moreover being of no commercial interest, a land accustomed for several centuries to a Muslim Arab currency, arguments admissible for the Danişmendids are not so for the Artukids, and by implication put in doubt even those which might otherwise be acceptable for the Danişmendids. As will later appear, the Turks did not share the Arabs' dislike of these representations, but those found in their own works of art are not in the Byzantine tradition; consequently this is not an explanation of the present problem. It may be admitted that the Artukids like the Danişmendids had handled an abundance of Byzantine coins as a result of raids in Asia Minor, and some of their own coins are perhaps copies of such models; but it is difficult to admit the persistence of this situation through several generations. Obviously one cannot dismiss the influence of the Byzantine tradition, nor yet that of wartime booty and tribute (which was not in copper), but there is still no explanation of why it was so strong and durable, and this author has no suggestions to make on the subject.

Furthermore these reasons would be equally valid for the Seljukids, whose coins are (apart from the lion image) more steadfastly Muslim. It may be that at the outset they were content with the Byzantine coins which were in circulation, or which they had in their possession. This would explain why there is no specimen of their coinage before they set up a Muslim monarchy; subsequently the wish to have a Muslim currency appears clearly. It may seem astonishing that the Seljukid sultans, whose relatively peaceful policy towards Byzantium had been indicated, should appear to have been more intransigent in this matter than the Danişmendids, who represented the *gazi* spirit of the Turcomans. It will however appear that their political attitude was in no way an impediment to an effort at islamization in the classical sense, whereas the Turcomans were in contact with the indigenous peoples as much in peace as in war, and were little preoccupied with monetary islamization.

We have a silver coinage from Kılıc Arslan II onwards, which probably signifies that the opening or reopening of the mines should be dated to his reign. In the following century Simon of St Quentin was to make much of the quantity of coins which the sultans could mint, thanks to these mines. This minting of silver exclusively, apart from copper, for some time is easily explained and offers no problem, but should nevertheless be stressed as being somewhat singular. Silver had been for a fairly long period the predominant coinage in Iran, but at this time it had almost entirely given place to gold. In Byzantium too and in spite of difficulties, gold remained the fundamental metal until the thirteenth century – for large transactions of course. Gold, which began to be minted in Asia Minor in the thirteenth century, did not occur naturally in the country, and consequently could only be obtained by means of trade, and to some extent by tribute. There is thus evidence of the way in which trade progressed, which is all the more remarkable in that we are reaching the time when the Muslim states of the Near East and likewise Byzantium were beginning to have increasing difficulty in obtaining gold, and when its minting was to move to the Italian trading cities.

It is perhaps impossible to decide whether the early small denominations in copper were aligned in value to their Byzantine counterparts. The silver dirhams and the later gold dinars were so aligned by legal definition in the neighbouring Muslim countries. It does not seem that there were alloyed coins, as there were under the Ayyubids of Egypt in the same period – although for reasons which were not necessarily or uniquely connected with a scarcity of metal, at least as far as silver is concerned.

CHAPTER TEN

The system of land-tenure and taxation

Osman Turan was the first to perceive that the system of land-tenure in medieval Turkey presented certain original features differing entirely from the system in classical Islam. This is naturally a matter of the first importance for the entire social and institutional history of the country.

In the Byzantine Empire as in the Muslim states, there existed a clear division between private, essentially individual, property, and state property. In the Byzantine Empire as in the Muslim states, state domain had been reduced on the eve of the Turkish conquest because of grants made under forms resembling in practice gifts of property, while in private property large holdings had developed at the expense of small estates and of the free peasantry. Nevertheless, to avoid frequent misinterpretation, the distinction must be borne in mind between agricultural estates, almost always individually held, and the pastoral areas, unexploited or collectively used without individual tenure, on the one hand; and on the other hand the genuine domain of the state and its rights over private property, this latter category including the personal wealth of the sovereign. It must finally be borne in mind that, in fiscal matters, classical Islamic law contrasts territory subject to the land tax (*kharāj*) with that paying only tithe; the first being land which at the time of the Arab Muslim conquest belonged to native owners left in possession, the second being land which was henceforward Muslim, to which were assimilated in practice the *qaṭā'i'* (s. *qaṭī'a*) assigned to individuals from those parts of the public domain which were not retained for direct management by the state.

The Turks in Central Asia had become acquainted with these different types of property. Nevertheless for all those who remained organized according to tribal tradition, the notion of individual property, primarily agricultural and well defined both on the ground and by the administration, was an unintelligible or unacceptable concept, and they tended to consider all land as for collective use, or at most as regionally distributed among groups. It is hard to imagine that when they entered Asia Minor they were sufficiently surrounded by jurists of the traditional Islamic stamp to give up this way of thinking. The only question is to know whether, as in the Central Asian states which they had served previously, collective territories were assigned to them in unappropriated stretches of land retaining their classical administrative organization, or whether they considered themselves the masters of all they surveyed, apart from allowing the continued existence here and there of islets of subjected cultivators, locally retaining their previous structure. The second answer seems likely enough in view of the fact of the conquest, although it may be observed that at the conquerors' level of organization and intellectual development there is perhaps no clear practical difference between the two solutions. On the contrary the difference could and did appear afterwards to the officials who step by step established an administered state in the conquered land; they were men who had received some training in law and terminology inspired by classical Islam.

The example of what took place after the annexation of Ahlat makes it seem likely that in the first third of the thirteenth century at the latest a general cadaster of the land of Rūm was drawn up. At that moment, in accordance with a process of which there are many other historical examples, the state apparently deemed everything which was not individually held to be public domain, apart from the concession to certain nomadic or pastoral groups of the collective use of some territories, which were henceforward precisely defined. It is hard to doubt that this public domain included even a great number of agricultural undertakings, the cultivators of which were not regarded as proprietors. In such a course of developments, it is comprehensible that (in contrast to what happened after the Arab conquest) there was no place for distinctions either between Muslim and native property (i.e. between tithe land and *kharāj* land) or between the property of the state and state rights in private property, where it was a matter of two types of *iqṭāʿ*. Taken as a whole, perhaps with some individual or regional exceptions, there was a single state domain, in the framework of which alone different conditions could be provided for individuals or groups. From this domain private properties could even be reconstituted through alienation, but they were not generally the original ones; if by chance such they were, they could only be maintained by the legal fiction of a new grant by the state, the theoretical proprietor.

There is certainly another approach, and that is the possibility of continuity with the Byzantine system. The fact that the Turks often entered Rūm almost as the emperor's agents, in any case without the deliberate intention of destroying the imperial institutional framework insofar as it did not affect them personally, makes it impossible to avoid the question of possible continuity even in the system of land-tenure. There is in fact no contradiction here with the impressions gained from the conditions of the Turkish conquest. For one thing, it must be remembered that there remained hardly any Greek peasant proprietors in the regions where the Turks were to establish themselves (this was perhaps less true of the Armenians), and as the great landowners were absent or refugees, their tenants automatically fell directly under the domination of the conquerors, normally without their having any chance of reconstituting a small estate. For another thing, the evacuations, transfers of population and so forth in many regions created a gap between the Byzantine and Turkish regimes. Only an extensive study of agrarian structures and methods of assessment of taxes and dues (a study which because of the state of the documentation would have to cover several centuries) would warrant a decision as to the extent of some continuity existing between the Byzantine and Seljukid periods in the various regions. It can of course be admitted that there were cases of both continuity and discontinuity, but from the present point of view it is sufficient that the way in which things took place does not appear to contradict the conclusion reached previously.

In addition, the importance of the territories of the Ottoman imperial domain, the *mirî*, is one of the features so clearly brought to light by the work of Ömer Lütfi Barkan that there is no logical reason for surprise at finding the same feature existing already in the origins of Turkey; up to a point it is even an argument in support of its existence. The continuity is however less simple than might appear, for Osman Turan has shown that the Mongol protectorate altered the system of the Seljukid state domain, while on the other hand the Ottoman state comprised more than Anatolia. The continuity is thus probably less simple and more uneven than appears at first sight, but one should not conclude that it did not exist.

Taking all this into account, there was nevertheless some private property both Muslim and native before the Mongols. Confining the survey to documents anterior to 1242, of which both the authenticity and the interpretation are incontrovertible, there is, for example, a *waqfiyya* of 598/1201. This type of legal deed is interesting because a *waqf*, being in principle intended for a future limited only by the end of the world, cannot rest on revocable rights of usufruct, but only (in classical Islamic law) on freehold property or the like, and *waqfiyya*s are always drawn up conformably to the stipulations and in accordance with the forms of classical Islamic law. So in this *waqfiyya* the founder formally specifies that the possessions that he conveys in *waqf* are his full property; one may note in passing that they are for the most part urban, and that where rural possessions are concerned, they seem to be situated in the region of Konya. Another example may be taken from a passage in the chronicle of Ibn Bībī, who was too well informed about chancery usages to misapply a technical term. He specifies that Kay Qubādh gave certain villages in full freehold (*milk*) backed by a charter to Kir Farīd, the Greek governor of Kalonoros (Alanya) at the time of its surrender. Ibn Bībī distinguishes this grant from that of an *iqṭā*ʿ, which Kay Qubādh also made to him. It is probable that private property constituted in this way was made at the expense of the public domain, and shows the beginning of a process which was to accelerate under the new conditions of the Mongol protectorate. It moreover appears almost certain that the preceding observations apply to the open country, and must be distinguished from property in and around the towns as urban life recovered. For the present it is not necessary to say more about this, as a return will be made to the subject when dealing with the towns.

Waqf, mentioned above, was a classical Islamic institution, which almost certainly played no part in Asia Minor before the diffusion of traditional Muslim culture. Although the *waqf* might have private purposes as well as the public interest in Muslim lands, at the period under discussion *waqf*s were increasingly established for the benefit of a religious institution (or a social institution, which came to the same thing), such as a mosque, *madrasa*, caravanserai and so forth, and this seems to be the sole kind found in Asia Minor. *Waqf* consists of the alienation of property for the benefit of the institution in question, or rather of the persons who will ensure its maintenance and activities. The grant is in perpetuity and is consequently inalienable, although certain kinds of lease are inevitable. There were thus many *waqf*s in the Muslim world as a whole; in Asia Minor they are met with from the end of the twelfth century, although they were probably not widespread before the Mongol period. They then became numerous in order to ensure the safety of threatened families by bringing property under the cover of *waqf*, and to safeguard the income of institutions hitherto supported by their ordinary (but now endangered) budgets. In the rest of Islam *waqf*s were made in practice on private property, although perhaps under the Mamluks of Egypt at the end of the Middle Ages some were also established on state domain. In Asia Minor the latter practice appears of more frequent occurrence, precisely because of the importance of the public domain. For example when Ertöküş established various properties as *waqf* in 613/1216 for the benefit of a mosque in the recently conquered city of Antalya, and of other institutions in this province or its northern neighbour Burğlu, he probably did not do so as the individual owner of these properties but because as the semi-autonomous governor of all southern Anatolia, he was empowered to dispose of the public domain there.

Property constituted as *waqf* retained all its previous features. If cultivated land was concerned, the peasants there were subjected to the new beneficiary and its management as previously to the landowner or the state; hence they owed the same dues to the new beneficiary as to its predecessor. In the classical Muslim lands a property thus alienated as *waqf*, and which formerly paid *kharāj* or tithe to the state, continued to pay these same taxes in its new status, except in the event of their abandonment by the state, which became general at the end of the Middle Ages. In the system prevalent in Rūm, this stipulation was pointless: since in principle almost all land was state property, there was by definition confusion between tax paid to the state as the organ of government, and a due paid to the landowner, who was here the state itself. In these circumstances land however alienated is granted with the dues involved, even if these dues bear the name of classical taxes; it being understood that the state could also make partial grants reserving certain financial or other rights. This relates rather to the idea of *iqṭāʿ*, to be considered next.[12]

The word *iqṭāʿ* has been mentioned more than once. According to Osman Turan, the landed system in Seljukid Asia Minor involves the general use of the *iqṭāʿ* as an administrative procedure as the state was incapable of administering directly the extensive territories it possessed. Here is the idea, adopted by Turan, that the *iqṭāʿ* was of Seljukid and Turkish origin, characteristic of a specifically Turkish 'feudalism' since the word is freely translated 'fief'. This theory is unacceptable. There is in any case a difference between Asia Minor and the realm of the Great Seljuks, who as rulers of old Muslim lands never had at their disposal a public domain analogous to that of their kinsmen in Rūm. A particularized study is therefore necessary here.

When the so-called 'feudalism' of Seljukid Asia Minor is under consideration, there is, as in many other cases, confusion among the various uses of the term *iqṭāʿ*, and even between this term and its mistranslation in European languages. In the classical lands of Islam in the first place, *iqṭāʿ* could signify the quasi-ownership of a portion of the public domain, or simply the right to the dues of land in private ownership. In the former case it was automatically hereditary like all property, but this is alien to the original concept in the latter case, and was only extended in the twelfth century, giving for the first time a semi-feudal character to this type of *iqṭāʿ*. Furthermore a distinction must be made between the small *iqṭāʿ*s normally amounting to one or two villages, which were the equivalent of an army officer's pay, and the great provincial governorships, which in the twelfth century also began to be designated *iqṭāʿ*s insofar as they became autonomous and hereditary. The governorships however did not automatically possess these characteristics, and might be granted only to high officials, who were subject to dismissal, and might possibly be paid by an *iqṭāʿ* within the sphere of their administration. As regards Asia Minor, a distinction must as elsewhere be made between the small *iqṭā*ʿs and the provincial governorships. It will later be established that, in spite of what has always been said, provincial governorships in Seljukid Asia Minor had only exceptionally the character of an *iqṭā*ʿ. In any case the holder of a great administrative jurisdiction, however granted, was in the position of the state in regard to local property. What it is necessary to know here is whether the state was directly affected at the base by grants of *iqṭā*ʿ in the true sense as it was by gifts or sales of property, or the foundation of *waqf*s.

If a fundamental distinction is made, as seems necessary, between the independent Seljukid regime and the Mongol protectorate, there are few mentions of ordinary *iqṭā*ʿs. This may arise partly from insufficient documentation and a lack of interest in minor personages, and any statistical reckoning is impossible. What will be said about the army will support the view that in Rūm the *iqṭā*ʿ did not have the same military importance as in the surrounding Muslim states. However it may be, the *iqṭā*ʿ in Rūm necessarily differed from the *iqṭā*ʿ in the other states because, by reason of the great predominance of state property, it rested on this land, and not on fiscal rights in private properties. Nevertheless the organizers of the Seljukid state of Rūm were not unaware of how the *iqṭā*ʿ was practised around them, i.e. that it was not a grant of property but was deemed a source of income. So too the *iqṭā*ʿs of Rūm, which were carved out from the public domain like those of early Islam in the countries conquered by the Arabs, were not regarded as a grant of property but only of revenue, whether due or tax being vague here as has been seen. Furthermore these *iqṭā*ʿs were temporary in nature, sometimes linked to the exercise of an office but not necessarily military, sometimes for life but not normally hereditary; while the state could reserve such administrative or financial rights in their source as it pleased, and these were specified in the deed of concession. Even the great *iqṭā*ʿs of Kırşehir and Akşehir, set up for the princes of Erzincan and Erzurum in compensation for their dispossession, appear to have been of this kind. The holder of an *iqṭā*ʿ (Ar. *muqṭa*ʿ) had no right to alter the condition of the inhabitants in regard to their taxation or otherwise. The *muqṭa*ʿ in Asia Minor was in some respects similar to the *muqṭa*ʿ in Egypt, where in general the land was in the same way particularly firmly held by the state.

The preceding restrictions did not mean that some great officers and officials were unable to acquire great fortunes through various revenues drawn from their functions by regular or illicit means, e.g. the possession of immense herds in the uncultivated lands. It will be seen how ruthless Kay Qubādh was against intolerable abuses of this kind. These however were just those men who held *iqṭā*ʿs perhaps by reason of their offices, but precariously. In any event they were not independent *muqṭa*ʿs.

To sum up; in Seljukid Asia Minor almost all the land except on the outskirts of towns may be deemed to have been basically public property. The state might however gradually alienate portions either as freehold (*milk*) or as *iqṭāʿ*, the latter being most often linked to service, especially military service, and thus not finally granted away. Developments in the Mongol period show that these grants of *iqṭāʿ* for the army had become fairly extensive from the time of independence; but statistics are lacking, and in any case it must be stressed that these were small *iqṭāʿ*s which were not prejudicial to the state's direct ownership. They were not *iqṭāʿ*s of the governmental type, of which more will be said when provincial administration comes under consideration.

In the Ottoman period the state distributed landed concessions without real public authority to its troopers. These were intended to supply their needs, and bore the name of *tımar*. It is more or less implicitly admitted that there was some relationship between the *iqṭāʿ* and the *tımar*, but here it is important to agree on what is under discussion, and to pay attention to some aspects of research methodology. If one simply means to say that certain estates which formed *tımar*s in the Ottoman period might have some continuity of system with what they had previously under the name of *iqṭāʿ*, this may well be so, although no actual example seems to have been provided. This however does not necessarily mean that the concept of the *tımar* was born from that of the *iqṭāʿ* with a mere verbal change. This view has found support because the word *tımar* appears in the *Selcukname* of Yazıcıoğlu ʿAlī, but there is no justification for using his term for the Seljukid period. He wrote a Turkish adaptation of Ibn Bībī's Persian *al-Awāmir al-ʿAlāʾiyya fiʾl-umūr al-ʿAlāʾiyya* in the Ottoman period, and scholars more familiar with Turkish, working from Yazıcıoğlu, have committed a grave fault of methodology. In fact research on the name and institution of the *tımar* is back at the start. The word is Persian, *tīmār* signifying 'much forethought, means of providing for one's needs, concern for one's needs'. The transition from this meaning to the technical sense given above is comprehensible, in the same way that the Latin word *beneficium*, 'benefaction' was used to designate the European fief. *Tīmār* in the technical sense seems to be unattested in any pre-Ottoman Persian text, either under the independent Seljukids or in the Mongol period. It is possible that the Ottomans borrowed the usage directly from the Byzantines as a translation of the Greek *pronoia*, which has exactly the same meaing as *tımar*. The matter does not need discussion here, but it is clearly unjustifiable to deduce certain ideas on the Seljukid *iqṭāʿ* a priori from those about the Ottoman *tımar*. Some elements of continuity certainly do not indicate identity.

A better knowledge of the system of taxation would assist a better reconstruction of the landed system. However, to have a clear idea of the problems awaiting solution in the light of the available information, it is important to bear in mind the fiscal system in the classical Muslim lands and the Byzantine Empire.

In the classical Muslim lands at the time of the Arab conquest, those estates which were not included in the state domain, i.e. the domain of the previous states or the great estates of private owners who had disappeared, were generally left to their previous owners subject to the payment of a land-tax called the *kharāj*, which moreover corresponded to what they had paid to the previous regimes. At the time this tax could be regarded as characteristic of non-Muslim status since the conquering Arabs were still the only Muslims; but in fact it was still maintained when the owners became Muslims on the grounds that the nature of the land did not change. At this time, however, a distinction, which had existed in some but not all regions, became general. This was between the land-tax and a poll-tax, the *jizya*, which disappeared in the event of conversion to be replaced by the *zakāt*, a contribution (originally voluntary) to the needs of the Muslim community. The practical difficulty of recognizing the cases in which there was a general tax, and those in which there was a distinction between two taxes, lies in the fact that the two terms designating them had not received their precise technical sense in administrative usage, and so even at a very late date *jizya* and *kharāj* are used interchangeably, or for a single undistinguished whole.

The land-tax could admittedly be levied on landowners, to whom were assimilated *de facto* possessors who held their estates on conditions practically equivalent to *de jure* ownership. Those peasants who were not landowners were sharecroppers (Ar. s. *muzāriʿ*) to the owner, to whom was due an amount roughly equivalent to the *kharāj*, but recorded by the administration in the landowner's name. Moreover sharecropping was often the system, not of *kharāj*-land but of tithe-land, tithe (Ar. *ʿushr*) being an ancient tradition but held in Islamic law to represent the *zakāt*, when this tax was levied on land. The land was deemed tithe-land and not *kharāj*-land if at the time of the conquest it was the property of a Muslim. Strictly speaking this was rarely the case outside Arabia proper, but to these Muslim properties there had been assimilated the *qaṭīʿa*s, the estates distributed abundantly by the new Islamic state from its domain land, which was too extensive to exploit directly. In such cases there was an important discrepancy in favour of the owner or quasi-owner between the due paid by his sharecroppers and the tithe due to the state, so that the grant of a *qaṭīʿa* became the commonest means of conferring material advantages on a notable. The sole condition was that he should ensure the exploitation of the land by settling cultivators on it, if there had not been any previously.

The Muslim states had of course also brought in numerous taxes on trade, industry and so forth under various names; but they lacked the fiscal importance of the fundamental taxes described, and they may be ignored for present purposes.

In the Byzantine Empire also the land-tax was the basic tax, as is normal in all countries where the land has remained the principal source of wealth, whatever the development of trade. The problem of knowing the extent to which there was a distinct poll-tax remains obscure, and is of no concern here. The majority of the peasants however had become sharecroppers of the great landowners, and paid a due to them rather than to the state. This was perhaps less clear in Armenia and the western valleys than in central Anatolia.

In fact there is evidently no information on the system which came into being at the start of the Turkish occupation. The Byzantine system of taxation was disorganized, and it is possible that in some places people had paid nothing legally for some time. It is however self-evident that the conquerors exacted payments which, although apparently not definitely institutionalized, must nevertheless have been burdensome, if one takes into account the devastation of those very districts where the presence of the conquerors made their exactions most frequent and unavoidable. Then a *modus vivendi* must have been institutionalized, which as the administrators became islamized must as always have produced little by little a progressive inclination towards the classical Islamic models wherever possible. There exists hardly any direct information about what then ensued, but it can be partly deduced from accounts of the Mongol period because these texts sometimes specify whether what they report corresponds to the Seljukid tradition, or on the contrary is an Ilkhanid innovation. Moreover the Ilkhanid system was never fully applied in Asia Minor, which, even when it was administered by Mongols, retained some autonomy in this respect. Finance is what a conqueror always has difficulty in changing.

Aksarayi, writing in the Mongol period, states that the *jizya*, an essential item of the Seljukid fiscal system, was so still in the time of the Mongol protectorate, and he ridicules the newly arrived Ilkhanid officials, who were completely ignorant of it. This ignorance may be connected with the fact that in the states under direct Mongol administration the *jizya*, classically the poll-tax on non-Muslims, no longer existed because the Mongols, before their conversion to Islam, had suppressed this sign of a relative confessional inferiority. It is however possible that they suppressed it in the eastern half of Asia Minor itself. However important a poll-tax may have been in a country with a non-Muslim majority, it is hard to believe that it was more so than the land-tax. In the Ottoman Empire in consequence of the verbal confusion already mentioned, the term *jizya* is generally used to signify the land-tax, or the combined land-tax and poll-tax paid by the non-Muslims. The word *kharāj* is rarer, and paradoxically signifies the poll-tax in the strict sense. It is tempting to believe that this was already the usage in the Seljukid period, and that Aksarayi's remarks thus refer either to the land-tax, or to the compound total tax paid by the non-Muslims, if the two elements were explicitly combined, which is by no means certain. The word *kharāj* is found occasionally in Aksarayi but still more vaguely, being applicable to any tax. In such a case the tax is paid in kind, which is one possible method of payment of a land-tax (*kharāj*) often of a proportionate amount, and is inconceivable for a poll-tax of fixed amount. On the other hand, the classical *kharāj* on land implies its payment by a landowner, i.e. it could not legally be demanded of a sharecropper. If, however, one starts with the idea that there remained few indigenous landowners, and that a great part of the soil was state domain, it is difficult to think that the word *jizya* should be attached to Muslim landowners, while it is equally inappropriate in regular terminology for the dues levied on sharecroppers of state land. On the other hand, it is normal for such dues to be paid in kind, whether in proportion to the harvest or not. It is difficult not to think that there was a good deal of verbal and institutional confusion; more exactly, that traditional Islamic terminology was applied to a state of affairs differing from the classical Islamic system, that the Seljukid officials no longer knew whether the *jizya* was a tax on landowners or a payment by sharecroppers, nor whether the rights of the state were those of a landowner or the public treasury. There is no reason to think that the sharecroppers were held to be free taxpayers, but the legal terminology concerning free taxpayers is applied to them. In Ibn Bībī, when dealing with the time of the independent Seljukid state, the normal tax on Christians (i.e. Greeks) and Armenians, a principal source of state revenue, is called *kharāj*. There is of course no mention anywhere of tithe-lands, since the *iqṭā*ʿ paid nothing.

All the same, the very little that is known of Seljukid taxation before 1243 thus corroborates the impressions gained from an examination of the landed system. There were of course other taxes, particularly in the towns, which correspond to what is mentioned under the vague general term *ʿawāriḍ-i dīwanī*. On the other hand, the landed and fiscal systems proper to Anatolia should not be extended to territories annexed in northern Syria and northern Mesopotamia, both regions which had known the regular Muslim practice. In the texts attention must be paid to distinguishing both between regions and periods; for example by not extending to the whole of Asia Minor the distinction between sharecropper and free landowner, the latter sometimes a village chief (*dihqān*). This was a term of varying significance which was current in Iran; its existence for the Ahlat region is attested by Ibn Bībī.

For the rest an attempt will be made to penetrate somewhat more deeply into the actual determination of the land-tax whatever its name. Several relevant passages of Aksarayi, although relating to a late period, may be of interest here, since they do not appear to deal with a Mongol innovation. These show that the levy on cultivable land was by *juft-i 'awāmil*, a Persian expression, but where the Arabic noun has a meaning that translators do not seem to have understood. The phrase means 'a yoke of plough-animals'. The word *juft*, whence the Turkish *cift*, is indeed known in Iran under the Ilkhanids, but it seems only to have been used in its original sense of 'a pair', the agrarian unit remaining as in the past, the *jarīb*. By contrast, in the texts relating to Asia Minor mentioned above, as much later in the Ottoman Empire, the term refers to a unit of land defined as what can be ploughed by a yoke of oxen; similar terminological and economic usages are found in many countries. In fact the Byzantine fiscal authorities taxed by 'yoke', in Latin *iugum* and in Greek *zeugarion*. This would seem to be a clear example of Byzantine-Turkish continuity, an impression which is perhaps confirmed, pending a more precise investigation, by the resemblances later presented by Ottoman to Byzantine law in these matters, both for the previously Turkish parts of Asia Minor as for the provinces directly annexed from Byzantium.

Whatever the case may be for this last question, the yoke could be taxed in different ways: in kind, proportionately to the harvest, in which case the agrarian unit is not of great importance; in cash for a fixed amount according to surface area by agrarian unit; finally, in kind but for a fixed sum. In Muslim countries generally private sharecroppers paid proportionately and in kind; cultivators or landowners chiefly paid the tax for a fixed amount on the agrarian unit, sometimes in cash, sometimes in kind for a calculated value. In thirteenth-century Asia Minor there is no doubt that the grand total of the taxes of a district were stated in cash; it is hard to believe that this was not also the case with the yoke, which in one passage of Aksarayi is said to be taxed at 1 dinar, although others report a tax by *taghar*, a Byzantine word meaning a measure of capacity for grain amounting in weight to 10 *manns*; the value of the quantity could naturally be calculated at a price fixed by the administration or the market. The tax based on the surface area is in general the Byzantine system; it is also frequent in Islam. But it is self-evident that the same surface area would bring in different amounts according to soil, climate or cultivation, and should therefore be taxed differently. In yoke regions this was often achieved by the yoke signifying different areas according to circumstances; while in the regions where the surface area was fixed, it was the rate of taxation which varied. Unfortunately however the system of Rūm is quite unknown. As for the sharecroppers of private landowners, they seem most often to have made proportionate payments; a *waqfiyya* of Karatay (made some years after the battle of Kösedağ) gives instructions that the demands are not to exceed one-fifth – in classical Islam this was the proportion paid by mediocre land requiring irrigation or otherwise difficult. This *waqf* was in the Kayseri region, and one cannot say whether the share was the same everywhere. In any case, and contrary to what has been believed, firm conclusions about the tax cannot be drawn from it.

In certain cases an agreed fixed sum (Ar. *muqāṭaʿa*) was substituted for the tax as normally calculated. Such was the case of the monastery of Mar Bar Sauma to the south of Malatya, the residence of the Jacobite patriarch. No doubt this applied also to the Turcoman groups, especially on the frontiers. It may be supposed that they paid in animals; this in fact would agree with the classical Islamic rule for pastoral nomads, but nothing is known about it. Tribute paid by vassals was of course a different matter.

Insofar as a precise estimate can be made for the total budget of the Seljukid state in the thirteenth century, it was (according to the later Ḥamdallāh Musṭawfī Qazwīnī) under the Seljukids 15 million dinars, i.e. of his own time, but after a decline of 3.3 per cent as will appear.[13]

At the beginning of the Ottoman Empire there existed in Asia Minor a group of regions which broadly coincided with the former Seljukid territories, and had a system called *malikâne-divani*, and so has been considered to be of Seljukid origin. Some remarks are due on this subject.

The taxes and dues as a whole there as elsewhere fall into two categories: the legal (Ar. *qānūnī, sharʿī*), and the customary taxes (*ʿurfī*). The first were concerned with land, the second with personal occupations. This does not mean that they differed from the taxes of other regimes, but that for collection they were shared out between two groups of beneficiaries, on the one hand private landowners, on the other the state. Does this system derive purely and simply from the Seljukid period? In this case it would aid us to form a more precise idea of the system in the twelfth and thirteenth centuries as described above. If it is hard to believe that there was no continuity from one to the other, it is not less so to think that the upheavals in these two centuries failed to produce any evolution in this respect. The expression *malikâne-divani* is sometimes met with in Mongol Iran, where it seems merely to signify the traditional Islamic fiscal system. It seems to have been met with in Asia Minor once only, without precise meaning. This is a subject for research which should be taken into account, but affording at present no precise deductions.

CHAPTER ELEVEN

The towns

As has already been said, from the mid-twelfth century urban life revived in Rūm, and in the thirteenth century probably reached a higher level than had been known during the last Byzantine centuries. In the mid-thirteenth century Simon of St Quentin asserts that there were a hundred towns in the Seljukid state, and Ibn Saʿīd says that there were twenty-four metropolitan centres, each provided according to regulations with its governor, *qāḍī*, mosque, baths and textile merchants. They do not list these towns, and perhaps neither was capable of doing so, but the impression is explicit and there is no difficulty in compiling almost the required number of names from the chroniclers and the travellers' accounts.

In general, and in spite of the undeniable break in their history made by the period of the Turkish conquest, the Seljukid towns are virtually the same as the Christian ones, whether there was unbroken continuity of settlement, or the site was reoccupied. In a country once highly urbanized, geographical conditions would rarely allow a choice of completely new sitings. Continuity is often marked by the name itself, and one must be heedful of cases where the *modern* name does not correspond to the one formerly used in Seljukid times but is of later introduction. Thus Colonea, south of Trebizond, continued as Kuğuniya but is now Şebinkarahisar, and even Ankara, while preserving the former name, Ancyra, used to be called Ankuriya, which is closer to the older form. The biggest cities among others retain to the present their ancient names somewhat corrupted, e.g. Konya (Iconium), Sivas (Sebastea) and Malatya (Melitene). In some instances the corruption is more marked, or the name has been completely replaced by another of pre-Turkish origin and due to the Armenians or the Arabs, e.g. Erzincan (Keltzine), and Erzurum, a neighbour to the former Qālīqalā (Arabic), and also called Theodosiopolis. Finally, and especially in western

Asia Minor, new Turkish names came into use, especially for small and middle-sized towns, although unfortunately there is not always evidence of the circumstances of the change. In some cases it was not accompanied by any interruption of settlement; in other cases this may have occurred, e.g. between Byzantine Archelaus and Turkish Aksaray. In yet other cases a neighbouring site may have taken the place of the old one; thus Denizli (spelt Tunguzlu) grew up in place of Laodicea ad Lycum (Lâdik), and strangely Eskişehir (meaning 'Old Town') arose three kilometres south of the ruins of Dorylaeum, likewise also Beyşehir in the place of Karalea. It does not seem that there were any true foundations of towns in districts where there had been none previously, but there might be re-foundations, e.g. Aksaray, or official renaming, e.g. Alaya for Kalonoros in honour of 'Alā' al-Dīn Kay Qubādh. Finally, of course, a town might not have the same relative importance as previously.

The towns were inhabited by elements of the diverse peoples of Asia Minor. It is reported that at Antalya the Greeks, Jews and Turks each inhabited their own quarter, but the fact that this is reported suggests that it was not the case elsewhere; in fact although an 'Armenian tavern' is mentioned once at Konya, there is no impression of any segregation. This was indeed rare at that time, and still less frequent in Byzantium than in Islam. The special case of Antalya may be explained by its being more of an international port, and perhaps by the conditions of its capitulation long after the rest of the country. The presence there of Jews moreover appears exceptional for Asia Minor, although there were some at Konya. It is not known if there were any at Sinop, also a place of international resort but where there is no indication of separate quarters for the different ethnic and religious groups. The members of each group would naturally tend to stick together, but without any systematic segregation. In a large Armenian city such as Erzincan, it was the Muslim group which was isolated.

Neither in the Byzantine Empire nor in the Islamic world did the cities enjoy the autonomy which they had possessed in classical antiquity, or which they regained in the medieval West. It does not follow that they lacked vitality or a certain kind of community spirit; nor does it follow that no care was given to the public works they needed. All that is simply an inherent part of the general structure of the state, and Islamic law does not recognize as legal entities collective organizations intermediate between the individual and the state, even where such exist. To dwell on these general concepts is needless here; they have been discussed many times. It is important simply to remember that on the whole in Asia Minor as elsewhere, and more for the Muslims than for the indigenous inhabitants, the city was the centre of all administration and culture. The Turcomans, who were physically outside the city, were at this time also truly outside society and culture, or at least formed another society and another culture in the broad sense of the word.

Thus it was in the city that the governor resided with his garrison; it was in the city that were to be found the mosque and the *qāḍī*, who rendered justice, and whose appointment was sought among the eminent jurists. The *muḥtasib* will be discussed elsewhere, but something must be said here about him and the organization of the trades. The *muḥtasib* was in law a subordinate of the *qāḍī* with special responsibility for public morals, the control of the non-Muslims, and above all for the smooth course of trade. This was the case throughout the Muslim world in the Seljukid period, and it is not surprising that the state of Rūm adopted the institution. Unfortunately we do not know when this took place, nor whether it had some peculiar features there arising from the number of indigenous merchants, who had their own traditions, and were more numerous there than elsewhere. Insofar as they did not positively harm Islam, their traditions were respected.

An account attributed to Jalāl al-Dīn Rūmī will serve excellently as an introduction to both the scene and the social structure of a great Seljukid city:

> At Konya the chief men, the dignitaries and the notables have thousands of houses, castles and palaces. The houses of the merchants and *ikdīsh* are more elevated than those of the artisans; the palaces of the emirs are more elevated than those of the merchants; the domes and palaces of the sultans are yet more elevated than all the others.

To this may be added various passages from the chronicle of Ibn Bībī enumerating the notables, the *ikdīsh* and the *ahi*s, sometimes the men of religion also.

So at the summit were the emirs, the governor and so forth, all the representatives of authority and the dominant class, but below the sultan in the city where he resided. As in the Italian cities, so in some Muslim cities, the height of the dwelling was duly proportionate to social rank. There is no difficulty in recognizing the social category concerned; with the other categories which follow, it is rather different.

The word *ikdīsh* (T. *ikdiş*), which was Iranian and Turkish before it was adopted in Arabic, properly meant a gelding or crossbreed, in particular a mule. Thence it acquired the meaning, especially in Iranian and Turkish countries, of a human half-breed.[14] So in Asia Minor it particularly signified children whose father was a Turk, or perhaps a Muslim of other nationality, and whose mother was an indigenous woman – a situation which, as has been indicated, was necessarily more frequent than the reverse. Perhaps, but there is no proof of this, the term *ikdiş* included native converts pure and simple, or young Christians levied from the population for training as Muslim soldiers like the Ottoman janissaries. If this were the case however it would be surprising not to find it mentioned in the Christian writings.

Whatever their ethnic origin, it is striking to see that these *ikdiş* belonged on the whole to the urban aristocracy, where they formed a special corps under the command of a Muslim *ikdişbaşı* or *amīr-i akādīsh*, often the son of a native convert, several of whose names are known. When they are mentioned in the chronicles, it is because in or beside their place in the army, properly speaking, they carried out military operations of a local character. From this has arisen the belief that they were a military corps; but it seems that they were no more so than any police force or militia normally assigned simply to the maintenance of order in the city. Perhaps they had this function; it even happened on one occasion that an *ikdiş* of Ankara was temporarily entrusted with the guarding of a defeated pretender. Otherwise a model diploma of investiture drafted towards the end of the thirteenth century and a letter of Jalāl al-Dīn Rūmī show the *ikdişbaşı* and the *ikdiş* acting as collectors and even assessors of urban taxes. Thus they had a fairly large share in urban administration, and this is mentioned in a sufficient number of towns to suggest that it was a general system. In short, it was by means of this local aristocracy of mixed blood that the sultans kept a grip on the urban population, in the lower ranks of which non-Muslims predominated, but if need be even Muslims.

Nevertheless with the passage of time this social category lost its distinctness and its *raison d'être*. After several generations there could no longer be the same distinctions between Muslims by origin and the descendants of converts or mixed unions as at the start. From the fourteenth century the word *ikdiş* disappears in its social sense, and, as will be seen, the *ahi*s alone remained as the local police force. But before dealing with the *ahi*s, some consideration must be given to the merchants, the artisans and their connections. To begin with, the question must be more extensively dealt with.

The organization of trades and professions in Asia Minor touches on a problem of wider territorial range. It is impossible here to enter into matters of detail, but the broad object must be indicated. Both in Byzantium and in the later Roman Empire to which it succeeded, there was a state organization of occupations in the sense that they were distinguished from one another, but their regulation belonged to the state, and the persons directing them were state-appointed. It was quite different from the system which began to develop in Western Europe contemporaneously with the Seljukids. There professional corporations came into being, i.e. collective but private organizations, which were disregarded by the states, but elaborated their own regulations, chose their directing officers by themselves, and for these reasons provided a framework for the general life of their members by mutual aid and religious activities in a way of which the Roman *collegia* were incapable. On the basis of a very superficial examination which confuses things, periods and countries, it has often been believed that such professional corporations were known in Islam. For the so-called classical periods of Islam, the opposite is certainly more or less true; there existed administratively powerful states, which, like the Byzantine Empire, governed without admitting intermediate bodies. The occupations were administratively distinct, but their direction was a matter for the state, i.e. for the *muḥtasib*. It is true that there were heads of trades (Ar. *ʿarīf*, *amīn*, *raʾīs*) under him, but these were his subordinates, not elected by the trades, and there is no trace of a wider role played by the trades in the lives of their members. Any groupings they formed (e.g. the *fityān*, shortly to be discussed) lay outside their professional bodies. In the twelfth and thirteenth centuries, Syria and Egypt (as also Muslim Spain) saw the compilation of manuals of *ḥisba*, the function of the *muḥtasib*, the purpose of which was just to set down exactly the *muḥtasib*'s obligations from a purely administrative point of view.

From the end of the Middle Ages, however, some degree of evolution must be admitted. In modern times when the states had less power, even in the Ottoman Empire, even at Istanbul, and apparently as a consequence of originally different circumstances, the trades had a semi-corporate organization, and there arose a combination of some degree of state control and some private activity. It is possible that Iran and Central Asia, which had probably not exactly the same traditions as the former Roman possessions such as Syria and Egypt, were further advanced in this evolution than the rest of the Islamic world. This hypothesis should at least be taken into account. It now remains to set Asia Minor into this general picture.

Without completely excluding the possibility of traditions brought by the Turks from their distant Central Asian homeland, it would seem reasonable to admit that the life of artisans in the towns of Seljukid Asia Minor resulted at the outset from the juxtaposition or contact of Greek and Armenian artisans on the one hand, and Iranian immigrants on the other. As the Iranian Muslims occupied the essential place in the formation of the administration, it may be granted that at least the framework of professional life was conceived according to their ideas and traditions, even if the particular customs of any occupation in native hands may have retained the character it had before the coming of the Turks. This having been said, what do we really know? Of the Seljukid period itself, practically nothing, even though it is likely that each trade had its own alley or quarter. At the end of the Mongol period, Ibn Baṭṭūṭa brings information which is both important and difficult to interpret. First however the *ahi*s require introduction.

The organization of the towns is in fact linked to that of the *ahi*s. For reasons which will appear, this only appears in full light and force under the Mongol regime, although it existed previously. It is a very interesting institution but raises many problems, so that it must be considered at some length.

Here the *futuwwa* must be mentioned, or rather the *fityān*, commonly called the *ʿayyārūn*, who claimed to go back to it. They were corporate groupings with a popular but not an occupational membership, showing strong solidarity, moved by social rather than religious considerations, somewhat violently at odds with authority and the aristocracy (although some aristocrats tried to make use of them), and powerful when the government was weak. Thus they were a true militia at such times, more covert at times of strong government but still surviving. Every city in Iraq and Iran, i.e. those lands which had once been possessed by the Great Seljuks and traversed by the Turks of Rūm (who still felt the influence), had its *fityān*, who were sometimes the real masters of local politics. If the cities of Byzantine Asia Minor had nothing really equivalent, nevertheless it was normal for a *futuwwa* to appear as urban life was reorganized by peoples of different origins.

Nothing is known of the existence of the *futuwwa* in the twelfth century, before the closing years of which it must have been unimportant. The moment in which, however, it makes its real appearance is that when the Caliph al-Nāṣir (575–622/1180–1225) in Baghdad tried to institutionalize the *futuwwa*, and to turn it into an organization for social cohesion by attracting both high and low with precise and modified regulations, and by encouraging all the neighbouring rulers to make a similar effort under his aegis. It has been mentioned above (p. 52) that this was the reason why the caliph sent to Kay Kāwūs I the great Shaykh Shihāb al-Dīn ʿUmar al-Suhrawardī, one of his advisers in this matter, who made a great impression on the Turks of Konya, or at least those in government circles. This coincided with the time when the Seljukid sultanate was being organized as a Muslim state, and was concerned to present itself as orthodox, and thus to receive the caliph's blessing. Hence Kay Kāwūs joined the *futuwwa* as renovated by al-Nāṣir, and it may be granted that in some unknown manner there resulted a drive for the organization of the Anatolian *futuwwa*, for an organization perhaps closer to the caliph's wishes than that in the old cities, overburdened as they were with too rigid a tradition.

In Asia Minor and some neighbouring regions to the east, however, another problem arises about the beginning of the *futuwwa*. In this country as in the north-west of Iran, i.e. that part of Iran where there had been most Turkish penetration, the usual name for the *fityān* (or perhaps more precisely their leaders) is *ahi*, which has no equivalent in the rest of the Islamic world. There is no doubt that the two terms had the same meaning in the thirteenth century, but it cannot be positively asserted that this was so from the start. Even the origin of the word is uncertain and was unknown to the *ahi*s of the later period on which alone there is serious documentation. Writers who discuss this have thought to find there the Arabic *akhī*, meaning 'my brother', but the forms assumed by this word in Persian and Turkish texts, possibly even Arabic, at least exclude its conscious use in such a sense. The illustrious modern Turcologist Jean Deny has suggested an etymology for it which would be linguistically admissible, but an historian must query it because the first known *akhī*s, situated in north-western Iran in the eleventh century, clearly appear to have been Iranians, from whom the Turks would have picked it up. In any case they were purely mystics, who seem to have been unconnected with any kind of *futuwwa*, and certainly not with a *futuwwa* of the urban *fityān* as mentioned above. Whatever may have been the early meaning of the word, unimportant moreover since it seems to have been unknown, there is a problem in the conjunction of *ahi* and *futuwwa* in Seljukid territory which differs from the history of the *futuwwa* in other lands.

It is clear that it is not purely a matter of words. It is known that particularly from the eleventh century onwards, when mysticism established itself in orthodox Islam and tended to be organized in brotherhoods, some of the *fityān* were open to some forms of mystical thinking, while on the other hand some mystics adopted in their own way the idea of communal life implied by the *futuwwa*. Shaykh 'Umar al-Suhrawarḍī is an example of this kind of convergence. The so-called *futuwwa* literature, of which more will be said, is interesting and surprising in this respect. As only the literate wrote, we are given only their point of view on the matter. In practice this appears in the fact that at the very time when the chronicles and other texts show the *ahi*s as acting in positive, indeed violent, ways, the *futuwwa* literature speaks almost wholly of initiation rites and theoretical moral and religious considerations to such as extent that, were it the only source, one would hesitate to believe that it could be dealing with the same matters and men. The *futuwwa* literature produced by al-Nāṣir's circle was to have a particularly great influence on that of Anatolia. It is certain in broad terms that, as elsewhere in Islam, there was an interpenetration of a certain kind of social action and a certain kind of mystical way of life, a taking-over of some social organizations by some groups of 'mystics', with due regard to the possible differences in the significance of that word. That is all that can be said at the moment.

Beside *fityān* and *ahi*s, terms were used in popular speech which, like all jargon, varied from time to time and place to place. In this period *'ayyārūn*, used in previous centuries, is found, but the term most in use in the Seljukid dominions was *rind* (Ar. pl. *runūd*; Pers. pl. *rindān*), meaning 'rogue'.

The *akhī*s in general had as ancestor a certain *Akhī* Faraj Zanjānī, from Zanjān in north-western Iran, who lived in the first two-thirds of the eleventh century; but the Turkish *ahi*s claimed as their ancestor one *Ahi* Turk (if the reading of the name is certain) of Urmya on the frontier of Ādharbāyjān and Armenia, who must have lived in the twelfth century. The headship of the community including the *fityān* remained to some extent in his family until the thirteenth century, at least in Konya. The oldest *ahi*s of whom there is knowledge are in fact in other cities, the first to be attested being at Antalya only a few years after its conquest in 1207. This shows that the organization was introduced at the same time as the Muslim immigration, and so was really already a part of every Muslim urban community.

Nevertheless the role of the *ahi*s is not fully apparent in the sources, and evidently reached its political, if not its economic, apogee only in the periods of the breakdown of authority. Since furthermore it happens that the *futuwwa* (T. *fütüvvet*) literature begins in Asia Minor only at the end of the thirteenth century, little is known about the *ahi*s and *rind*s before the Mongol period, when it will be possible to complete and substantiate these generalizations.

On the question of connections between the *ahi*s and the trades, a glance at the Mongol period is permissible because a source of that period poses a problem extending to the whole of the Turkish, and even of the Muslim, Middle Ages. It is the account of the travels of the famous Ibn Baṭṭūṭa.

The problem is this. As has been said, the *futuwwa* organizations in the Muslim world as a whole before the end of the Middle Ages, even while bringing together men who were mostly tradesmen, were not occupational organizations, since a specific trade or profession does not seem to have been the framework either of their activities, or of the distribution of their membership among sub-groups. There were the trades on the one hand, and the *futuwwa* on the other, even if the membership of both was largely identical. Nothing at least seems to show that it was different before the thirteenth century. In the Ottoman period, however, there is no doubt that in Turkey proper as well as in the non-Turkish provinces there was a convergence of the two organizations. The trades of Istanbul as described by the Turkish eyewitness Evliya Çelebi in the seventeenth century are bodies of initiates of the *futuwwa* type, while the handbooks dealing with the trades of Ottoman Egypt are entitled handbooks of *futuwwa*. The identification is not total; perhaps it varied from one country to another, but that they converge is undeniable. Thus there is a major problem about the reasons for this development, the way it came about, and its chronology. In this respect the evidence of Ibn Baṭṭūṭa is of capital importance.

As he passed through Anatolia soon after 1330, Ibn Baṭṭūṭa was struck by the importance of the *ahi*s in almost all the towns he visited; this will be further discussed. What touched him personally is that these *ahi*s practised the virtues of hospitality and fellow-feeling for which he as a stranger had nothing but praise. These qualities were told of the first *fityān* of Islam, but less indeed of their descendants. He almost always found accommodation in their communal house, where he was sumptuously received. So he observed their practices, to which we owe the details he gives us. What is important at the moment is that according to Ibn Baṭṭūṭa the membership of a group of *ahi*s, although readily open to any kind of bachelor, was in the first place constituted within the framework of practitioners of the same trade. Such was at least his general introductory description; although when he speaks immediately afterwards about the *ahi* chief who received him at Alanya, he is less clear, for he writes that the chief was a cobbler, and that he was surrounded by 200 artisans of various trades, who had chosen him as their leader. The example of Lâdik (Denizli) proves however that all the trades were not necessarily or normally united in a single group of *ahi*s, as there was competition between two groups, but evidently more than two trades. At the festival of the Breaking of the Fast, however, they marched bearing arms and with a band, trade by trade, after the sultan's troops. Confirmation of these matters is provided with less precision in the information he gives on Aksaray and Sivas. The conclusion is that in Ibn Baṭṭūṭa's time there could be rival groups of *ahi*s organized on identical principles, but that within each group containing members of a large number of trades there was a structural distribution by trades, and that the collectivity of these trades formed the substance of the *futuwwa* of *ahi*s. In all his travels Ibn Baṭṭūṭa never found the like. Even in Iran, where the trades seemed to him more autonomous and distinctive than elsewhere, there was no systematic link with the *futuwwa*, although it was well known there.

In the light of all this, it is important to know whether the picture which Ibn Baṭṭūṭa gives of the fourteenth century can be retrojected to the one preceding. If so, it probably signifies a certain originality within the Muslim world, the reasons for which would be worth investigating. If not, then there would have been an evolution, and one would wish to know whether it was self-generated, or had undergone influences from the Mongol regime or otherwise. Nothing can be said of this at the moment, but it is important that the questions should be clearly posed.

The *ahi*s had not a specific religious connection any more than any other organization. In general however they traced their origin back to ʿAlī b. Abī Ṭālib and, like the Caliph al-Nāṣir and his heirs, seem by preference to have given the leadership of the principal groups to ʿAlid families, even of more or less Shīʿī complexion. In the fourteenth century, in the time of weakness of any authority in the Anatolian plateau, a sort of *ahi* republic existed at Ankara, remote from all the great political centres of the period. Family tradition traced the governing 'dynasty' to the second half of the twelfth century, when it was called upon by Kılıc Arslan II to organize the Muslim tradespeople newly arrived in that city. It may previously have been established at Khoi in the marches of Ādharbāyjān, and it boasted of descent from the Eleventh Imam at the same time as did some Zaydīs of Ṭabaristān. In fact its earliest known member is one Ḥusām al-Dīn (d. 695/ 1295–96), whose tomb has been preserved. However unreliable the rest of the story may be, it remains indicative of a certain socio-religious atmosphere, and perhaps also of the encouragement given by the sultans, in the thirteenth century at least, to this form of corporate organization.

It seems that the *ahi*s were exclusively Muslims either by origin or conversion. There were also more or less professional groups among the non-Muslim parts of the population, e.g. among the Armenians of Erzincan.

The largest city under the Seljukids before the Mongols was apparently Konya, which already owed to Masʿūd the first attempts to make it the capital. Certainly it was so when Frederick Barbarossa's crusaders passed by in 1190. One of them describes it as being the size of Cologne, and as having a city-wall and a citadel. The Great Mosque, begun by Masʿūd, was repeatedly increased in size by all the sultans until Kay Qubādh, under whom it reached the state in which it can be seen today. A *waqfiyya* of 598/ 1201 mentions two small mosques founded by rich merchants. There is no reason why this chance document should list all the mosques, and there were surely others; even though three only, including the Great Mosque, can be reckoned before 1243, insofar as it is possible to date monuments which do not always have inscriptions, and excluding mausolea, *madrasas* and so forth. The *waqfiyya* also makes mention of the new market beside the old one, showing the growth of the city and its business, while *waqfiyyas* of the period mention tradesmen of all kinds.

Kay Qubādh judged the existing fortifications to be inadequate, and had them all more or less reconstructed at the expense of the treasury and the great emirs. The hill of the citadel is the site of the royal foundations, the tombs of Masʿūd, Kılıc Arslan II, Rukn al-Dīn Süleyman II and Kay Khusraw I, and the lost palace of the sultans, of which the important ruins were still extant and described by various travellers in the nineteenth century. In the suburbs were gardens and monasteries, the most famous of which was the so-called convent of Plato, the Charition (see below, p. 128). The descriptions of the *Tārīkh-i āl-i Saljūq* and Eflaki for the second half of the thirteenth century, even allowing for exaggeration and vagueness, give the impression of a city of economic, political and cultural activity, with certainly some tens of thousands of inhabitants.

The second city of the sultanate was probably Sivas, an international centre for merchants, also fortified by Kay Qubādh at the expense of the emirs. This he did at Sinop as well. Kayseri, which was to dazzle the troops of Baybars, the Mamluk sultan of Egypt, in 1277, was little inferior to it. Antalya should also be regarded as a great city, well described by Ibn Baṭṭūṭa. Erzincan was a great Armenian city, and Malatya a great city housing various confessions. There were many other towns which, although apparently smaller, were reckoned as truly cities, e.g. Erzurum, Amasya and Aksaray.

CHAPTER TWELVE

The non-Muslims

However numerous the Turkish population may have been, it is clear that there were still many non-Muslims, who were probably the majority almost everywhere – in the proportion of ten to one, according to William of Rubruck. It has been shown on several occasions above that in spite of, or sometimes because of, the depredations committed by the first conquerors, the natives had not been systematically hostile to them, but that they had viewed the conquest less as an ordeal for themselves than a punishment for Byzantium, and moreover that some Byzantines had called Turks in aid against other Byzantines; thus there had everywhere definitely been collusion as much as resistance to the Turkish conquest. It has been shown that in the regime as it was organized little by little after the conquest, there stood native notables, even Greeks, as well as refugees from outside, beside the Muslim masters, just as in other Muslim countries. All this is enough to suggest that, without failing to recognize the sufferings in the eleventh century and some subsequent tribulations or difficulties, there was on the whole in Turkey, when it was organized, a symbiosis akin to what existed in other Muslim countries but perhaps even better, and certainly more wide-ranging by reason of the numbers involved. It is unnecessary to return to the social aspects of the regime, but a word should be said about the religious situation.

A more precise study of the situation is rendered difficult by the fact that, apart from the Jacobites (who were important only for the province of Malatya and its neighbourhood), our only sources about the relevant confessions come from outside Seljukid territory. Furthermore it is necessary to take care not to be misled by documentation from the Mongol period. The pro-Christian attitude of the first Mongol rulers in Muslim lands, and the alliance of the Palaeologi with the first *īlkhāns* of Persia in fact allowed something to be regained by the Church; hence the mention of a community, a diocese and so forth at the end of the thirteenth century does not by itself justify the conclusion that they existed at the beginning of the previous century. Certain facts do however appear.

It is difficult for a present-day mind to grasp the possibility of the coexistence in twelfth- and thirteenth-century Asia Minor of the convictions and behaviour of *gazi*s together with a degree of religious toleration superior to that in the rest of the Islamic world. Some consideration must certainly be given to the difference of outlook between the Turcomans and the ruling elites, but this is not the whole of the matter since this coexistence was present among the Turcomans also.[15] As far as the rulers were concerned, to repeat: the Holy War quickly appears as an activity alien to their general tendency, one undertaken under the pressure of particular circumstances. This had happened many times in the history of other Muslim states, e.g. eleventh-century Syria, but at the period under consideration this attitude was reversed in Syria and Egypt because of the struggle against the crusaders and the Latin East. The Turks of Asia Minor were completely indifferent to this struggle. Even when at the start of the Frankish occupation or under some of the Ayyubids, there was a search for a détente and the acceptance of peaceful coexistence with economic profit, a family alliance between Muslim and infidel rulers was there inconceivable. Furthermore the brief and semi-legendary hint of an alliance with Richard Lionheart, suggested by Saladin, to be sealed by a marriage between their families, had no sequel. In contrast to this (as mentioned, p. 10), Malik-Shāh proposed the like to Alexius I Comnenus. Subsequently such marriages became common among the Turks of Asia Minor, not only at the start when beautiful captives were brought it but later, when marriages were concluded with agreement between equals, at least with Greeks and Georgians. The sultans' family also is full of Christians both male and female. The mother of Kay Khusraw I was a Greek and so was that of Kay Khusraw II, two of whose sons, if not three, had a Christian mother. It is true that one of these, a Georgian princess, later married to the Pervane Mu'īn al-Dīn Süleyman, was converted to Islam. This however was not a general obligation, and opposite cases were also known. The influence on the young Kay Kāwūs II of his Christian uncles, and even Michael Palaeologus is well known. Armenian women alone are missing from the list of Christian wives; they could represent no political power. On the other hand, there was a plan to marry a French kinswoman of the Latin emperor of Constantinople (above, p. 69). Whether by temperament or out of interest, the sultans protected their Christian subjects against those who might violate their religious freedom, while Muslim travellers to towns with a Christian majority and a weak Muslim colony, such as Erzincan or Erzurum, were indignant at the atmosphere they found there with wine, pork, religious processions and so on.

This coexistence is more difficult to understand, although not less certain, in the Turcoman territorial fringes. War against the unsubjected infidel did not exclude protection of the infidel subject, nor did it even exclude profitable commercial exchanges between one raid and the next. In these circumstances indigenous Christians came to seek an understanding with the Turcomans more willingly than the protection of the Byzantine government, which was often haughty and inefficient, and was accompanied by heavy taxation. History is full of these little exchanges between neighbours, who subsequently turn up as allies against their respective rulers.[16] In addition it was almost entirely a matter for the Greeks, as the Armenians had all become the sultan's subjects, as had all the small Monophysite groups, while the Georgians were too remote from the centre and difficult of access. To the Byzantines, the collusion of the Armenians and Monophysites with the Turks in the time of Alexius I Comnenus appeared so well established that they avenged themselves on the members of these communities settled in Constantinople.

The rulers of neighbouring states at this period revived from time to time the restrictions on non-Muslims which strict Muslims regarded as linked to the commands of Islam, particularly regarding sumptuary distinctions and the construction of new churches. The first of these measures almost always fell into abeyance, while dispensations in regard to the second could be obtained by financial means. It does not seem that before the conversion of the Mongols to Islam at the start of the fourteenth century, any measure of this kind was contemplated in Rūm, where its application would have been pointless or impossible according to time and place.

The cross-currents of politics and religion could at one time or another favour or prejudice good relations between the Turks and one or other of the Christian Churches in their states; but taken as a whole it is certain that in one respect the non-Greek Christians felt an improvement in their lot when they passed under their new masters, inasmuch as they no longer had to submit to vexation from the Byzantine Church. As it was, Süleyman I had turned over to the Monophysites churches at Antioch that had formerly been Byzantine, and Atsız had done the same at Jerusalem. Michael the Syrian in particular expresses satisfaction. The Turks were indifferent to the divisions among Christians, and held an even balance between them.

It must be emphasized that all this did not of course mean that the sultans were in any way lukewarm in their Islam. Those same rulers whose toleration is extolled did their best to promote Islam. At the very time when they left the Christians of their towns to profess their faith in peace, they were creating a model, and purely Muslim, city at Aksaray. Perhaps in proportion to the acculturation of the dominant circles they felt the maintenance of their domination was bound up with the consolidation of their

Islam, both culturally and as the political and social cement. The Greek Church might perhaps have thought of attempting their conversion in the very earliest days of the Turkish occupation. It did not, and that was the end of the matter.

Clearly it was the Greek Church which suffered most at the start. It was not that the invaders systematically wished to challenge it more than the others, since, as has been said, they took over the state of Rūm rather than wishing to destroy it. Yet all the same, in every conflict the Greek clergy seemed more closely linked with the government they were fighting than did the indigenous clergy. Above all, the Greek Church was often held in low esteem by the Armenians and Monophysites, who considered the Turkish invasion as the deserved punishment of the Byzantines, and sometimes came to terms with it. The Greek clergy, who had the possibility of withdrawing to Constantinople or elsewhere when life appeared too hard either morally or materially, were not held back as were the other clergy, who remained with their flocks, devoted to saving what could be saved, and restoring the shattered situation once the storm was over. One gains the impression that on the whole, even when it would have been possible to return, the Greek prelates judged their churches to be too impoverished, and preferred to seek in other provinces of the patriarchate of Constantinople posts as administrators of churches or monasteries which were more suitable to the maintenance of their positions. It is difficult to tell whether consideration of 'the barbarians' already had weight in 1082 in discussions about the maintenance of two small autonomous bishoprics opposite respectively to Ancyra (Ankara) and Heraclea of the Taurus (Ereğli); difficult also to tell whether the trials of the churches of the interior caused the promotion of Antalya to an ecclesiastical metropolis a little later, for there are similar promotions without such reasons. On the other hand, it is known that on the death of the metropolitan of Caesarea (Kayseri) and the arrival of the Turks, the archdeacon fled with precious relics; that in 1082, as the metropolitan of Gangra (Çankırı) could reside there no longer, he received the administration of the bishopric of Amastris (Amasra) on the Black Sea coast; that in 1093 or 1108 Alexius I Comnenus secured by decree the same rights to bishops exiled from their sees as those resident. In these circumstances the fact that the proceedings of twelfth-century synods at Constantinople were subscribed by the titulary metropolitans of Caesarea (Kayseri), Tyana (Niğde), Heraclea (Ereğli), Mokissos (Kırşehir), Ancyra (Ankara), Neocaesarea (Niksar), Amasea (Amasya), Gangra (Çankırı), Iconium (Konya) and even Melitene (Malatya), as well as the bishops of Sasima, north of Niğde, and Nazianzus, proves only that the patriarchate continued to nominate them, but not that they actually resided there. It is known that in 1157 a bishop who had been metropolitan of Amasea and then transferred to Ancyra, finally administered the simple bishopric of Kerasos (Giresun) on the Black Sea coast, which was still in Byzantine hands. At the end of the twelfth century the canonist Theodore Balsamon, commenting on the councils and decrees of Alexius I Comnenus regarding non-resident bishops, takes as one example of these the bishop of Iconium; and he states that in view of the distress of the church at Ancyra, it had to be linked with that of Nazianzus in the Seljukid Taurus. However, it should not be concluded from this general situation that even in the twelfth century there was a total desertion by, or exclusion of, the Greek clergy. In regard to this, there is extant a document which has received hardly any attention, and is of sufficiently great interest.

This is the report of an action for heresy brought before the patriarchal court at Constantinople against two bishops, Leo of Balbissa or Balbiatus (an unknown place) and Clement of Sasima or perhaps Sosanda (? Soanda, near to Nevşehir) on the complaint of the metropolitan of Tyana, supported by the priests of his church and also of one Nicephorus of Palatinon and a certain Basil of Monogrotton in the metropolitan province of Mokissos. The accused were at first charged with having, after their election at Constantinople, received ordination solely from James, a former metropolitan of Tyana, whereas the canons required ordination by several prelates; furthermore and above all they were challenged with various practices linking them to Bogomilism. They denied most of the charges, but Leo in answer to the complaint that he had handed Christian women over to the infidels, admitted that he had given one of his flock as a slave to the emir because she was an adultress. The evident conclusion from these records is that, at least in Tyana and two of its dependent bishoprics, prelates resided in Seljukid territory, but were not prevented from visiting Constantinople, where they were elected, and where their orthodoxy could be judged. There was, however, perhaps some difficulty in assembling the number of prelates canonically necessary for an ordination. Hence the Seljukid regime accepted Greek prelates, and even allowed them to maintain contact with Constantinople. Süleyman I and Shāhānshāh had similarly allowed the Greek patriarch of Antioch to remain in the city, and he made several visits to Constantinople. In this the Seljukids of Rūm went further than the other Muslim states, whose subjects following the Greek rite belonged to the arabized Melkite patriarchates of Antioch, Jerusalem or Alexandria, not to Constantinople, with which they had consequently few relations. The Danişmendids, apart from Mehmed, appear to have been of the same mind. Most often the only bishoprics sure to disappear were those in the east, which were political implants into populations attached to their own churches, and so had no longer any reason to exist. One must also naturally distinguish between the bishops who fled and the priests (not to mention their flocks) who had to stay. The trial of 1143 also suggests that owing to their relative isolation, some whiffs of ancient heresy might smoulder on, but there is too little evidence to be sure of this.

The return to internal order, and the improvement of political relations with the Greeks in the thirteenth century, probably promised some resurgence to the Greek Church, in which Greek nobles in the sultans' service or family might be interested. When in the middle of the century Michael Palaeologus, the future Emperor Michael VIII but then a refugee in Rūm, was allowed to return to Nicaea, it was through the intercession of the metropolitan of Iconium. At the same time the 'convent of Plato' at Charition, so-called because the philosopher was believed to be buried there, enjoyed a reputation which attracted pilgrims from all the countries around; even the Muslim notables of the city made excursions there. Moreover the legend of Plato became a traditional theme of inter-confessional folklore, traces of which have been revealed in our own day. At the end of the twelfth century the strongly anti-Romanist Theodore Balsamon judged it better to submit to the Turks, who had respect for souls, than the Franks, who menaced even these.

Another kind of documentation gives some information about Greek Christianity, especially in Cappadocia. It is well known that owing to a topography abounding in cliffs, subterranean 'rock churches' were built (or rather excavated) there, to be rediscovered as one of the great events of the twentieth century for the history of Byzantine art. The great majority of these churches predate the Turkish invasion, but it does not seem that they suffered any far-reaching alteration from this episode. Furthermore there are a few cases of construction, repair or decoration which were carried out in the Seljukid or perhaps the Danişmendid period. It is not possible to enter into the details of specialist discussion, the dating of the works, except in the few cases where there are dated inscriptions, being a tricky matter as isolated rural artists may retain past themes, forms and traditions out of fashion elsewhere. But some are certain, and the approximate dating of some others probable. Three dated inscriptions from the reign of Theodore I Lascaris (1204–22) and John III Ducas Vatatzes (1222–54) have been believed to prove that Cappadocian territory was re-annexed by the Empire of Nicaea. The hypothesis is unsustainable, and has been refuted; but when the names of the Emperor Andronicus II Palaeologus (1282–1328) and the Sultan Mas 'ūd II (1282–1304) are found later side by side, the conclusion must be not only of a good relationship between these rulers as attested elsewhere, but also of a certain sentiment among Greek Christians that their admitted political subjection to the Seljukid government did not exclude a kind of overall membership of the 'Roman' community.

Perhaps the churches of Cappadocia should be associated with the necropolis of Obruk, mentioned by several Muslim travellers of the twelfth and thirteenth centuries. In this site between Konya and Aksaray were tombs where could be seen at that time well-preserved mummies, which were apparently Christian and to which there was access, forming a place of inter-confessional pilgrimage. This necropolis may not have been the subject of recent notice or excavation, but there is no reason to think it all simply legendary.

This is perhaps the place to stress the presence in the sultans' entourage of aristocrats, Greek by origin, who were temporary refugees or permanently employed, and often in high office. The sojourn of Andronicus has been mentioned (p. 21), also the conversion and settlement of his son John, whose descendants are unknown. Later there was Mavrozomes, devoted to Kay Khusraw I and Kay Qubādh I, who through some obscure but possible kinship was styled in Rūm 'the emir Comnenus'. He remained a Christian, and in a church near Konya there is the epitaph of a young male descendant of his who died there in 1297. The future Emperor Michael VIII Palaeologus lived for some years in Rūm under the name of Comnenus. Less attention has perhaps been paid to the Gavras family, kin of the great Armenian Byzantine family of the Taronitae, most of whom dwelt in Trebizond and governed it, whether loyal or rebellious to Byzantine authority. At the beginning of the twelfth century, as mentioned, one of these governors sought Danişmendid support against Alexius I Comnenus, and twenty years later another was allied with Mengüçek of Erzincan against Gümüştekin, the son of Danişmend. Then in 1146 there was a Gavras who was brought up among the Turks, and was one of their provincial governors. In 1176 a Gavras carried offers of peace to Manuel I Comnenus, which he, after rejecting them, was glad to accept after Myriocephalum. This same Gavras or his son, called in the texts Ikhtiyār al-Dīn Ḥasan b. Gavras, negotiated with Saladin in 1180, and in 1187 brought him his master's congratulations on the capture of Jerusalem, before dying tragically as has been described (p. 90). From his name, he was probably a Muslim, and he seems to have been Kılıc Arslan II's vezir, or in any case his chief helper and adviser. However, the fact that on the eve of his death he asked to retire to the Mengüçekids, who inherited his wealth, suggests that care for the family's riches may have lain behind his conversion.

Besides these one might also mention Kir Farīd, the former lord of Kalonoros, who became Kay Qubādh I's father-in-law and his governor of Akşehir; and Fakhr al-Dīn Siwastus, perhaps a former freedman of Kay Khusraw II's Greek mother, one of Rukn al-Dīn Süleyman II's emirs. One of his sons is known from an inscription of 671/1272 from Afyonkarahisar. There is also the intermediate case of the two uncles of 'Izz al-Dīn Kay

Kāwūs II. They were indigenous notables who, before accompanying him to Constantinople, exhorted him, although Greek, to fight the Mongols with the aid of the Turcomans, against the advice of some Muslims, who had rallied against them to Rukn al-Dīn Kılıc Arslan IV, although he was vassal to the heathen Mongols.

Anyone reasoning from other histories may find it hard to believe, but it is the fact that relations between Greeks and Turks, in spite of their conflicts, were for several generations perhaps closer than between any other two Christian or Muslim princes. As has been seen, Greek rebels sought support from the Turks, and it is doubtful whether Byzantine history can show as many doing so from the Slavs, for instance, who were also powerful neighbours. On the other hand, it is still more remarkable that Turkish rulers from Asia Minor, when forced into flight abroad, very rarely went to the Muslims of Syria, Mesopotamia or Iran, even when the rulers there were Turks. On the contrary, they normally fled to the Byzantines or sometimes to the Armenians of Cilicia. There was a descendant of Kutlumuş in Byzantium. The Turks of Asia Minor were certainly Muslims, but in a sense were more or less consciously integrated in the entity called Rūm. They aspired to dominate it but it was because they felt part of it, and felt themselves at home there rather than in Dār al-Islām, even when they were among infidels. Is it exaggerated to propose some such formulation as this, which has clearly no explicit backing in the texts? At least a suggestion of the sort may be deduced from them.

The relations between Turks and Armenians appear somewhat differently from those between Turks and Greeks. Although there were Armenians in Konya itself, they were on the whole massed in the eastern half of the country, where the sultans did not normally reside, and they lacked the backing of political power. For both these reasons their role in Seljukid politics was less than that of the Greeks, but less also were their difficulties with the Seljukids once the first wave of devastation had passed. They acted almost as loyal subjects and, feeling themselves to be decently treated, mourned the rulers' deaths. The feelings of a more recent past should not be retrojected into earlier history.

Our information on the Armenian Church is not very complete. It is certain that some of the great centres of its life were to be found in the little state of Lesser Armenia, which gradually emerged in Cilicia, and others in the north-west of Ādharbāyjān, incorporated in the thirteenth century in Georgia, a Christian kingdom, but of another Church and another language. The Armenian hierarchy however survived in Turkish Asia Minor. The existence of bishops of Kayseri, Malatya, Sivas, Niksar and Cucusus (sometimes held by the Armenians of Cilicia) is known from the synods. As they played no part in Cilician history, there is no reason to suppose that they were not resident in their sees. On the contrary for example, Anania of Sivas with the strong support of Sultan Kay Kāwūs I elevated his bishopric into a rival catholicate, while John VII, the other catholicus, who lived at Qal'at al-Rūm (Armenian, Hromgla) on the Euphrates at the meeting-point of Ayyubid and Seljukid territories, and was in conflict with King Leon I of Cilicia, similarly appealed to Kay Kāwūs. Furthermore, extant manuscripts testify by their script and occasionally their illumination to the existence of monastic centres of culture at Erzincan, Erzurum and elsewhere. From the Mongol period there is a chronicle written at Sivas. An Armenian physician speaks to us nowadays through Arabic, Armenian and Syriac inscriptions telling of his foundation of a caravanserai, still standing north of Malatya. The role of Erzincan and its bishops under the Mongols will appear, and that of its artisans has been mentioned (p. 91).

It was the Monophysites who occupied the smallest place in Seljukid or Danişmendid territory. They were the most highly arabized Christians, the majority lived in Arab lands, they attained no more than a modest social level and they had no political memories or aspirations, no specific state for backing. Hence they caused no trouble; they would have been easy to persecute, but gave the least reason for persecution. They openly rejoiced at the Arab and Muslim conquests, achieved at this point at Byzantine expense; and it is they who today, without Armenian grandiloquence, live in the best symbiosis with their Turkish masters. This makes a diffused appearance throughout the chronicle of their patriarch, Michael the Syrian, and appears very explicitly with regard to Mas'ūd I in a statement by Sawīris b. al-Muqaffa', the historian of the Coptic patriarchs of Alexandria, who, as he belonged to a sister Church, was informed about Rūm. Sawīris says, 'The majority of [Mas'ūd's] subjects are Greeks; because of his justice and good government, they prefer to live under his administration', while Michael observes, 'As the Turks have no idea of the sacred mysteries . . . they are not accustomed to make inquiry into professions of faith, nor to persecute anyone on these grounds, in contrast to what is done by the Greeks, a bad and heretical lot.'

The Monophysite patriarch's principal residence, the convent of Mar Bar Sauma, lay in the mountain at the extreme end of the eastern Taurus in a region long disputed by the Franks of Edessa, then their Muslim Aleppine or Artukid successors, and the Danişmendid or Seljukid rulers of Malatya; several of their bishops frequently changed their political masters. In truly Seljukid or Danişmendid territory, bishops are mentioned at Malatya, Arka, Elbistan, Tzamandus and Kayseri. Michael the Syrian was personally on the best terms with Kılıc Arslan II; he received his visits, discussed religion with his *'ulamā'*, and later had letters from him. He was delighted at this, as he was delighted at the conquests gained by the Turks from the

Byzantines. The fact was all the more remarkable since he was one of the finest minds of the time, and in regard to other Churches the most inclined to Christian ecumenism. Michael succeeded in thoroughly restoring the convent of Mar Bar Sauma, which had moreover obtained a favourable rate of taxation, and likewise the cathedral of Malatya. This city and Mar Bar Sauma continued to be centres of Syriac monastic culture. Before Michael the theologian and historian Dionysius bar Salibhi had lived there, as some time after him did the greatest and last of the medieval Monophysite scholars, Bar Hebraeus (Ar. Ibn al-ʿIbrī). There is a Syriac Gospels produced at Malatya *c.* 1200, and no doubt a systematic investigation would result in the location of other Syriac and Armenian manuscripts in Asia Minor.

To say in conclusion something about the relations between the Seljukids and the Roman Church. The Seljukids had of course no Catholic subjects, and since also, unlike the Muslims of Syria, they had no quarrel with the Franks, who belonged to the Roman Church, they might simply have abstained from any relations, good or bad, with Rome and the Latin clergy. The relations which did exist should neither be exaggerated nor misinterpreted. Kılıc Arslan II possibly, and Kay Khusraw II certainly, corresponded a little with contemporary popes for political reasons. Whether political relations with the Byzantines were good or bad, the sultans could see no harm in these Latin propagandists coming to rival the influence of the Orthodox patriarch's clergy with their Greek subjects. So when Gregory IX and Innocent IV started to send missionaries to the East, they were well received. Although for the time being this might have been the case in Syria and Mesopotamia also, it is quite possible that the welcome was warmer in Asia Minor, where there were also Latin merchants and soldiers. Doubtless this fact is also connected with the enthusiasm of Simon of St Quentin's account of the several years he spent in Rūm, which is the source of some valuable information.

It does not seem that there were many Jews in the interior of Asia Minor under the Byzantines. There were some in Antalya, and they were still to be found there after the Seljukid conquest, as has been seen. It is normal that the court of Konya should have attracted some in due course, but only at the time of Jalāl al-Dīn Rūmī are they known to have had rabbis and a quarter where wine could be found. It is not known if there were any in the commercial centre of Sivas. Aksarayi seems to have had an unfavourable view of them, but does not say whether he had dealings with individual Jews. In any case their role does not seem to have been important, even at the time when the *īlkhāns* gave the vezirate to a Jew and a convert from Judaism respectively. Bar Hebraeus, the son of a Jewish physician of Malatya converted to Monophysite Christianity, was born in Rūm.

The evidence provided about the toleration enjoyed by the non-Muslims does not mean that there were no conversions. Apart from the special cases of slaves and *ahis* there were genuine conversions from time to time. They took place among the aristocracy, no doubt for career reasons; we have mentioned the Gavras, the Comneni and the wives of sultans, who included both converts and the unconverted. There were yet others. Although Eflaki, the hagiographer of the Mevlevis, evidently exaggerates, his reports of individual or mass conversions through the sole influence of Jalāl al-Dīn Rūmī are not purely imaginary; moreover at Rūmī's mystical level adherence was easy, perhaps not always implying a genuine and formal passage from one faith to another. Several other instances are known, perhaps occasionally of priests or monks. It is certain that, when the Turks arrived, some of the indigenous peoples had only an imperfect knowledge of Christianity, and the increased isolation caused by the conquest facilitated conversion by weakening their faith still further. The investigation of some modern groups suggests that there may be cases of syncretism going back to the Middle Ages. The Karamanlı people of the province of Karaman seem to have been an ancient autochthonous group, who adopted the Turkish language but remained Christian.

CHAPTER THIRTEEN

The central political institutions

There has been controversy between scholars holding that most of the institutions of the Ottoman Empire were of Byzantine origin, and others rgearding them as of Islamic or Turkish origin. The dispute was basically somewhat misconceived because, while a number of examples were cited, there was no clear distinction of the fields, and it may consequently be thought that the solution is not necessarily the same at the level of the central organization and the underlying social organization. As far as Seljukid Asia Minor is concerned, the problem is not quite the same as for the Ottoman Empire; first of all because the period was different, but secondly and more especially because the conditions of establishment and growth were not the same. The Ottoman Empire was established in a kind of symbiosis with what was left of the Byzantine Empire, and was a European before it became an Asian power. Institutional unification was never fully realized; the regime in Asia Minor was not that of the Balkans nor of the Arab lands, and the Islamic models, so far as they existed, had been mediated only through the Seljukid-Mongol regime. The Seljukid state also was more limited in size; it underwent at one and the same time the influence of traditions of local or Byzantine origin, and of the Iranian Islamic lands through which the Turks had passed, which continued to send them experts, and in which the empire of the Great Seljuks had become renowned as a model for the future. Furthermore it had of course its own character and specific evolution. It is these three elements which must be recognized in any study of institutions without reaching conclusions based on assumptions.

In regard to this some precautions are required. It should not be automatically concluded that, even if some organizations have an indigenous personnel, an indigenous tradition has continued to exist in its entirety. Care must also be taken to see things as they really were, and not to be led by superficial similarities of terminology to include institutional similarity: the same words have not always and everywhere the same meaning. It is no less indispensable not to assume that all the Seljukid regimes were identical. The Turks who colonized Asia Minor certainly were kinsmen of those who founded the state of the Great Seljuks, and they had passed through Iran. Certainly also immigrants from Iran came to Asia Minor, and the example of the Great Seljuks, or of the model set out in Niẓām al-Mulk's *Siyāsat-nāma*, was studied there. This influence however becomes clear only in the thirteenth century, when many of the features of the Seljukid state in Rūm were already determined; in their determination, local conditions and the consequences of the conquest evidently count for at least as much as contributions from outside. The regime in Anatolia must thus be studied for itself, avoiding assumed assimilation to others.

Finally, it is absolutely indispensable to distinguish carefully between periods. This must be stressed, as fundamental confusion has been caused for lack of this precaution. It so happens that the sources which are most helpful to an understanding of Seljukid institutions come from the Mongol period. Since the dynasty continued under the Mongol protectorate and the new masters did not intend to overthrow the old regime, Seljukid and Mongol-Seljukid institutions have generally been treated together as if they were undifferentiated. An investigation which is careful of the distinction clearly shows that in some matters at least the situation is quite otherwise, and thus that the interpretation to be made from the facts under consideration is wholly different from what has been believed.

Distinctions of the same kind should probably be made between the very beginnings of the Seljukid state and its companions, and its further developments. It would be important to delineate the origin of institutions as they appear when better known. To some extent the task is hopeless here for lack of documentation; so it must be undertaken all the more carefully in all the particular cases where data are available.

. . . . .

The Seljukid regime in Asia Minor was of course headed by the sultan. The term, originally a colloquialism, became official, and since the caliph had lost effective power, it was used for the holder of power as distinct from the caliph. The distinction is in no way that between pope and emperor, as said by some medieval and modern writers, because the caliph had nothing of the pope about him, and because among Muslims there is no separation of temporal and spiritual power. Particularly if his realm did not include Baghdad, the sultan enjoyed the plenitude of power in both religious and political matters, saving the general theoretical reservation in Islam that the God-given Law cannot be made or changed, even in details, by man.

Usually the sultan paid respect to the caliph, sometimes finding it to his advantage to stress this, but that was all. The caliph had the unique and indefeasible right to legitimate the sultan's power. Others held the sultanate to be self-justified, while the actual holders of power were little troubled when some reason or other prevented them from obtaining legitimation. The caliph generally accorded his legitimation, which safeguarded the appearance and principle of his authority. An active caliph would also show a care for the good order of the religious institutions, and try to extend it by moral authority beyond the frontiers of his own state, if he had one; but he could not enforce his intervention.

That the first Turkish chiefs in Asia Minor received any kind of ʿAbbasid legitimation is, as has been seen, not credible. Their successors did apparently have it, but it is difficult to know from what date, as the only fact explicitly known was the sending of the insignia of *malik* to Gümüştekin b. Danişmend in 1135.

The title of sultan was recognized by usage, and perhaps even by the Byzantine chancery, at the beginning of the reign of Alexius I Comnenus for Süleyman b. Kutlumuş; and it may be supposed that Kılıc Arslan I held or took it when he decided to oppose his kinsman, Muḥammad, in Mesopotamia itself. Perhaps Muḥammad recognized it for Shāhānshāh. Masʿūd used it on a coin dating probably from the end of his reign, and Kılıc Arslan II in an inscription immediately after his accession; but this does not necessarily prove that it was by official grant, and moreover the significance it held is uncertain. While writers of the period occasionally use the title of sultan, they generally entitle the Seljukids of Rūm only *malik*, but they do the same for Nūr al-Dīn b. Zengi, who was evidently and officially sultan. It may have been felt that the title of sultan was not very different from the function of *malik*, which alone is found on the coins and in the inscriptions of the period of the sultanate. When the title of *malik* was granted to Gümüştekin, it is unlikely that this was regarded as an anti-Seljukid act, since Masʿūd was on good terms with him, and it is difficult to take literally the title which Masʿūd gives himself on a coin of 'king of all Anatolia and Romania'. Was Masʿūd considered as 'sultan' to be above a *malik*, or as another *malik*? At present this must be an open question.

The titulature of the inscriptions and, in the second place, of the coins and other sufficiently official sources, is interesting to study in every way. Kılıc Arslan II is styled there, among other things, as 'sultan of the Arabs and the ʿAjam'. The last word no doubt implied the Turks, without their being named explicitly beside the ordinary ʿAjam, i.e. in the Arabic-speaking East, the Persians. He is further 'the Champion in the Holy War', which in view of the events recounted above should be taken with some reserve; 'the Guardian of the land of God', i.e. that he regarded his realm, even if it was still called Rūm, as now forming part of the *Dār al-Islām*, the land of Islam; 'the Helper of the Caliph', a title which he had no doubt received from the caliph, who gave it to all rulers who acknowledged his name; finally, 'Sultan of the land of Rūm, of the Armenians, of the Franks, and of Syria', which in the fashion of the times expresses the wider ambitions of one who has nibbled at an alien realm, and claims their legitimacy – in the present case, ambitions directed characteristically towards the south-east as well as the whole of Rūm, i.e. Asia Minor. If there is a reference to the Holy War, the term *ghāzī* (T. *gazi*) is nevertheless absent, although it was used by the Danişmendids, the Saltukids and the Mengüçekids. Absent also are titles in Turkish, which at that very time were used not only by the Mengüçekids but also by some Zengids and Artukids. Did they appear too narrow in scope for the idea of a sultan?

The insignia and setting of sovereignty were the same as in all the Muslim East. The sovereign had a slightly elevated throne; for exceptionally grand occasions he wore a sort of crown, but ordinarily wore a large turban; his signet ring enabled him to authenticate anywhere documents presented to him for signature. When he travelled, he was protected by a black canopy, the ʿAbbasid colour. The canopy was little more than a vast parasol, which was appropriate to an individual ruler, and accompanied him to his tomb. Banners and a band marked the procession, in which slaves and guardsmen took part. He generally dwelt in a palace, each large city having one for his reception, used in his absence by the governor. He had also pleasure domes, such as Qubādhābād on the lake of Beyşehir, north-west of Konya, Fīlūbād near Konya, Kayqubādhiyya near Kayseri – all built for Kay Qubādh I.

In the times of the great sultans these palaces contained storerooms and treasures of every kind. Alanya, sheltered against revolts and invasions by land, was particularly planned for this purpose, as also at different times were Antalya, Tokat and others. However, great tents were also pitched for the sultan at the entrance to towns for use in his receptions and banquets which of course it was his duty to give. He could also enjoy the pleasures of music, wine and the harem, but nothing in particular is said about this; for wine especially, it is possible that the attitude of the Seljukids of Rūm was above the average. Like all contemporary aristocrats, they loved hunting and certain sports, especially on horseback, for which hippodromes were provided near the cities. The sultan had naturally the monopoly of the mint. There is little doubt that like all the great contemporary rulers he had a workshop for the manufacture of textiles and luxury garments for presentation to foreign princes, but evidence of this is lacking.

Among the Seljukids of Iran and Iraq young sultans had *atabeg*s at their side. So likewise had their successors, but without their effective powers.

The dignity of *atabeg* is also found in Rūm, but there it never reached the heights attained among the other Seljukids. Kılıc Arslan I had an *atabeg*, Khumartash al-Sulaymānī, whose name shows that he was a freedman of Süleyman b. Kutlumuş, not a Turcoman chief; but he is indeed known only as the governor of Mayyāfāriqīn, the capital of Diyār Bakr, which was given him by Kılıc Arslan when he conquered it in 1106 and 1107. The young Seljukid of Malatya had several *atabeg*s in succession, chosen as husbands by his mother in the years 1102–13 and subsequently, and so followed a more traditional role.

The Danişmendids had no *atabeg*s. The next to be known among the Seljukids is the *ispahsālār* Badr al-Dīn (Shāhānshāh) b. Arslan Doğmuş, who so styles himself in an inscription of 1177. It is not known of whom he was the *atabeg*, and in this he appears as governor of Niksar, which had recently been taken from the Danişmendids. It is not known if one of the sons of Kılıc Arslan II (perhaps the one who was later to have Niksar in the succession partition) was theoretically the holder in title of this place under the guardianship of its effective master, Badr al-Dīn. The thirteenth-century *atabeg*s are also known to us only by title with other functions: e.g. Mubāriz al-Dīn Armaghān-Shāh, the head of the army of Amasya at the time of Baba Isḥāq's revolt, and *atabeg* of ʿIzz al-Dīn b. Kay Qubādh with orders to put him to death; and Karatay, a freedman of the Mongol period.

The sultan had a deputy, *nā'ib* (*al-sulṭān*), but it is not clear whether he held office temporarily, e.g. during the sultan's absence or sickness, or permanently.

Among the sultan's personal assistants was the *pervane*. This official, whose poetic name (from the Persian *parvāna*, meaning 'moth') is a little surprising in this context, has an equivalent only in Mongol Islam. There however it is much less important, and appears in the form *pervaneci*, suggesting that *pervane* is a derived and shortened form. In any case, it signifies the person who carries the ruler's personal messages, whether it is the messages or the messenger who deserves the name of 'moth'; he is literally the distributor of the favours. It is obvious that with skilful management this post could lead to an exalted career, and notable *pervane*s are known from the beginning of the thirteenth century. Care must nevertheless be taken not to make the error about the power of the office which has sometimes been made because of the personality of the Pervane Muʿīn al-Dīn Süleyman, who was a veritable dictator under the Mongol protectorate. He continued to be known usually by the title under which he first obtained recognition, but it was not as *pervane* that he obtained all his power.

The sultan had an entourage of office-holders and court dignitaries, some possibly identical with holders of posts in the political and military hierarchy, and in any case members of the same caste. Almost all had partly Persian titles which were already known under the Great Seljuks. The *amīr-i jāndār*, was the chief of the *jāndār* (i.e. the guard), the *amīr-i silāḥ* the chief of arms, the *amīr-i shikār* the chief huntsman, the *amīr-i ʿalam* the standard-bearer, the *amīr-i ākhūr* (also its Latin-Byzantine equivalent, *kondestabl*, i.e. constable, even if the office-holder was a Muslim) the chief of the horses. The *ustādhdār* was the chief of the palace, while the *amīr-i majlis* organized receptions, audiences and so forth. The *chāshnīgīr* was the taster and the *sharābsalār* the cupbearer, but these were sinecures of great office-holders. Finally, the chamberlains (Ar. *ḥājib*) had at their head the great chamberlain (*ḥājib al-ḥujjāb*), who was also and especially a general in the army.

In most of the Muslim states in the East contemporary with the Seljukids, there was a clear ethnic and career distinction between administrative office on the one hand, and political or military and official functions on the other. While the latter were reserved for the military caste, which was essentially Turkish, sometimes Kurdish, and only exceptionally from other ethnic groups, administrative functions were kept for the indigenous peoples, who alone were competent to discharge them and were theoretically excluded from bearing arms, at least in the regular army. To pass from one career-group to the other was quite exceptional. The judiciary, which formed a third career-group, was also recruited from the indigenous peoples; to pass from an administrative to a judicial career was unusual but not impossible.

In the Seljukid state of Rūm, the circumstances were somewhat different from the other Muslim states in the region. Here the indigenous peoples were Christians and, while it is quite certain that they held some posts, difficulties were caused not so much by their religion, which was no obstacle either in Egypt or in Iraq, as by their ignorance of Arabic and Persian. A career was thus open, at least in the thirteenth century, for a good number of Iranian immigrants from Khurāsān or north-western Iran, and occasionally from Iṣfahān and elsewhere. Furthermore, as will appear, the military career in the Seljukid state also lacked the simplicity it possessed, for example, among the Great Seljuks or the Zengids and Ayyubids. Political and military office was however usually given to the Turks, although some of them may also have entered upon administrative or judicial careers in later generations as the sons did not necessarily follow their fathers' military vocation, and the Turks became part of the native population. This of course required their mastery of the necessary languages and administrative skills. On the whole however the distinction among the different careers remained valid.

At the head of the civil administration was the vezir (Ar. *wazīr*). If the title was not misapplied by the Arabic chronicler who provides the information, there is evidence of the vezirate from Süleyman b. Kutlumuş in the eleventh century, and there were one or two vezirs during the twelfth century.

At all events its formal existence is certain from the time when the sultanate was firmly established, for the conception then was that the installation of a vezir was a manifestation of sovereignty. Even in the thirteenth century our knowledge of the vezirs remains incomplete; and nothing gives the impression that the holders of the title ever possessed (even when they were occasionally active in political affairs) the vast powers enjoyed by some vezirs in other countries, and by Niẓām al-Mulk under the Great Seljuks. Was this due to a lack of personality among the vezirs, or rather because the organization of the government limited them strictly to administrative duties which still lacked development? Perhaps something may be allowed for the fact that the early vezirs included natives, who had been converted but were mistrusted by the ruling Turks. In any case, vezirs of real importance are lacking before the Mongols, and then in the context of a wholly different organization. As elsewhere, the vezir bore the title of *ṣāḥib*.

The *mustawfī* was previously known throughout the Muslim East as *ṣāḥib al-zimām*, the chief accountant. He checked the actual returns of taxes and expenses, and his assistance was indispensable to the vezir who chose him, sometimes until he himself became vezir. It is more difficult to define the duties of the *mushrif*, apparently the superintendent of the royal domain, or of the *nāẓir* (controller), who was perhaps his assistant. They probably existed under the Seljukids as they did in the neighbouring Muslim states, since on the whole there were parallel organizations and titles; but there is evidence of them only in the Mongol period, and they may have been an innovation, if not by the Mongols themselves, then at least by the Iranian agents who were influential at that time. In the Seljukid period, on the other hand, but not under the Mongols (perhaps because of the reduction of the army), there is evidence of an *ʿāriḍ* as in all the neighbouring states. Like them astride the civil and military administration, he must have been responsible for inspecting the army with the sultan at reviews, and distributing pay on these occasions. Only one holder of this office is known by name. Like its neighbours, the Seljukid state had its official postal system, the *barīd*.

As in all the neighbouring countries, the administration was composed of departments (Ar. *dīwān*; T. *divan*) under these officials. A special part was played by the writing office (Ar. *dīwān al-inshāʾ*), which drafted both political correspondence and diplomas. Among the Great Seljuks the *ṭughrāʾī*, who inscribed the sultan's monogram (Ar. *ṭughrāʾ*; T. *tuğra*) on state documents, was rapidly identified with the *munshiʾ*, the head of the *inshāʾ*. The title of *munshiʾ* does not seem to appear among the Seljukids of Rūm, where the *tuğrai* was the real chancellor. Only one holder of this office is known by name.

The Seljukid writing office or chancery seems normally to have drafted its letters and diplomas in Persian; at least, extant specimens in the original language are only in Persian, so that this seems likely. There are however exceptions. First, Muslim legal documents, not originating from the chancery but from *qāḍīs*, are required to be drafted in Arabic, and extant specimens prove them to be perfectly correct in their formulation. It is most improbable that even in the chancery there was no clerk capable of writing in Arabic to Arab rulers; it must be conceded, however, that the letter written to congratulate Saladin on the taking of Jerusalem (if it is genuine) is written in Persian. Inscriptions on monuments and coins, which place the object under the protection of Islamic law, are normally in Arabic; only in the Mongol period do rare exceptions to this rule begin to appear. Fiscal documents are themselves in Arabic; the principal ones are translated into Persian under the Mongols. Treaties with foreign states, where Arabic or Persian was unknown, could be drafted in the two languages; but it cannot be said by whom the translation of the original was drafted, although it is virtually evident that the Seljukid state had at its disposal interpreters in several languages. Letters are extant written in Greek in the name of Kay Kāwūs. Even if another copy in Persian was kept in Konya, they were no doubt directly drafted in Greek there, and are not translations made by the addressees as in the case of Franks of Cyprus, who had Latin translations made. Ibn Bībī even mentions *nūtar*, i.e. *notaroi*, notaries in the *divans*, evidently meaning Greek clerks. We do not know the language used by a Seljukid sultan when writing to a non-Muslim high dignitary among his subjects, such letters as those of which Michael the Syrian gives a Syriac translation.

It is known that the Seljukids of Iran and Iraq authenticated their documents with a symbolic sign called the *tuǧra*. As would be normal since the Ottomans were also to have their *tuǧra*, it existed also among the Seljukids of Asia Minor. The arched form, the meaning of which was variously interpreted, is attested by a passage of Ibn Bībī, who had some special knowledge in this field; although in one document (but in Greek and for foreign use) it uniquely appears as a particularly solemn way of writing the sultan's title. It is strange that although the title of *tuǧrai* remained in use, and was held by persons of high status, the word *tuǧra* itself was sometimes confused (e.g. by the Arabic-speaking Mamluks of Egypt) with the Arabic word *ṭurra*, meaning a margin. This in fact corresponds to the method of authenticating signatures used by the Mamluks but never apparently by the Seljukids.

The Seljukid clerks of the Mongol period used models of administrative styles or collections of documents left by their illustrious predecessors. It is through some extant collections of this kind that some pre-Mongol pieces are available, but it cannot be confidently stated that any collection was made in the period of the independent sultanate, such as are known from the other Seljukids or their Khwarazmian heirs.

Did the task of the administrative departments become heavier under the Mongol protectorate, or was there a spontaneous and unjustified proliferation of the number of employees? Complaints resounded against this proliferation, which, if they are to be believed, culminated in a fourfold increase in comparison with the time of the great Kay Qubādh I – twenty-four high officials where there had been no more than six.

As in the neighbouring Iranian Muslim states, beside the ordinary justice of the *qāḍī*, which existed in Rūm as everywhere else, there was justice dispensed by the sultan and a chief magistrate (*amīr-dād*) for cases of *maẓālim*, i.e. for the repression of administrative and other abuses. Here again, only one holder of the office is known by name.

It has been said that the military sector provided most of the office-holders and court dignitaries who have been mentioned, as well as the *nā'ib* and the *atabeg*, although not the *pervane*. It also provided the provincial military commandants, of whom more will be said.

It is somewhat difficult to form a clear idea of the *beglerbegi*, i.e. the *beg* of *beg*s, chief *beg*. It is perhaps he who is called the archisatrap (in twelfth-century Greek literary texts), the *ispahsālār* or *amīr kabīr*. In the thirteenth century the term is normally the equivalent of *amīr al-umarā'*, more commonly *malik al-umarā'*, the *amīr* of the *amīr*s, king of the *amir*s; both titles are attested in different texts or even in the same one. Only one is mentioned in any given time; and, when in the Mongol period there is an explicit account of the different office-holders, there is always a single *beglerbegi*. In the period of independence, however, there are sometimes names of persons appointed alternatively as if they coexisted. Since one of them was the chief of the great Turcoman province of Kastamonu, it may be thought that he held the title in virtue of this. It might also be thought that the *beglerbegi* was specially charged with the general control of the Turcomans, whose chiefs were entitled *beg*s, but there seems to be no confirmation of this hypothesis; moreover a Comnenus is to be found among the *beglerbegi*s, and it is hard to think of him as having this function, however assimilated he may have been. Evidently the *beglerbegi* had essentially a military role, but this does not signify that he was a sole commander-in-chief; the *atabeg*, for example, undertook this task fairly regularly when his ward, the sultan, was not in a position to command the troops in person.

It does not seem that there is anything special to say about the ordinary course of justice in Rūm. The installation of a *qāḍī* wherever there was a Muslim community was already assured by Süleyman b. Kutlumuş, but little can be said about the actual working of the institution where there was indeed no reason for it to have a special character. Throughout Islam the *qāḍī* stands outside the state (although he is state-appointed) in the sense that he administers a law which is independent of the state, and that the funds at his disposal are in part essentially religious funds, over which the state has in theory no rights. The extant *waqfiyyas* display the *qāḍī* as the guarantor and supervisor of the *waqfs*, as he was everywhere. In each provincial capital there was a *qāḍī*, who might have deputies elsewhere. It is not clear whether there was a chief *qāḍī*, who might be, as in other states, the *qāḍī* of the capital, or whether this was the responsibility of the *amīr-dād*. As regards witnesses to the authenticity of deeds, it is known only that in Rūm there were signatories at the base of the *waqfiyyas*, but their number apparently exceeded that of the official witnesses (*shuhūd*). As in the neighbouring oriental states, there was particular *qāḍī* for the army, who required special legal and linguistic knowledge, and was called *qāḍi'l-'askar* or *qāḍī-i lashkar*. Around the *qāḍī* were expert jurists, who might serve as consultants (Ar. *muftī*), but virtually nothing is known of them in Rūm at this period.

Occupations have been discussed earlier. Throughout Islam they were controlled by an agent of the *qāḍī*, the *muḥtasib*, and the existence of this functionary is attested in Rūm at this time. He was perhaps accompanied everywhere by special deputies for the supervision of the individual trades. This may have been the case in Rūm, but there is a problem here which has been encountered elsewhere (p. 114).

The army is an institution almost certainly affected by the Byzantine model, albeit somewhat paradoxically by the classical Iranian model and the ancient Turkish tradition as well. A distinction of periods must evidently be made. At the start the only military force was that of the Turcomans, who more or less retained their autonomous organization. They continued, as has been seen, to play a part on the frontiers throughout Seljukid, to say nothing of later medieval history. This was sometimes on their own account, regardless of Seljukid policy. But another army was constituted in the twelfth century, and developed in the thirteenth. The rate and methods of its organization cannot unfortunately be precisely stated. It is certain that, like the other Muslim Near Eastern armies, whether Seljukid or not, it comprised slaves who were later manumitted. Here, however, it is known that many of them, instead of being Turks as elsewhere, were Greeks captured in frontier raids, especially in the province of Kastamonu. The reason why their recruitment appealed, especially for the guards and the main garrisons, was the same as in all the neighbouring states: politically, the need for loyalty, and simultaneously the technical need for specialists in ways of fighting unknown to the Turcomans, so that the Seljukids might confront comparable hostile armies, and conduct siege operations. But there was another element in the army which appeared in the thirteenth century, and had no parallel among the other Near Eastern Muslims, i.e. men of mixed ethnic origin, and also foreign mercenaries.

It has sometimes been thought that there was a corps of *ikdiş*, but, as appeared when speaking of the towns (p. 115), this arose from a misunderstanding. If they were occasionally able to act as a militia, they did not normally form part of the army. It must not be thought that there was any anticipation of the Ottoman janissaries, i.e. native children levied to be brought up as Muslim soldiers. Of course the participation of Christians was excluded as in all Muslim countries; under the Mongols, who were not Muslims, and who favoured the Christians in some ways, the claim of the Armenian bishop of Erzincan to contribute a corps of fellow-Christians to a composite army aroused an outcry. The Seljukid state however was not precluded from employing foreign Christians as mercenaries. It is not always possible to tell from the texts whether contingents of this kind were in fact mercenaries or corps sent by vassal rulers; even where Franks are concerned, they may have been Frankish subjects of the Armenians of Cilicia. Such were not lacking, for it was partly because of them that the *Assises* of the principality of Antioch, a collection of its laws and customs, were translated into Armenian for governmental purposes. There might also have been intermediate cases when, because of urgent danger from the Khwarazmians or Mongols, the Seljukid government might take wholly or partially into its pay troops sent by its allies or vassals additionally to the ordinary levies.

There is however no doubt that, as in the Byzantine army, there were mercenaries in the exact sense of the term. The Byzantines were unacquainted with military slavery, and employed as mercenaries Turks from the Russian steppes, Slavs, Scandinavians and Franks, especially Normans from Italy, among other foreign soldiers. It may seem very strange to a modern mind that the Seljukids' chief mercenaries at the time of the Crusades were Franks. Here again it is important to distinguish between the Muslims of Syria (and possibly of Upper Mesopotamia and Egypt) on the one hand, and the Turks of Asia Minor on the other. The former were directly in conflict with the Franks of the Latin East as the latter were not after the fall of the border county of Edessa, except when a crusade went through their territory. Indeed they were sometimes allies; although there are some alliances between the Franks and the Muslims of Syria, these were regarded as scandalous exceptions. There are one or two cases of Frankish mercenaries in the service of the Muslim rulers of Syria and Egypt, but as a general rule the Church, however vainly it excommunicated traders selling arms to the Muslims, would certainly not have permitted soldiers to go to fight for them, even against other than Frankish opponents.

There is however a parallel case in the Muslim West, particularly in Almohad Morocco, where the papacy tolerated the existence of real

European mercenaries in exchange for guarantees of Christian worship. It may be doubted whether this parallel was known to the Seljukids, or had any influence on them. It is certain that there were Frankish mercenaries who sometimes played an important part, in which the missionary Simon of St Quentin takes pride, as has been seen. Among their chiefs was a Venetian, who was also a businessman, another Italian from Piacenza, a Norman of Sicily and a Gascon. What had they come to do, and how had they got where they did? It remains unknown. Some perhaps had reached Cyprus at a time of unemployment. Others were among the former hangers-on of the Byzantine state, and had now by way of the Latin Empire reached the Seljukid Turkish state which, it must be constantly repeated, did not appear alien or hostile like the states which lay beyond. Others had been prisoners of the Syrian rulers, and were liberated during the campaigns of Kay Kāwūs and Kay Qubādh. Obviously the Mongol conquest ended the possibility of employment in Rūm, and nothing more is heard of them after 1243.

The titles of the military chiefs generally followed the Arabic, Persian or Turkish traditions somewhat interchangeably, and used to a greater or lesser extent in the different periods. The Arabic *amīr* paralleled the Turkish *beg*, often indicating a Turcoman; *amīr al-umarā'* paralleled *beglerbegi* and the Persian *ispahsālār*; the Turkish *subaşı* had the same significance as the Persian *sarlashkar*, and the Arabic *shiḥna* was reused to mean the head of a garrison, and so forth. A title of Western origin may have been introduced by way of the Byzantines: the chief of the cavalry, often designated by the Arabo-Persian *amīr-i ākhūr*, was sometimes called *kundestabl*, constable. One or two of its holders may have been Greeks, but this proves nothing as others were Muslims. Although this may have been a purely onomastic influence, it bears witness nonetheless to the cultural climate, and as such deserves some emphasis.

These military influences are particularly interesting as they exist in the field where one would have expected the Turks to have been sheltered from such temptations of borrowed terms by reason of their universally recognized superiority. Exaggeration should however be avoided; the Seljukid army was not the Byzantine army, and the Turks beat the Byzantines. Their manner of fighting was in any case typically Turcoman in the twelfth century, even in the regular army, as Myriocephalum shows. At the battle of Erzincan against the Khwarazmians in the thirteenth century, or at Kösedağ, where the armies were more composite and contained few Turcomans, the character had evidently changed. The armies were like those throughout the Middle East, and need no special remark.

The military and provincial commands were generally linked, and more must now be said of the provinces.

CHAPTER FOURTEEN

The administration of the provinces

It is often said that the provincial organization of the Seljukid state of Rūm was 'feudal', i.e. that it was based on the *iqṭāʿ*, which has been regarded as equivalent to the fief in medieval Europe.[17] There is also a tendency to think that the administrative system that existed among the Seljukids of Iran could be transferred automatically to Asia Minor. For a correct appreciation of Seljukid history, this demands further consideration.

There is first a question of terminology. Historians in search of an evolution by universally social types or periods, whether or not they are Marxists, tend to call any regime 'feudal' which falls chronologically between 'primitive slavery' and modern capitalism, and in which the labour of a more or less servile peasantry is exploited for the benefit of great landholders. So regarded, there were evidently a great number of 'feudal' regimes, and that of the Seljukids of Rūm could at least be so considered. However, without in any degree underestimating this aspect of the feudal regime, it must be affirmed that an infrastructure of this very type, considered very loosely on broad lines, may be accompanied by superstructures too different to be grouped under a common designation without danger of abuse. In fact, what those historians who speak of 'Seljukid feudalism' have in view is not the territorial economy of the system, but the relationship between the landowners or local magnates and the authority of the state. In this sense a state is feudal if it surrenders or delegates the essential public powers in the provinces to magnates, who hold them as a sort of hereditary property. Hence there is opposition between the idea of 'feudalism' in this sense, and that of a strong, centralized state; opposition in practice between a state which can keep the reins of power in its hands even in the provinces, and one which, whatever its ideal, is incapable of doing so. While taking notice of the power of the Seljukid sultans, historians have generally thought that they reigned over a feudal state (there being in fact moments in the history of different countries when there has been sufficient harmony among the different interests, sufficient balance among the various forces, for there to have been monarchies which could be described as at once strong and feudal). As regards Seljukid Rūm, this view is false, and is explained by the methodological error, already frequently noted, of treating under the same head the Seljukid period proper and the Mongol period, extrapolating to the former period data from the latter. It will also appear that even the 'feudalism' of the Mongol period is of a special character. The error arises also from the neglect of the precise sense of words, the treatment of terms as identical when their acceptation is in reality different. It is indispensable not to get lost in vague generalities, but to take Asia Minor for itself, period by period, and not to see a feudal lord in a governor liable to recall, or a prince of the blood holding an apanage.

From this point of view, the history of Turkish Asia Minor from the conquest to the Mongol period can be divided into four periods:

1 The simultaneous establishment of the Turcoman chiefs and the Seljukid prince at the semi-tribal stage, without well-established territorial or personal links of dependence.
2 The progressive absorption of the Turcoman groups, and the constitution of apanages.
3 The resumption of apanages and marcher territories under direct government.
4 The break-up of the system resulting from the way of functioning of the Mongol protectorate (see Chapter 16).

The first period

This does not require further treatment. The account of the conquest has shown how the various chiefs established themselves, and gives no reason to think that they were all originally considered as vassals of the Seljukid sultan. It is possible that theoretically a certain dependence applied to the chiefs of the far west, but their subsequent historical importance is weak since the Crusade and the Byzantine reconquest eliminated them. The actual power was still exercised over semi-tribal groups rather than territories, even though the old tribal groups had broken up.

The second period

As the unifying conquest of Asia Minor by the Seljukids proceeded, they set up apanages for the benefit of princes of the blood. This was the outcome of several considerations: their estimate of the difficulty of suppressing a degree of autonomy and the specific tribal grouping in the territory acquired, while at the same time they sought to maintain their own dynasty; also perhaps the retention by the Seljukids of the idea that all their living members had a right to the partition of their inheritance. At all events, the idea that partition was necessary prevailed among the Danişmendids perhaps until Mehmed, or at any rate until the last reigns, as the late ruler's eldest son was no longer the senior member of the family as a whole. The same idea was found among the Mengüçekids. There is little sign of it among the first Seljukids, where there is only the case of the peripheral principality of Malatya; then, under Masʿūd, Ankara and Çankırı (which had been recently acquired from the Greeks, and were briefly the possessions of an otherwise unknown person) were formed into an apanage for the benefit of Shāhānshāh, the brother of the future Kılıc Arslan II. Finally, under this ruler, who as heir to the throne governed for a while the recently acquired Syrian marches, they were conferred before 1173 on his uncle, and later resumed.

At the end of the twelfth century however there took place the celebrated partition of Kılıc Arslan II's realm among his eleven sons and near kinsmen. It is possible that some provinces had already been allotted to some of them in principle, although without concession in fact. Provision was made for their registration in the *Divan* of Konya, and the establishment of a double apanage for Quṭb al-Dīn perhaps signified that he was intended to be his brothers' future overlord, or so at least he was resolved to interpret the matter. What ensued has been seen. Kay Khusraw I nevertheless allotted Malatya and Tokat to his sons Kay Kāwūs and Kay Qubādh respectively, but Kay Kāwūs ended the last traces of the system. Meanwhile a collateral (hardly a vassal) dynasty had been set up at Erzurum after its conquest by Rukn al-Dīn Süleyman II, to be brought to an end by Kay Qubādh I at the same time as the Mengüçekid dynasty. In the twelfth century, there does not seem to have existed any great command held other than by members of the royal family, except, to prove the rule, by the *atabeg* of a prince. No doubt one or two non-princely provincial governors are mentioned, but there is no indication that they were not liable to dismissal, as were most of their like in the thirteenth century, and there does not seem to be any question of extensive jurisdictions under such governors.

The third period

Experience had shown the dangerous power of holders of apanages. Although the Iranian officials came from a land which had experience of this type of grant, they traditionally had a feeling for administration secured, if possible, by governors drawn from the category of officials, and directly dependent on the central power. The recruitment of such governors had now become possible in Rūm. It can hardly be doubted that reasons of this kind led the thirteenth-century Seljukids to substitute the appointment of governors liable to dismissal for the apanage system. This already existed in some instances but now became general. As this has not been demonstrated previously, it must be emphasized here.

For a clear understanding of the difference, it must be borne in mind that in the Seljukid state a person might receive a position of command in one of three ways. The post might be an *iqṭāʿ* in the full sense, as in the late Iranian state and its successors, i.e. it might confer authority over a given district as *de facto* private and hereditary property. It might be a more or less complete concession of limited duration, e.g. for life but not hereditary, or linked as remuneration to the exercise of a function, and lapsing with its withdrawal. Finally, it might be simply a delegation of power to a notable, who did not exercise any authority by personal right, and might be dismissed.

Each provincial capital was the base of a military command exercised by an officer given various titles in the texts, combining the three languages of the Muslims of the country: *subaşı* (Turkish) and *sarlashkar* (Persian, T. *serleşker*) meaning the chief of the army, while *shiḥna* (Arabic), a term already used by the Great Seljuks, had the primary meaning of the head of a garrison. Simpler and vaguer are terms such as *amīr* and *beg*. These functions might be conferred in *iqṭāʿ*, but in no way is this automatically implied. When there is no clear statement that such was the case, it probably means in general that a command could be rescinded, and was not an *iqṭāʿ*. It is thus completely wrong to see such commanders as evidence of feudalism. The way to be sure of this is to list carefully the known commanders of as many provincial capitals as possible and, when the nature of their command is not explicitly stated, to detail the duration of their commands, and particularly the identity of the commanders, and whether or not their commands were inherited. This necessarily entails the detailed survey which follows.

What in the first place are the cities which are known to have been conceded in *iqṭāʿ*, and not merely to have had ordinary governors? The kingdom of Erzurum is a special case. Under the Seljukid princes at the beginning of the century it was independent in fact, even if Rukn al-Dīn Süleyman, who set it up, had meant it to be a vassal principality. Annexed by Kay Qubādh I, it nevertheless remained a peripheral possession distinct from his proper dominions, until the moment when, because of the devastation caused by the warfare on the approach of the Mongols, he judged it opportune to concede it to the Khwarazmian refugees with the obligation to defend it. The attempt failed, as has been seen, and in the following years Erzurum was directly annexed, and put under the command of a *shiḥna*.

The last Mengüçekids of Erzincan and Divriği looked on themselves as vassals of the Seljukids. When Kay Qubādh brought their rule to an end, one of them (to judge from an inscription) perhaps kept Divriği, but within the framework of the Seljukid state; it was in any case a city of the second rank. As for Erzincan, it was at first annexed directly, then briefly conceded in *iqṭāʿ* to a Khwarazmian chief, and finally resumed when the Khwarazmians fled. The *serleşkers* who are known there subsequently, Sharaf al-Dīn Masʿūd to 1246, then Muʿīn al-Din the Pervane, were royal officials.

After its reconquest in 1201, Malatya was apparently directly administered. In 608/1211 Kay Kāwūs I gave it to the *ispahsālār* Ḥusām al-Dīn Yūsuf al-Sulṭānī, who on the evidence of an inscription was still there four years later. However, the fact that Kay Kāwūs kept his brother, Kay Qubādh, under guard as a prisoner in this city would seem to imply that Ḥusām al-Dīn was a governor, and not a *muqṭaʿ*. The whole history of the city in the following three decades similarly implies that the sultan held it in direct possession; the *subaşı* known in 1237 anyhow was certainly a royal official. Khartpert was acquired in 1233, and similarly had a *subaşı*, never being conceded in any other way. It does not seem that things went differently for the late conquests in the marches of Mesopotamia after the end of the time when in some, such as Samosata, a ruler who had formerly been outside the Seljukid sultan's dominions transferred his allegiance to him.

The situation was perhaps different at Elbistan, a place of strategic importance on the route to Syria. In 609/1211 Kay Kāwūs I gave it to Abu'l-ʿIzz Mubāriz al-Dīn Çavlı al-Sulṭānī, the grant being linked with that of Malatya to Ḥusām al-Dīn (above). This may have been an ordinary command. All the same, an inscription indicates that Mubāriz al-Dīn was still governor of Elbistan in 639/1241 and since he was also *chāshnīgīr*, the possession of the city may have been connected with that court office, at least for him personally. In 1254 Elbistan had an ordinary *subaşı*. On the other hand, the province of Maraş, which lay more directly on the Syrian approaches, had the status of an *iqṭāʿ* either temporarily or permanently in the twelfth century. From 608/1211–12 to past 630/1232–33 at least it was held by *malik al-umarāʾ* Nuṣrat al-Dīn Ḥasan b. Ibrāhīm. In 1258 it fell into the hands of the Armenians; after which its lord sought in vain to cede it to Kay Kāwūs II in order to safeguard it from the Turcomans.

Towards the north were the directly governed Seljukid cities with some slight differences as to the former Danişmendid cities of Tokat, Niksar and Amasya. The position of Niksar is certain; towards 1240 the then *chāshnīgīr*, its *subaşı*, is merely a royal governor. Tokat was for a time the residence of the son of Sultan Rukn al-Dīn Süleyman; then the centre of Kay Qubādh's apanage in Kay Khusraw I's lifetime. Under Kay Kāwūs I there is an inscription which mentions one Zayn al-Dīn Bashārā al-Ghālibī (probably not identical with the *amīr ākhūr* Zayn al-Dīn Bashārā) who is styled in 612/1215–16 *ṣāḥib* of Taqit, which may be Tokat.[18] On the other hand, it is certain that Tokat was held directly by Kay Qubādh, who sent important prisoners there, and by Kay Khusraw II, who in 1243 deposited his treasure and harem there for security in view of the Mongol danger. Later the Pervane Muʿīn al-Dīn Süleyman was in this patrimony of the Seljukids. The outcome of all this is that it is doubtful if Zayn al-Dīn was anything but a governor; and it is certain in any case that from Kay Qubādh on Tokat had only royal governors.

Lastly, the situation at Amasya was no doubt more complex. In 606/1209–10 the emir Mubāriz al-Dīn Bahrām-Shāh was there as the deputy governor, and also in 612/1215–16 but without a superior, at the head of the provincial emirs. He is well known in history as *amīr-i majlis*, but is not shown in the chronicles as having any special connection with Amasya. He died in 1228. Amasya was afterwards given in *iqṭāʿ* to the Khwarazmian chief Berke, and the sultan resumed it on Berke's arrest. At the time of the Bābā'ī revolt, the *sarlashkar* of the city, Armaghān-Shāh, was killed. The city belonged directly to the sultan in 1243, when the vezir fled there; and also at the time of Kay Kāwūs II's disagreement with his brother, Kılıc Arslan IV, whom he placed under surveillance there. The inscriptions of the period give no clear data. It cannot therefore be asserted that Mubāriz al-Dīn Bahrām-Shāh held Amasya otherwise than as its governor, unless the city was granted to him in connection with his court office of *amir majlis*.

Sivas and Kayseri were naturally always directly administered Seljukid cities. Governors of Kayseri, who were unrelated to one another, bore the titles of *ḥākim*, *wālī*, *shiḥna*, or more often *subaşı*, one perhaps simply *amīr*. By contrast, little is known of the governors of Sivas, although documents on this city are not lacking. In the inscription of 612/1215–16, which lists the great emirs who collaborated in the construction of the ramparts of Sinop, the others such as the city governors only appear anonymously at the head of the city notables; three however are named for Sivas and 'the provinces of Sivas'. Thus it seems that this city had a special administration, perhaps like Konya, of which no details are available.

Cities along the important frontier of the Cilician Taurus show more variety. The chief of them was Niğde. In 608/1211–12 it was given, in the same equivocal conditions as the other grants of this year, to the *amīr ākhūr* Zayn al-Dīn Bashārā, without its being apparently linked to his office. He was put to death early in the reign of Kay Qubādh I, shortly after 620/1223–24, and thereafter Niğde was certainly held directly of the sultan, who subsequently conceded it in *iqṭāʿ* to one of the Khwarazmian chiefs in his service. This did not however preclude the *pervane* Tāj al-Dīn from commanding the regular provincial army a little later. On the flight of the Khwarazmians, Niğde was resumed. At the start of the reign of Kay Kāwūs II, it was allotted to one Ṣamṣām al-Din Kaimaz, then to one of the sultan's slaves, before undergoing various vicissitudes under the Mongol protectorate. Lu'lu'a, which had been a dependency of Niğde since the conquest, was always a royal fortress. At Ereğli a *ṣāḥib* was known in 612/1215–16. Lârende (now Karaman) was granted in 1231 for a while to a Khwarazmian chief, and thus was a possession of the sultan, who resumed it later like the other Khwarazmian *iqṭāʿ*s.

Further to the north, Aksaray, Kırşehir and Akşehir were temporarily given as *iqṭāʿ*s; the first in 612/1215–16 to an obscure *ṣāḥib*. When Kay Qubādh I annexed the kingdom of Erzurum, it was given as compensation to the deposed ruler; but there is no doubt that from Kay Khusraw II to the beginning of the fourteenth century (when Aksarayi, a native of the city, has much to say about it), it always belonged directly to the sultan. Kırşehir was given in the same conditions by Kay Qubādh to the Mengüçekid of Erzincan. When he died in the time of Kay Khusraw II, it was resumed by the sultan, since it formed the emirate granted to the vezir Muhadhdhab al-Dīn and other vezirs after him. Ayyubhisar, lying between the two, had been joined to Aksaray for the former prince of Erzurum but to Kırşehir for the vezirs. Akşehir had been given in *iqṭāʿ* to Kir Farīd, the former lord of Kalonoros; then, presumably after his death, to the Mengüçekid Dāwūd-Shāh. There can be little doubt that it was then resumed by the sultan.

In the northern provinces, Ankara, after forming part of Kay Qubādh's apanage under Kay Khusraw, reverted as usual into the royal domain. In 1235 it belonged as *iqṭāʿ* to Tāj al-Dīn the *pervane*, but whether this was a personal link or ex officio is unknown. In any case, when it was taken from him at this date, the executions and imprisonments ordered by the sultan's vezir clearly appear to signify that it was kept in the royal domain, and this is confirmed by subsequent history.

It is more difficult to reach a firm conclusion about the vast frontier province of Kastamonu. Ibn Saʿīd in the mid-thirteenth century describes the city of Kastamonu as 'the Turcomans' capital'. In the fourteenth century it was the seat of the Turcoman dynasty of the Isfendiyarids, and at the end of the thirteenth century the province more or less belonged to the descendants of a person already known under the independent Seljukids. It would be easy to conclude from this that here as elsewhere a Turcoman emancipation took place, but here with origins going back to the start of the century, were it not incontrovertible that at the same period Kastomonu belonged to the sultans, who had their governors there, and then under the Mongols to the non-Turcoman powers who partitioned among themselves the fragments of the Seljukid state. There is thus a question which requires clarification.

The problem begins with Ḥusām al-Dīn Amīr Çopan, *beglerbegi* from perhaps 608/1211 and in any case *c.* 625/1228, and by reason of this office or concurrently, master of the whole or part of the province of Kastamonu and its Turcomans. By reason of this, he was commissioned like other *beglerbegis* for an expedition, in this case the celebrated expedition to the Crimea. Half a century later Ibn Bībī says that his son and grandson inherited the whole or a part of this region; this might be deemed an exception for an exceptional region, and as the *de facto* admission by Kay Qubādh of the formation of an autonomous Turcoman family power. There is however nothing to say that these people were Turcomans and, if in fact they held real power in these parts during the last quarter of the thirteenth century, the continuation of the family and the extension of their authority are much more debatable, as will be seen. Moreover in the Mongol period, Kastamonu and its province came under agents of the Seljukid-Mongol power, or of the famous Pervane Muʿīn al-Dīn Süleyman. Çopan might therefore have been merely a governor for a long period, with Kastamonu being directly under the sultan's authority during the independent Seljukid regime. This was certainly the case of Sinop. Perhaps Saymara in its hinterland, which had a *ṣāḥib* in 612/1215–16 and 615/1218–19 was in a different situation; it was in any event a place of minor importance.

In the rest of the Anatolian periphery, Alanya and Antalya in the south were winter residences of the sultans, where their treasures were deposited, and they could not be alienated. This was however a Turcoman frontier zone requiring particular vigilance, so a general command of the southern territories was created. From 603/1206 it was held with its extensions over more than twenty years by one of Kay Khusraw I's freedmen, Mubāriz al-Dīn Ertöküş; in the hinterland his authority included Isparta, and almost extended to Burğlu. There was a similar situation in the Mongol period. In the intervening time, it seems that Kay Qubādh I took over this command or divided it, as it is no longer mentioned. Ertöküş never fell from favour, but there is evidence that in the end his power may have seemed excessive. Promoted *atabeg* by Kay Khusraw, he was sent to fight the Mengüçekids, and played no further part in the south. He was perhaps replaced at Antalya by one of Kay Qubādh's freedmen, Armaghān-Shāh.

Further to the east, the province of Ermenek, increased by new conquests, was given by Kay Qubādh to a certain Qamar al-Dīn. He must have held this newly formed province for a long time, since it kept his name, but of the man himself nothing further is known.

In south-western Asia Minor, the base of Seljukid power was for long after its conquest Burğlu, the Byzantine Sozopolis and the modern Uluborlu. Somewhat supplanted in this respect by Antalya on the one hand, and by Denizli on the other, it remained a place of importance in the direct possession of the sultans, as proved by the incarcerations within its walls. Denizli linked with Honaz (Chonae), once possessed by Mavrozomes, was governed in 612/1215–16 by a certain Asad al-Dīn Ayaz al-Ghālibī, possibly identical with Rashīd al-Dīn Ayaz b. Abdallāh al-Shihābī, known there in 627/1229–30. Whether or not it was partly alienated, it was subsequently held by the sultan, who may have placed Karatay and his brother, Karasungur, there as governors. Before the start of the Mongol period, it was briefly surrendered to the Greeks before its permanent reoccupation by the Turcomans. In 634/1236–37 and 641/1243–44, Kütahya had as governor the *amīr ispahsālār* 'Imād al-Dīn Hazārdīnārī, of whom nothing further is known. The governors of Karahisar (now Afyonkarahisar) were probably Ṣābiq al-Dīn Abu'l-Wafā' Ilyās b. Uğus before 606/1209–10, and then his son, one of whose brothers was at Karacaviran in 607/1210–11. Subsequently it was held by the sultan, who disposed of it at the start of the Mongol period in favour of the family of the vezir Fakhr al-Dīn 'Alī. Its almost unknown history is complicated by possible confusion with similarly named places in the Taurus and the mountains of Trebizond. The places on the Syrian approaches may be ignored. They were precariously held, and were normally dependencies of the principality of Aleppo. The chief of them was Tall Bāshir, the Turbessel of the Crusaders.[19]

So it does not seem that the general impression can be denied, whatever doubts may remain in some cases, that the Seljukids governed their state with the aid of officers, who might be retained in their posts, but who were nonetheless, except in special cases, liable to dismissal, and were in fact dismissed or transferred. Before the Mongol invasion, the sultans were strong enough to do this, and consequently the complexion of their regime, far from being 'feudal' in this respect, was on the contrary deliberately anti-feudal.

It is true that there was one important exception, but it would be an error to consider it the norm, to which it was the opposite, namely the Khwarazmians. It has been seen how, after the death of their chief, Jalāl al-Dīn Mengübirti, most of the Khwarazmians in disarray entered the service of Kay Qubādh I, who was glad to withhold them from possible rivals, and might possibly use their warlike qualities against the Mongol threat. After some hesitation, the sultan granted them in *iqṭā'* the provinces of Erzincan, Amasya and Lârende, situated on exposed frontiers or important strategic routes, and lying outside the western half of the realm. The degree of authority conceded to the Khwarazmians in their *iqṭāʿ* is nevertheless unknown and, as will appear, it was not necessarily total. The circumstances moreover were exceptional, and any speculations about normalization are somewhat otiose, since in fact on Kay Qubādh's death, as the immediate danger had diminished, and the new masters were perhaps more conscious of the difficulties which had come to light, the Khwarazmians were expelled, and the system was not followed up.

The impressions drawn directly from an examination of the facts before the Mongol protectorate are indirectly corroborated by other data in the latter period. It will appear that as the personal powers of the sultan then vanished almost completely, the real authority under Mongol control fell to some of the great officers of state, who, on the pretext of securing the revenues needed for the fulfilment of their duties, divided up the provinces, and turned them into a sort of family fief. It is clear that such an enterprise would have been impossible if 'feudal' powers had existed there beforehand. These great officers would have had difficulty in suppressing these powers by force, which was lacking to the reduced Seljukid state. More generally, it would have been inexplicable that the disaster of Kösedağ was not followed by any sign of revolt or local independence (apart from the frontier Turcomans), if there had previously existed great lords of a 'feudal' type. No doubt the Mongols would have paid little heed to such risings, but no text indicates that they had to struggle with them in conjunction with, or in the place of, the Seljukids. Some might develop little by little, but the inevitable conclusion is that there were none immediately following 1243.

There was indeed one exceptional category, which however formed a special case, not affecting the interior of the state before 1243: namely the Turcomans. On the whole under the Seljukids of the first half of the thirteenth century, in spite of the tragic and revealing episode of Baba Isḥāq, the Turcomans were held under firm control. It is certain however that they enjoyed a fairly large degree of autonomy within their own territories. In some instances these may have been granted them under the legal form of *iqṭāʿ*. Nevertheless this term does not truly characterize the reality of their regime. It must first be noted that the Turcomans were particularly numerous on the frontiers, or in any case that it was only on or, one might say, straddling the frontiers that they had a special regime. They lived there in a sort of administrative no man's land, where their effective autonomy derived from the fact that they did not own Seljukid, Byzantine or Cilician Armenian authority and, if one encroached on them, they could take refuge with another. Administrative vocabulary and practice made a clear distinction between the real lands of the state and this belt of country of the men of the *uc* (literally 'border', 'frontier'), and the Mongols made the difference even clearer by deliberately sacrificing these regions.

The Seljukid administration however tried gradually to establish itself in these territories where Turcoman independence could have hidden dangers, and which in any case it did not like to deem beyond its control. Following the Turcoman expansion, agents of Seljukid power were gradually installed in the chief towns. On other occasions, in order to populate territories conquered by the regular Seljukid armies, such as the western Taurus, Turcomans were installed in a region where the administration was set up in advance or simultaneously. By one or other of these procedures it is certain (and this is noteworthy) that when Seljukid power was at its zenith, there was no province of true state territory, even if it contained autonomous groups of Turcomans with land open to their movements and activities, which did not have at its summit a royal authority set over them. Later the holders of the Turcoman principalities were concerned to spread the belief that they had received genuine provincial commands from the sultans, and authors who wrote under the influence of these notions in the confusing changes of circumstances are in danger of deluding us into believing this. Care must be taken to judge only on the evidence of data clearly relating to the time under consideration.

The *iqṭāʿ*s here discussed are the great *iqṭāʿ*s. The small *iqṭāʿ*s, which have already been dealt with, should not be confused with these.

CHAPTER FIFTEEN

Cultural and religious life

The rhythm and manner of acculturation in Muslim Asia Minor are difficult to follow. Only with the latter half of the twelfth century do its signs make a clear appearance, and only in the thirteenth century does it produce work which will henceforward be of recognized importance. A distinction must admittedly be made between two spheres almost lacking in intercommunication: that of the Turcomans, as yet hardly touched by traditional Muslim culture, and for that very reason almost unknown to us before the Mongol period; and that of the townspeople of ethnically mixed origins, the only ones of whom something can be said because they alone left written records.

It has already been said that the earliest Seljukids of Rūm show in the political play of their times a tendency towards opposition, or at least indifference, to the militant Sunnism of their kinsmen, the Great Seljuks. Among the influences which had penetrated the Islam of their Turcoman subjects, some were Shīʿī as well as others Sunnī, not to mention the barely disguised survival of ancestral beliefs previous to their islamization. These popular ideas, to which we shall return, did not prevent the Seljukids from speedily seeking a rapprochement with the ʿAbbasid caliphate. This implied a profession of faith which was at least superficially Sunnī; then gradually they presented themselves as good Sunnīs, and especially as heirs to the policy of the Seljukids of Iran after their disappearance – whatever may have been the import which they or those about them placed on this interpretation. Like their kinsmen of Iran, they had in their entourage Khurāsānī Ḥanafī religious advisers from an early period. The earliest known of these (in 1108) was a *faqīh* from Herat, sent on an embassy to the caliph to negotiate for the release of Shāhānshāh. Others came independently or by request from different regions, often north-west Iran. Süleyman I asked Tripoli in

Syria, a Shīʿī city, for a *qāḍī* for Tarsus after its conquest in 1084; and there was a chief *qāḍī* at the accession of Kılıc Arslan II, who like the Danişmendid Yağıbasan also had *imāms*. On several occasions Seljukid rulers persuaded foreign scholars visiting them, such as ambassadors, to stay permanently in Asia Minor.

The first Muslims in the towns of Asia Minor certainly worshipped in small makeshift buildings, no doubt disused churches or parts of such. Islamization cannot be dated from the appearance of mosques, although this bears witness to the progress and official recognition of Islam. Their date cannot always be fixed precisely, especially in the case of modest buildings without inscriptions. A pulpit for the mosque at Konya, made by a townsman from Ahlat (or at least ordered from him there), carries the date 550/1155, and the other oldest mosques in Seljukid, Danişmendid, Mengüçekid and Saltukid territory appear at about that date or a little later.

Furthermore, throughout Sunnī Islam from the time of the Great Seljuks there spread the institution of the *madrasa*, organized for the teaching of orthodoxy to those in training for key positions. The first one known in Asia Minor, at Kayseri, has a foundation inscription dated 589/1193. At this time *madrasa*s were so abundant in all the cities of the Arab and Persian Near East that the Aleppine writer ʿIzz al-Dīn Ibn Shaddād enumerated more than forty in his own city. There may even have been some earlier than that of Kayseri, such as perhaps the one mentioned in the colophon of a manuscript copied in 591/1195 in a Seljukid *madrasa* in Sivas. A systematic search among the manuscripts might reveal others. Nevertheless it is improbable that the general picture would be profoundly changed. Even in the thirteenth century, the number of *madrasa*s to be known in Asia Minor remains fairly limited.

As is well known, Arabic literature is immensely rich in biographies of scholars. Persian literature is less so but it has some, especially of the Sufi orders. Of these thousands and thousands of biographical notices, practically none relates to Asia Minor. If indeed a scholar died there, remote from colleagues accustomed to write biographical notices and obituaries, his name was in danger of being forgotten. All the same, the simplest explanation is generally that there were as yet hardly any such people in Asia Minor, that the few who were there had no real reputation before their move, and that they had not maintained contact with the scholars of neighbouring countries, to whom their scholarship might have seemed mediocre. This being so, it will however be a useful preliminary to the citing of those mentioned in the texts. It is possible that the Ḥanafī *faqīh* of 1108 noted above may be identical with the jurist ʿAbd al-Majīd b. Ismāʿīl b. Saʿd of Herat, who was well known in Muslim lands as the author of works on Ḥanafī theory, and who died at Kayseri in 537/1142 after having acted as a *qāḍī* in Rūm. Kayseri, which was in easy communication with Syria, was perhaps one of the first centres of islamization; it had also one of the earliest mosques. A little later Malatya, although it was always an important Christian city, had another scholar, no doubt because of its easy contacts with Upper Mesopotamia. This was Muḥammad al-Mawṣilī, who, after seeking masters and colleagues throughout Syria and Mesopotamia, pressed on to Malatya, but felt no need to go further. It will appear that several authors seem to have lived there. Previously in the middle of the century another jurist, al-Kāshānī, sent by Nūr al-Dīn to Sultan Masʿūd, was detained by him for a time. Kılıc Arslan, like many others, had a Christian physician, who came from Edessa.

These authors, who were chiefly concerned with the religious and legal sciences, wrote in Arabic as was usual in this field, although they were Iranian by birth. Soon however Persian writers appeared in the entourage of the Seljukids and their emulators. Real activity seemed to reign around the aged Kılıc Arslan II and his sons in the last years of the twelfth century, together with a whiff of heterodoxy, perhaps facilitated by contact between sects and the weakness of the traditional religious organization. Michael the Syrian knew a Persian philosopher in Kılıc Arslan's entourage, who was capable of sensible discussion with Christian scholars. This can hardly have been the distinguished Illuminationist philosopher, Shihāb al-Dīn Yaḥyā al-Suhrawardī,[20] but it is almost certain that it was to Kılıc Arslan or his son, Rukn al-Dīn Süleyman II, that this author dedicated his book *Partaw-Nāma.* Rukn al-Dīn had in any case the reputation of being a 'philosopher', a discourteous term in the mouths of the orthodox of his day. Among other authors mentioned as being in the company of these rulers was Sharaf al-Dīn Ḥubaysh Tiflisī of Tiflis (Tbilisi), an old Muslim city conquered by the Georgians. He compiled for Kılıc Arslan and his son, Quṭb al-Dīn, typical compendia of medicine, astronomy (much to the taste of the Seljukids), oneiromancy and *adab,* i.e. general culture. Another was Muḥammad b. Ghāzī, who compiled for Rukn al-Dīn at the time of his capture of Malatya (1201) an adaptation of the well-known Persian work, the *Marzbān-Nāma,* under the title of *Rawḍat al-ʿuqūl,* while preparing another collection of tales for Kay Khusraw. Finally, Abū Ḥanīfa ʿAbd al-Karīm wrote for Muḥyī al-Dīn of Ankara, another of Kılıc Arslan's sons, an anthology of *rubāʿiyyāt,* the genre of poetry made famous a century earlier by ʿUmar Khayyām. This shows at least that a real intellectual life existed in some centres in Anatolia, attracting foreign writers and no doubt also some indigenous people. Witness is borne to the commencement of iranization by the fact that Kılıc Arslan II gave one of his sons the legendary Persian name of Kay Khusraw, and he in his turn gave similar names to his three sons. It should however be observed that another of Kılıc Arslan's sons was called Qayṣar-Shāh, hinting at a 'Roman' past. Somewhat later a 'mirror for princes' was compiled for Kay Qubādh I. Its author had lived for fifteen years previously in Erzincan, i.e. in Mengüçekid country.

There is no evidence of a similar cultural appeal among the Danişmendids. Their outlook was perhaps different, and in any event they disappeared too soon. It appeared a little later among the Mengüçekids, especially during the long reign of Bahrām-Shāh at Erzincan. Although this city was to remain a great Armenian centre for a long time yet, there was an active little Muslim circle in the entourage of this ruler, which perhaps, like those around the Shaddadids at Ani, did not reject inter-confessional relations. However this may be, at the start of Bahrām-Shāh's reign the *Makhzan al-asrār* (Treasury of secrets) by the great Persian poet, Niẓāmī of Ganja, seems to have been dedicated to him, and he may have known another poet, Khāqānī. A little later the famous physician and philosopher from Iraq, 'Abd al-Laṭīf al-Baghdādī, stayed at Erzincan for twelve years, returning to his homeland only after Kay Qubādh I's annexation of Erzincan. The extracts from his autobiography preserved in later sources unfortunately contain no information on his life at Erzincan or the activities of its cultural circle; however, whatever the facilities extended to him by the ruler, it is doubtful that 'Abd al-Laṭīf would have accepted exile in an intellectual desert. It is possible that a minute study of his minor works, now beginning to receive attention, might yield some fresh information about this.

The study of cultural life in Rūm in the thirteenth century (and indeed in the fourteenth and fifteenth centuries) is difficult and hardly yet sketched out, and only a very imperfect account can be given here. In restricting it to the pre-Mongol period the Turkish language will not require attention, inasmuch as it did not as yet offer any written work. It must however be stressed that there was an oral literature (which will be discussed later), while literary activity in Persian and Arabic was restricted to urban society. Whatever its intrinsic value, this reduced its range, and created a gap between the two elements of the population, the townspeople and the Turcomans; other manifestations and other dangers of this gap have already been shown. Even within the sphere of Arabic and Persian literature, it cannot be said that there has yet been drawn up a real inventory of the intellectual life. For lack of Anatolian biographical works similar to those produced in the neighbouring Muslim countries, the latter must be patiently scrutinized for what they may contain about people who passed some time in Rūm. There should also be drawn up, particularly in the libraries of Istanbul and other places in Turkey, a list, not only of works written in the country (which has largely been done) but also of works copied there, where this is specified, and the date when possible. There is, for example, a Qur'ān written for Kay Qubādh. Again, it is instructive to record that, not by chance, the majority of the known manuscripts of the works of the numerous Central Asian Ḥanafī jurists are in Turkish libraries, and that many of them were copied there. Others may also have been brought from Central Asia, particularly by refugees fleeing before the Mongol irruption, or by immigrants attracted by Seljukid favours, and so forth. In this respect it is important to pay attention to readers' notes, which are often to be found at the beginning and end, or in the margins of manuscripts. From this one could have a better idea, not only of the limited amount of material written in Rūm, but more widely of what was taken into consideration there, and consequently influenced what was written. Perhaps one would escape from the impression, which is certainly excessive at the present, of a spiritual life almost monopolized by a few great figures, and would be able to present a more diverse and differentiated picture.

With matters as they are at present, spiritual life in Asia Minor in the mid-thirteenth century, particularly at the beginning of the Mongol period but already a little earlier, appears from our documentation to be centred around the figure of Jalāl al-Dīn Rūmī, or secondarily on those who 'announce' him. It is not a matter of diminishing either the great poetical and religious value of his extant work, or even the social importance of the mystical order at the origin of which he stood. It is quite simply a matter of recognizing that he was not alone, that he had predecessors and contemporaries who, although less easy to know, had probably not less importance.

Jalāl al-Dīn Rūmī and his circle wrote in Persian, and there is no doubt that in general throughout the history of Turkey the role of Persian was greater than that of Arabic. This is explained by the fact that the first Turks, or at least their aristocracy, had some idea of Persian from having lived in contact with Iranian societies; and then because the immigrants who contributed to the formation of Anatolian culture were in the great majority Iranians, or Central Asian peoples who expressed themselves in Iranian. Nevertheless there were Arabs also, and in any case the study of the Sharīʿa was in principle a realm reserved to Arabic, and having its own importance.

As already suggested in passing, it was largely on the basis of Central Asian works on Ḥanafī law that the jurists of Asia Minor constructed their knowledge of the Sharīʿa. The Sivas manuscript already referred to consists of several short works originating there. One of them is due to that Kāshānī who was later an ambassador from Nūr al-Dīn, and was held for a while by Masʿūd; the manuscript was purchased by a reader in Erzurum. It is not however remarkable that the jurists who established themselves in Asia Minor might now come from other regions, particularly those near at hand. From Egypt came Afḍal al-Dīn al-Khunajī, at first as an envoy from al-Kāmil. Under Kay Qubādh I and Kay Khusraw II he was chief of the *fuqahā'* of Rūm until he fled before the Mongols. 'Umar al-Abharī (d. 663/1265) and Sirāj al-Dīn al-Urmawī (from Urmya on the lake of that name in Ādhārbāyjān) divided their lives between Mesopotamia and Asia Minor, while a certain Muḥammad al-Ṭāliqānī, who died as a *qāḍī* in Rūm in 614/1217, came from Qazwīn in north-western Iran. Moreover it was from the Iranian east that Yūsuf b. Sa'īd al-Sijistānī came to Anatolia, but it was at Sivas that he wrote in 639/1241–42 his *Munyat al-muftī*, a considerable treatise on law, which was to be highly successful throughout the Muslim East. It seems needless to insist on an enumeration having as its essential object to emphasize the existence of a kind of activity which was less illustrious than some others.

It is rightly considered that mysticism has particularly flourished in Iran, and consequently found expression in Persian. This Persian mysticism was to come to Asia Minor, but it was not the exclusive influence there. There lived in Egypt at the start of the thirteenth century a great Arab mystic of Spanish origin, Ibn 'Arabī, whose prestige was immense throughout the Muslim lands. There is no doubt that he exercised great influence in Seljukid Asia Minor. Perhaps this influence was to a slight extent the effect of the passage of Maghribī pilgrims through Asia Minor. They were sufficiently numerous to have a small mosque of their own at Konya – it is not very clear why. More directly, Ibn 'Arabī himself travelled in Anatolia, twice to Malatya in 602/1205 and 613–15/1216–18, where he composed a short work, and even in 612/1215 to Sivas and Konya, where he had an audience with Kay Kāwūs I. His Maghribī disciple, 'Afīf al-Dīn Sulaymān al-Tilimsānī (of Tlemcen), was later to stay in Rūm for years, and it would be worthwhile to know its attraction. But it is not necessary to turn to this foreigner to find Anatolian disciples of Ibn 'Arabī. He had been the guest there of a shaykh who declared himself to be his disciple. This was Majd al-Dīn Isḥāq, whose credit was great, and whose son, Ṣadr al-Dīn Konevi (of Konya), was to be the master of the mystical theologians of Rūm, and always remained true to the object of his father's devotion. By contrast almost nothing can be said of another Arab mystic and contemporary of Ibn 'Arabī, 'Umar b. al-Farīd. It is known however that a man from Farghānā, Sa'īd b. 'Alī al-Farghānī, wrote a commentary on his works.

It is also under the heading of Arabic mysticism that we should to some extent place the influence of 'Umar al-Suhrawardī. This person, better known as the spiritual adviser and ambassador of the Caliph al-Nāṣir, and one of the promoters and ideologists of the *futuwwa* as revived by this caliph, was also the founder of the Sufi mystical order of the Suhrawardiyya. He first made himself known in Asia Minor as the caliph's ambassador when he went there in 1221, bringing very ceremoniously the insignia of the sultanate sent by al-Nāṣir. How he acquired the personal ascendancy which he subsequently had there is unknown. Witness is borne to it by the fact that the expenses of his tomb at Baghdad were defrayed by Karatay, Kay Qubādh's faithful servant and the regent for his two grandsons. Kamyar is also said to have been his disciple, as also of Sirāj al-Dīn al-Urmawī for *fiqh*.

One or two physicians from Arab lands were employed by some of the sultans. The illustrious botanist, Ibn al-Bayṭār, collected plants in Rūm; the expert on jugglers, impostors and fraudulent practices, al-Jawbarī, brought his followers there from Syria. Nothing of this contradicts the fact (of which Baybars's campaign in 1277 gives positive proof) that as a general rule the magnates of Rūm did not understand Arabic. This evidently restricts the influence, or at least the direct influence, of the Arabs to a relatively narrow sphere; by contrast most of the magnates, and even a good number of the townsmen, understood Persian, hence Persian works and Iranian influence acquired a wider range. Before the Mongol conquest there was no historical work devoted to Muslim Asia Minor. However, when the Iranian Rāwandī completed a history of the Seljukids of Iran and Iraq, the death of the last of them prevented its dedication to him. So Rāwandī turned to Kay Khusraw I, and added some additional matter and panegyrics of the patron he sought to the original work. The work cannot have been well known in Rūm, as it does not seem to have been used directly by any later historian there, but it is proof that the Seljukids of Rūm regarded themselves as the heirs of the Great Seljuks.

A little later however a refugee from Khurāsān, Aḥmad b. Muḥammad al-Ṭūsī al-Qāni'ī, wrote an important *Saljūq-nāma* for Kay Qubādh and Kay Kāwūs II, but no doubt this dealt only with the eastern Seljukids. Otherwise it would be hard to explain why Ibn Bībī says that he found no work about the first Seljukids of Rūm, and this was also evidently true of Aksarayi and the anonymous author of *Tārīkh-i āl-i Saljūq*. On the other hand, there can be no doubt of the interest the Seljukids of Rūm had in the eastern Seljukids. As has been seen, the writings of the great eleventh-century vezir of the Great Seljuks, Niẓām al-Mulk, were read and appreciated, and in principle at least his teachings were willingly heeded. The verses of various Persian poets were also known; while, as already mentioned, almost all the thirteenth-century sultans had names that were not Turkish, but taken from Iranian legend.

In return an appreciable number of Iranians found a second homeland in Rūm. Attracted by its rulers, and at first fleeing before the Mongols, later arriving with them, it was essentially there that they ended up, rather than in the other Muslim lands, which were older, richer and to a greater degree inhabited by Muslims. As a historical fact, in several cases a sort of Turco-Persian symbiosis came about, but never a Turco-Arab one.

So it is not surprising to come on the titles of different kinds of works edited in Persian in Central Asia, e.g. an adaptation of *Kalīla wa-Dimna* by the same al-Qāni'ī whose *Saljūq-nāma* has just been mentioned. It is however mystical works which provide the most interesting examples. Najm al-Dīn Abū Bakr b. Muḥammad al-Rāzī (of Rayy), called Najm al-Dīn Rāzī Dāya, arrived at Malatya in flight from the Mongols (618/1221), and met 'Umar al-Suhrawardī there. He was for some time in the service of Kay Qubādh at Kayseri, and in 620/1223–24 wrote at Sivas a mystical work called *Mirṣād al-'ibād*, and later a small work of the same kind, *Sirāj al-qulūb*. He was a disciple of Najm al-Dīn Kubrā, the great mystic who founded the order of the Kubrāwiyya in Iran. His success in Asia Minor is attested by the number of manuscripts of the *Mirṣād* still to be found in Turkish libraries, and by the fact that it was subsequently translated into Turkish. The Iranian mystic, Awḥad al-Dīn Kirmānī, may have stayed for some time at Kayseri and Konya.

Najm al-Dīn al-Rāzī finally settled in Konya, where he was acquainted with Jalāl al-Dīn Rūmī and Ṣadr al-Dīn Konevi. These are better considered in the Mongol period, but it was while the Seljukids were still independent that Jalāl al-Dīn's father, Bahā' al-Dīn Veled (Ar. Walad), himself a mystic, and his later spiritual guide, Shams al-Dīn Tabrīzī, settled in Rūm. Bahā' al-Dīn Veled, a preacher in Balkh, emigrated towards the west in consequence of obscure disagreements with the last Khwārazm-Shāh of Central Asia, Muḥammad. He was at Malatya in 614/1217–18, Sivas in 616/1219–20, Akşehir of Erzincan until 619/1222–23, and at Lârende (Karaman) until 626/1228–29. There his wife died (her tomb is still extant), and his son, Jalāl al-Dīn, born at Balkh *c.* 604/1207–8, married. At the invitation of Kay Qubādh, Bahā' al-Dīn finally went to Konya, where he died after 628/1230–31. He wrote sermons, some of which are extant, but relate particularly to the period of his life in the East. He also had a mystical side, perhaps related to the Malāmatiyya, which his former disciple, Burhān al-Dīn Muḥaqqiq, contributed towards passing on to Jalāl al-Dīn. Burhān al-Dīn however settled at Kayseri, and died in 638/1240–41. During these years Jalāl al-Dīn passed some time at Damascus in order to perfect his training, and he may there have met Shams al-Dīn Tabrīzī, the great Persian mystic. It was only later however that Shams al-Dīn influenced him most fully.

Naturally all this remained strange to the Turcomans of Asia Minor, even if these mystics had popular contacts in the Iranian lands. Place must here be found for Baba Isḥāq, and perhaps Baba Ilyās for more remote influence. Nothing is known directly of what they taught the Turcomans, and it is only possible to observe those who might be their heirs in the Mongol and post-Mongol period. They will therefore be discussed at the appropriate time. All the same, some names of mystics have come down from the period before the Mongols: those of a certain Aḥmad-Faqīh, a townsman who became a hermit, and somewhat later Shayyād Ḥamza, who translated the story of Yūsuf and Zulaykha. The importance of this work does not lie in its content, but in the fact that it is evidence of the first appearance of written Turkish in Asia Minor – a century later than in Central Asia.

It is by no means easy to solve the problem of the existence of a Shī'ī movement in thirteenth-century Asia Minor. It must be considered in view of the importance of some forms of Shi'ism among the Turcomans in the eastern half of the country during the following two centuries. To judge from the texts from which the history of Asia Minor can usually be reconstructed, there arose no movement hostile to the Sunnī policy of the authorities apart from that of Baba Isḥāq, which was equally remote from both Shi'ism and Sunnism.

Some hitherto unnoticed evidence helps to confirm the existence of Shī'ī circles of some importance. In what may be described as the memoirs which the conjuror al-Jawbarī wrote about his itinerant career, he says that when he found himself among Shī'īs in Rūm at the beginning of the thirteenth century, he gave himself out to be the reincarnation of a descendant of 'Alī, evidently to a public of the common people. It has already been said that at the start of the conversion and migration of the Turks there were both Shī'ī and Sunnī agents, pro-Shī'ī as well as pro-Sunnī activity, but there is no information on developments in later generations. Perhaps the Mongol protectorate aided the Shī'ī cause, in the first place through Mongol indifference towards the divisions of Islam, of which the *īlkhāns* were not adherents. This might do some harm to the persistence of offical Sunnism. Then on the other hand the Mongols tended to rely politically on elements of the population which had been maltreated or held in contempt by the preceding regimes, the Shī'īs in particular – such as Naṣīr al-Dīn Ṭūsī. Then, further, at the start of the fourteenth century, after the conversion of the Mongols to Islam, some of them, including rulers, became Shī'īs.

In reality the situation was probably more confused. There can be no doubt that so-called Shī'ī elements penetrated Anatolian Islam as will appear, but it does not follow that they were consciously felt to be Shī'ī, i.e. anti-Sunnī. Among the uneducated everything was mingled together without distinction between orthodox and heterodox elements. Even among the more cultivated, the pious adopted some elements of Shi'ism, without being any the more regarded for that as Shī'īs. It must be admitted that before the official reorganization of Shi'ism in Iran by the sixteenth-century Safavids, it is sometimes hard to distinguish indisputable Sunnism from indisputable Shi'ism. The Caliph al-Nāṣir's influence together with that of the *futuwwa* may have helped the confusion; the caliph by the ʿAlid, or at least syncretistic, tendencies which characterized his attitude, and for which he was blamed by strict Sunnīs; the *futuwwa* by its open admiration of ʿAlī as the traditional initiator of the *fityān*. So it is not surprising that a little later popular stories, such as the Turkish version of Abū Muslim, combine a pro-ʿAbbasid attitude with veneration of the twelve Shīʿī *Imams*. It may be imagined that in such conditions the question of the specific existence of Shiʿism in Asia Minor assumes a somewhat particular appearance, but this can only be usefully discussed in the Mongol period.

There is a more delicate problem. As is known, there exists a whole sector of groups devoting an exaggerated respect to ʿAlī from the Nuṣayrīs of Syria to the ʿAlī-ilāhīs of eastern Iran. Little is known of any of these sects, essentially because they guard their secrets jealously; there are only some indications that their adepts were more widespread than it may seem at the first glance. Now it is a fact that important groups of believers called Alevis (ʿAlawīs) survive to the present day, and have as an essential characteristic precisely this exaggerated devotion to ʿAlī. It is hard to see how the Turcomans of Central Asia could have found that idea and brought it thence, not to speak of even more popular beliefs capable of combination with it. It might thus be supposed that these ideas were introduced into Asia Minor by propagandists of the ʿAlid sects. This is of course pure speculation, but the supposition is hard to avoid.

It does not seem that the Assassins had much effective propaganda in Asia Minor; nevertheless there is proof that relations existed between Kay Kāwūs I and ʿAlāʾ al-Dīn *Naw-Musulmān*, the head of the Assassins of Alamūt and grand master of the order, with whom the Caliph al-Nāṣir had found the means of concluding some sort of armistice implying mutual recognition. It is also known that the Turkish rulers of Asia Minor, no doubt as a precaution, came to send tribute to Alamūt, and the grand master required them to transfer this to his underlings in Syria to simplify matters. A writer at Sivas completed or wrote a little treatise on the Ismāʿīlī doctrine. The Mongol conquest of the Near East and the destruction of Alamūt did not cause the sect to disappear, but suppressed even its secret activity in the Arab lands and Asia Minor.

The non-Muslim communities have been discussed in connection with some manuscripts, and some of their writings are mentioned in the historical sources of the present work. It has also been seen that there were occasional exchanges of correspondence between the sultans of Rūm and some indigenous notables. However, it must be noted that there appear to have been hardly any cultural exchanges between these communities and the Muslims of the country, nor any influence of the one group on the other. In this respect there were virtually watertight bulkheads.

The history of art in Muslim Asia Minor is a subject which it is important to approach without preconceived ideas. No Muslim art had existed there previously, so that insofar as art had to be Muslim, the guiding models had to be sought in the old Muslim lands – in practice essentially Iran. There was indeed a native art, which as has been seen could still produce original works, and the remains of which were visible, but which being Christian could only provide contributions of detail to the new Muslim art, and not the guidelines. It is difficult to know to what degree it was extant, or whether the new masters wished to employ native specialist technicians. In the few cases where the names of architects or other workers are known, there are some native names but more of Muslims from nearby Ādharbāyjān. Hence it might be said that the art of Asia Minor generally designated Seljukid was only a division of Iranian or Irano-Seljukid art. This would however be an over-simple conclusion. In the remains visible in Asia Minor, there are echoes of Iranian or Turkish art from Khurāsān or beyond, but there exist particularly local conditions as to materials, climate and specific social development, which are not to be forcibly assimilated to those in Iran or Central Asia. Finally, without ignoring the wider aspects of the study, it is of primary importance to consider without any preconceptions the remains of Anatolian art in themselves, and then to determine their specific qualities by comparing them with those of neighbouring regions. There can be no doubt that it is somewhat pointless to try to know what should or should not be called 'Turkish' in an art to which so many different and closely interwoven elements have contributed.

It will be enough for the present to give some words of guidance. In addition, part of what might have been said here has found expression in discussing the originality of some workmen's techniques, the activities of sultans and their magnates as builders, the network of fortresses and caravanserais, the role of the *madrasas* and so forth. It remains to suggest some ideas of a more particularly technical or aesthetic nature.

Naturally no traces exist of any art immediately following the Turkish conquest of Asia Minor. The oldest go back to the second quarter of the twelfth century, and the blossoming begins with the start of the thirteenth century, and is prolonged during the first generation of the Mongol protectorate.

The civil architecture is both difficult to know and badly known. The excavation of the palaces of Konya and Qubādhābād (Beyşehir) and old pictures make possible an idea of the Seljukid residences as being a collection of pavilions set in gardens and surrounded by a wall, thus bearing a resemblance with due proportion to the Ottoman Saray in Istanbul. Military architecture is more abundantly represented in the form of city walls and isolated fortresses. No study has yet been made either of what they owe to the numerous previously existing Byzantine or Armenian fortresses, nor of how they profited from eastern contributions, or followed (perhaps preceded) some of the advances made in a Syria disputed between Crusaders and Muslims.

The religious architecture is better known, although there are no completely intact remains. This division should in a sense include buildings with a lay purpose, e.g. caravanserais, hospitals, baths and so forth, which were regarded as religious foundations. Strictly religious architecture comprises particularly mosques, *madrasas* and tombs. As the towns where they were constructed were of moderate size, the effect aimed at, and always successfully, was less of grandeur than of elegance. The principal mosques surviving from before the Mongol protectorate are those of Kayseri and Sivas from the first half of the twelfth century; that ascribed to ʿAlāʾ al-Dīn Kay Qubādh I at Konya, which was actually undertaken in Masʿūd's time, and enlarged by his successors, whence a certain heterogeneity of plan; those of Niğde and Divriği, and finally that of Malatya, completed in 1247. The principal ancient *madrasas* are those of Niksar, built by the Danişmendid Yağıbasan in the mid-twelfth century; that of the amir Altın Apa at Konya at the end of the same century; the Gök Madrasa (Blue *Madrasa*) of Amasya *c.* 1240; finally, at Konya again, the *madrasas* of Karatay (1251), and of the vezir Fakhr al-Dīn ʿAlī *Ṣāḥib ʿAṭā* called *Ince Minare* (1258). Among the characteristics of these monuments may be noted the frequent use of stone with wood for the flat roofs, and hence a smaller part was played by domes. By contrast Iran and Mesopotamia built in brick, and except on the northern fringes the Arab world and most of the Iranian world used brick almost entirely. Furthermore, the climate entailed the predominance of closed mosques without a court, and the installation of the ritual fountain within the building. With regard to external decoration, which was concentrated around the main doorway, great but essentially ornamental use was made of bands of almost illegible script; also above the doorways and at the bases of the domes were 'stalactites' (Ar. *muqarnas*), which then triumphed throughout the whole Muslim world. Finally, the *madrasa* often contained a small mosque around the founder's tomb, as elsewhere in the rest of the Muslim world from the thirteenth century onwards. However, there also developed the type of mausoleum coming from Central Asia and northern Iran, which consisted of a circular building surmounted by a conical roof. The adaptation in Asia Minor of the technique of painted tiles for interior decoration has already been mentioned; this explains the appearance of 'Blue' or 'Green' in the names of so many mosques.

Although the extant direct evidence is often not great, it may be affirmed that almost all the minor arts practised in neighbouring countries attained a high quality in Asia Minor. Apart from ceramics and carpets already mentioned, this applies in particular to metalwork and carpentry using the natural resources of the country, the binding of manuscripts in leather, and even their illumination by both Muslims and Christians, while among the productions of craftsmen were marvellous mosque pulpits. There is no doubt of the general relationship of the inspiration to that of the neighbouring countries, the Muslim lands of course, but perhaps also Armenia to a small extent; even Georgia and Byzantium were also related. Special stress should probably be laid on the role played in every branch of art by the representation of living creatures, animals and even men, beside arabesques, and geometrical and calligraphic motifs. Such representations had indeed been practised in Islam, especially Iranian Islam, particularly in metalwork (perhaps above all under Turkish domination and in the regions of some turcicization), in the decoration of textiles and in miniatures. The Arabs also enter into consideration there, but again it was perhaps a development under Turkish influence. However, in addition to coinage, which has already been examined, the frequency of these representations, their role up to the level of monumental sculpture (e.g. the jinn decorating the gates of Konya) and the nature of some animal motifs, suggest that beside Byzantine models there were traditions from the steppes of Central Asia. So, perhaps more easily than in literature, where the confessions coexisted there developed an interpenetration of composite influences which yet culminated in an art of unquestionable harmony.

PART THREE

General History of the Mongol Period

CHAPTER SIXTEEN

The establishment of the Mongol protectorate: the time of troubles (1243–65)

The end of Kay Khusraw II's reign

As night fell on Kösedağ, all might have been thought lost. However, the vezir Muhadhdhab al-Dīn, who was in the vicinity of Amasya, went on his own responsibility (because of the sultan's youth, says Ibn Bībī) with the city *qāḍī* to find Baiju. He had left for Erzurum, whence he took them to Chormaghun in the Mūghān, who was paralysed with his wife acting for him. Muhadhdhab al-Dīn succeeded in demonstrating respectfully that a direct conquest of the whole of Asia Minor would have been a heavy task for the Mongols by reason of the Seljukid realm's resources; the region was certainly too remote to be necessary or even advisable for them at the moment. So peace was granted, conditionally on an alliance and annual tributes of gold and cattle of all kinds. Ibn Bībī says that this was fixed, but it appears that if he was right, Baiju and the Mongols continually increased their demands in the following years. It may moreover be thought, although confirmation is lacking, that, having regard to numerous similar cases and the consideration paid by the Mongols to the vezir's son, Muhadhdhab al-Dīn stood in a kind of personal dependence on them, which made him their representative as well as the sultan's. This might take the form of the grant of a *yarligh*, i.e. a decree by the ruler, and a *paiza*, a tablet of authority, evidently intended to inspire respect from any rival in Rūm, while requiring of any Mongol chief more consideration than would be shown to a mere foreign vassal. However that may be, Muhadhdhab al-Dīn returned, and was welcomed by the sultan with joy and due regard. On hearing of the Mongols' withdrawal, Kay Khusraw had returned to Konya.

Chormaghun was not however the supreme ruler of the Mongols, and Muhadhdhab al-Dīn had not been officially sent by Sultan Kay Khusraw. Being too weary on his return to set off again himself, he had a new embassy sent by the sultan, this time to Batu, who, although not yet the Great Khan, was at least the chief of all the Mongols of the West. The principal ambassador was Shams al-Dīn al-Iṣfahānī, who had returned to Rūm as soon as he heard of the Mongol withdrawal and Muhadhdhab al-Dīn's negotiations, having succeeded in recovering part of the pay distributed for now useless assistance, and in rallying a certain number of deserters. He had simply made a detour to pass by Malatya in order to effect a rendezvous with the former ruler of Āmid, al-Masʿūd Mawdūd, who had asked to be escorted by him from fear of the Mongols, Turcomans and Kurds, but on arrival there had allowed himself to be persuaded by an envoy of the ruler of Aleppo to return to Syria. From Malatya al-Iṣfahānī returned to Konya, where Kay Khusraw conferred on him the post of acting vezir, pending Muhadhdhab al-Dīn's return, in addition to his own office of *nā'ib*. So he now set off for Batu in the steppe between the Don and the Volga. He was accompanied by the *qāḍī* of Amasya and an interpreter. They returned, accompanied by a Mongol ambassador, with a *yarligh* appointing Kay Khusraw as Batu's lieutenant in Rūm, to find that Muhadhdhab al-Dīn had died. Al-Iṣfahānī was appointed to succeed him by the sultan, who also gave him as a special favour the government of Kırşehır. It was subsequently planned to send Kay Khusraw's young son, Rukn al-Dīn Kılıc Arslan, to Batu. One might have the impression that the worst had been avoided, and that the Seljukid sultanate was reviving.

Disorder among the Turcomans and Kurds however remained. Their unrest on the eve of the disaster of Kösedağ shows that following the battle it was not a passing disturbance, but a wish to profit from the regime's disarray to resume the free life natural to them. Could the disorder in central Asia Minor already mentioned, and that now noted at the south-western end of the Taurus, have more in common than just their nature? Had they some actors in common through the interplay of migrations, such as those from precisely the first to the second of these regions as the bard of the Turcoman dynasty of the Karamanids in later times ascribes to its ancestors? In such a hotchpotch of impossible details, one seeks in vain to extract a real historical memory. Like the eastern Taurus, the western Taurus is in any case one of the theatres in which the Turcomans were to achieve most importance after Kösedağ, as will appear.

At this juncture a Turcoman known as Aḥmad to Ibn Bībī, and less comprehensibly as Coterinus to the missionary, Simon of St Quentin, revolted in the mountains between Konya and Alanya, and devastated the fields of those two cities with a force of some 20,000 men for some three months. He had rallied them by asserting with his mother's backing that he was a son of Kay Qubādh, and by claiming the throne that his 'brother' Kay Khusraw was no longer worthy to occupy after defeat. In order to dispose of him, Kay Khusraw was forced to have recourse to the good offices of Constantine of Lampron, a kinsman of the king of Armenia but in revolt against him, who also had an interest in keeping the Turcomans quiet. The claim by both Ibn Bībī's Aḥmad and Simon's Coterinus to be the son of Kay Qubādh leaves little doubt that they were one and the same person. However, Simon, who wrote several months after the event, says that he was taken and put to death during Kay Khusraw's lifetime while, according to Ibn Bībī, who in general is well documented, the incident occurred only after the sultan's death, and he says nothing about the rebel's fate. In any event, this episode was not the end of Turcoman agitation; several months later, at some unspecified place on the frontier, Ibn Bībī speaks of a new and equally vague *malik* named Vāyūz.

Was there some connection between these affairs and the campaign undertaken by Kay Khusraw in 1245 against the Armenians of Cilicia? His army was guided by Constantine of Lampron. The sultan had however a personal reason for his campaign. At the time of Kösedağ the Armenians had captured some fugitives and, still worse, had handed over to the Mongols Kay Khusraw's mother, who had taken refuge with them. It was moreover good to show the world that Seljukid power still existed. A campaign was organized, perhaps with Mongol authorization, and led stubbornly against Tarsus. To obtain peace, King Hetoum had to cede Bragana and some other fortresses which completed the Seljukid occupation of the Isaurian hinterland, and perhaps facilitated the maintenance of the sultan's authority over the Turcomans. But, at the moment the army regained the Anatolian plateau, Kay Khusraw, who had gone ahead, died at the end of 1245 or in 1246.[21] The Armenians strengthened their links with the Mongols, becoming effectively their agents on the Mediterranean coast, and sheltered themselves from further attacks of this kind. Two years later they regained Bragana, while Constantine of Lampron was reduced to taking flight to his Turkish allies.

ʿIzz al-Dīn Kay Kāwūs II. The vezirate of Shams al-Dīn al-Iṣfahānī

Kay Khusraw had three sons. The eldest, 'Izz al-Dīn Kay Kāwūs, his son by the daughter of a Greek priest, was eleven years of age; Rukn al-Dīn Kılıc Arslan, his son by a Turkish woman of Konya, was nine; and 'Alā' al-Dīn Kay Qubādh, his son by the Georgian princess, was seven. It was this last son whom Kay Khusraw had designated to succeed him, but he was the youngest and a weakling. Shams al-Dīn al-Iṣfahānī seated 'Izz al-Dīn Kay Kāwūs II on the throne with his two brothers on his right and left. He then divided up the offices among his friends: Karatay was *nā'ib*, Shams al-Dīn Khāṣṣ-Oğuz, a distinguished Rūmī Mamluk, *beglerbegi*, Asad al-Dīn Ruzbih *atabeg* and Fakhr al-Dīn 'Aṭṭār Abū Bakr *pervane*. On this occasion Shams al-Dīn Maḥmūd, known from his office as Baba Tuğrai also makes his appearance; he seems to have been the vezir's *éminence grise*. The emirs were not, it seems, unanimous over the enthronement of 'Izz al-Dīn. Shams al-Dīn al-Iṣfahānī was too openly ambitious for power, while there were personal rivalries, such as the opposition to their colleagues of Khāṣṣ-Oğuz and Ruzbih, who were linked by marriage.

There may have been a conspiracy. In any case the sultan, who in the circumstances could have only a small bodyguard, and al-Iṣfahānī felt themselves threatened by the power of the emirs. Kay Kāwūs's tutor and intimate, Fakhr al-Dīn 'Aṭṭār, and al-Iṣfahānī's crony, the *amīr-dād* Nuṣrat al-Dīn, accused Ruzbih and Khāṣṣ-Oğuz. In his anxiety al-Iṣfahānī thought of absconding with with Kılıc Arslan, whom Kay Khusraw had decided, when living, to send to Batu. Finally he appears to have given a free hand to the enemies of the two emirs. They were tricked into an ambush prepared with the help of the *rind*s of Akşehir and Abgurum (obtained by promises of favours and *iqṭā*'s), and were put to death. Some of their partisans shared their fate, while others were plundered and arrested by the *rind*s, even Constantine of Lampron was imprisoned briefly. But had Shams al-Dīn al-Iṣfahānī, who was generally held responsible, intended to go so far? Did he judge it opportune, in the face of unrest among the emirs, to appear to condemn the crime? Did he feel threatened by the victorious party? He turned against his two collaborators. The victims' sequestrated possessions were restored to their children. On the advice of Baba Tuğrai, he appointed Sharaf al-Dīn Maḥmūd, *serleşker* of Erzincan, to succeed Khāṣṣ-Oğuz and invited him to lead his troops. This is an indication that, when confronting the *rind*s of Konya, his own troops were neither adequate in number nor sufficiently reliable. It was then decided in agreement with Sharaf al-Dīn and Baba Tuğrai to leave for Sivas, where Kılıc Arslan's journey would be organized. Fakhr al-Dīn 'Aṭṭār and Nuṣrat al-Dīn opposed this in vain. Judging himself to be in danger among the emirs, 'Aṭṭār, once outside the city, obtained permission when the cortège left to return to Konya. There he tried to foment a revolt of the *rind*s and *ahi*s who had served him previously, but came up against a refusal to rise against the sultan because of private quarrels. In addition, Shams al-Dīn Yutaş was sent by the vezir, who was informed of this, and he won them over. 'Aṭṭār tried to flee to

Cilicia, but was taken and imprisoned, as was his son, and Nuṣrat al-Dīn, who was arrested on arrival at Sivas. Kılıc Arslan could then be sent off. He was accompanied by the *qāḍī* Kamāl al-Dīn al-Khutanī and Bahā' al-Dīn Yūsuf b. Nūḥ Erzincani, his *atabeg*. The journey was all the more urgent as it was clearly necessary to give Batu every clarification and satisfaction over the succession to Kay Khusraw.

However, during Kılıc Arslan's absence al-Iṣfahānī's ambition provoked a conflict with Sharaf al-Dīn Maḥmud in his turn. Al-Iṣfahānī had married the sultan's mother without informing Sharaf al-Dīn, and had offended many of the emirs. Also it so happened that he rebuked Sharaf al-Dīn for putting to death one of the emirs, a grandson of the Ayyubid al-Malik al-Ashraf. Thereupon Sharaf al-Dīn withdrew to Erzincan. Al-Iṣfahānī, who did not want to break off relations, proposed an agreement, which was concluded before the *qāḍī* of Sivas. It recognized Sharaf al-Dīn as *serleşker* of Erzincan and Niksar, together with a charge of 300,000 dirhams annually on the sultan's private domain as a contribution towards his expenses. Sharaf al-Dīn however was filled with mistrust, and revolted at Niksar. The vezir sent Shams al-Dīn Yutaş, who had been *subaşı* of Niksar, against him. Sharaf al-Dīn was beaten, and sought refuge at Kemah. Besieged there by all the *serleşkers* sent by the vezir, he obtained a safe-conduct. He was to be taken to the vezir, but on the way he was beheaded on al-Iṣfahānī's orders, and his head sent to Sivas. Fakhr al-Dīn 'Aṭṭār and his son were simultaneously strangled in prison. For some time thereafter al-Iṣfahānī was all-powerful, and Ibn Bībī has described his court of scribes, men of culture and religion, and emirs. There was only one cloud on the horizon – the Turcomans continued to be ungovernable, and this distracted part of his forces.

According to Simon of St Quentin, the amount of tribute due from the Seljukid state to the Mongols was fixed in this year. While Ibn Bībī says that it was fixed from the start, and perhaps not always very effectively. Simon seems to have started from the gathering of the tribute at Sivas, perhaps in connection with Kılıc Arslan's departure, about which he was informed by a witness. He states that the annual tribute was 1,200,000 *hyperpyra* (? dinars), 500 horses, 500 camels, 5,000 sheep, 500 pieces of silk brocade, half being of mixed silk and gold thread, as well as expenses for the entertainment of the Mongol envoys amounting to 60,000 (? 600,000) dinars for the two previous years. In any event it is certain that the demand bore heavily on the Seljukid treasury, and that there were frequent visits from Mongol envoys to intervene in the affairs of Rūm. The Mongols did not forbid the Seljukids to have all the troops they could get, but availability remarkably limited the possibilities. This had the consequences already seen, arising from the inadequacy of these troops in facing Turcoman or urban insubordination, and the state's difficulty in keeping control of the chiefs whose *iqṭā*'s had not yet been demanded by the Mongols.

Kılıc Arslan however returned from Batu. Enemies of the vezir, and indeed of Kay Kāwūs, had slipped into his entourage. The *atabeg* Bahā' al-Dīn Yūsuf had made allegations to Batu that al-Iṣfahānī's executions and even the sending of Kılıc Arslan were intended to isolate and exclude someone who had as much right to the sultanate as Kay Kāwūs. Batu gave orders for the vezir's arrest and the appointment of Kılıc Arslan to the sultanate. When Kılıc Arslan IV's return was announced, al-Iṣfahānī, lacking previous intelligence, sent ahead the former governor of Malatya, Rashīd al-Dīn Juwaynī, who was now *amīr-'āriḍ*. He, on learning of the appointment of the new sultan, hastily shut himself up in Kemah, and then fled to Aleppo, whence however Bahā' al-Dīn Yūsuf obtained his extradition. He was then imprisoned in a fortress where the prisoners were generally thrown from the ramparts. He exceptionally left it to regain afterwards his post as *amīr-'āriḍ*. Meanwhile Kılıc Arslan IV, accompanied by a corps of 2,000 Mongols, was proclaimed as he advanced at Erzincan, Khartpert, Āmid, Sivas, even at Kayseri. Karīm al-Dīn Alpsarı and Fakhr al-Dīn Sīwāstūs brought Batu's *yarligh* to Karatay. Although Karatay was disinclined to accept anything from the Mongols, he thought that on this occasion he had no course but to accept it for his own sake and that of the Seljukid state. While Tāj al-Dīn Sīmjūrī went to rally the army of Isauria on his behalf, he himself forced the anxious al-Iṣfahānī to go to Kay Kāwūs's palace. The sultan was perhaps not displeased to be rid of his overweening minister, who was arrested, imprisoned and tortured, while his possessions were sequestrated. Shortly afterwards, on 8 Dhu'l-Ḥijja 646/25 March 1249, he was beheaded, perhaps against Karatay's wishes.

Al-Iṣfahānī's fall was followed at once by his opponents' revenge on his partisans. Sayf al-Dīn Tarantay and Türkeri (both later known as henchmen of Kılıc Arslan IV), and the Kurdish emir, Ḥusām al-Dīn Bijār (who had fled to Rūm before the Khwarazmians) are mentioned as having their possessions plundered. Then the *qāḍī* Kamāl al-Dīn al-Khutanī took the *yarligh* about the sultanate to Konya. It is not clear whether the decree ordered the three brothers to be jointly installed upon the throne, or whether it established a partition between eastern Asia Minor, given to Kılıc Arslan IV, and Anatolia, left to Kay Kāwūs II. According to Ibn Bībī, the Mongol envoys were won over to an undivided realm by the hostility shown by Karatay and the emirs to any partition of Seljukid territory. This was in any event the system after the battle of Aksaray (see below); but according to Bar Hebraeus, apparently confirmed by Aksarayi and the *Tārīkh-i āl-i Saljūq*, the undivided realm was only adopted after this battle. In any case it is certain that it was then preferred by Karatay and the emirs for the sake of concord, and no doubt for the same reason by the Mongol envoys. It appears that the second version permits a better account of events. This in fact settled the matter. The Mongol corps of envoys withdrew, feeling that it had fulfilled its mission. Bahā' al-Dīn Yūsuf, on his own and out of favour with the emirs, who feared to be included in his reprisals, was set aside; likewise the *qāḍī* of Kayseri, ʿIzz al-Dīn Muḥammad Rāzī, who however was made vezir on Karatay's advice when al-Iṣfahānī fell. A new government was set up, composed chiefly of al-Iṣfahānī's friends. Sirāj al-Dīn became *beglerbegi*; Tarantay became governor of Malatya, and Türkeri of Sivas in Kılıc Arslan's share, if there was a partition; the vezirate passed to Niẓām al-Dīn Khurshīd. But even the agreements between the sultans or their emirs did not last. Kılıc Arslan was on the way to Konya when Kay Kāwūs arrived at Aksaray to encounter him. Each had his small army.

Once reunited, the emirs of both sultans felt much less enthusiastic about a partition. They were two armed camps, and it came to a pitched battle in spite of the Mongol envoys' endeavours. On Kay Kāwūs's side, the army was commanded by Arslan Doğmuş the *amīr-ākhūr*, Nūr al-Dīn Yaʿqūb the *amīr-jāndār*, and Shams al-Dīn Yutaş; on Kılıc Arslan's side by Tarantay and Türkeri. The latter were defeated; Tarantay and Türkeri were made prisoners, likewise Kamāl al-Dīn al-Khutanī, whom Arslan Doğmuş put to death. Kılıc Arslan himself was captured, and taken to his brother (1 Rabīʿ I 647/14 June 1249). It was then, if we are not mistaken, that Karatay and the emirs definitely adopted the undivided sultanate of the three brothers. The government was again reorganized, and the real master was Jalāl al-Dīn Karatay, the support of the sultanate as Kay Kāwūs's *atabeg*.

The government of Karatay and the revolt of Kılıc Arslan IV

Karatay was a freedman of Greek Christian origin, perhaps attached to Kay Kāwūs I, and in any case in the sultan's personal service from the start of Kay Qubādh I's reign. He was the sultan's *ṭashtdār*, then *amīr-dawāt*, and was a pious man who seems to have enjoyed a fairly high reputation and to have kept himself above the factions, even when he became the *nā'ib*. He thought that in order to restore agreement, it would be advantageous to give the vezirate to a holy man who stood outside the parties, Najm al-Dīn Nakhjavānī. One of the vezir's first initiatives however was to seek a reduction in his own salary from the 40,000 dirhams received by Muhadhdhab al-Dīn to 700 (perhaps in order to be able to effect a reduction in payments to the magnates), but Karatay opposed this. It was also necessary to resume the struggle against the Turcomans (this is the time when Ibn Bībī speaks of the *malik* Vāyūz); Arslan Doğmuş and Yutaş dealt successfully with the matter. Finally new envoys arrived from Batu to investigate al-Işfahānī's execution, which had been perpetrated without authorization in the orders he had sent. Baba Tuğrai, al-Işfahānī's intimate collaborator, was sent off to give Batu all necessary reassurance. The instigators of the murder, Bahā' al-Dīn Yūsuf and Karīm al-Dīn Alpsarı, were taken to Batu on his orders. They were escorted by Rashīd al-Dīn Juwaynī, who had now been released, the *ra'īs al-baḥr* Shujā' al-Dīn 'Abd al-Raḥmān, Najīb al-Dīn Dalikhānī and Khaṭīr al-Dīn Zakariyyā Sivasi, all four clients of al-Işfahānī. At the same time the first regained his post as *amīr-'āriḍ*, the second became *nā'ib*, the third became, or was already, *mustawfī* and the last *serleşker* of Haramlu. Then Najm al-Dīn Nakhjavānī, ill at ease as vezir, retired to Aleppo; Baba Tuğrai, on his return, became his successor. It is remarkable that all these functions were conferred by *yarlighs*, i.e. by virtue of Mongol sovereignty, and subsequently other emirs who did not receive *yarlighs*, such as Yutaş, complained bitterly to the sultan. Furthermore it seems that in the past the vezir and perhaps other high officials had received an estate in *iqṭā'* as salary; it now appears that there was a systematic partition of territory among the office-holders. For some this counted more than the effective discharge of their functions, the limits of which overlapped with some confusion. While the clients of Baba Tuğrai and the *mustawfī* installed themselves at Konya, the others made a fresh start in the territories which they had administered previously; Shujā' al-Dīn 'Abd al-Raḥmān at Sinop, Rashīd al-Dīn Juwaynī at Malatya, Khaṭīr al-Dīn Zakariyyā at Haramlu.

This was still not the end of quarrels and intrigues. There were bad relations between Baba Tuğrai, whose tongue ran away with him, and Najīb al-Dīn the *mustawfī*. A scene ensued between Karatay and the vezir, who threw his official inkwell in his face. It happened that a son of the former vezir Muhadhdhab al-Dīn, named Mu'īn al-Dīn Süleyman, who was now *serleşker* of Erzincan (perhaps since the fall of Sharaf al-Dīn Maḥmūd), now went with Tarantay to Baiju, with whom he was in favour for his father's sake. This seems to show that the emirs of Rūm went privately to pay court to the victor, without regard to the government agents of the Seljukid protectorate. Baba Tuğrai, who had long been on good terms with Mu'īn al-Dīn, wrote in his favour to Baiju. The letter fell into hostile hands, and was taken to Karatay. It was in cipher, and was deciphered. Thereupon Karatay, in a plenary assembly of the emirs in the sultan's presence, ordered Baba Tuğrai to be kept in rigorous confinement in the palace, whence he was sent in captivity to Antalya. Although one of his clients was sent by the emirs in the suite of bribed Mongol envoys to Baiju, who had him liberated, he never regained the vezirate.

The succession to Baba Tuğrai was once again given by Karatay to a holy man, one soon to become a martyr, the *qāḍī* 'Izz al-Dīn Muḥammad Rāzī, whom he had previously appointed to the office for a few days on al-Iṣfahānī's death. Like Karatay himself, 'Izz al-Dīn had of old good relations with the caliphate. Karatay sent him as ambassador to Baghdad in 649/1251–52. In return an envoy from the Caliph al-Musta'ṣim brought the usual presents. It is impossible to know what serious questions were discussed, but it is hard to believe that the situation of Islam in the Seljukid country under the non-Muslim Mongol protectorate was not considered. It is curious that on most of the Seljukid coinage of 647–55/1249–57, where every ruler's name is lacking, the name of the caliph alone, formerly associated with that of the ruler, makes an appearance, while there is no sign of the Mongol suzerainty. It is certain that, in rendering to the Mongol Caesar what was inevitably his, Karatay's government endeavoured to maintain and strengthen links with the free Muslim world for the sake of Anatolian Islam. He kept up good relations with al-Nāṣir of Aleppo, who married a Seljukid princess in 1253. Consequently his relations were less good with al-Mu'izz Aybak, the Mamluk sultan who had overthrown the Ayyubid dynasty in Egypt, and he gave asylum to dissident Egyptian amirs.

In this respect the *waqf*s founded by Karatay are also remarkable. Even in Baghdad he had at some date made a contribution towards the construction of a tomb for 'Umar al-Suhrawardī, whom he had ceremoniously and respectfully received when in Kay Qubādh's service. During the vezirate of al-Iṣfahānī immediately after Kay Khusraw's death, he had founded a remarkable caravanserai which was famous on the road from Kayseri to Syria, a region where the ungovernable Turcomans had doubtless recently made the utility of a substantial shelter particularly appreciable. A little later he established a mosque and a *zāwiya* at Konya, and committed its construction to his brother, who was also the founder of a *madrasa*. In 651/1253 Karatay too founded a *madrasa* in the presence of the vezir, the *qāḍī* 'Izz al-Dīn. Its administration went to his other brother, who was long the governor of Denizli, and known there as the founder of a caravanserai. Finally, a hospice (*dār al-ṣulaḥā'*) at Antalya owes its existence to Karatay. All were richly endowed, bearing witness to the wealth of their donors, but also, like the foundations of others, to their traditionally Muslim orientation.

On the other hand, it was probably about 1254 that Karatay and the vezir 'Izz al-Dīn sent an embassy to the Great Khan Möngke led by the *amīr-dād* Fakhr al-Dīn 'Alī, who was destined to a brilliant future. They were disturbed to see Baiju and other Mongol military chiefs continually sending demands for tribute which, if there was a fixed amount, either surpassed it or was beyond the possibility of payment by the country. The embassy's business was to ask the suzerain for a reduction or a limit. Their success will appear in due course.

Was this embassy due to the situation of a government the attachment of which to Islam might appear politically troublesome, or to the intrigues of Baba Tuğrai, or was it simply because the Mongols normally required the personal attendance of the rulers from time to time? In 1254 ambassadors from Batu came to summon Kay Kāwūs, no doubt because he had attained what might be thought his majority at the age of nineteen. There might have been fears that the recent intrigues had alienated the Mongol ruler from Kay Kāwūs, and so it was judged useful that he in his turn should make the journey from which Kılıc Arslan had recently profited; but it might also be felt that in his absence some loyalties might grow cold. For the young sultan, encouraged as it was said by Türkeri, was leading a life of debauchery and disregarding the virtuous instruction that Karatay and the vezir tried to give him, and was distributing emirates to his favourites. So many complaints were made to Karatay about Türkeri that he had him banished, and put to death. Those who were dissatisfied also brought up the expensive, but perhaps unavoidable, multiplication of interpreters and *munshī*'s, and recalled that Kay Qubādh I at the height of his power had only two or four; so, for example, spoke the emir Shams al-Dīn Altınbeh. In the circumstances a meeting of the three sultans to discuss the Mongol summons was organized at Kayseri, to which Kay Kāwūs went from Aksaray. In the end it was decided to send the youngest, 'Alā' al-Dīn Kay Qubādh II, to make excuses for his brothers. He was accompanied by Tarantay, Shujā' al-Dīn the *nā'ib*, the *khwaja lâla* Muṣliḥ, and a certain Nūr al-Dīn 'Abdallāh. The two other young sultans remained at Konya.

There they soon quarrelled. Kay Kāwūs, it will be recalled, was the son of a Greek mother. He had Greek uncles, and furthermore he had perhaps married a daughter of John III Ducas Vatatzes. It is certain that subsequently he sought refuge and sometimes advice in the Empire of Nicaea. The malcontents followed normal practice in turning to Kılıc Arslan IV, the son of a Turkish mother, even though he represented the party of unconditional submission to the Mongols, as contrasted with Kay Kāwūs, who was trying to salvage something of the past. One of the magnates who had accompanied Kılıc Arslan to Turkestan encouraged him to flee from Konya to Nuṣrat al-Dīn, the son of Sinān al-Dīn Kaimaz Rūmī, the *subaşı* of Develi, and to summon there Ṣamṣām al-Dīn Kaimaz, the *amīr-'āriḍ* and *subaşı* of Kayseri, who was ill-disposed towards Kay Kāwūs because he had taken Niğde from him for the benefit of a little slave. This was done. Kılıc Arslan was enthroned at Kayseri, where other partisans gathered, including Bijār the Kurdish chief. At the caravanserai of 'Alā' al-Dīn, a stage from Aksaray, they burnt to death a group of nomads who resisted them. Yutaş the *beglerbegi*, sent by Kay Kāwūs in pursuit of Kılıc Arslan, they threw into prison at Develi. But at the same time Mu'īn al-Dīn Süleyman and Khaṭīr al-Dīn Zakariyyā reached Konya from the vicinity of Kayseri. The vezir 'Izz al-Dīn opened the treasury, and an army set out by way of Kırşehir in the province of Tuzağac. At the same time the illustrious Shaykh Ṣadr al-Dīn Konevi and Humām al-Dīn Shādbahār, the *nāẓir mulk*, were sent to restore peace with Kılıc Arslan, who was then on the campaign trail by Sivas, Malatya, Khartpert and Āmid. The plotters dragged out negotiations on the plain of Ahmedhisarı until Kılıc Arslan arrived with his army. There was a battle, which ended with the defeat of the rebel supporters of Kılıc Arslan. Nuṣrat al-Dīn and Ṣamṣām al-Dīn were captured, and put to death by order of Kay Kāwūs's uncles. In trying to reach Cilicia, Kılıc Arslan was taken by Turcomans, and handed over to Arslan Doğmuş, sent by Kay Kāwūs. A spectacular reconciliation of the two brothers ensued at Kayseri. Kılıc Arslan had to choose between living at Burğlu or Amasya. He chose the latter, but was nevertheless soon transferred, perhaps at the end of 1254, to Burğlu in order to be more remote from Mongol contacts.

It will be observed that the name of Karatay does not appear in the account of Kılıc Arslan's revolt. In fact Bar Hebraeus, Aksarayi and the author of *Tārīkh-i āl-i Saljūq* say that he died previously, the last giving the precise date of 28 Ramaḍān 652/11 November 1254. This is actually the date of his last extant document, the appendix to the *waqfiyya* of his *madrasa*. It is not impossible that, as Ibn Bībī says, he was involved in the decision to send Kay Qubādh, even if he was not still alive at the time of the mission's departure. Ibn Bībī, who gives no date for the revolt, puts Karatay's death in an account of events which at least can hardly be anterior to the revolt, and which he in fact places after it. It may be admitted that Karatay, who seems to have settled at Kayseri, had perhaps been ill recently, and in no position to take part in Kay Kāwūs's government at Konya.

Kılıc Arslan's revolt is difficult to date with certainty. According to Bar Hebraeus it was also in 1254. Neither inscriptions nor coins are of any help for these years, particularly as the fiction of the undivided sultanate was maintained. If Karatay's death might have left the young sultans under the influence of troublemakers, Kay Kāwūs's victory meant that no change of government resulted. The holders of high office named by Aksarayi at this point are those which were established by Karatay after the crisis of 1249, with the addition of one person as *mushrif*. Of greater importance, if it is accurate, is the mention of the real influence exercised by Mu'īn al-Dīn Süleyman and Fakhr al-Dīn 'Alī by reason of their *yarligh*s. The former may have had the honorary rank and pay of a vezir because of his father. Unfortunately it is impossible to be sure that Aksarayi has not pre-dated events in this period.

After his victory, Sultan Kay Kāwūs received embassies from the Caliph al-Musta'ṣim, the rulers of Mosul and Mardin, the Franks and the Byzantines. With his *atabeg* Arslan Doğmuş at Antalya, he gave himself up to the amusements of his age, but government went on. It seems that shortly after his victory, Fakhr al-Dīn 'Alī brought the *yarlighs* and *paizas* which had been requested for the determination of the financial obligations. On his return, incidentally, he had shown them to Baiju, who let him know that he knew how to get round them – it will soon appear how. In addition the ungovernable Turcomans had to be fought. The *Ağaceris* of the Maraş region were waylaying the caravans, and for years had plundered both the marches of Cilicia and northern Syria, and the Seljukid territories in this sector. The lord of Maraş, 'Imād al-Dīn, not knowing where to turn, offered his city to the sultan and to the ruler of Aleppo, to prevent its falling into the hands of the Turcomans or the Armenians. As others failed to do so, the Armenians took it in 1258. The vezir 'Izz al-Dīn and the *beglerbegi* Yutaş were on their way to fight the *Ağaceris*, when grave news arrived.

Baiju's expedition and the ensuing troubles

'Izz al-Dīn and Yutaş were suddenly made aware then that Baiju at the head of all his troops was invading Asia Minor. The reason did not lie in the internal disputes in the country, nor in the complaints which the Mongol chief might frame against Sultan Kay Kāwūs, but in the development of the Mongol empire. The Great Khan Möngke had appointed his brother Hülegü to govern Iran and to complete the conquest of western Asia, and had added the Seljukid protectorate to his sphere of action, whereas it had formerly been a dependency of Batu, the chief of the Mongols of Russia. At the beginning of 1256 Hülegü established himself in Iran. He brought with him important new troops, who needed pastures. Baiju received an order to leave the Mūghān meadows to them, and take his own beasts to pasture on the plateaux of Asia Minor. Was Hülegü ignorant or heedless of the fact that Möngke or his predecessors had made grants to the Seljukids which contradicted this, grants which furthermore were concerned with the revenue due to the Mongols, not with where they lived? This renders comprehensible what Baiju had shortly beforehand intimated to Fakhr al-Dīn 'Alī.

Baiju did not want war. He demanded the right for his troops to quarter themselves permanently in Asia Minor; but it was evident that this would be a serious matter for the Seljukid state because of the loss of resources, and the effective military control secured to the Mongols to the detriment of the Seljukid magnates. Then the internal disorder of Rūm would necessarily interfere with these events. Although it had long been decided to send 'Alā' al-Dīn Kay Qubādh to Möngke, and he had proceeded to the eastern provinces to make preparations for his journey, his departure had been delayed by the collection of presents and his brothers' hesitations, so that he was still in Armenia when Baiju's preparations became known. During the interval his brothers had wondered whether Möngke, who would see him without them, would make him their overlord. Kay Kāwūs was now certainly able to enjoin the ambassadors to make his excuses for the new reason of the death of Karatay, who had forbidden him to leave in view of the Turcoman danger.

But there were other matters. As has been seen, Mu'īn al-Dīn Süleyman was *persona grata* to Baiju. Perhaps Baba Tuğrai had also been in contact with him, and had conveyed unfavourable opinions of Kay Kāwūs. Niẓām al-Dīn Khurshīd, whom Kay Kāwūs had sent to negotiate with Baiju, brought back a new requirement, that Mu'īn al-Dīn should be appointed head chamberlain (*ḥājib al-ḥujjāb*) – in practice the controller of the sultanate. As 'Alā' al-Dīn Kay Qubādh set out for Batu, from whom he was to proceed to Qaraqorum, he wrote on seeing the Mongol forces, telling Kay Kāwūs to yield at any price. At Konya some were for submission, but the supporters of resistance won the day. They were of several categories: personal slaves of the sultan, who no doubt feared for their privileges; rigorous Muslims, partisans of the *jihād* against the Mongols, whose direct government would mean the treatment of Islam on the same level as other religions, and even perhaps favours to Christians; and, in spite of that, perhaps also the Greeks of Kay Kāwūs's entourage, who doubtless thought that the joint support of the Byzantines of Nicaea and the frontier Turcomans would allow resistance to be organized. Among these Greeks was the future emperor, Michael Palaeologus, a recent fugitive from Nicaea. Lightly armed contingents, partly recruited from the Turcoman tribesmen, were actually mustered, while Michael Palaeologus commanded the indigenous Christians.

Baiju was advancing rapidly, and all the great cities opened their gates as the plundering began. To the south of Aksaray, Yutaş and Arslan Doğmuş offered battle at the caravanserai of 'Alā' al-Dīn. As always in hostilities with the Mongols, there were desertions, here perhaps aggravated by Kay Kāwūs's behaviour towards the womenfolk of some emirs. Arslan Doğmuş had probably been in touch with Baiju, and changed sides during the battle. The vezir 'Izz al-Dīn found an appropriate death as a martyr. The Seljukid army was crushed on 23 Ramaḍān 654/15 October 1256. Michael Palaeologus and Yutaş fled to the latter's territory of Kastamonu. King Hetoum of Cilicia, who was returning from Qaraqorum, accompanied Baiju in this campaign before going to his realm.

While Sultan Kay Kāwūs fled, some of the magnates who had remained at Konya were trying to limit the disaster by conciliating the victor. While the treasurer, the *ustādh-dār* Niẓām al-Dīn ʿAlī b. Iltutmış (?), was occupied with containing the possible disorder of the *rinds*, Muʿīn al-Dīn Süleyman, Niẓām al-Dīn Khurshīd, Arslan Doğmuş and the *khaṭīb* of Konya obtained from Baiju, through his wife's mediation and the payment of tribute, freedom for Konya from pillage. They then went to Burğlu to find Kılıc Arslan, whom they brought to Konya. A certain Shams al-Dīn Kadıcık was nominated vezir, but died soon afterwards. Niẓām al-Dīn Khurshīd became *nāʾib*, being succeeded as *pervane* by Muʿīn al-Dīn Süleyman, to whose name this title (by which he will now be designated) was to remain attached in popular usage.

Kay Kāwūs himself had fled to Antalya, where he collected for himself and his household the priceless treasures of cash, letters of credit and precious objects amassed there, some since the time of Kay Qubādh I. He fled thence with his partisans, Uğurlu the *amīr-ākhūr*, Ḥusām al-Dīn the *ṭashtdār* and Hacı Baba to Lâdik by Denizli in the midst of the frontier Turcomans. In vain did Kılıc Arslan get Baiju to send a thousand Mongols under the command of his grandson in an attempt to capture him, or to negotiate with him while he was at Lâdik, and in vain did he write him a letter before Dhu'l-Qaʿda 654/*c.* December 1256. Kay Kāwūs was not safe however in Turcoman country, and moved on into Byzantine territory, with which his uncles had evidently secret contacts. It was no doubt at that time that the accession of Kılıc Arslan as sole sultan was proclaimed at Konya; his coinage with this title begins only in 655/1257. However, Baiju did not feel confidence even in Kılıc Arslan and his advisers. Among the *noyans* who accompanied him were two named Engürek and Khwāja *noyan*. The second was greedy, and one day he was found apparently poisoned. Niẓām al-Dīn was accused (with the Pervane as an accomplice, according to Aksarayi), and Baiju had him put to death. According to the same partial author, the Pervane succeeded in satisfying the Mongols without disorganizing the administration. In the spring Baiju withdrew. Before leaving Konya, he required the Pervane to dismantle the city's defences, which was done.

Baiju's departure was due to his recall by Hülegü, who was preparing for operations in Mesopotamia. It might be thought that Anatolia proper would not see him again for some time. Moreover, Kılıc Arslan preferred Kayseri or Tokat with the Pervane to living in Konya. These places were perhaps less afflicted, and in any case closer to the Mongols, with fewer links to Kay Kāwūs. He went there, but not to stay on this occasion as he had been brought to realize the need to go and do homage to Hülegü. This for the moment left the door wide open for the return of Kay Kāwūs. He had no wish to profit from the opportunity. Attempts were made in vain to induce him to come back. Just in time 'Alī Bahādur, whose duty it was to join him, returned to Konya to welcome back his old master. There was indeed no resistance in Anatolia to Kay Kāwūs. He had obtained significant Byzantine reinforcements from Theodore II Lascaris of Nicaea, to whom he ceded Lâdik by Denizli in return, and the Turcomans were not slow to occupy it. Back in Konya on 14 Rabīʿ II 655/2 May 1257, Kay Kāwūs caused Uğurlu the *jāndār*, his *amīr-ākhūr*, to put to death the *serleşker* installed by Kılıc Arslan at Niğde. From the year 655/1257 there are again coins struck in his name at Konya, Ankara and Gümüşpazar. It is also noteworthy that Yutaş, who used his influence on Kay Kāwūs for the holy war against the Mongols as protectors of the Christians, seized Tokat, the Pervane's home.

As regards Malatya, Kay Kāwūs had raised the Turcomans and Arabs of this province, perhaps after Baiju's invasion, and had more particularly drawn in the Kurds, two of whom received Malatya and Khartpert from him. These were Sharaf al-Dīn b. Shujāʿ al-Dīn Dāwūd Balas al-Hakkārī al-Maʿmūrī and Sharaf al-Dīn Muḥammad, perhaps a son of the famous Shaykh 'Adī, venerated by the Hakkārī Yazīdīs.[22] They were certainly not accepted by the people, who had rallied to Kılıc Arslan. Ibn Balas however pillaged the region of Claudias (Q̱ālāwdhiyya) with the monasteries of Mar Madiq and Mar Asya, and then went on to defend Āmid, which in the meanwhile had been attacked by the Artukids of Mayyāfāriqīn and Mardin, claiming to anticipate the intrigues of Badr al-Dīn Lu'lu' of Mosul. He fell into an ambush set up by the attacking army, and he and many of those with him were killed, and Āmid fell. Sharaf al-Dīn Muḥammad however marched on Kemah, but there he came up against the Mongol Engürek *noyan*, and lost his life also.

Thereupon Kay Kāwūs, now back in Konya, sent forces under the command of 'Alī Bahādur in a special attempt to put an end to the ravages of the *Ağaceris*. He succeeded in occupying Adiyaman and Malatya, in restoring order in the country of the monasteries of Mar Madiq, Mar Asya and Mar Dimat, and in capturing the Turcoman chief, Shuti Beg. However, a Mongol army in the service of Kılıc Arslan occupied Malatya and Elbistan, and obliged him to entrench himself in Kâhta, whence he escaped thanks to the Mongols' departure for Mesopotamia in September 1257. In 1258, now helped by the *Ağaceris*, he retook Malatya through famine, and executed the notables. Then he fled again before a new Mongol threat, killing on the way two persons evidently suspect in his eyes of complicity with the Mongols. As for Maraş, during these troubles King Hetoum of Cilician Armenia was authorized by Möngke to receive it from its lord, 'Imād al-Dīn, who, as has been mentioned, lacked the power to defend it against the *Ağaceris*.

Kılıc Arslan had however reached Hamadhān, where he received a *yarligh* from Hülegü confirming him as sultan of Rūm. Back in Erzincan, he learnt of what had happened in Konya. He distributed the villages of Erzincan in *iqṭāʿ* to his soldiers, promising them that in the event of victory they should have them in allod. The Pervane, who according to Ibn Bībī was 'the support of his rule', brought a thousand Mongols to extricate his family, who were in Tokat. He was beaten at the Yıldızdağ between Sivas and Tokat by a certain Shāh-Malik, and saved only by a relieving force brought from Erzincan on Kılıc Arslan's orders by one of his slaves. He then went to ask for more significant help from the Mongols, and received 10,000 men. They occupied Niksar, where they installed Kılıc Arslan, and then advanced on Tokat, where they invested the garrison commanded by Yutaş. At that point the embassy sent with 'Alā' al-Dīn Kay Qubādh to Möngke returned.

The embassy had had a lively time. Baba Tuğrai had rejoined it at Batu's court, along with the mother of Kay Khusraw II and others. He had forged a letter, allegedly from Kay Kāwūs, ordering Tarantay and his companions to give place to the new arrivals for the duration of the embassy. In spite of his endeavours, Batu decided to send both groups together to Möngke. After some days on the way, Baba Tuğrai and the young prince became separated from Tarantay, who was in charge of the baggage. During this time 'Alā' al-Dīn Kay Qubādh was found dead one night in the sole company of Muṣliḥ the *lâla*. He was sickly, but Muṣliḥ was accused and also, by some, Kay Kāwūs and Kılıc Arslan, who were said to have ordered this crime out of fear that Möngke might prefer their brother. Tarantay himself formally accused Baba Tuğrai to Möngke, who ordered an inquiry on their arrival. Tarantay convinced Möngke in the end, and consequently obtained satisfaction on the objects of his embassy. Kay Kāwūs was confirmed as sultan, the tribute was fixed and the Mongols were forbidden to cause damage to the country in other respects. Tarantay received a golden arrow from Möngke, his suite silver arrows and a *yarligh* and *paiza* for his master. Unfortunately for him, at this moment and simultaneously with bad news from Qubilai in China, Möngke received a report from Baiju of the resistance he had encountered in Rūm. Möngke was enraged and, before the inquiry into 'Alā' al-Dīn Kay Qubādh's death had finished, Baba Tuğrai demanded that the sultanate should be transferred to Kılıc Arslan. Möngke finally decided that it should be divided between the two brothers. He had moreover an underlying reason. For the great western expeditions which Hülegü was to carry out, it was important that there should be no internal rivalries to weaken the vassals whose help he needed. No doubt the double sultanate for Asia Minor appeared the least bad solution.

So the embassy returned to Asia Minor, and went to Kılıc Arslan, who granted Baba Tuğrai Ayyubhisar and Kırşehir, which he certainly did not occupy. Then Kay Kāwūs was invited to a conference on the carrying out of Möngke's decisions. He answered by sending his *pervane*, Tāj al-Dīn, while Kılıc Arslan sent Tarantay. Baba Tuğrai forbade the continuation of the war. In the end a treaty was concluded giving Kılıc Arslan the eastern provinces with Sivas, Kayseri and Sinop, while Kay Kāwūs kept the rest. The coins and inscriptions confirm this partition, perhaps made at the end of 1257. Moreover at that time it was more theoretical than real, as in both parts the same individual held the vezirate. This was Baba Tuğrai, restored to the post he had never resigned, and he now obtained Kastamonu as his remuneration. For a while the dominant influence on Kay Kāwūs was exercised by the constable, Michael Palaeologus, who was perhaps promoted to *beglerbegi*. He encouraged the sultan to settle at Antalya and, it is said, to neglect his duties as a Muslim. But with the reconciliation of Kay Kāwūs and Kılıc Arslan, and the simultaneous death of the Emperor Theodore II Lascaris, Michael was allowed through the mediation of the head of the church in Konya to return to Nicaea, where he was soon to acquire the throne.

There remained the making of peace with Hülegü, who had invested Kılıc Arslan not long before. The two sultans went to him; Kılıc Arslan with Baba Tuğrai and the Pervane. Hülegü made no difficulties over confirming the partition which Möngke had ordered in principle, or over the boundaries decided in advance by the two brothers. Āmid, which had been handed over to him by al-Kāmil's deputy, he passed to Kılıc Arslan. Baghdad had now fallen,[23] and Hülegü was now preparing to conquer Upper Mesopotamia and Syria, so peace on his Anatolian flank was particularly valuable to him. The two sultans were ordered to participate in the campaign, and so were present at the capture of Aleppo and Damascus, while other Mongols attacked Mardin and Mayyāfāriqīn whose lord had broken with the Mongols. Kay Kāwūs vainly attempted to persuade him to accept an attempt to mediate, while on the other hand he resisted the endeavours of al-Saʿīd of Mardin to get him to raise a revolt in Asia Minor. The other activities of the two sultans in regard to the Mongols consisted in expending (and hence in borrowing from the Mongol treasury) sums which were long to be a source of difficulty – all the more so since Baba Tuğrai for his part borrowed as much to ease his start as vezir. To repay the loans, it was expected that they would pay annually, in addition to the normal tribute, 200,000 dinars in cash, 3,000 bars of gold or their value, 500 horses, 500 mules and finally 500 pieces of textiles, perhaps of Antalya. To these were later added Baba Tuğrai's debts, since he left no personal fortune when he died. When Hülegü left for Syria, he gave the two sultans leave to return to Rūm, one to Konya, the other to Tokat or Kayseri; but he mistrusted Kay Kāwūs, and made him hand back to Kılıc Arslan the *yarligh* and *paiza* he had received from Möngke. At about this time in 1260, Baba Tuğrai died.

These two events inaugurated new tension between the sultans. In the first place, the single vezirate could not be retained. Kay Kāwūs appointed as vezir Fakhr al-Dīn ʿAlī, whom he had made his *nāʾib* at the time of his reconciliation with the Mongols. He was succeeded as *nāʾib* by Amīn al-Dīn Mīkāʾīl, hitherto the *mustawfī*; while with Kılıc Arslan, the vezirate fell to the Pervane, who continued to hold his former title in addition. This nomination was made by virtue of a *yarligh* from Hülegü, as was also that of Tāj al-Dīn Muʿtazz as *beglerbegi*. He was a son of Mujīr al-Dīn Ṭāhir, former chief *qāḍī* of the Khwarazmian realm, who had been sent on an embassy from Jalāl al-Dīn to Kay Qubādh I.

The situation of the two Seljukid territories in regard to the Mongols was not identical. It is evident that Kılıc Arslan's share could be, and was, much more directly under their control. Moreover Tāj al-Dīn was essentially the agent for the *īlkhān*'s interests in Rūm and, with the chief Mongol envoy, his business was the repayment of the loans made to the sultan and Baba Tuğrai in accordance with the agreed terms. He began by going to Kay Kāwūs, who was then at Qubādhābād on the way to his residence at Antalya; but Kay Kāwūs, according to Aksarayi, had under the Greeks' influence neglected the collection of the money due. Tāj al-Dīn went on to Kılıc Arslan, where the Pervane paid his claims in full. Kay Kāwūs was accused of concerting a revolt with the Turcomans. The future was indeed to reveal links with them, but there were also difficulties; and at this very time he was fighting a disastrous campaign in the mountain country between Antalya and Alanya against the Turcomans of Mehmed Beg (said by Aksarayi to be the chief of the frontier Turcomans), who detested the sultan's Byzantine alliance. Kay Kāwūs was also accused of negotiating with Egypt. It is certainly true that he did so when he felt himself threatened, going so far as to offer half of his realm to Baybars, the Mamluk sultan, who was to decide on the boundaries. It is also true that Baybars sent him a force of 300 horsemen, but too late. For the time being, Tāj al-Dīn returned to Hülegü, and delivered a report hostile to Kay Kāwūs, to whom the *īlkhān* sent a letter filled with disturbing threats.

Scenting the Pervane's intrigues, Kay Kāwūs attempted a rapprochement with Kılıc Arslan, and sent Fakhr al-Dīn ʿAlī to negotiate. But it was already too late. A strong Mongol army was arriving from the east. With Kılıc Arslan and the Pervane, it reached Aksaray, then Obruk. Fakhr al-Dīn ʿAlī judged resistance to be impossible. The Pervane sent him an offer of the vezirate of the whole Seljukid state, if he would go over to Kılıc Arslan. He yielded to the seductive offer. At the news of this, Kay Kāwūs hastened to Konya, picked up his treasures and, while ʿAlī Bahādur reached the frontier country beyond Sivrihisar, went to Constantinople, followed by Uğurlu the *amīr-ākhūr*, Ḥusām al-Dīn the *tashtdār* and Hacı Baba, the companions of the first exile, and at least one of his uncles. But if he had hoped to reconquer his realm from there, he was to be cruelly deceived; the policy of the Emperor Michael VIII Palaeologus, who had entered Constantinople a short while before (August 1261), was to ally with the Mongols of Iran against those of Russia, for the two groups had recently broken off relations. So he showed little interest in his frontier in Asia Minor, so that he would neither clash with the Mongols, nor with the Turcomans as his sole possible allies in the event of a Mongol threat. Thus Kay Kāwūs ended by becoming an embarrassment to him in Constantinople, or even with the sultan's companions displaying a possibly dangerous opposition to him. He was imprisoned, then liberated by troops of the Mongols of Russia. Thenceforward he lived in the Crimea until his death in 1279–80. His sons were later to try their luck in Asia Minor.

Kılıc Arslan entered into possession of Konya on 14 Ramaḍān 659/13 August 1261, but he was far from being the master of the whole of Anatolia. Kay Kāwūs's partisans still infested a number of provinces. Uğurlu and 'Alī Bahādur provoked a rising in the region of Çankırı and Ankara, and even advanced on Konya, but were defeated at the caravanserai of Altınbeh. Uğurlu certainly escaped, since he reappeared at Constantinople, where he was compromised in a conspiracy for which Kay Kāwūs was blamed, and was blinded on the emperor's order. At the same time Shāh-Malik, who, as mentioned, was recently operating in the Danişmendid province, revolted. He capitulated on the promise that his life would be spared, but was put to death by the Mongols. Another rebel stirred up some parts of the same province and that of Kastamonu. The *amīr-ākhūr* Asad installed himself in the fortress of Selime in the province of Aksaray, where he ended by being taken and put to death by Nūr al-Dīn Jibrīl b. Caca, the new governor of Kırşehir. With the possible exception of the last, these risings could only have been carried out with the cooperation of the northern Turcomans. The first two rebels may have been Turcoman chiefs themselves. All these revolts however were ultimately crushed, even if the Turcomans were not destroyed.

The situation of the Seljukid-Mongol government was more serious in regard to the Turcomans of the west and south. Mehmed Beg, who seems to have been the chief of almost all the Turcomans of the south-west, found himself at war to the east of his own territory with Kay Kāwūs in alliance with the Byzantines, as will appear. He had hanged some of the sultan's men from the walls of his chief city, perhaps Denizli. This city had recently been ceded by Kay Kāwūs to the Greeks, and retaken from them by the Turcomans; Mehmed Beg certainly held it. At the time when Kılıc Arslan was installed in Konya by the Mongols, Mehmed Beg with his brother, his son-in-law and another kinsman in fact requested Hülegü to let them hold their territories directly of him. These comprised Lâdik-Denizli, Honaz and Dalaman lying opposite Rhodes. Hülegü agreed, and sent them a diploma and a flag, as well as a military commander. Shortly afterwards he summoned them to come in person to his court. Mehmed refused, so the Mongol army of Rūm set out with Kılıc Arslan to fight him. He was crushed in the plain of the lower Dalaman, thanks to his son-in-law's treachery and, although he had surrendered on the promise that his life would be spared, he was put to death at Burğlu. His brother-in-law became the chief of the Turcomans of the south-west under the suzerainty of Kılıc Arslan, and it is said that the authority of the Mongols was recognized as far as the frontiers of Istanbul (660/1262).

The situation in the Isaurian and Cilician Taurus was still more serious because of the strength of the Turcomans in this sector, and their proximity to the vital centres of the Seljukid state. As has been seen, there had been trouble from this direction since shortly after Kösedağ. Other chiefs of Turcoman bands had come into prominence on the Armenian front in the following years. In the hinterland of the coastal stronghold of Korykos (Corycus) an Afşar and another Turcoman are particularly mentioned in 1254 and 1258 respectively. It will be remembered that in 1258 Turcomans more to the north-east captured Kılıc Arslan. From this same period a new and more important chief is mentioned. He was Karaman, and was to be the founder of a dynasty, but it is impossible to know his relationship to the Turcomans previously mentioned.

Later bards of the Karamanid dynasty tell stories of its origins in which, it would seem, there are real historical memories, but with the generations and homonyms confused, mingled almost inextricably with imaginary matter intended to glorify the rulers for whom they worked. Around Karaman revolve, in their presentation, almost all the eponyms of the Turcoman dynasties, even Mongols of Asia Minor and beyond, not to mention Kurdish notables, Christian converts and so forth. Their possessions also are represented as deriving from Seljukid grants (although not without episodes of disagreement), and in particular as from the most glorious of them, Kay Qubādh I. They bring Karaman's ancestors from the far north of Ādharbāyjān, with a halt of several years in the region of Sivas. Although this cannot be verified, it may be true of several groups. Karaman's father is named Nure Sufi (Nūr al-Dīn), who is depicted like the Turcoman shaykh who with Baba Isḥāq stirred up the movements among the Turcomans of central and eastern Asia Minor twenty years earlier. The real connections among these various Turcomans will be discussed later. While we cannot be as ready as the bards to grant their hero the lordship of the whole province of Ermenek from Lârende to Korykos (which was then in the hands of the Hospitallers), the few scraps of available information do indeed show them in this region, i.e. in the region of Turcoman settlement resulting from Kay Qubādh's conquests. This renders unlikely the immigration stories taken as a whole.

Neither, naturally, had the *Ağaceri*s of the eastern Taurus been subdued before 1261. In 660/1262 Hülegü sent Baiju to carry out a systematic harrying of these parts, and many Turcomans fled to Syria. Others remained; the Mongols were always suspicious of them, but they were no longer to cause serious trouble. The same agitation of the Turcomans could also be seen on the other frontiers, e.g. those of Georgia. 'Turks of Syria', i.e. of the Euphrates borders, held sway in 1258 in the region of Ani, as did others claiming to be under 'the sultan of Erzincan', perhaps meaning Kılıc Arslan. In these parts, which adjoined the Mongols' lines of communication, order was no doubt vigorously reestablished, and we hear of no further trouble. However, the Turcoman world was everywhere in motion, not only because of the enfeeblement of the Seljukid state, but also because of difficulties among the Turcomans themselves, arising from or provoked by the Mongols.

For the moment it might seem that the Pervane and the Mongols had succeeded, if not in suppressing, at least in containing the Turcoman danger. Moreover, there had been brought to light the complicity with the Turcomans of some of Kay Kāwūs's former adherents, although others might have incurred suspicion simply for having served him, or might have been regarded with jealousy by the Pervane for personal reasons. So he proceeded to an internal purge, and ordered the execution of the *mustawfī*, the *mushrif*, the army judge and other high officials. The *mustawfī* was replaced by Majd al-Dīn Mehmed b. Ḥusayn, the *mushrif* by Jalāl al-Dīn Maḥmūd (later to become *mustawfī*), the son of the *amīr al-ḥājj*. Amīn al-Dīn Mīkā'īl remained as *nā'ib*, and Fakhr al-Dīn 'Alī vezir, which in no way signified their pre-eminence over the Pervane. He remained in fact the absolute head of the government, whether or not he assumed, as in an inscription, the title of 'King of the emirs and the vezirs'. Above all, the government of the provinces was resumed by establishing more widely than before almost autonomous marchlands for the benefit of the magnates of the realm. Fakhr al-Dīn 'Alī's sons received Kütahya, Sandıklı, Gurgurum and Akşehir. Bahā' al-Dīn, the Pervane's son-in-law, became *malik al-sawāḥil* for all the southern coastal provinces. He resided at Antalya, and under this title no doubt took part in the mopping-up operations against the Karamanids and Mehmed Beg's Turcomans. The Pervane himself took Tokat, Amasya and Niksar, and was soon to add Sinop in conditions that will appear. His old client, Sharaf al-Dīn Mas'ūd b. Khaṭīr, received the appointment of *beglerbegi* with the *iqṭāʿ* of Niğde, which kept watch over the central Taurus. It seems that henceforward there were always Mongol troops quartered in Asia Minor to maintain order beside Seljukid troops, which from now on were insufficient and possibly opposed to them. At the same time the Mongol troops were ready to join in battles in Syria, and must have had royal demesne land (*injü*) assigned to them, by so much diminishing Seljukid potentiality. Finally, Tāj al-Dīn Muʿtazz returned and, as security for the celebrated loans, or to establish his position, obtained Kastamonu, formerly belonging to Baba Tuğrai, then Aksaray and Develikarahisar. The Mongol envoys were always at his side.

Only a gap remained in the external reconstruction of the state. In 657/1259 the ruler of Trebizond, the Grand Comnenus, had regained Sinop, profiting from the disorder in Asia Minor. In Ramaḍān 663/June 1265, according to Ibn Shaddād, the Pervane, who had gone with Kılıc Arslan to do homage to Abaqa, the new *īlkhān*, obtained permission to reconquer Sinop, and duly organized the enterprise. Aksarayi places the reconquest just after Abaqa's accession, but the narrative does not exclude the possibility that it had been taken before this. However, Bar Hebraeus, Ibn Bībī, Aksarayi and the *Tārīkh-i āl-i Saljūq* agree that the reconquest was before the death of Kılıc Arslan. If these writers place his death in 664/1265–66 (according to the last, Jumādā II 664/March–April 1266), Ibn al-Fuwaṭī by contrast places it earlier, in 663/1264–65. This date appears to be confirmed by a coin of Kay Khusraw III dated 663, unless there has been an error of the mint or the publisher of the coin. There is even an inscription from Sinop itself, the text of which indicates that it was made just after the reconquest and dated 661/1262–63, if the reading is correct. Ibn Bībī indeed claims that the reconquest took two years, perhaps meaning all the operations in that province. The writer is inclined to admit that the enterprise was made during the lifetime of Hülegü and Kılıc Arslan, but that the administration of Sinop was finally regulated only after Abaqa's accession. However it may be, the campaign consisted of combined operations by land and sea, for the Turks had not lost all the coastlands, and they possessed Samsun. A certain Tāj al-Dīn Kılıc is distinguished among the attackers; while the Greek governor, Ghidrān or Ghidrās, defended himself fiercely and died in the defeat. The war was fought with troops recruited in the Danişmendid province, the Pervane's territory, so he awarded Sinop to himself personally. Inscriptions prove that he set to work at once to reconstruct it on a firm Muslim basis by constructing or restoring a mosque, a *madrasa* and so forth.

In the history of all the years during which his name occupied so large a place, Kılıc Arslan appears as no more than a puppet. It was wearisome to him to be an adult. He and his brother were blamed for their orgies, and in his anger he began to attack the magnates. He brought about the death of Kay Kāwūs's Greek uncle, who had been the governor of Burğlu when he was a prisoner there, but who was also the father of a daughter-in-law of Fakhr al-Dīn ʿAlī, which turned Fakhr al-Dīn against him. He was so enraged against Sharaf al-Dīn b. al-Khaṭīr that he saved his life only by the payment of a great fine. He even spoke unwisely to Tāj al-Dīn Muʿtazz. Finally he let it be known that the Pervane's appropriation of Sinop was offensive to him. Sharaf al-Dīn easily convinced the Pervane that the sultan was hatching a plot against him, and intriguing with Baybars. Perhaps the Pervane spoke of this to Abaqa, who may have authorized him as his deputy to take action against traitors, whoever they might be. In any event, he reached an agreement with Tāj al-Dīn Muʿtazz, perhaps Fakhr al-Dīn ʿAlī, and Nabski *noyan*, the chief of the Mongols, then at Kırşehir, and other Mongols. They advanced on Aksaray, where they were joined by reinforcements from Niğde and bands of miserable wretches brought together by Ibn Caca from Kırşehir. Kılıc Arslan went out to meet them, and had a stormy argument with the Pervane. On the initiative of the Mongol commander, he was brought under duress to a banquet given by the Pervane. There he was given drink, and strangled, perhaps in 663/1265. His son, Kay Khusraw III, aged from two to six years according to the sources, was installed in his place with the Pervane as his tutor and regent.

CHAPTER SEVENTEEN

The government of the Pervane

Did the failure to condemn Fakhr al-Dīn ʿAlī, the military checks of the Mongols, and the authoritarianism and financial demands of their representatives in Asia Minor lead the Pervane to harbour some mistrust and animosity towards them? His ambition and perhaps the interests of the country might have induced him to be the sole representative of the Mongol power. It can only be said that the preliminaries to a breach are visible from about 1272 with, as a counterpart, the establishment of contact with the Mamluks by the Pervane. Unfortunately there is no information on the subject in any source from Asia Minor, and only two contemporary biographies of Baybars by Ibn ʿAbd al-Ẓāhir and ʿIzz al-Dīn Ibn Shaddād respectively are available without being subject to outside control.

According to these sources, in Shawwāl 770/May 1272 Baybars received in Damascus an embassy sent jointly by the Pervane and Samaghar *noyan*, the Mongol chief in Rūm. Its purpose was the establishment of peaceful relations (according to Ibn ʿAbd al-Ẓāhir), which may be the court biographer's gloss on a demand for submission, which is Ibn Shaddād's version. Baybars forthwith sent off two envoys, who met Samaghar near Sivas, then the Pervane in Konya, and he conducted them to Abaqa. The negotiations, such as they were, proved ineffective. According to Ibn Shaddād, Baybars rejected the idea of submission to Abaqa, and called on him to hand over the Muslim territory he held, while Ibn ʿAbd al-Ẓāhir asserts a more positive threat. According to him, the Mamluk envoys told Abaqa that Möngke Temür, the khan of the Golden Horde, had several times suggested that Baybars and he should jointly attack Abaqa, and partition his lands. An embassy from Abaqa in Ṣafar 771/August–September 1271 was coldly received by Baybars in Damascus and sent back. In the following month the *īlkhān* sent an invading force into northern Syria, and the frontier town of al-Bīra (now Birecik) was laid under siege. Troops from Rūm participated in the action, and comprised 3,000 horsemen led by the Pervane, the *beglerbegi* Sharaf al-Dīn b. al-Khaṭīr, the *atabeg* Arslan Doğmuş, and the *nā'ib* Amīn al-Dīn Mīkā'īl. Baybars himself led the successful relieving action, and Mongol forces withdrew. The sultan's exploits in the battle are celebrated at length in prose and verse by Ibn 'Abd al-Ẓāhir. No doubt a lightning attack by the Mamluks on the territory of Claudias (below Malatya), noted in 1273 by Bar Hebraeus, was a reprisal.

While the Pervane was with Abaqa, he complained to him about the *īlkhān*'s brother, Ajay, who, he said, threatened his life. He obtained a promise that Ajay and Samaghar would be replaced by Tuqu *bitikçi noyan.*[24] The promise however was not fulfilled, and the Pervane feared that Ajay had heard, and was preparing vengeance. So he sent an appeal to Baybars, promising to become his vassal if the sultan would undertake a campaign to rid him of Ajay and Samaghar; but, when Baybars replied and laid down his conditions, Ajay and Samaghar had in fact been recalled. This ended negotiations for the time being, at the end of 672/spring 1274.

Perhaps Fakhr al-Dīn 'Alī's journey to Abaqa, which took place at this time, was connected with the recall of Ajay, who had been implicated in his fall. Ajay's successor, Tuqu, in any case recovered the vezirate for him. It is impossible to know whether the Pervane had sought a reconciliation with Fakhr al-Dīn 'Alī in his own interest, or had been deceived. However it may be, Ajay's designated successor was indeed Tuqu, assisted by one Tudun. It would certainly be easier for the Pervane to confer with *noyans* than with a prince of the blood, and one also feels that the replacement of Ajay and Samaghar by Tuqu and Tudun was also that of one clientele of friends by another. It must not be assumed however that there was any relaxation of the Mongol grip. When Tuqu, perhaps somewhat later, reached Asia Minor, he had an order from Abaqa (who no doubt was not fooled by the Pervane's honeyed phrases) to send him a precise statement of the finances of Rūm, and to maintain control of the whole administration, including that of the Pervane.

The Pervane in fact renewed his contacts with Baybars, inciting him to turn Ajay's recall to profit by an attack on the Mongols, at least in the shape of an attack on their allies, the Armenians of Cilicia. While King Leon II had given one of his sisters in marriage to the Pervane, the operation suggested would allow the latter to continue his double game better than direct Mamluk intervention in Asia Minor with its uncertain outcome. Perhaps the Pervane thought of profiting from the proximity of the Mamluk troops to prepare for a revolt but, as there appeared to be no sign of resistance to Tuqu's demands, he could only defer to circumstances for the time being.

Naturally, as all this is probably derived from the accounts given in Egypt by the Pervane's envoys, it is consequently in danger of depicting him as more at variance with the Mongols than he actually was, and of giving the impression that the Mongol residents made innovations where there were precedents of which Ibn Shaddād and Ibn 'Abd al-Ẓāhir were unaware. Immediately after the accession of Kay Khusraw III, Aksarayi notes a division of the taxes into four categories, which he inserts there either without its being an innovation, or because on the contrary he intends to present it as such without saying so explicitly. As one, if not two, of the taxes mentioned bears a Mongol name, it is not difficult to conclude that there was at least a partial reorganization of the Seljukid fiscal system, which cannot easily have occurred before the firm and unified establishment of the Mongol protectorate around 1261. It is hard in every way to see the fiscal interventions of Ajay and Tuqu as unprecedented, but no doubt the earlier instances lacked detailed record in the fiscal officials' registers.

However this may be, in 674/1275–76 Ajay, who had not accepted his recall, reappeared in Asia Minor, where his stay was doubtless not unprofitable. Tuqu, the Pervane, and the sultan himself were again summoned by Abaqa, and it may only have been then that Tuqu obtained Fakhr al-Dīn 'Alī's return to the vezirate. On their return to Rūm, they learnt that Ajay had executed some agents of the Pervane and of Ḍiyā' al-Dīn Maḥmūd b. al-Khaṭīr, and informed Abaqa. He again recalled Ajay, who wrote to his brother that the Pervane and Tuqu were plotting against him. The Pervane, who had his suspicions, and feared that Abaqa's reply would be dangerous, succeeded in taking the *īlkhān*'s envoy by surprise. He made him drunk, and seized the letter to find that Ajay was given authority to put him to death. So at least the story was told by his envoys to Baybars. While sending presents to Ajay to disarm his suspicions, the Pervane recorded before a *qāḍī* the plan of Ajay to murder him and Tuqu, which, he said, would have been followed by the handing over of the country to Baybars. Thereupon in an effort to settle these intrigues, Abaqa summoned Ajay, Tuqu, the Pervane and the *beglerbegi* Tarantay, as well as the Armenian bishop of Erzincan, Mar Hisya Sarkis, in whom he had sufficient confidence to hand over to him the government of the city, and who had accompanied the Pervane and Tuqu on their previous visit to the *īlkhān*. The Pervane, who mistrusted Tarantay, granted him Erzincan in *iqṭā'*, according to Ibn Shaddād, as well as the guardianship of the sultan, in order to conciliate him. Sarkis had asked for Erzincan, promising a contingent of 500 horsemen in return, but had to be content with compensation, as no *iqṭā'* had ever been granted to a cleric. As for the disputes in Anatolia, for the moment all that is known is that Abaqa kept Ajay at his side. Such at least is Ibn Shaddād's presentation of events. It must however be borne in mind that this writer must have learnt of developments retrospectively from the reports of a succession of embassies, and thus there is the possibility of some overlap of accounts, in particular those of the first and second struggles between the Pervane and Ajay – if indeed there were two. As Ibn ʿAbd al-Ẓāhir's account of the events of 674/1275–76 is almost wholly lost, it cannot be used to complement Ibn Shaddād.

In any event, it was necessary for Abaqa to settle the disputes in Anatolia in order to prepare a new enterprise against al-Bīra. Half of the attacking army was composed of non-Mongol contingents, among which those of Rūm were again led by the Pervane in person. A small troop which he had sent to make a sudden attack happened to seize some envoys from Baybars in their vicinity. They were carrying letters which alluded to the previous negotiations. The letters were brought to the Mongol chief, Atabay *noyan*, who threatened to massacre all the Muslims in the army, but then let himself be persuaded that it was a ruse thought up by King Leon of Cilicia. Nevertheless he sent the letters on to Abaqa. As the resistance of al-Bīra continued, Atabay sent to ask the advice of Tarantay and Ḥusām al-Dīn Bījār. Convinced by them, he raised the siege, which had lasted from 8 to 17 Jumādā II 674/29 November to 8 December 1275, and withdrew to Malatya.

According to Ibn Shaddād, collaboration with the Mongols now appeared impossible to the Pervane and his adherents. A group of conspirators comprising Ḥusām al-Dīn Bījār, his son who was *muqṭaʿ* of Diyār Bakr, Sharaf al-Dīn Masʿūd and Ḍiyāʾ al-Dīn Maḥmūd b. al-Khaṭīr, and Amīn al-Dīn Mīkāʾīl, swore an alliance with Baybars, while the *atabeg* Majd al-Dīn and the *mustawfī* Jalāl al-Dīn refused to cooperate, and Tarantay held himself incommunicado. An envoy was sent to Baybars with a copy of the oath, requesting his armed intervention, on condition that Kay Khusraw should remain sultan of Rūm, but should pay the Mamluk sultan the tribute which he paid to the Mongols. Baybars however politely rejected the invitation on the grounds of the aridity of their country, but expressed the hope of coming the next spring. The Pervane was intensifying his policy of duplicity and reinsurance; it was dangerous but hitherto successful, and it was perhaps the only practical one.

Already, and especially in the struggles between Kılıc Arslan IV and Kay Kāwūs II, Anatolian emirs were seen to take sides against the Mongols because of what they regarded as their excessively pro-Christian attitude, while the Mongols in return, as has just appeared, suspected all Muslims of hostility towards them. There was now a dramatic episode which illustrated this antagonism, and provoked fresh defection to Baybars's profit. The very old Kurdish *muqṭaʿ* of Khartpert, Ḥusām al-Dīn Bījār, may have had a grudge against Bishop Sarkis, Abaqa's protégé, who was killed in an ambush together with his son. Bar Hebraeus attributes this to Bījār in 1276, while Ibn Shaddād places the murder in Ramaḍān 675/February 1277, and names as responsible a brother of the Pervane, the governor of Erzincan, acting on the Pervane's express order, as he complained of Sarkis's anti-Muslim influence with Abaqa. Bar Hebraeus adds that Bījār had to flee to Egypt; but according to Ibn Shaddād, who confirms the flight, it was brought about by his son, Bahādur. He was brother-in-law to two brothers, Mongol officers, who had recently, and with his complicity, put to death a third brother, who was still a nomad. He had demanded wealth from them, and threatened to complain to Abaqa. The murder was perhaps instigated by the Pervane. At all events, Bahādur and the two Mongols accompanied Bījār to Egypt, taking a year's taxes from Diyār Bakr, Bahādur's *iqṭāʿ*. Thereafter they were among the keenest instigators of Baybars's intervention in Rūm. Their flight was however probably not to the Pervane's taste as he was just then under the obligation to be absent, as will appear, and feared that it would bring him prematurely into disfavour with Abaqa. His son, Muhadhdhab al-Dīn, who was his deputy during his absence, sent the Mongol chief, Nabshi *noyan*, still in Rūm or perhaps back again, to follow up the fugitives, but he was too late to catch them.[25]

At the same time, however, whether on Abaqa's initiative or that of the Pervane is unknown, a marriage was arranged between the *īlkhān* and a sister of Kay Khusraw III, who had to be escorted to the Mongol court. The *atabeg* Majd al-Dīn, the *mustawfī* Jalāl al-Dīn and Tarantay accompanied the Pervane to Sivas, and then returned to Kayseri to keep watch over the sultan and the country, while the Pervane went on his way, accompanied by the *nā'ib* Amīn al-Dīn Mīkā'īl and the vezir Fakhr al-Dīn ʿAlī. During his absence, the military defence of the Seljukid territory was placed particularly in the hands of Tāj al-Dīn Kivi, the *serleşker* of the Danişmendid province, which was under the command of the Pervane, and Sinān al-Dīn, son of the *atabeg* Arslan Doğmuş, the commandant of the frontiers. Apart from Tarantay, others no doubt lacked serious military forces at their disposal.

Up to that point, all these intrigues had gone on under cover. Now the drama was about to unfold, although one cannot tell the extent to which it had been organized or foreseen by the Pervane, or whether it was directed against him, or done without his knowledge.

During his absence, early in Muḥarram 675/June 1276, a body of Baybars's troops under the command of Baktūt al-Atābakī appeared on the Seljukid borders, summoned by Sharaf al-Dīn Masʿūd b. al-Khaṭīr directly after the Pervane's departure. What had led him to do this? It is most likely that, being compromised in the Pervane's previous intrigues, he feared that any reconciliation of the Pervane with the Mongols would be at his expense.

Moreover as *muqṭaʿ* of the province of Niğde, he was the best situated of any to have the support of numerous Turcomans, and to effect a junction with the Mamluk forces. He had evidently to act quickly to take advantage of the Pervane's absence.

Baybars naturally did not wish to embark on such an adventure without a guarantee. Baktūt brought letters to the principal emirs of Rūm intended to obtain a specific oath of fealty from each of them, and to agree upon a rendezvous at Kayseri when his arrival was imminent. Ibn al-Khaṭīr set out for Elbistan by way of Pınarbaşı on the pretext of defending the frontier. The army of Elbistan easily overcame the few Mongols in the region, and joined the Mamluk troops, which it accompanied into Syria pending the real offensive. Ibn al-Khaṭīr however turned about, and marched on Kayseri by way of the caravanserai of Karatay. Although Tāj al-Dīn Kivi was one of the emirs sounded out by Baybars, and Tarantay had translated Baybars's letters to the emirs who knew no Arabic, neither seemed to have remained in agreement with Ibn al-Khaṭīr longer than was necessary to learn his plans, and to denounce them. Perhaps following instructions given them by the Pervane, anticipating Ibn al-Khaṭīr's insubordination, they hastened to Kayseri in order to arrange with Muhadhdhab al-Dīn, the Pervane's son and deputy, for the murder of Ibn al-Khaṭīr and his son as they approached. However, Ibn al-Khaṭīr received warning through agents of his brother, Ḍiyāʾ al-Dīn Maḥmūd, in Muhadhdhab al-Dīn's entourage. In the interview which he had with Tāj al-Dīn and Sinān al-Dīn, the son of Arslan Doğmuş, the *subaşı* of Konya, who had come to summon him to appear before the sultan, it was he who ridded himself of them by murder.

Muhadhdhab al-Dīn's behaviour was equivocal. On the one hand, he gives the impression of participating in the anti-Mongol movement, if (as reported by Ibn Shaddād, evidently according to Diyāʾ al-Dīn Mahmūd) he had the Mongol subordinates of Nabshi and Tuqu arrested. In the light of subsequent events, it is difficult to imagine that they had been won over to Ibn al-Khaṭīr. On the other hand, he was in conflict with Ibn al-Khaṭīr, and perhaps the arrest of the Mongols was due to the sultan acting under other influences; for after Ibn al-Khaṭīr had vainly begged Tarantay to reconcile him with Muhadhdhab al-Dīn, he had no difficulty in being received by the sultan, whereas Muhadhdhab al-Dīn entrenched himself in the family stronghold of Tokat. Ibn al-Khaṭīr's agreement with the sultan entailed the adherence of Majd al-Dīn the *atabeg*, Tarantay, the *mustawfī* Jalāl al-Dīn Maḥmūd and the *amīr-dād*. Ibn al-Khaṭīr took them all, including the sultan, to his *iqṭāʿ* of Niğde. At the same time he sent his brother Ḍiyāʾ al-Dīn to Baybars at Ḥimṣ, urging him to hasten as otherwise his accomplices would be crushed (Ṣafar 675/July–August 1276). Ḍiyāʾ al-Dīn was accompanied by the sons or brothers of Majd al-Dīn the *atabeg*, of

Tarantay, and of Jalāl al-Dīn the *mustawfī*. They went under duress, more or less as hostages.

Unfortunately for the accomplices, Baybars deemed it impossible to undertake the campaign at the height of the summer dry season. Reproaching them for having acted precipately, as his plans with the Pervane were for the end of the year, he advised them to entrench themselves in their strongholds, and await his coming in the winter. The chief of the small force which he sent them, however, retraced his steps on the frontier at al-Ḥadath al-Ḥamrā' on hearing of the approach of Mongol forces which he was incapable of resisting.

The Pervane was in fact on his way back, accompanied by Mongol troops. Informed on his arrival at Erzurum of what had happened, he accelerated his march. The presence of those troops left him no option for the moment but to play for a Mongol victory and turn to account, in the event of an Egyptian victory, that he had led the Mongol troops into a trap. Tuqu and Tudun were in command of these troops, now under the personal direction of Abaqa's brother Qongqurtay. Ibn al-Khaṭīr's camp was sometimes at Niğde itself, sometimes in the basin of Develikarahisar. He was unable to prevent encirclement by a Mongol army, but just succeeded in escaping to the fortress of Lu'lu'a, where he had taken the precaution of hoarding supplies. The Pervane however regained possession of the sultan. An armed detachment under Sayf al-Dīn Jālīsh went to summon the commandant of Lu'lu'a to hand Ibn al-Khaṭīr over with his associates, and he complied, although he was a former *ghulām* of Ibn al-Khaṭīr. The prisoners were taken to Qongqurtay in his winter quarters on the Delice, a tributary of the Kızılırmak, and the trial of the rebels was held in a judicial assembly in Mongol style, in the presence of the Pervane, Tuqu, Tudun and Karay, a Mongol chief. Sultan Kay Khusraw, the first to appear, excused himself on the grounds of his youth and his powerlessness to resist the great emirs. Tarantay and Jalāl al-Dīn the *mustawfī* alleged duress, as proved by the murder of Tāj al-Dīn Kivi, and obtained pardon on condition of the payment of fines or the confiscation of goods. The Pervane however killed Kibe, the sultan's *lâla*, in cold blood, perhaps because he knew too much, or because he was responsible for the sultan's faults. Finally, Ibn al-Khaṭīr defended himself by accusing the Pervane himself of being the source of the whole plot. He withdrew the accusation under torture, and designated his accomplices. All were executed. Ibn al-Khaṭīr's head was sent to Konya, one of his hands to Ankara, the other to Erzincan. Meanwhile in the other camp, Baybars incarcerated the son of Tarantay, the brother of the *atabeg* and the brother of the *mustawfī*, as a reprisal for the adherence of their father or brother respectively to the cause of the Pervane and the Mongols. They were set free in the following year, on Baybars's death.

If the events of 1276 had consisted solely of the revolt and repression of a few notables, they would have had no great repercussions. But to back his rising, Ibn al-Khaṭīr had left the way open to the Turcomans, and even encouraged them, particularly the Karamanids, who also entered into direct communication with Baybars, and who, one might think, did not wait to be asked. 'Then the brilliant Seljukid state was brusquely thrown to the ground', as Aksarayi says. Mehmed b. Karaman and his people were not content to fall upon some Mongols who oversaw their territory, such as the commandant of the garrison at Maden. Ibn al-Khaṭīr had welcomed them at Niğde. He had removed the governor, Badr al-Dīn Khutanī, and the Turcomans no longer recognized the administration and refused to pay taxes. After Ibn al-Khaṭīr's fall, Badr al-Dīn, acting against the Pervane's advice, but with Mongol and Iranian reinforcements provided by Tuqu and Tudun, attacked them by way of Lârende, after refusing a request for peace, for which they offered 100,000 dinars. He was defeated in the gorges of the Göksu, north of Ermenek; his treasure was captured, and he was reduced to shutting himself up in a fortress upstream of that place. The encouragement this gave to the rebels may be imagined. Reinforcements sent from the Delice under Amīn al-Dīn Mīkā'īl the *nā'ib* and the sons of Fakhr al-Dīn 'Alī, who had come from Karahisar (now Afyonkarahisar), succeeded in releasing Badr al-Dīn, but not in reducing the Turcomans to submission. On the contrary an important caravan of Frankish and native Christian merchants coming from Cilicia was captured by the Turcomans near to Ereğli. It was in the state interest that this outrage should be punished. The *mustawfī* of Antalya, who was the Pervane's uncle and Badr al-Dīn's deputy as *malik al-sawāḥil* while he was defending Konya, set out to attack the Turcomans. They also rejected an offer of agreement, and they too were crushed. The winter was favourable to the Turcomans, and made serious operations impossible. Amīn al-Dīn, who had fallen back on Konya, hoped for the organization of a stronger expedition with the Pervane and the Mongol troops themselves in the spring, but Baybars's invasion came to thwart that project, and the Turcomans remained unsubdued.

It was at this moment that, despite the misadventure of his imprudent partisans, Baybars hoped to realize his long-envisaged project, for which he still no doubt counted on the Pervane himself, other emirs and the Turcomans. Later the Pervane was accused of having underestimated to the Mongols the danger of the invasion, so that preparations for resistance in Asia Minor remained insufficient in spite of warnings from Leon of Cilicia. Tuqu and Tudun advanced on Elbistan from Kırşehir, as did the Pervane with native contingents, but Baiju's grandson, who had wintered at Niğde, had not joined them when they learnt of the approach of the Mamluk army. Ibn 'Abd al-Ẓāhir, Baybars's head of chancery and biographer, transmitted in a letter to the Mamluk sultan's *wazīr* a journal of its march.

The Mamluk expeditionary force arrived by the pass between al-Ḥadath al-Ḥamrā' and Elbistan. An initial clash between the vanguards of the two armies was unfortunate for the Mongol commander, Karay. The real battle took place on the upper course of the Ceyhan, below Elbistan. The Mongols numbered 10,000 men, augmented by a corps of 1,000 Georgians. The Pervane's army, set aside because of mistrust, also took part in the battle. The first charge was made by the Mongols, whose chiefs were Tuqu, Tudun and others. After a furious mêlée, in which Baybars risked his life, the Mongols were crushed. Tuqu was killed, Tudun and other chiefs captured. In all, it is said, 6,000–7,000 lay dead and almost all the rest were prisoners. The prisoners from the Pervane's army included his son, Muhadhdhab al-Dīn, a grandson, and a number of other notables such as Nūr al-Dīn Jibrīl b. Caca, the brother of Majd al-Dīn the *atabeg*, a brother of Tāj al-Dīn Kivi and finally Shihāb al-Dīn Ghāzī b. 'Alī Shīr, a Turcoman whose name will appear again. Ibn al-Khaṭīr's brother, Ḍiyā' al-Dīn Maḥmūd, who fought in the Mamluk ranks, was killed by an arrow, said to have been shot by a wounded man when he was inspecting the dead after the battle, which took place on 10 Dhu'l-Qa'da 675/16 April 1277.

There was now nothing to oppose the advance of the conquering army. The Pervane passed hastily through Kayseri, taking the sultan, the vezir Fakhr al-Dīn 'Alī, the *atabeg* Majd al-Dīn, the *mustawfī* Jalāl al-Dīn Maḥmūd, the *nā'ib* Amin al-Dīn Mīkā'īl, his own nephew the *tuğrai*, and his wife, Gürcü Hatun (the Georgian widow of Kay Khusraw II), together with all the servants, treasures and so forth that he could. He proceeded to entrench himself with them all at Tokat, the family stronghold. During this time, other emirs came in to submit to Baybars: Ibn al-Khaṭīr's son and grandson, his brother, Sayf al-Dīn Jālīsh b. Isḥāq (previously devoted to the Pervane) and others. On 15 Dhu'l-Qa'da/21 April Baybars and his army reached Kayseri, where Kay Khusraw's tents stood ready in his garden. Baybars solemnly took his seat on the Seljukid throne, following the customary ceremonial for the arrival of a ruler in Asia Minor, and coinage was struck in his name. The Mamluks admired the monuments, the Kāshānī earthenware, the Georgian carpets, the markets of the southern suburb, the *khānqāhs*, the *madrasas* and what they learnt of the wealth of the vezir Fakhr al-Dīn, the Pervane and his wife from the spoils that fell into their hands (17 Dhu'l-Qa'da/23 April).

Yet a throne was not enough to make Baybars's victory durable. If he had the support of the Taurus Turcomans, who sometimes flew his flag, his envoys had failed to incite the indispensable rising in Rūm. No doubt there was still fear of the Mongols; also perhaps Baybars had discouraged some potential Muslim allies at the outset by opposing attacks on the native Christians, whom they regarded indiscriminately as the Mongols' accomplices. At Malatya there was fighting between Turks and the troop sent to protect the bishop of Mar Bar Sauma. Above all, the army had to be fed, and even if the storehouses of Kayseri were full, they could not last for long; the Turcoman disorder compromised provisioning, and prices rose to dizzy heights. To take decisive measures and draw in the hesitant, it would have been necessary for the Pervane to have come to him, as Baybars perhaps expected; but at most he sent a letter, asking Baybars to have patience. The Mamluk sultan well knew that the Mongol army which he had defeated was not the whole of their forces, and Tudun had taken it upon himself to tell him that the *Ilkhān* Abaqa was personally bringing an army which was powerful in other respects also. It was no doubt the imminence of Abaqa's arrival which kept the Pervane from making the leap. In the circumstances Baybars could only regard his message as a trap and, if he stayed, the situation was in any case very risky.

It was better to withdraw at once without getting his fingers burnt or abandoning the booty. The withdrawal from Kayseri began on 22 Dhu'l-Qaʿda/27 April, after which there were some anti-Christian activities. The Mamluk forces used a new route, which was not entirely lacking in subsistence. As he passed the caravanserai of Kay Qubādh, Baybars sent orders to burn Comana and massacre the Armenians there, who, he was told, were guilty of concealing some Mongols. The army reached the desolate battlefield of Elbistan, and resumed the line of their outward march by way of al-Ḥadath al-Ḥamrā' and so on to Syria. Baybars entered his Syrian capital of Damascus on 5 Muḥarram 676/8 June 1277.

However, the Karamanids, reinforced by the Eşref and the Menteşe (of whom this is the first mention in history) had launched a great offensive in liaison with Baybars, whose flag they had received, and perhaps flew. After the failure of a sudden attack on Aksaray, they attacked Konya, which was remote from Mongol aid. In the end they broke the resistance of the *nā'ib* Amīn al-Dīn Mīkā'īl, who was killed in flight, and they entered the city, which was delivered up to pillage in Dhu'l-Ḥijja 675/May 1277. It seems that Amīn al-Dīn had refused to organize the defence of the city by relying on its *ikdiş* and *ahi*s. Their chiefs had offered their services, but he suspected opposition, and perhaps collusion with the Turcomans. The Turcomans had discovered a person subsequently to be known in history by his nickname of Cimri (i.e. 'the mean'), who claimed to be a son of the former Sultan ʿIzz al-Dīn Kay Kāwūs II. The departure of Baybars no doubt made it urgent to have a more visible sovereign of legitimate descent as a rallying point for enthusiasm. There had been a project, which was perhaps carried out, to negotiate with Kay Kāwūs himself or his sons in the Crimea, for the sending of one of them, but this naturally proved too protracted. The evidence of a merchant back from Sughdāq was deemed sufficient to establish Cimri's lineage, and he was proclaimed sultan with regalia taken from Kay Qubādh's tomb; he was then married to a daughter of the late Sultan Kılıc Arslan IV. Cimri naturally made Mehmed b. Karaman his vezir and distributed offices to the Turcomans. It is remarkable, even if the cause lies essentially in the Turcomans' ignorance of Arabic and Persian, that a sort of practical resistance to the dominant turcicized Muslim community appears in the drafting of his diplomas in Turkish: such had never been the case under the Seljukid or Mongol administrations.

On the news of the fall of Konya, Bahā' al-Dīn *malik al-sawāḥil* and Fakhr al-Dīn 'Alī's two sons prepared a counter-attack from their *iqṭā'* of Karahisar, supported by the Germiyan, who had probably been recently settled in that region in order to keep an eye on the restless Turcomans. The Turcomans took the initiative. They occupied Akşehir and Abgurum. A battle took place near Tuzağac in the district of Altıntaş on 23 Dhu'l-Ḥijja 675/29 May 1277, in which Fakhr al-Dīn's two sons were killed, as was the *khawaja* Yūnus near Sivrihisar. Karahisar suffered a brief attack. Bahā' al-Dīn also met his end in one or other of these battles. These events naturally encouraged every form of disorder; a *muqṭa'* in the region of Aksaray, Kızıl Ḥāmid, gathered a band of Turcomans, and seized the city, which he plundered.

It was then that news came of the approach of the great Mongol army. Abaqa himself led it by way of Erzincan and Divriği. He had hoped to fall on Baybars's army as it withdrew, but he arrived some eight hours too late to accomplish more than the capture by his vanguard of some stragglers and Turcomans, and he did not deem it opportune to invade Syria with the Turcoman revolt on his flank. He could only contemplate the lugubrious scene of the battlefield of Elbistan, where he indignantly noted the absence of Anatolian victims. At Divriği the children of the Mongol chief Tāj al-Dīn Zirek had been killed; he had those guilty arrested, and razed to the ground the fortress from which arrows had been aimed. He had over a hundred captives executed on the battlefield. Turning to Kayseri, he proceeded to execute Muslims suspected of pro-Mamluk sympathies, among them the grand *qāḍī*. The Turcomans found there also suffered. By contrast, he had all the Christian captives who could be found redeemed in the markets. There were also some reprisals at Sivas.

There remained the Pervane. It was difficult for recent events not to lead to his being accused at least of bad advice, and they would bring to mind the hitherto disregarded reports of his intrigues with Baybars. Abaqa would however take into account the quality of the Pervane's government in Rūm, and the difficulty he would have in finding a native of equal merit, or in governing without a native. He might also fear that a condemnation would bring about a general rising of the Muslims of Asia Minor. Without doubt the Pervane counted on such considerations, or on his own skill in management; to believe his partisans, he wished to the very end to limit at the risk of his life Mongol reprisals against the Muslims, or at the least to secure some inheritance for his family. It is certain that he could have fled, but he did not attempt to do so. On the contrary, he went to place himself at the *īlkhān*'s service when Abaqa arrived at Kemah. After his stay at Kayseri, Abaqa withdrew by the Kösedağ to Kuğuniya, one of the Pervane's *iqṭā*ʿs. He demanded its surrender, and the Pervane came to give the order. But the governor of the citadel declared that he would surrender the place only to the Pervane's children, then in Egypt, on the pretext that the Pervane was not free, and was responsible furthermore for the killing of many of the Muslims of Asia Minor. The Pervane may secretly have been his accomplice. The sons of Tuqu and Tudun accused him of their defeat. There was again talk of the killing of Kılıc Arslan IV, and of the failure of the Anatolian army to take part in the battle of Elbistan. There were witnesses to the Pervane's negotiations with Baybars. Finally, Abaqa decided to have him executed with three other notables on 1 Rabīʿ I 676/2 August 1277. Whatever orders were given in regard to his property, we find his sons in possession of a good territorial inheritance.

The Pervane's death may be regarded as symbolizing the end of an era, and of this his contemporaries were well aware. It is with reason that Aksarayi groups around his death quite a series of others which occurred about this time: the *atabeg* Majd al-Dīn, who died of sickness at Sivas towards the end of 1277, and likewise Tāj al-Dīn Muʿtazz; the two *qāḍī*s of Sivas and Kayseri, executed by Abaqa, as also the *qāḍī* of Konya; Tāj al-Dīn Kivi and a few years previously Jalāl al-Dīn Rūmī and Ṣadr al-Dīn Konevi. It seems that the whole generation which grew up politically and spiritually in the time of Seljukid splendour and retained some of its traditions had gone down into the tomb in a short space of time. The vezir Fakhr al-Dīn ʿAlī alone survived, and his personal political role (if indeed he had any) appears less important to us than his ardour as a builder. His two sons had fallen in the defence of 'legitimate' authority.

As regards the Pervane himself, the evident importance of his role and the incontestable power of his personality render it all the more regrettable that we cannot yet truly present it from the available documentation.

CHAPTER EIGHTEEN

The crisis of 1277–79

During this time the redress of the recent misfortunes began, first in military matters. On the Syrian side there was no difficulty, for Baybars died in Muḥarram 676/June 1277, and his successor, his son al-Saʿīd Baraka (Berke) Khān, was in no position to risk a further adventure. The only incident (which lacked consequences) was the concession in Ṣafar 676/July 1277 of Malatya to ʿIzz al-Dīn Aybak, a fugitive Syrian amir, who, after accumulating a year's taxes, fled back to safety in Egypt.

There was however all that part of Anatolia where the Turcomans reigned as masters. There Abaqa sent his brother, Qongqurtay, accompanied by the *noyans* Kahurkay and Arqasun, the *īlkhān*'s vezir Shams al-Dīn Juvaynī, the vezir of Rūm Fakhr al-Dīn ʿAlī, and Sultan Kay Khusraw III, who had come without delay to put himself at Abaqa's service. To begin with, Qongqurtay reduced Tokat and Kuğuniya. Then, as Kızıl Ḥāmid had drawn the whole population into revolt, 6,000 of the inhabitants were indiscriminately reduced to slavery for the benefit of the Mongols, to equal the losses in the battle of Elbistan. Then the army marched on Konya, whence the Turcomans judged it prudent to withdraw in Muḥarram 676/June 1277. At the same time it captured Akşehir and Abgurum, where the Turcoman commandants were executed. Cimri, Mehmed b. Karaman and their followers were then pursued to the basins of Ermenek and Mut, numerous prisoners being taken. The summer, and perhaps disarray at the news of the Pervane's execution, delayed operations; and the Mongol army abandoned Konya for the better watered and more central region of Kayseri. The Turcomans turned this to profit with a new attack on Konya in Ṣafar/July. The city, led by the *ahi* chiefs Aḥmad and Aḥmad-Shāh, put up a brave defence, and avoided being retaken by skilfully spreading the rumour that the Mongol army was returning. A third attack took place in Jumādā I/

October. Meanwhile the fields were of course laid waste. This time the Turco-Mongol army really appeared, and pursued the scattered Turcomans. Encircled in a mountain forest, Mehmed b. Karaman and his two brothers were killed, and the rest of the party were massacred. It was then possible to send orders to the frontier provinces of doubtful loyalty for the payment of taxes.

Cimri had however succeeded in escaping, and the winter allowed him to rebuild his fortunes among the Turcomans of the west of Anatolia with Karahisar as centre. Officially this region formed the *iqṭāʿ* of Fakhr al-Dīn ʿAlī's family. Hence its reconquest was of particular concern to him, and he cared little about the activities of the Mongol army which ravaged the country. He obtained from Qongqurtay the sole responsibility for the region together with the sultan. Leaving the Danişmendid province, they went to Ankara, where they were now able to assemble contingents of emirs from all the Seljukid territory, some former slaves of the Pervane, and the Germiyan led by ʿAlī Shīr's family. The battle with Cimri's forces took place on 7 Muḥarram 677/31 May 1278 or 7 Muḥarram 678/20 May 1279. The parasol of Kay Qubādh I, which had been carried off by Cimri, was recovered, and finally the Germiyan took the pretender himself. Cimri was flayed alive, and his skin, stuffed with straw, promenaded on a donkey through every city in Rūm.

At the same time Trebizond delivered a new attack by sea on Sinop. However, the governor succeeded in repulsing it, thanks to reinforcements from the Turks of Ḥusām al-Dīn Amīr Çopan, who will appear again. At this period they must have been in agreement with the Seljukid-Mongol government, as will soon be proved by their behaviour towards the sons of Kay Kāwūs II.

On the other hand there remained the Turcomans of Burğlu and Denizli, who, if they had not joined Cimri's movement, had refused to take part in its repression. The Seljukid army invaded their territory; their chief was taken and executed at Karahisar. The sultan stopped briefly in this city, of which the grandsons of Fakhr al-Dīn ʿAlī regained possession; he then went on to Sandıklı, and returned to Konya. However, as Aksarayi remarks, if the Seljukid state had risen again, and the Turcomans had been repulsed, they were by no means destroyed; although they were contained in their territories, there they were definitely autonomous.

Another attempt made at this time was to restore order to the administration. This was now done under the management of the Ilkhanid authorities. Six weeks after the Pervane's death, Abaqa sent his own vezir, Shams al-Dīn Juvaynī (as has been seen), to take advice with the *mustawfī* of Rūm on the necessary measures, particularly in matters of finance. He concerned himself with the restoration of the ruined towns and the destroyed buildings; he revised, re-established, or set up general registers of financial accounts and properties, introduced into Rūm the innovation of the *tamgha*, and at the same time took part, as has been mentioned, in the first struggles against the Karamanids. So far as one can tell from Ibn Bībī's vague phraseology, he seems to have suppressed abuses, reduced considerably the payments owed by the state for the redemption of loans from the time of Baba Tuğrai and revised the alienations of crown property in *injü* in the province of Erzincan.

Naturally this does not mean that the Mongol treasury no longer had any right to the revenues of Rūm. In 679/1280–81 Mujīr al-Dīn Mehmed, the son of Tāj al-Dīn Mu'tazz, came to Rūm armed with the necessary *yarligh*s and *paiza*s to levy as his father had done the revenues of the *injü*s, the *muqāṭa'āt* and the *balish* for the Ilkhanid treasury. Furthermore, immediately after the sultan's return to Konya, the *mustawfī* Jalāl al-Dīn, who had been at the *īlkhān*'s headquarters, brought back the nomination of Fakhr al-Dīn 'Alī as the *īlkhān*'s *nā'ib*, and his own as the *nā'ib* of the sultan. Shortly afterwards 'Azīz al-Dīn the *tuğrai* went in his turn to the *īlkhān*, and returned as *beglerbegi*. So even appointments within the government of Rūm were now made by the Mongols, or in any case ratified by them, and some important posts were occupied by their personnel in Rūm. In 680/1281–82 or 681/1282–83 Shams al-Dīn Juvaynī sent his own son to pick up the post of *pervane* with the administration and revenues of everything attached to that office under Mu'īn al-Dīn Süleyman. This was no doubt a personal concession, since in the end the post went back to the emirs of Rūm. On the other hand, the *īlkhān*'s *nā'ib* remained a man of Rūm, although he was always assisted by Mongol military commanders. After Tuqu's death and Qongqurtay's departure, the *nā'ib* was no doubt Samaghar, assisted by Kahurkay.

CHAPTER NINETEEN

The growth of direct Mongol control

Apart from some ruins, some frontier territorial changes, and the increasing substitution of Mongol authority for local autonomy (which was both logical and unavoidable from the moment when the Mongols shattered the framework of the country, and broached its resources), a stable regime seemed to have been re-established with some kind of continuity with the previous period. But the history of the subsequent years was to show how fragile and shallow it was, and how the new forces which had seemed defeated came back almost without a crisis.

The Karamanids continued to exist. Had they a single chief? If so, after the death of Mehmed Beg, was he the Güneri Beg, who was in any event their chief a few years later? This remains unknown. However, in 1279 the Egyptian army on its way to besiege Qalʿat al-Rūm (Rumkale) on the Euphrates, obtained by threats freedom of passage through the kingdom of Cilicia from a Karamanid chief, which proves that the Turcomans were still there, that they maintained or renewed the links established in the time of Baybars, and so remained, as in the past, the unsubdued adversaries of the Seljukid-Mongol regime.

This lasting encouragement given by the Mamluk rulers to the trouble-makers of the southern frontier regions might count, along with all the other reasons of policy outside Asia Minor, in leading the Mongols to organize another powerful expedition against the Mamluks of Syria. Abaqa entrusted it to his brother, Mengü-Temür, who received reinforcements from Rūm, but was defeated near Ḥimṣ in October 1281. Then Abaqa and Mengü-Temür both died in 1282. A settlement on the frontiers could only be obtained by peace. The new *īlkhān*, Tegüder Aḥmad a Muslim, sought to profit from this in negotiations with the Mamluk sultan, Qalāwūn.[26] An embassy was sent, two of its three leaders being from Rūm, but the attempt was a failure. There had been a Mamluk raid on Malatya in 1281, and oddly enough the Jacobite monks of Mar Bar Sauma were accused of having supplied the invader, but succeeded in exculpating themselves. In 1283 there were more raids, which reached as far as the province of Khartpert. They were aimed particularly at the Armenians, who were everywhere the most favourable to the Mongols.

At this point a new complication was introduced into Anatolian politics. Kay Kāwūs II died in the Crimea, probably in 678/1279–80, perhaps after exhorting his sons to reconquer the Seljukid heritage. The Cimri affair showed the possibilities. The eldest son proclaimed himself sultan as Ghiyāth al-Dīn Mas'ūd II, and received oaths of loyalty in the Crimea. One of his brothers, probably Siyāwush, acting as his precursor, disembarked at Sinop towards the end of 678/spring 1280, but was hunted down by Ḥusām al-Dīn Alp Yürük, the governor of Kastamonu, and was taken prisoner near Amasya. Mas'ūd himself disembarked at the beginning of 679/summer 1280, and won over Alp Yürek's son, the emir Yavlak Arslan. He had his brother set free, and went on his way to the *īlkhān*'s court, where he stayed for some time. At an unknown date the Mongols perhaps decided on a partition of territory, which appears not to have been effective. Kay Khusraw III retained the sultanate of Rūm proper, but Mas'ūd was given the government of the province of Qamar al-Dīn, i.e. of the Karamanids. Meanwhile, however, a nephew of Mas'ūd named 'Alā' al-Dīn Kay Qubādh had disembarked, apparently without his knowledge, among the Karamanids, who had presumably kept up their links with Kay Kāwūs II's family in the Crimea. After being recognized and proclaimed as sultan by the Karamanids at Lârende, he was defeated by the Pervane's son and Fakhr al-Dīn 'Alī's grandson, Sa'd al-Dīn Çelebi, who had mustered a force at Niğde, no doubt on Kay Khusraw's orders. He was forced to flee to Cilicia, where he long remained in obscurity, but was to reappear. Was there some connection between these events and the grant of the Karamanid territory to Mas'ūd? He does not however seem to have shown any inclination to go there. Kay Khusraw set out for the *īlkhān*'s court in order to combat his cousin's intrigues, and to demand reinforcements against the Turcomans as the Karamanids and Eşref were threatening Konya and Eskişehir. He returned in Rabī' II 681/July–August 1282 by way of Erzurum, accompanied by Mongol troops under the orders of Qongqurtay and the emir Aqbuqu. Taking the Turcomans by surprise, he decimated them, followed them up to Mut and Ermenek, and laid waste the Karamanid country. The hollowness of the victory of 1277 was clear, and henceforward it was of no significance.

Unfortunately for Kay Khusraw, Abaqa died at that point, and Qongqurtay rose with his troops in Asia Minor against his successor, the *Ilkhān* Aḥmad, as did Aḥmad's brother, Arghun, in Khurāsān. Qongqurtay died during his enterprise, having been accompanied by Kay Khusraw as far as Erzurum. So Aḥmad, who may in any case have decided on his accession to partition the Seljukid territory between Kay Khusraw and Mas'ūd, sent the latter to Konya, where he received oaths of loyalty in agreement with Fakhr al-Dīn 'Alī, who had perhaps not taken part in the revolt. This was at the end of Dhu'l-Qa'da 682/end of March 1284. Kay Khusraw was put to death by the emirs and Aḥmad in agreement, as it seems.

Then in Jumādā II 683/October 1284, Aḥmad was overthrown by Arghun, who sent his brothers Hulachu and Geikhatu to govern Rūm, and hear with favour a request for the partition of the sultanate, presented by Kay Khusraw's widow on behalf of the two young sons he had left. Escorted by one Bahā' al-Dīn Wurukardī and a Mongol envoy, the princess and the two children proceeded to Kayseri, where they met Sultan Mas'ūd and the vezir Fakhr al-Dīn 'Alī, who had no choice in the matter. The young princes were installed at Konya, while it seems that Mas'ūd stayed at Kayseri. Thus was replicated Aḥmad's partition, itself like those of Hülegü's time. This was at the end of Ramaḍān 683/beginning of January 1285.

However, the princess, who was no doubt aware of the hostility of the establishment, had the idea of obtaining Turcoman support. She sent Kılıc Arslan IV's former *rikābdār* to offer the titles of *beglerbegi* and *nā'ib* respectively to Güneri Beg, the Karamanid chief, and Süleyman Beg, Eşref's son. In consequence the Turcomans reappeared at the gates of Konya. Thereupon Fakhr al-Dīn 'Alī, the *ahi* chiefs, and the uneasy royal slaves resolved to defend the city, and a demonstration against the princess was ordered. Nevertheless the *ahi* chiefs, Aḥmad and Aḥmad-Shāh, and no doubt the vezir as well, succeeded in avoiding a clash. A solemn session was held at the beginning of Rabī' I 684/mid-June 1285, at which the two little princes were enthroned with Güneri and Süleyman beside them, in the presence of the combined forces of Konya and the Turcomans.

But the magnates remained hostile, and Mas'ūd had not given up hopes of regaining the lost half of his realm, which he announced that he was going to ask again of Arghun. Immediately after the enthronement session, the princess thought it prudent to get there first. Unfortunately Bahā' al-Dīn, whom she had left with one of the children at Konya, died there unexpectedly a few days after her departure. A troop of Sultan Mas'ūd's men, led by 'Izz al-Dīn Khāṣṣ Balaban, a eunuch of Fakhr al-Dīn 'Alī, who was perhaps an accomplice, hastened to seize the city and the child, whom they sent to Mas'ūd's mother, then at Aksaray. This seems to prove that the princess had hardly any real power outside Konya, an impression corroborated by Aksarayi's complete ignorance of this incident, and the absence of any inscription or coinage in the names of the young princes. It took place in Jumādā I or II 684/August or September 1685. Meanwhile the Mongols, who had doubtless been won over in advance, sanctioned the facts. They sent Kay Khusraw's widow to govern Sivrihisar, and put the child accompanying her to death on 4 Rajab 684/1 October 1285. The other child in the keeping of Mas'ūd's mother must also have been disposed of on his orders, after having been taken to Konya in Shawwāl 684/January 1286.

Meanwhile the government of Konya remained in the hands of the *mushrif* Fakhr al-Dīn and the *amīr-dād* Niẓām al-Dīn. According to the citizen of Konya who wrote the *Tārīkh-i āl-i Saljūq*, they misused their positions. In any event, the arrival of Mongol commissioners to check their accounts alarmed them, and they fled, the former to the Eşref, the latter to the Karamanids (which may indicate that contacts had continued), while the mob pillaged their homes. The arrival of the Mongols was probably connected with that of an army, led by Geikhatu to Kayseri and Aksaray. He had previously been settled in Erzincan with Hulachu, who was recalled to Iran. The presence of this army was justified by the events of which eastern Anatolia was the theatre at that time.

It does not seem that the return of Mas'ūd produced a reaction by the Karamanids and the Eşref as might have been expected. There was, however, for the first time, a rising of the Germiyan, who attacked the province of Gurgurum, then held by the Eşref. As there is no evidence of the presence of the Eşref in the counter-attack, one must conclude that they and the Karamanids, always their allies, had an agreement with Mas'ūd. It is noticeable that there had actually been no indication of difficulties between them previously, and perhaps Mas'ūd, client of the Mongols though he was, appeared preferable to their adversary, Kay Khusraw. Perhaps the *Īlkhān* Aḥmad, taking in everything the opposite course to Abaqa, had recommended peace there as elsewhere. As the Germiyan had appeared in 1277–78 as enemies of the southern Turcomans, and as the transient bid for power by Kay Khusraw's widow did not change the essential factors in the situation, it is comprehensible that the Germiyan should intervene against Mas'ūd at this point. Perhaps it all went back to the revolt of Qongqurtay and Kay Khusraw, which they may have supported, but all this is clearly speculative.

However that may be, a few months after his restoration Sultan Mas'ūd had to march against the Germiyan assisted by a Mongol army commanded by Baltu, the son of that Nabshi who had several times intervened in Rūm in the previous two decades. The vezir Fakhr al-Dīn 'Alī also soon came to join them. He had spent a large part of his personal income on the subsistence of the Mongol army during its stay in Erzincan in 684/1285–86, and of course now the next year in Anatolia, since Mujīr al-Dīn Mehmed (usually called the Amīr-Shāh), who represented the interests of the Mongol crown, and even the *beglerbegi* Azīz al-Dīn, had refused to take any official responsibility for the expenses. They said that it was not for them to contribute to the costs of a campaign, the essential aim of which was to hand over their domain to the grandsons of Fakhr al-Dīn 'Alī, who had been partially dispossessed by the Germiyan.

After success the Seljukid army was surprised and defeated in mid-Ramaḍān 685/beginning of December 1286. A new campaign ended with the amassing of loot in the Germiyan country but not in seizing the enemy, who had escaped. It would be hard to define the results of short campaigns against semi-nomadic opponents. Once the army had left for Kayseri, the Germiyan reappeared. Fakhr al-Dīn's grandson, Sa'd al-Dīn Çelebi, who had retained Karahisar, wanted to fight them; he was crushed and killed by the Germiyan chief Barguş Bahadır in 686/1287–88. Once again it was necessary for the aged Fakhr al-Dīn to hasten with the sultan at the head of a Seljukid-Mongol army. Once again the Germiyan escaped; the army could do no more than pillage the frontier territories, then return to Karahisar, maintained as always at the expense of Fakhr al-Dīn's family. The sultan and Fakhr al-Dīn then returned to Konya on 7 Shawwāl 686/ 15 November 1287, and went on by way of Kayseri to report to Arghun on the situation.

They received his order that they were now to fight the Karamanids, who had attacked Cilicia, where King Leon, also a vassal of the Mongols, had asked for aid. But it was no more possible there to seize an enemy who had taken refuge in the mountains. Unable to do more, they were content to pillage the city and district of Lârende, which proves that these parts had come into Karamanid possession since at the earliest 681/1282–83 (see above, p. 203). This was in Dhu'l-Ḥijja 686/February 1288. Elsewhere the Eşref attacked Abgurum from Gurgurum in Muḥarram 687/March 1288. This place had belonged to one Balaban, a former slave of its *qāḍī*, who had seized it at the time of the Turcoman expansion, perhaps in 1277. On his death it was given to Badr al-Dīn 'Umar, the former cupbearer of the vezir Fakhr al-Dīn 'Alī, as *subaşı*. He had however been killed, and succeeded by Balaban's son, who defeated the Eşref. Thereupon the two chiefs of the Karamanids and Eşref respectively sought to resume their fealty to the sultan, who feared a ruse, and accepted it only outside Konya, and surrounded by a good armed guard. The Germiyan ruler, Badr al-Dīn Murād, maternal grandson of the son of 'Alī Shīr, came to Konya, which the sultan had just left to visit the *īlkhān*. His deputy, Khāṣṣ Balaban, received the Turcoman chief, and peace was established there also for the moment in Jumādā II 687/July 1288.

Did the sultan wish to discuss Fakhr al-Dīn 'Alī with Arghun? At about the same time the *amīr-shāh* Mujīr al-Dīn, who was decidedly at odds with

Fakhr al-Dīn, went to the Ilkhanid court, and had obtained the nomination of a new vezir. Arghun appointed Fakhr al-Dīn Qazwīnī, but, although he went to Konya, there ensued no diminution in the old vezir's immense personal authority according to Aksarayi. However, Fakhr al-Dīn 'Alī died shortly afterwards in Shawwāl 687/November 1288. In him there passed away the last important survivor of the Seljukid old guard. Although the sources do not show him as particularly outstanding, he was a man who certainly had an important part. His was a prestige increased by his longevity, rare among politicians, and his influence both realist and traditionalist for moderation towards both the Mongols' adversaries and themselves, and for fidelity to Islam, is demonstrated by numerous foundations where inscriptions extending over forty years still recall his memory. He had the positive outlook of an administrator who respected the mystics but did not participate in their movement, and was sorely tried by his descendants, whose fortune he had made and which the survivors were to keep until the beginning of the next century.

Fakhr al-Dīn Qazwīnī, though no scholar, was a good accountant and not lacking in generosity; but, hungry to acquire a fortune or under pressure from his clientele of Iranian newcomers, he gave the impression of being above all an insatiable tax-collector. Moreover he did not enjoy full power, for Mujīr al-Dīn as *nā'ib*, and backed by an important clientele inherited from his father, had in fact superior authority. When the unpopularity and economic dangers of Qazwīnī's fiscal policy caused him some unease, he obtained the partition of the administration of Rūm once again into two parts, the western half from Kayseri remaining Qazwīnī's responsibility, the eastern with the Danişmendid province increased by Sinop and Samsun going to Mujīr al-Dīn. Each had its Mongol military resident. The appointment of Qazwīnī is especially remarkable in that it signifies the direct tenure by an Ilkhanid bureaucrat of a post hitherto held by a Seljukid official, and this moreover without reference to the sultan. Seljukid personnel naturally looked with disfavour on this foreigner (although they were themselves partly of somewhat distant Iranian origin), and they sourly pointed out the ignorance of Qazwīnī's clients regarding the financial and administrative regulations of this unfamiliar country. Qazwīnī was accused of innovations, which in part could only be the introduction of Ilkhanid practices, while the sultan also had naturally no love for this imposed vezir.

Apart from this there was a revival of Turcoman disturbances, due perhaps to Fakhr al-Dīn 'Alī's death. This time the Germiyan made an appearance in the direction of Denizli, where the *beglerbegi* 'Azīz al-Dīn defeated them, and their chief, Badr al-Dīn Murād, was killed. At about the same time the army of Fakhr al-Dīn 'Alī's heirs took the son of Balaban of Abgurum, and put him to death in the wilderness of Konya. Denizli fell to

Fakhr al-Dīn's grandson in Jumādā I 688/June–July 1289. At this time indeed ʿAzīz al-Dīn thought it good to go to Geikhatu, and then the Germiyan raids were resumed. At least the sultan endeavoured to give force to the agreement which appeared to hold with the Eşref by marrying a daughter of their chief to his brother, Siyāwush, whom he summoned from his residence at Sinop. However, at the meeting between Siyāwush and the Turcoman chief near to Viranşehir, the chief took Siyāwush prisoner. He was freed through the mediation of Güneri Beg, but it is not known whether there was a reconciliation, or whether the marriage took place. The Karamanid chief came in person to renew his fealty to the sultan in a solemn session at the gates of Konya in the presence of the vezir Qazwīnī.

Perhaps because of Siyāwush's popularity with the people of Konya, the announcement of his captivity produced a stirring among the *rinds*, who were the masters of the streets. They had an establishment in the suburb; the *shiḥna* proceeded to blockade them, and set it ablaze. All there perished apart from the chief, who managed to escape (1 Rabīʿ I 689/16 May 1290). The course of events clearly proves that this bloody episode concerned only a group of extremists, and that the *ahi* chiefs were in no way compromised. It appears on the contrary that the sultan, who no longer had a serious army, relied to some extent on these *ahis* to counterbalance the Mongols.

Qazwīnī was away, and his return coincided with a devastating storm connected with an earthquake at Erzincan and a flood at Amasya. His unpopularity grew, and his subordinates added uncontrollable indiscipline to the abuses for which he was blamed. In defiance of custom the sultan, using a rising of the *rinds* as pretext, did not go to welcome the vezir at the gates of Konya; he had himself incited this rising. It was noted that at a reception the vezir did not open his mouth. An attempt was made to pacify him with small gifts, which he rejected. He carried out fresh cadastral surveys and multiplied the taxes according to the *Tārīkh-i āl-i Saljūq*. The chief of the *ahis*, Aḥmad-Shāh, headed a delegation of youths, heads of families and dervishes, which he received scornfully. The people murmured. As they jeered, the vezir decided to go to the sultan; on the way he met Sultan Veled and his disciples, who laughed at him. Then he fell from his horse, which was seen as ominous.

His arrival at the palace coincided with that of Mongol commissioners, who had come for Qazwīnī's accounts. They took him first to an assembly at Sivas, then to the *īlkhān* in Jumādā I or II/May–June 1290. The influence with the *īlkhān* of a certain Shams al-Dīn of Konya, and the jealousy of Arghun's new vezir, Saʿd al-Dawla, led to Qazwīnī's condemnation, it is said, and he ended by being beheaded at Tabrīz or on the Aladağ in Shaʿbān 689/August–September 1290. Mujīr al-Dīn Mehmed was arrested at the same time, but with his loyal following of clients he was able to protract the affair, and was saved by Arghun's death. The Mongol residents and two other chiefs were also recalled about this time, reaching the *īlkhān* in Ramaḍān/September–October. The next month Aqbuqu was sent back to Rūm.

The immediate successor of Qazwīnī was one Shams al-Dīn Aḥmad Lākūshī[27] under the general supervision of Samaghar, the former resident who had been dismissed by Abaqa at the Pervane's demand. He had however continued to command the Mongol troops in the west, for example in 1283 when he is mentioned near Malatya. From 1278, perhaps under the general direction of Qongqurtay or in his absence, he had taken over from Tuqu, who fell in the defeat of 1277. Both Aksarayi the official, and the townsman who wrote the *Tārīkh-i āl-i Saljūq* speak as well of him as the former spoke ill of the vezir and his clique. In Jumādā II 689/June–July 1290 he sent a deputy to Konya of whom the author of the *Tārīkh-i āl-i Saljūq* speaks equally well – particularly, it is true, because of the influence he allowed to the *mustawfī* Nāṣir al-Dīn Yavlak Arslan, the favoured protector of the author. Samaghar himself bore the title of *yarghuchi*, i.e. chief judge of the Mongols of Rūm; the title itself was not new, but does not seem to have appeared previously among the Mongol chiefs of this territory. It is remarkable that the author of the *Tārīkh-i āl-i Saljūq* says that the government was conferred on the sultan and Samaghar. This terminology is evident witness to the abasement to which the sultanate had fallen in regard to the Ilkhanate; on the other hand, it is possible that it indicates a wish to concede a minimum reality to the sultanate as a reaction to the power of the preceding quasi-autonomous vezirs. At this time, in any case, Arghun sent a princess of his family as a bride for Mas'ūd. The origin of the new vezir, Lākūshī, is unknown, but he was linked to a notable family of emirs of Rūm known as the Sons of Kilavuz, who were dependants of the Ilkhanid regime.

Samaghar was soon recalled for no clear reason. Arghun ordered his son, Geikhatu, to assume the government of Rūm, and to send Samaghar back. Geikhatu met Samaghar at Tuhal on 2 Shawwāl 689/8 October 1290, and despatched him to the *īlkhān*. Nāṣir al-Dīn the *mustawfī* however retained his confidence, and came to meet him at Aksaray, where he remained for some time while the sultan went to Konya to prepare for Geikhatu's state entry. This took place on 25 Dhu'l-Qa'da 689/29 November 1290. The Karamanid Güneri Beg came to pay homage, and, according to the *Tārīkh-i āl-i Saljūq*, Mongol discipline and Nāṣir al-Dīn the *mustawfī*'s *savoir faire* prevented any clash with the population.[28] As well as to Mas'ūd, Güneri Beg also offered his homage to Geikhatu. Thereupon Geikhatu set out for Akşehir. During Samaghar's term of office, the sultan had had an interview at this place with the chief of the Germiyan, who feared a breach of relations, and confirmed the recently made peace. At Akşehir Geikhatu sent the sultan to the coastal regions, where he rejoined him later after a brief return to Konya. During this short progress from Muḥarram to Rabīʿ I 690/January–February 1291, he received only declarations of homage as painless as shallow. The *Tārīkh-i āl-i Saljūq* praises the justice of Nāṣir al-Dīn, whom Geikhatu had made his *nā'ib*, as well as his ability to guarantee order, and his love of men of religion. To Geikhatu himself the work ascribes justice, perhaps because the essence of the work was written during his reign. The fact that Nāṣir al-Dīn's name is not mentioned by either Aksarayi or Eflaki leads one to think that his administration was of no great importance.

However this may be, Geikhatu's rule did not last, for in Jumādā/*c.* May 1291 a messenger arrived to report the death of Arghun (10 March 1291), and was quickly followed by Samaghar, who had been sent to tell him of the choice of Baidu as the new *īlkhān*. Geikhatu left in haste to dispute the succession. He left the military command in Konya to one Qutluja, appointed *shiḥna*s to the other principal cities, and entrusted the supervision of the whole to a certain Fakhr al-Dīn Masʿūd. He installed Sultan Masʿūd at Kayseri, which he deemed nearer and more controllable than Konya. Nāṣir al-Dīn accompanied Geikhatu.

As might be expected, the simultaneous departures of Geikhatu, the sultan and the *mustawfī* was followed by a reaction at Konya. The internal and external discontents gave mutual encouragement. Within, the rule of Qutluja was borne uneasily by the *rind*s, some magnates such as Khāṣṣ Balaban, the sultan's confidant, even the sultan's brother Siyāwush, who had stayed at Konya. They accused Qutluja of an inquisitorial approach. It was easy to convince Siyāwush that Qutluja wished to kill him, and as early as 2 Jumādā II 690/2 June 1291 Qutluja was put to death. His place was taken by Khāṣṣ Balaban with a certain Asad al-Dīn as *amīr-dād*, and as *nā'ib* one Jamāl al-Dīn, who had been left by Geikhatu as *ḥākim*. But the *rind*s ruled the streets.

The rising had been encouraged by reports of Turcoman attacks, which no doubt Qutluja did not appear to wish, or to be able, to overcome. The Turcoman forces may also have encouraged some people to take action against the Mongols. For the first time known the differences between the Eşref and the Karamanids culminated in real warfare. Güneri Beg took Beyşehir, and captured Eşref's son Süleyman, who (as proved by the inscriptions) had held the city from at the latest 687/1288–89. But the Turcomans regrouped around Süleyman's son, and drove Güneri back; the inscriptions prove that Süleyman was released six years later at most. The Karamanids also disturbed the approaches to Konya, which suggests an alliance of the Eşref with Konya. Appeals to the sultan in Kayseri were fruitless, as he had to repress similar disturbances by the Turcomans of the Syrian borders between Jumādā II and Rajab 690/June–July 1291.

Thereupon an attack by the Germiyan under Khalīl Bahadır took place. The emirs and *ahi*s of Konya, not daring to confront them in open country, were restricted to the defence of the city ramparts. An unfortunate sortie on 2 Sha'bān/31 July resulted in the Germiyan following on their heels into the city, which they pillaged for three days. The citadel however held out, and the arrival of Mongol representatives announcing the approach of an Ilkhanid army caused the attackers to flee. But the army delayed; the Germiyan came back, and resumed the pillage. The citizens of Konya then sought the aid of the lord of Lâdik-Denizli, the maternal grandson of Fakhr al-Dīn 'Alī. He came with his army of frontiersmen at the risk of stripping his territory. At the same time Siyāwush went to Kayseri, probably bringing back some reinforcements. The combination of these forces with those of Khāṣṣ Balaban made it possible to defeat the Turcomans, and regain the cattle they had raided, first at the gates of Konya, and a second time after an enemy attack near to Gurgurum. Another counter-attack was then carried out below Lârende, but the Karamanids encircled the army of Konya, which suffered heavy losses including that of Khāṣṣ Balaban. The Turcomans also lost one of their notables, but they came back to raid Konya.

Sultan Mas'ūd then sent an appeal to Geikhatu, who, having gained the throne by the elimination of his rivals, probably needed no incitement to return and secure his domination over Asia Minor, where he had so long commanded the Mongol forces. At the beginning of Dhu'l-Qa'da 690/November 1291 the sultan greeted him at Kayseri. This campaign however was not like its predecessor; at the head of a powerful army, the *īlkhān* wished to leave a feeling of terror in the region as he massacred Turcomans and non-Turcomans alike. This was the fate of the district of Ereğli; then from 19 Dhu'l-Qa'da/13 November, of the city of Lârende, which was burnt to ashes, and its people both Muslims and non-Muslims massacred without pity, apart from the women and children, who were led into captivity. A Mongol chief followed the Karamanids up into the mountains, without however being able to catch up with them. Then it was the turn of the country of the Eşref from 16 Dhu'l-Ḥijja 690/10 December 1291 onwards. Seven thousand women and children were brought in from the two regions. Next the Mongols reached the city of Lâdik-Denizli, where the terrified people shut the gates. The city was taken, and there was no quarter; blood flowed for three days. From this it may be concluded that it was no longer in the hands of Fakhr al-Dīn 'Alī's family. Finally Geikhatu reached the country of Menteşe, pillaging and slaying as he went. Then with his herd of captives, he returned to Konya at the end of Muḥarram 691/January 1292. The seventeen days of the Mongol passage through the country left a memory of terror to its people. At last, after a new raid into Karamanid country, the terrible ruler left for Kayseri on 16 Ṣafar 691/7 February 1292.

In reality, ruins were the only result of this expedition. The Turcomans were not destroyed. Two Karamanid raids had to be answered in Shaʿbān 691/July 1292 by a counter-raid, in the course of which two members of Güneri Beg's family were killed; but when Alanya shortly afterwards fell to a sudden Frankish attack, the Karamanids seized it, and informed the Mamluk sultanate that the *khuṭba* would be made there in his name. Then it was the turn of Khalīl Bahadır of the Germiyan, who threatened Konya from Kırkpınar on the Feast of Sacrifices. Siyāwush armed the youths, and the city escaped with a bad fright. But again in Dhu'l-Ḥijja 691/ November–December 1292, the Eşref laid hands on the fortress of Kavala, the key to the Konya district, and Siyāwush with the *nā'ib* Jamāl al-Dīn had to undertake a campaign to regain it on 29 Muḥarram 692/10 January 1293. Disorder reigned everywhere, and on top of this came a revolt by Siyāwush.

A very detailed report given by Aksarayi cannot be called into question. According to this, an army of Muslim troops of Asia Minor, under the orders of the sultan, Mujīr al-Dīn Mehmed (liberated on Geikhatu's accession, and favoured by him), and Najm al-Dīn, newly appointed by Geikhatu as vezir for Rūm, together with Mongol troops commanded by Anit, Göktay and Giray, proceeded to block the mountain passes of Kastamonu. As the Turcomans fell back, they pursued them. Returning to the offensive, the Turcomans surprised the vanguard commanded by Giray, causing Göktay to retreat. They then killed Anit, and captured Sultan Masʿūd, who was taken to Kastamonu. Giray however resumed the attack, routed the Turcomans, and liberated the sultan; then, grown prudent, he withdrew below Osmancık.

The reports given by *Tārīkh-i āl-i Saljūq* and Aksarayi are difficult to reconcile. According to the former, Siyāwush had won over the emirs of Kastamonu.[29] According to the *Tārīkh* also, the revolt followed on Geikhatu's departure, while according to Aksarayi it was due to the fear of him, and was at the same time as his arrival. This latter point is inadmissible, given the precision of the *Tārīkh*, but it remains possible that the origin of the breach goes back to the execution of Qutluja and the excesses committed by Geikhatu's Mongols, or to differences between Masʿūd and Siyāwush on these occasions. Siyāwush's presence in Konya during Geikhatu's stay is not mentioned, and it is possible that he had left by then; however, it is clear that he returned afterwards. He has been mentioned above as colluding there with Jamāl al-Dīn, who after visiting Geikhatu continued for some time to represent him there. That Siyāwush's revolt occurred previously is thus very unlikely.

Somewhat curiously, Aksarayi's report becomes brief at this point, so that he says nothing about Siyāwush's ultimate fate. According to the *Tārīkh*, however, matters went much more easily for him. At some date Geikhatu, while keeping Jamāl al-Dīn as *ḥākim*, appointed a new lieutenant-general for Rūm, named Tash-Temür. According to Aksarayi, he was appointed towards the end of 691/1292. While Jamāl al-Dīn stayed to administer Konya, Tash-Temür and the *mustawfī* (still perhaps Nāṣir al-Dīn Yavlak Arslan) marched on Burğlu (here meaning no doubt Safranbolu), which Siyāwush had made the centre of his revolt. An envoy from the *mustawfī* may have been enough to recall him to obedience. In any event, he allowed himself to be brought to Kayseri, where the two brothers were reconciled, and in the end Siyāwush even went back to Konya. Apart from the evident embellishment of the role of the *mustawfī*, there is no reason to refuse credit to this account. Aksarayi does not attest that Siyāwush played a direct part in the operations he describes; the disturbances among the Turcomans of the north might have other causes than Siyāwush's incitement, and he may only have exploited them. Aksarayi's campaign is one thing; the report of the *Tārīkh* another. It may be admitted that the insufficient success of the Turcoman revolt may subsequently have contributed to making Siyāwush's actions more comprehensible; the operations in Kastamonu may have been a replica of Geikhatu's personal campaign against the Turcomans of the south.

Two years later however, at the time when Geikhatu sent Baltu to Rūm (below, p. 225), fresh complaints against Siyāwush were carried to the *īlkhān*, according to the *Tārīkh*. Mas'ūd was easily persuaded to take action against him. Siyāwush fled to Develikarahisar. Sayf al-Dīn Sungur, the sultan's *çaşnigir*, persuaded him to surrender once again. Baltu thought him a good fellow, and gave him his daughter in marriage. So once more Siyāwush got out of a scrape.

As for Tash-Temür, he did not enjoy a good reputation at Konya. He was accused of exactions, and the sultan and *mustawfī* proceeded to arrest him. As Geikhatu does not seem to have been troubled about this, and did not restore him, he was presumably no longer attached to him. We are told that after this incident, the sultan went to Ankara with the *mustawfī*. This may perhaps have been for further measures of pacification after Siyāwush's revolt.

In spite of the partiality of the author of the *Tārīkh*, who moves the disorders in the administration forward to Geikhatu's death, it seems clear from Aksarayi's evidence that the deterioration, the roots of which lay far back, accelerated in his reign. Tash-Temür was succeeded by two persons, but the real head of the administration was increasingly Mujīr al-Dīn Mehmed as the *nā'ib* simultaneously of the *īlkhān* and the sultan; he also had an associate, but it was his brother. According to Aksarayi, this division of posts among several holders was general at all levels and, as each individual endeavoured to augment his income, and had his clients to provide for, reciprocal jealousies poisoned the functioning of the services, which only dealt more or less efficiently with petty current matters. Moreover each high official paid court directly to the *īlkhān* instead of attending to some sort of uniformity of management for Rūm, so it became ever less possible to speak of a real government of Asia Minor. This disintegration also assumed a territorial form with each individual levying on his own account the taxes of the region where he was master; consequently any central budget became increasingly illusory. Finally, Geikhatu multiplied the misappropriation of territory and revenue for his favourites, one of whom received in 692/1293 the general control of the government of the provinces, and another of the property in *injü* (royal domain), in some ill-defined relationship with Mujīr al-Dīn. The impression of disorder and discontent was thus general when the news arrived of the overthrow of Geikhatu by Baidu in 694/1295.

The intermezzo with Baidu was even worse. In reality there was a general movement of insubordination. Moreover the new ruler was, it seems, violently anti-Muslim, and Muslim institutions could be violated with impunity and misappropriated, if Aksarayi is to be believed. But Baidu was in his turn overthrown by Ghazan after a few months of rule later in 694/1295.

It will have been observed that little has been said of events in eastern Asia Minor. This is no doubt partly due to the fact that the two chroniclers who provide practically all our information come one from Aksaray, the other from Konya. But the lack of events there is not entirely because of this, since the rare and brief allusions by more general chroniclers show the same disproportion, Bar Hebraeus in particular, himself a resident in the eastern provinces and neighbouring countries. It is broadly evident that eastern Asia Minor, directly and firmly under Mongol control, having moreover no important Christian frontier, had less Turcoman activity and less insubordination of the native magnates, and was more integrated in the whole history of the Mongol world. Nevertheless the historians of the Mongol world say very little of it, perhaps because, being administratively distinct, it provided them with fewer facilities for documentation.

The narrative of events becomes tedious but it conveys an atmosphere. It was necessary to combat the Karamanids, who at this time regained for themselves the coastal stronghold of Alanya, which had been seized by a body of Franks from Cyprus. It was necessary to dispute Kavala, the key to the Konya basin, with the Eşref. During this period, Sultan Masʿūd had to fight the Turcomans of Kastamonu, and was almost held captive by them. As a matter of course we hear less of them than of the Turcomans of the south and south-west, perhaps simply because as the capitals were not so close to them, the Mongol-Seljukids and they left each other in more quiet.

On this occasion the war was partly caused by the revolt of Siyāwush against his brother, of which neither the chronology nor the details are clear. The brothers were reconciled like Kay Kāwūs II and Kılıc Arslan IV in the previous generation, in order to fall out again two years later, and again to be reconciled. Always there was a pretext for the Turcomans to increase their advantages, and to demonstrate that, apart from the exceptional moments when the Mongols approached their homeland, it was they who were truly the principal factors in the public life of Asia Minor.

The impression of growing disintegration was everywhere, certainly accelerated by the behaviour of Geikhatu, further accelerated when he was overthrown by Baidu, and Baidu by Ghazan. For reasons of mutual control, Geikhatu had systematically divided between two holders most of the official posts, including that of Mujīr al-Dīn, charged as always with the interests of the Mongol treasury. The sole consequence was an increase of quarrels, disorder and fraud. Every court official paid court directly to the Ilkhanid government, so that there was no unity of policy in Asia Minor, the administrative autonomy of the country became a pure fiction, and each district tended to turn into a personal lordship.

It was unfortunate for Asia Minor that the strengthening of the Mongol grasp occurred at the moment when the Mongol state itself began to show cracks, and these themselves evidently stimulated the rulers to increase their watchfulness over all their possessions. Precisely because the Mongol forces in Asia Minor were becoming more important, they were to play a greater role in the internal affairs of the Ilkhanid state. We have seen incidentally the failure of Qongqurtay's revolt and the success of Geikhatu's; and we have seen how the sultan and others were necessarily implicated. The chronicle of the end of the century and the following years, unfortunately ever less and less complete, shows Asia Minor as essentially a function (in mathematical terminology) of the risings of the Mongol chiefs who were there, and says little about what was happening among the people themselves. This is partly due to the gaps in the sources, but also to the fact that, by reason of the Mongol troubles, the emancipation of the Turcomans (whose chiefs were sometimes allies of the Mongols) henceforward became undisputed. Emancipation by a Mongol governor would not necessarily have been harmful if stabilization had ensured, for there would have been opportunities of correcting the abusive exploitation of the country for the benefit of an alien power. Attempts at overall emancipation however failed one after another, and Asia Minor only regained its independence, and that moreover after the fall of the Ilkhanid empire, in the form of a nebula of disunited principalities.

Ghazan had hardly seized power before a Mongol chief named Tagachar, formerly an adherent of Baidu, was trying to make himself independent in

Rūm in complicity with the Pervane's descendants. Combated feebly by ʿArab, Samaghar's son, and more energetically by Baltu, also the son of a former Mongol chief in Rūm, he was beaten in 694/1295. Baltu revolted in turn with some help from the Karamanids, and the impotent Sultan Masʿūd was drawn into his activities. Defeated by Sülemish, a grandson of Baiju, he fled to the Armenians of Cilicia. Not desiring to arouse the anger of the *īlkhān*, they handed him over, and he was beheaded in 696/1297. Although Masʿūd obtained a personal pardon, he was detained at Tabrīz, and he was replaced in Rūm by his nephew and former rival, ʿAlāʾ al-Dīn Kay Qubādh III. Of Kay Qubādh's career since his flight into Cilicia, nothing is known, but perhaps he was put forward by the Armenians. Next, Sülemish revolted in 1299 with help from the Karamanids. He was defeated by an Ilkhanid army at Sivas, which was resisting him, and fled to Syria. Fuller information about this than previous incidents is thus due to the Mamluk chronicles. Returning the following year, he was taken and executed. These men had apparently no original intention to revolt, but having become masters of the country by victory over a previous rebel, they exercised administrative authority which the *īlkhān* sought to bring under control. Wishing to escape it, they had no choice but to revolt. It will be observed that it happened particularly with men whose fathers or grandfathers had held commands in Rūm, which implies some degree of settlement there on domains acquired by whatever means.

Naturally each victor sacrificed the clients of his predecessor, and this applied to the sultans also. Kay Qubādh III for his part committed acts of vengeance which brought him into disrepute. He also went to pay his court to Ghazan, who sacrificed him. He was put to death, and Masʿūd returned in 702/1303 to a throne which brought him just enough to live decently and so was more devoid than ever of effective power. Power was exercised by Sutay and above all by Choban, one of the leading Mongol chiefs, to whom the victory over Sülemish was due. Then about 705/1306 power passed to Erenjen, a prince of the blood, sent by Öljeitu, the new *īlkhān*. It is at about this time that the sultanate disappears in so obscure a fashion that contemporaries do not mention it, while others trying to discern the event in retrospect disagree over both dates and facts. A sultan's death, even the lack of a successor, no longer had any practical importance. Descendants of the Seljukids survived, above all a number of women, and some notables prided themselves on a Seljukid pedigree. Politically however the era was at an end, or rather had been over for some decades.

On Öljeitu's death in 1312, Choban, the real master of the Ilkhanid empire, reappeared in Rūm in conditions which are not exactly clear, in order to assume the government. Erenjen was not however immediately set aside, but Choban, who could not stay, left the real power to his son, Temür-Tash. It is not easy to see why Temür-Tash revolted (722/1321), not merely as an opponent like several predecessors, but also as a religious adversary by proclaiming himself as the *mahdī*, who was expected by most Muslims, and particularly the Shīʿa. Choban, who was still all-powerful, was allowed to proceed in person to put him down, and he put to death some accomplices whom he held responsible. He took his rebel son to the *Ilkhān* Abū Saʿīd, and obtained not only his pardon but also his restoration to the government of Rūm. Aksarayi, who finished his chronicle as Temür-Tash's protégé after the restoration, passes over his rebellion, and ascribes the revolt to Erenjen against Temür-Tash, and ending in his execution. The result is that Temür-Tash's revolt, some of the causes for which might be sought in the Ilkhanid state and not in Asia Minor, remains unclear. Then in 727/1326, when Choban had fallen, Temür-Tash found himself driven to revolt again. This time in spite of a resistance at Sivas, he had to flee to Egypt like his predecessor Sülemish. But the international situation was not the same; peace had been concluded between the Mamluk sultanate and Abū Saʿīd. For this or some other reason, Temür-Tash was suspected of conspiracy, and put to death in 728/1327.

The account has been carried up to the fall of Temür-Tash without a break, because there are no profound changes in this period. It will no doubt be observed that here the narrative is only an outline sketch, and that in reality the centre of events lies on the one hand in a part of Mongol Iran, on the other among the Turcomans, who must now be more precisely discussed as far as possible.

Before starting this new topic, it may just be said that a new situation was produced on the death of Abū Saʿīd, the last *īlkhān*, in 1335. In theory at least, he had still reigned over the whole of the realm. After his death the succession was disputed by various pretenders; one of them, Ḥasan, Temür-Tash's son and grandson of Choban, known as Ḥasan-i Kūchak (i.e. Küçük, 'the Little'), briefly disturbed central and eastern Anatolia. In fact, apart from territories over which Mongol nomad tribes passed, nothing remained there of Mongol power except in the more or less enlarged province of Sivas, which was henceforward called Rūm in a narrow sense, and was in the hands of a former lieutenant of Temür-Tash called Eretna. He no longer cared about allegiance to any power outside Anatolia. A somewhat larger power was to be reconstituted in Iran by the Jalayirid dynasty, but they, in spite of some paper pretensions, never effectively extended their authority over Asia Minor. Perhaps some institutional continuity was maintained in the Eretnid principality, which, however, progressively allowed itself to be absorbed into the society around it, and was more or less turcicized once again.

CHAPTER TWENTY

The formation of the first Turcoman principalities

The preceding account of events shows that at the end of the seventh/thirteenth century there were three principal forces in Asia Minor: the Mongols, the urban Muslims and the Turcomans. The last had existed since the original Turkish conquest, but their numbers and importance had grown since the appearance of the Mongols. The three groups were in opposition to one another, with changing alliances which were complicated by the rivalries within each. The Mongol efforts to reduce the Turcomans had failed, especially in the western part of Asia Minor, apart from the central plateau. Little by little what had been no more than bands of nomadic pastoralists around cities which were still more or less governed by representatives of the central authority had become autonomous groups, and had taken possession of those cities. So principalities, still in a primitive stage of development, came into existence, and divided up the country. None of them had existed before the coming of the Mongols, and several of them were still gnawing at the remains of the Byzantine Empire and the realm of Nicaea. It is indeed very difficult to put their history together when it does not touch that of the Byzantines, the Seljukids and the Mongols. A fairly complete picture can only be drawn for around 1330, thanks to al-ʿUmarī and Ibn Baṭṭūta. However, this fact lends particular importance to the lists of Pachymeres and Nicephorus Gregoras for all the start of the fourteenth century, however rudimentary and sometimes obscure they may be.

The oldest of the principalities, and in this period the strongest or one of the two strongest, was that of the Karamanids. It too came into being after the arrival of the Mongols, but in the western Taurus, a region already strongly turcomanized. The origins and history of the Karamanids have already been dealt with because of their impact on Seljukid-Mongol history, particularly in the crisis of 1276–77. According to Eflaki, the historian of Konya in the fourteenth century, the invention of the white head-coverings which were generally fashionable in his time should perhaps be attributed to Mehmed Beg the Karamanid rather than his homonym of Denizli, thus being evidence of his influence. In any event, it was he who as master of Konya tried to introduce Turkish as the chancery language, as perhaps it was already for his minor correspondence. The reform had no immediate future, whatever seems to have been believed, but it was nevertheless not without significance. As has been seen, he deemed it necessary to legitimize his authority with that of a false or genuine Seljukid.

Mehmed Beg's successor from at least 1283 was Güneri Beg, perhaps a brother. This at least is the name given him by the author of *Tārīkh-i āl-i Saljūq*, who had a good knowledge of the history in which the Karamanid chief played a part. It is however strange that, anyhow under this name, there is no numismatic or epigraphic evidence of him, nor is he mentioned in the chronicles. He may have borne another name also, and the honorific of Majd al-Dīn, but textual information is lacking for the years from 683/1284–85 to 699/1299–1300 or 700/1300–01, where the *Tārīkh* places him. No doubt it is best to insert him between Mehmed and Maḥmūd, the last of Karaman's sons, who is known to have headed the clan at the beginning of the eighth/fourteenth century. The history of his relations with the neighbouring powers shows that like his father he was opposed to the Mongols, but concerned rather to act under the cover of the Seljukid sultans rather than revolt, if this were avoidable. In the Cilician and Isaurian Taurus he possessed Ermenek and Mut, the old seats of family power, but he added Lârende on the interior plateau and Alanya on the coast, while his influence extended to Ereğli and almost to Niğde. In 700/1300–01 an inscription of an otherwise unknown Karamanid shows that the family were starting to take an interest in urban religious foundations.

It has been shown that the Karamanids had several times sought to secure control over the Seljukid residence of Konya, the true capital of their frontier region. Once again, and in completely unknown circumstances, Mūsā, one of Maḥmūd's sons, occupied the city despite the resistance of its *ahi*s, and Choban retook it. Temür-Tash defended the region of Niğde against them, but Aksarayi (who knew the country well) goes on to say that the Mongol chief established peace with the Turcomans through his good relations with them – no doubt after his revolt. There can be little doubt that about this time Konya passed finally into the hands of the Karamanids. The Mongols were really no longer concerned about this region, or were no longer capable of acting effectively. Some of the townsmen finished by making the best of things, no doubt feeling that it was best to accept the inevitable, thereby reducing its inconveniences. Perhaps in some cases they preferred the Turcomans to the Mongols, and the Karamanids were visibly becoming more civilized.

The Eşref (more precisely, Eşrefoğulları) first made their appearance beside the Karamanids, but never equalled them in power. Perhaps mixed with Kurdish elements, they disputed with the Karamanids for influence at Konya, no doubt with a more general wish for independence. They proceeded to establish themselves further west on the marches of the province of Konya at Beyşehir, and at times occupied Abgurum, Kavala and other places. There is epigraphic evidence of Süleyman b. Eşref (d. 702/1302) in an inscription of 689/1290 over the refurbished fortress gate of Beyşehir. The city, renamed Süleymanşehir, was endowed with a mosque, of which the *waqfiyya* is extant, proving that he was a civilized prince. His son, Mubāriz al-Dīn Mehmed, extended his power over Akşehir and Bolvadin, endowed the former with a mosque, and in 1314 paid homage to Temür-Tash, a gesture which legitimized his power at no personal cost. However, in 1326 Temür-Tash rose in revolt, took Beyşehir and put Mubāriz al-Dīn to death. That was the end of the dynasty; not because the territory remained in the hands of the Mongols, but because in the course of events it was partitioned between the Karamanids and the Hamidoğulları.

The Hamidoğulları only appear in literary texts at the beginning of the eighth/fourteenth century, when they are said to hold Antalya, Eğridir and Burğlu. Epigraphy, useful also for the neighbouring Turcomans, shows that they were in these cities at the very end of the thirteenth century and the start of the fourteenth. The existence of numerous Turcomans in the hinterland of Antalya is known from the mid-thirteenth century from Ibn Saʿīd; but in the time of the Pervane the province of which Antalya was the capital was firmly held by one of his kinsmen or allies, Badr al-Dīn *Malik al-Sawāḥil* (i.e. King of the Coastlands), who restored for his own benefit the autonomous march of Ertöküş. It was no doubt around 1280 that Antalya passed from his successor to the Turcomans. Under the Hamidoğulları the territory was divided among three members of the family. The ruler of Antalya was defeated by Temür-Tash, but the principality was reconstituted by another member of the family who had taken refuge in Egypt.

It is also in connection with the Karamanids that the Menteşeoğulları are first mentioned. They were later established in the south-western corner of Asia Minor, and will be discussed later.

The zone comprising the central Anatolian wilderness and the high valleys running down to the sea formed a principality of a different kind in the last quarter of the thirteenth century. The Germiyanoğulları who were the possessors formed, as has been mentioned, a group of ethnic-social origin, probably of Kurdish descent but turcicized. It has been shown how the Seljukid-Mongol government brought them from eastern Anatolia about

1275 for help in its struggle against the Turcomans of the west. It was probably for this reason that for some time they came to be considered as having a certain predominance over the neighbouring principalities. It will also be remembered that the vezir Fakhr al-Dīn ʿAlī established an autonomous lordship around Karahisar for the benefit of his family, which he no doubt considered as relying on the Germiyan in case of need.

In consequence of the struggles among the pretenders to the sultanate, and their search for allies, the Germiyan effectively found themselves as much hostile to, as in agreement with, the official powers at Konya; and in the general disintegration of the state, they ended by becoming a principality like the others. However, Germiyan is the name of the people, and not as with the others that of the ruling family, who were known by their ancestral name of ʿAlī Shīr. Their centre was Kütahya; at the end of the thirteenth century Yaʿqūb, a descendant of ʿAlī Shīr, was a powerful chief. An inscription claims, perhaps ambitiously, that he controlled Ankara to the east, and to the west in particular Tripoli of the Menderes, Gümüşaşar, Sovriköy, Simav and Kula. Kinsmen or vassals held Denizli and Aydın; while Alaşehir (Philadelphia), which was under Byzantine sovereignty, paid him tribute. Al-ʿUmarī extols the resources of his state. Yaʿqūb built a mosque, and a romance of chivalry was dedicated to his son; but around the same time Ibn Baṭṭūta echoes rumours accusing the Germiyan of unorthodox Yazīdī tendencies. The descendants of Fakhr al-Dīn ʿAlī *Ṣāḥib ʿAṭā*, rulers of a small principality between the Germiyan and the Hamidoğulları, were still probably known to al-ʿUmarī under the corrupt form of his name, Ṣā'ib, due to a Genoese informant. Towards the middle of the eighth/fourteenth century their territory was incorporated in the Germiyan principality.

It has been seen earlier that Denizli was the scene of a first Turcoman attempt at autonomy, which failed. The city was retaken by the Seljukid-Mongol government, then briefly disputed between the Germiyan and the descendants of Fakhr al-Dīn ʿAlī. In the time of the *Īlkhān* Ghazan, Rashīd al-Dīn, the celebrated historian and vezir, perhaps with a touch of bluff considered it as firmly enough held to be a possible summer residence for the Mongol ruler.

It was principally from Germiyan territory that Turcoman penetration into Byzantine Aegean territory progressively took place. The attraction of this movement of expansion withdrew part of their warrior forces from the Germiyan, and contributed to their decline. This expansion had been helped by the return of the Byzantine government to Constantinople in 1261, which distracted it from attaching great importance to the insidious penetration of its frontiers in Asia Minor by Turcoman nomads. The country was already practically lost when the Emperor Andronicus II (1282–1308) decided to use the great Catalan Company, then in Greece. The attempt failed in the end, and after 1304 there were no longer Byzantine forces in the Anatolian hinterland of the Aegean Sea.

From south to north the front was then held by the principalities of Menteşe, Aydın, Saruhan and Karası, with Osman to the north-east. The principality of Menteşe appears to have been more or less established before 1290. This was not the case in 1277, when Menteşe, a Turcoman chief who had perhaps previously been settled in the Sivas region, was involved in fighting with the Karamanids. No doubt it was in connection with setbacks at this time or previous struggles against the Eşref that he migrated beyond Lâdik, where he was at war with others in 1282. At the beginning of the fourteenth century the territory of Menteşe included Milas, Muğla and other places, i.e. ancient Caria. At sea they confronted the Hospitallers, who had just established themselves in Rhodes. Naturally they picked up the traditions of the native sailors, and their expansion took the form of privateering and piracy.

The territory which was soon to form the principality of Aydın was the meeting-place of expansion from the south with Sasa, a vassal of Menteşe, and from the territory of Germiyan in the east under the sons of Aydın. Of Mehmed Aydınoğlu nothing is known before *c.* 700/1300. Of the Saruhan dynasty nothing is known at this period. Between them, the city of Alaşehir had an obscure autonomous status. The petty dynasty of Karası was perhaps a little later, resulting from both Turcoman infiltration from the south and the transfer of Turks from the Balkans by the Byzantines. The primitive principality of Osman around its kernel in Söğüt, the cradle of the future Ottoman Empire, was then nothing more than a little group like the others.[30]

Although geographical conditions were to allow these principalities to gain new power by gradually overflowing beyond the Straits and the Aegean coast, their activity did not differ at all from that of restless Turcoman groups which were waging war at the time around what remained of the state of Trebizond and westwards to Samsun. At the beginning of the fourteenth century they clashed at times with contingents of Mongols augmented by Georgians.

In the midst of the northern Turcomans an important bloc was formed by the principality of Kastamonu. As has been seen, the Turcomans were numerous there, and Kay Qubādh I gave the governor of the region an important role, culminating in the celebrated expedition to the Crimea. It is not clear to what extent the chiefs were autonomous during the thirteenth century, or were an integral part of the Turcomans as a whole.

According to Ibn Bībī, Muẓaffar al-Dīn Yavlak Arslan, the son of Ḥusām al-Dīn Alp Yürük, was a notable who held ancestral possessions from Ḥusām al-Dīn Amīr Çopan in the time of Kay Qubādh I. In the struggle between the sultans, Yavlak Arslan supported Masʿūd when he came from the Crimea, and was to find his death in the troubles of 691/1292. The cultural integration of the family and its political role are proved by the fact that to him were dedicated a treatise of popular astrology, an account of religious history and a collection of administrative texts. Nevertheless there is no doubt that in 1256 Kastomonu was dependent on a *beglerbegi* called Tutuş based in Konya; that in 1258 the province was taken over by Baba Tuğrai to meet the costs of his vezirate; that, because of this, Tāj al-Dīn Muʿtazz briefly held it as security for the repayment of Tuğrai's debts; that in 1272 it was administered by a son of the Pervane, and that his son, Mehmed Beg, again possessed it in 1295–99. In the same province Osmancık was evidently under the control of the Seljukid-Mongol government in 670/1271, since the vezir Fakhr al-Dīn ʿAlī was briefly imprisoned there. It must then probably be admitted that Alp Yürük, Yavlak Arslan and his son Maḥmūd only possessed Kastamonu during a fairly short period after the Pervane's death, doubtless as belonging to a family which exercised an older and more stable, if limited, power in the region. Their role in the revolts of Masʿūd II and Siyāwush has been described, and it is also known that around 1280 a Byzantine attack on Sinop was repulsed by the Turcomans. It does not follow that these rulers were Turcoman chiefs; on the contrary, these chiefs were raised against them by Siyāwush.

This would explain why it was definitely not this family that founded the durable principality of the Candarids, the eponym of which was a certain Candar (Jāndār), settled at Eflani to the west of Kastamonu, to whom later sources attribute the conquest of this city and of Sinop. But Sinop was independent until at least 1326, and Aksarayi states that Candar's son, Süleyman Paşa, was already master of Kastamonu in 1314, and did homage there to the *Īlkhān* Abū Saʿīd. The Greek writers seem aware of him from 1300, and say nothing of his father, known from a dubious inscription of perhaps 1289. Ibn Baṭṭūta met Süleyman Paşa, but on the occasion of al-ʿUmarī's visit he had recently been replaced by his son, Ibrāhīm. Significantly, however, al-ʿUmarī always calls the country 'the country of Sulaymān Pasha'. He sees no connection between him and the former dynasty of Kastamonu. The matter is further complicated by the fact that the Byzantine historians call the powerful chiefs of the region 'Amouroi', without making it clear of which dynasty they are speaking, one of the two mentioned, or that known at Girdebolu to the west of Kastamonu.

The history of Sinop before its incorporation in the Candarid state is hardly clearer. It is known that it formed part of the Pervane's principality, and that at the end of the thirteenth century it still (or again) belonged to his son, Mehmed Beg, then perhaps to his son Masʿūd Beg, who took Samsun at the beginning of the fourteenth century. At that time Sinop was in the hands of a certain Gazi Çelebi, of whom nothing is known. To the people of Trebizond and the Genoese, he was a notorious corsair; to Ibn Baṭṭūta and al-ʿUmarī, a wrecker of ships at Kaffa and in the Crimea as an underwater diver. According to writers in Ottoman times, he was a son of the Seljukid Masʿūd – the Masʿūd Beg just mentioned might also be borne in mind. According to his tombstone, he was the son of Masʿūd Beg or Çelebi. He was active until at least 1324. Sinop had been incorporated into the Candarid principality by the time of Ibn Baṭṭūta's visit.

There were other autonomous groups in the Syro-Mesopotamian marches at the beginning of the fourteenth century. Unstable and little known, they were in any case controlled by the then dominant Mamluk sultanate.

This is not the place to trace the further destiny of these nascent principalities. Most of them claimed that their rulers had been invested legally by the last Seljukids, even by the great Kay Qubādh I. More authentically, some chiefs are known to have paid homage to the *Īlkhān* Abū Saʿīd without any practical consequences.

PART FOUR

Society and Institutions in the Mongol Period

CHAPTER TWENTY-ONE

Ethnic, social and economic development

The new population elements which the Mongol invasion pushed into Asia Minor, first driving them forward and then carrying them in its ranks, have already often been incidentally mentioned: Iranians on the one hand, Turcomans on the other, and even the Mongols too in the east of the country and later in the central Anatolian plateau had settled down after 1256 with their animals and their families. Changes ensued in their numbers for which precision is difficult, changes also of a qualitative kind. In economic and cultural matters the new Turcomans, to say nothing of the Mongols, were not exactly akin to their predecessors.

An important question is to know the ethnic and tribal groups to which they belonged. It has already been stressed that the Seljukid expansion did not apparently bring in more than a part, albeit an important part, of the Oghuz. While the Turcomans already settled in Anatolia migrated more or less westwards towards the Byzantine Empire, the new arrivals often came more or less directly from Central Asia, where they had not undergone the same pattern of development as their kin in Asia Minor. It is impossible to say whether or not they had the tribal traditions which, as has been seen, were lacking among the Turcomans of Asia Minor; the texts of the Mongol period say hardly more of this than do their predecessors. It is possible that a certain tribal sense may have developed among the Turcomans when confronting the Mongols, but the evidence only becomes clear in the new conditions at the end of the fourteenth century. Moreover the place names that can be ascertained for the sixteenth century from Ottoman documentation show that broadly speaking there was dispersion rather than formation of tribal groups, as well as migration as the generations passed. Finally it should be noted that with the Mongols there were Turkish elements, particularly the Uyghurs, that were totally distinct from the Oghuz

Turcomans. The interest of these questions in the study of the western principalities has been seen. Kurdish migration also should not be forgotten. The various groups were neither entirely nor permanently identical economically; among them were shepherds and herders of camels, while some were partly sedentarized cultivators.

Whatever the tribal groups to which the Turcomans of Asia Minor may have belonged, the clear result of the events which have been described was that the impact of the Mongols accentuated the tendency, already apparent in the Seljukid period, for them to cluster in the frontier regions. In confrontation with the Mongols, who held the middle of Anatolia and the great route-centres, the Turcomans organized themselves on the periphery. In a sense Turkey lay on the periphery; and when the enfeeblement of the Mongols left the centre progressively lacking in any dynamism of its own, it was from the periphery that Turkey was reconstituted.

The Turcoman expansion of the end of the thirteenth and beginning of the fourteenth century does not display the same characteristics as that of the turn of the eleventh and twelfth centuries. The earlier expansion had been by warfare; the latter shows less of this character. In the plains it was rather an infiltration of pastoralists, with whom the native peasants more or less came to terms. The towns capitulated fairly quickly, or reached an understanding with the newcomers in order to avoid the ruin of the agricultural estates which fed them. Two great zones must be distinguished: that which had been Seljukid, which on the whole continued its previous existence, and that which had been acquired from the remains of the Byzantine Empire in Asia Minor, where the Greek peasants and townspeople remained without any brutal changes – so that the economic situation found by al-ʿUmarī's informants around 1300 did not differ radically from what it had been two or three generations before. The pastoral economy had certainly made an advance, but agriculture had not disappeared.

The political and institutional history of Asia Minor under the Mongol protectorate leaves an impression of disorder and ruin which cannot be entirely an illusion but must be qualified, inasmuch as the same period, particularly before the fourteenth century, saw an immense activity of commerce and culture. Warfare was neither continual nor ubiquitous, and the diminution of the resources of the Seljukid state might not signify the impoverishment of the country but simply a transfer of resources, partly to the Ilkhanid state (which made some compensating expenditure in Asia Minor), and partly to individual notables, who often undertook the upkeep of institutions hitherto funded by the state. So the various facts suggested by examination of the sources must be approached without prejudice.

As regards agriculture, did the Mongol presence and the Turcoman expansion modify the extent and structure of the cultivable areas? It was remarked previously that the arrival of the Turcoman pastoralists was not always in itself a factor prejudicial to agriculture. The situation is much less clear at the stage now reached. Generally speaking, it can hardly be denied that in the long or short run, the consequence of the Mongol invasion in most of the affected countries was an advance of pastoral nomadism to the detriment of agriculture. The newcomers appear to have respected less than their predecessors the cultivation and agricultural operations with which they had hardly lived in Central Asia; or they put such pressure on the peasants that they gave up, and abandoned the land to anyone wanting pasture – a situation from which the Kurds also profited. It is however possible that in some cases this eventuality may itself have been an incentive to some measure of Turcoman sedentarization, although it is admittedly not possible to follow the development in Rūm, if such occurred. Moreover it was not necessarily the same from one end of the territory to the other. Once the principalities had settled down in the fourteenth century, al-ʿUmarī's informants spoke favourably not only of the raising of stock, as was natural, but also of agriculture.

There are perhaps some better indicators of the exploitation of the natural resources of the country. There is no reason to suppose that either the products or the sites of exploitation underwent any necessary change, but in some cases change may have occurred in the organization of exploitation. The beginning of alum exploitation has been mentioned. In 1255 the missionary William of Rubruck found it in the hands of a Genoese of Syrian origin, Nicholas de Santo Siro, and a Venetian from Cyprus, Boniface de Molendino, who were partners in the monopoly. It is possible that, as the exploitation of alum had been undertaken especially in the interest and at the suggestion of Western traders, the management had from the start been committed to Westerners acting more or less autonomously; so that representatives of each of the two rival powers were paired to counterbalance one another, and to safeguard the Seljukid state against the abuse of an over-inclusive monopoly. It is also possible however that the concession of such a monopoly fell into the category of shared revenues which the notables were now making among themselves. This can only be a query; moreover we are in total ignorance whether the management continued in this form, or whether the state resumed the direct sale of alum in the years after William of Rubruck's visit. It is known that about 1275 the Zaccaria family of Genoa discovered and brought into exploitation a new alum field at Phocaea on the Aegean coast of Asia Minor, which was still Byzantine. Was this a result of difficulty in obtaining Turkish alum, or conversely did the new alum, situated almost on the embarkation wharf, threaten wholly or in part the exploitation of Turkish alum? It seems that, for a time at least, the Genoese were able to maintain the two alums side by side by using Trebizond and other ports, no doubt by a balance of prices.

As regards the other resources of Asia Minor, the principal evidence comes from the very beginning of the Mongol period, that of Simon of St Quentin, on which we drew to establish the list. All this is both confirmed and completed by later writers, who have no reason to speak only of the past. With regard to the Turcoman head-coverings, it is known that from about 1260 there were white ones in contrast to the red ones mentioned by Simon, but it is not known if they were also exported. The Italians found purchasers for Flanders cloth in Asia Minor, but Marco Polo was equally aware that the Greeks of Rūm made fine carpets and textiles of red silk and otherwise, and the Armenians of Erzincan a marvellous buckram. Fifty years later Pegolotti still knows of the buckram of Erzincan,[31] and Ibn Baṭṭūta makes a vaguer allusion to the beautiful textiles of this city. He also admired the woollen rugs of Aksaray, and also the cotton fabrics edged with gold embroidery from Denizli and Ayasoluk, continued or resumed by the Greeks from their Byzantine past. In this connection the correspondence of Rashīd al-Dīn enumerates various kinds of textiles, on the one hand from Rūm, on the other especially from Erzincan; among the former moreover are textiles coming from the Crimea and Russia. About the middle of the century again mention is made in the *Risāla* of Ibn Kiyā al-Mazandarānī of the woollens of Sivas and Kastamonu, together with the saddles of Tokat.

There is less information about the mines, but al-ʿUmarī, with data valid for about 1300, knew of three silver mines in Rūm at Gümüşsaray, Lu'lu'a and perhaps Baburt. Ibn Baṭṭūṭa knew of copper mines in the province of Erzincan, thanks to which vases and famous lamps were manufactured there. It is difficult to obtain clear impressions from scattered data of this kind about the level of artisan activity, its development or its decline, but in the final analysis there is no reason to conclude that there was any catastrophe before the fall of the Ilkhanid empire.

The commodities mentioned are hardly known except as objects of commerce. It is certain that commerce was really active, but largely in the hands of foreigners in transit, perhaps without much benefit to the country. In this respect the effects of Mongol domination are fairly complex, and one should not be in a hurry to celebrate the expansion of commerce because Marco Polo and other Italians passed that way, as is done somewhat frequently with a rather simple-minded enthusiasm. At least if there was an expansion for them, there was not necessarily simply an expansion for everybody. As has been seen, there was commercial activity before the Mongols. The creation of the Mongol empire, the incorporation of Asia Minor in its economic system, and the political decline of Konya certainly reduced, but without destroying, the role of the western part of the country to the profit of the eastern part. In 1255 William of Rubruck found Franks at Konya who were doubtless not soldiers. For the period of Jalāl al-Dīn Rūmī, Eflaki speaks of a merchant of Tabrīz who had come to Konya. The breach between the Mongols and the Mamluks of Egypt and Syria, which was more complete than the average in the wars of that time, must temporarily have threatened the trade of ports such as Antalya and Alanya, insofar as this breach had restrictive power where trade was not in Italian hands, or did not pass by way of Cyprus. This state of affairs continued at least until the formation (which it may have assisted) of the Turcoman principalities, which absorbed the ports, and were politically inclined towards Egypt.

Similarly the breach between the Mongols of Persia and those of Russia, and the close links between the latter, the Golden Horde and the Mamluks (for whom they procured *mamlūk* recruits through the Genoese) diverted to the Straits part of the transit-trade, especially in slaves, which would otherwise have gone by Asia Minor. This new route harmed such ports as Sinop and Samsun, and perhaps contributed to the birth at Sinop of that alternation of trade and piracy which characterized the activity of its ruler, Gazi Çelebi, at the beginning of the fourteenth century.

Finally, and perhaps especially, if Anatolian commerce played only a modest part before 1243 in the relations of Europe with the remoter East (if not in the relations among the eastern lands themselves), thereafter the eastern part of Anatolia was traversed by long-distance international trade, which linked Italy with Tabrīz, the residence of the *īlkhāns*, and sometimes with more distant parts; but, whereas before 1243 Anatolia was itself a goal for the merchants, they now tended to cross it without leaving any of their goods or their profits. The two ways of access by sea to the Ilkhanate were on the one hand Ayas (Yumurtalık) in Cilicia, on the other Trebizond at the far end of the Black Sea, both vassals of the *īlkhān*. From Trebizond the caravans only touched the edge of Asia Minor at Erzurum, which was ever less a real part of it. From Ayas the route went up by Kayseri to Sivas, before coming to Erzurum by way of Erzincan. Both these routes left Asia Minor proper to one side. Finally, however great Italian trade was with Tabrīz, the major part of the imports from the Indian Ocean to the Mediterranean passed through Egypt; while as for trade with China, there was rivalry between the Iranian route and the other which ran to the north through the territories of the Golden Horde, the adversary of the Ilkhanate.

Sivas retained a major, though perhaps a diminished role. This was probably partly due to the existing firmness of its organization, partly to the fact that it remained the crossroads for merchants who, instead of going to Tabrīz, went by way of Samsun, Vatiza (Fatsa) or Sinop to Kaffa in the Crimea (as did many Genoese), or who came from Tabrīz to Constantinople. There is a letter from Jalāl al-Dīn addressed to a merchant on his way to Sivas. In particular, chance has preserved some deeds drawn up by Genoese notaries at Sivas in 1274 and 1280, while staying in the inn of some Muslim colleague or other before moving on to follow the merchants to other staging-posts such as Vatiza for the Crimea or Erzincan for Tabrīz.

There is nothing to follow immediately, but in 1300 Genoa even set up a permanent representation at Sivas, which witnesses to the continued coming of the Genoese. Pegolotti explains that at each stage on the road there were Ilkhanid police officers, to whom a due had to be paid to secure a safe passage. On the other hand on one occasion, corresponding in date to the serious disturbances of 1276, a Sivas galley, i.e. a galley of merchants going to Sivas, was plundered at sea by corsairs. It may have been in reprisal for this kind of incident that Sinop was attacked by some Franks in 1298. On another occasion a caravan of Frankish merchants was pillaged near to Amasya, i.e. between Sivas and Sinop or Samsun. Another time, another of their caravans was plundered by Turcomans of the Taurus or the west. Yet it is certain on the whole that these occurrences were sufficiently exceptional to allow the Genoese (who were almost solely concerned) to continue their trade in Asia Minor as long as the Ilkhanate lasted. There are instances when they took on board their vessels merchants who were Ilkhanid subjects, and whose names indicate a variety of peoples and confessions. In 1271 several of them who had suffered losses because their ship had been pillaged by an Italian attacker received compensation. An anecdote about Jalāl al-Dīn shows him negotiating with a merchant who had been with the 'oriental Franks'. Another tells of a merchant who embarked at Antalya for Egypt, and had been captured by Franks.

As has been seen, caravanserais had been built before 1243, but many others were added during the period of Mongol rule. This is evidence of the vitality of commerce and the interest shown in it by the Seljukid and Ilkhanid governments, and by important individuals such as Karatay, but it also happened that in times of trouble some of these caravanserais were used as fortresses by rebels or bandits. The classification of the caravanserais of this period is interesting insofar as they may be accurately dated by inscriptions. Directly after the rout of 1243, the effects of which were not yet fully felt, several caravanserais were completed or built in south-west or western Anatolia, while by a celebrated act of foundation Karatay completed provision for the route linking Konya or Syria to Kayseri and Sivas by a caravanserai. A little later, evidently as a result of the Pervane's action, the connections of Sivas with Tokat and the Black Sea were secured by other acts of foundation, while Fakhr al-Dīn 'Alī continued to encourage the merchants of western Anatolia and Denizli. As well as the caravanserais, there were also *ribāṭ*s, fortified posts or dervish convents. Attention was also paid to the upkeep of roads and bridges, such as the bridge of Choban, the Mongol governor, between Erzurum and Tabrīz. At each stage on an important route there was a police detachment under the orders of a *kōtwāl*, to whom the merchants paid a protection-due. As has been mentioned, the Mongols introduced the *tamgha*, a sort of tax imposed in Iran but perhaps without a precedent under the Seljukids.

It is doubtful whether the Genoese or others were able to establish links immediately with the Turcoman principalities of the west and south, although relations can never have been entirely interrupted between Cyprus and Antalya or Alanya. However, when the principalities became stabilized, merchants were no doubt favoured by the rulers. This was not a matter of large-scale commerce but of interregional maritime trade, which was more and more falling into the hands of the Italians, or of acquiring the produce of the country, such as the alum of Kütahya, at this time especially through Ayasoluk. Ayasoluk (Altoluogo) on the one hand, Antalya and Alanya (Candeloro) on the other were deemed worthy by Pegolotti to be included in his treatise, which says that some time previously the Bardi of Florence, arriving on Pisan ships at Antalya, had obtained important reductions of duties which placed them almost on a level with the Cypriots. The Provençals also frequented Antalya. It is even possible that the Genoese had penetrated the hinterland of these ports, for a Genoese named Domenico Doria, who fell into the hands of the Egyptians, gave al-ʿUmarī half of the very remarkable data which he transmits on western and central Asia Minor and its different principalities as they were around 1330.

The incorporation of Asia Minor into the Mongol system entailed as time passed the alignment of its money with that of the *īlkhāns*. They, while allowing the dinar currency, newly based their monetary system on silver, but on a different rate of exchange from the classical system and from the systems prevailing in the neighbouring states. At first the Seljukid state of the coinage was retained, at least in principle, but according to Rashīd al-Dīn (who is only partially confirmed by the numismatic collections) the percentage of silver was enormously reduced, as was the tendency in the Mamluk state also. A similar condition of disorder existed under the *īlkhāns*, and was due to general factors rather than to their particular policy.

It is well known that in 1294 the *Ilkhān* Geikhatu, when attempting to reform his realm, tried to introduce a sort of paper money modelled on that current under his kinsmen in China. The technical and psychological preparations were naturally both inadequate, and the reform could not be maintained. Its introduction into Asia Minor was started, and Aksarayi echoes the complaints which arose. Thereupon Ghazan issued a new currency with a dinar at about half of the legal Muslim dinar, and a dirham at one-sixth of this dinar. The Mongol coinage was introduced into Asia Minor at the same time in the context of the strengthening of direct administration. The result was that the new Mongol system with the names of the Anatolian mints became current in this country also.

CHAPTER TWENTY-TWO

The development of the landed and fiscal systems

The Mongol protectorate of Asia Minor, followed by direct rule, stimulated fairly profound changes alike in the landed and fiscal systems. Too many investigators have imprudently confused the issue by considering the institutions of the Mongol period and those of the time of Seljukid independence as being one and the same. The development which actually occurred was due partly to the internal conditions of the administration in Asia Minor, and partly to the introduction of Iranian Mongol practices from the Ilkhanate. These practices in their turn were introduced at first simply because of the presence of Mongol agents in Asia Minor, later and more systematically to set right the marked decline in the administration of the country by means of a tendency towards the unification of institutions in all parts of the Ilkhanid empire.

It has already been shown that at the highest level of the state, the provinces had been partly distributed among the nominal ministers and magnates of the government. At this level it is difficult to tell whether there was a partition into principalities or a distribution of estates. Below this level there were also alienations which transferred state rights and possessions to private notables, either directly by the constitution of new private estates, or in a more complex manner by the transformation of *iqṭāʿ*s into estates.

The sultans distributed state lands as estates in order to win or keep partisans in their internal quarrels. Kılıc Arslan IV in particular appears to have been prodigal in largesse of this kind, which, as has been seen, was not entirely new, but had never been practised on so large a scale. There is extant a deed of grant to a shaykh, but it is known more generally that in one of his conflicts with Kay Kāwūs II, he promised all the emirs of his following that he would grant them the *iqṭāʿ*s of their rivals and, if victory crowned their endeavours, he would convert them into estates. In fact at the end of his short life he made many gifts of this kind, and this contributed to the rousing of anxiety and to the hastening of his assassination. In other cases the sale of state domains might be a means of procuring funds, and this time it is Kay Kāwūs II who provides examples: in 657/1259 and 660/1262 he sold a village in the province of Sivrihisar to one emir and another in the province of Amasya to another, and the deeds of sale are extant. There is also evidence that land acquired as estates could of course be alienated, e.g. to found *waqfs*. It is also very probable that in addition to regular concessions, numerous straightforward acts of usurpation occurred in times of troubles. When the *Ilkhān* Ghazan and his famous minister, Rashīd al-Dīn Faḍlallāh Hamadānī, endeavoured a general reorganization of the empire about 700/1300, an attempt was made to recover the lands illicitly appropriated in Asia Minor; but this as it stood had to be given up as the holders of the lands revolted. They were however obliged to pay large sums in compensation.

Nevertheless under Ghazan's successor, Öljeitu, the vezir for Rūm, Shams al-Dīn Aḥmad Lākūshī, himself sold some public domain lands to high state dignitaries, evidently with the intention of restoring the soundness of the treasury. Osman Turan has apparently justification for saying that the state domain nevertheless remained superior to that of neighbouring states, but statistics are lacking.

The passing of some lands into private ownership slightly, if not perhaps materially, modified the legal position of the peasants who cultivated them. This is perhaps expressed by a deed of 697/1298 in which parcels of land constitute an emir's salary; they are then his property, and what was formerly called so-and-so's *faddān* becomes the *muʿākara* of someone else. In this deed *faddān* is an Egyptian term, used by the scribe as the Arabic equivalent of the Turkish *çift*, both words signifying a unit of cultivable land. Here it meant the parcel of state domain formerly held by the person named, which has become land taken by someone else in *muʿākara* (a classical Arabic term), i.e. as a sharecropper. The change of persons may be due merely to the passage of time, or it may signify the replacement of the former occupiers. Both persons have Muslim names, indicating a process of Turkish sedentarization rather than the conversion of Christian natives.

The allusions made to the *iqṭāʿ* suggest that it was affected by two contrary tendencies. On the one hand the *iqṭāʿ*s disappeared because they were transformed into estates, but on the other hand it appears (without mention of distributions made by provincial governments under the name of *iqṭāʿ*) that a larger proportion of *iqṭāʿ*s was distributed to officers because of the growing difficulty of securing salary paid directly, and because of the now purely regional nature of recruitment, apart from foreign mercenaries.

Nevertheless in the end it is probable that the *iqṭāʿ* had fallen low because, whatever its form, it had become impossible for the Seljukid state to keep a large army in being; the Mongols did not wish it and, even if they had, it would have been financially impossible. To some extent the fact that henceforward the Mongol army would itself undertake some military duties in Asia Minor released the Seljukid state from the burden, so that there was a transfer of expenses rather than an increase or diminution. But the Mongol army was not maintained by the *iqṭāʿ* system, and even when this was brought in under Ghazan, it does not seem that it was really extended to Asia Minor. There the Mongol army subsisted partly on tribute regularly paid by the Seljukid state, and partly but less regularly on its quartering in the eastern pasture-lands of the country, on levies and so forth, which the efforts of the Seljukid officials never succeeded in defining very precisely or very effectively. This system of quartering was evidently equivalent to the withdrawal from the public domain of the lands where it existed. The lands were however not distributed in *iqṭāʿ*, and might occasionally be recovered by the treasury of Rūm after the Mongols' withdrawal. Of course Mongol chiefs acquired possessions in Rūm, illicitly or otherwise, and these could hardly have been other than estates.

What has been said indicates that the landed and fiscal system of Asia Minor did not develop solely within the framework of the Seljukid administration, but also in consequence of intervention by the Mongols. It is necessary to pay attention to this factor because, when this has not been done sufficiently, outgrowths of the Ilkhanid regime may have been taken as Seljukid features. The tribute and the obligation to maintain the Mongol troops were not the sole reason for this situation. It will be remembered that in 658/1260 the two brother-sultans, Kay Kāwūs II and Kılıc Arslan IV, as well as their vezir Baba Tuğrai, had been forced to borrow heavily from the Ilkhanid treasury, when they were detained longer than expected with Hülegü, who was conquering Syria. The Mongols did not treat such matters lightly, and were not satisfied with vague promises of repayment. The repayment was to consist (in addition to the tribute already fixed at 400,000 dinars) of an annual payment of 200,000 dinars in cash and 300 bars of *zerkub* gold or their equivalent, as well as beasts and textiles. The Mongols appointed Tāj al-Dīn Muʿtazz (p. 190 above) as commissioner for the service of the debt. To guarantee the payment of the agreed sums, Tāj al-Dīn obtained the concession in *iqṭāʿ* of the entire province of Kastamonu, as well as Aksaray and Develikarahisar. It was at Aksaray that the historian Aksarayi, who was a financial official, made the acquaintance of his son and future successor, thanks to whom we owe this information.

On Tāj al-Dīn's death in 676/1277 this son, Mujīr al-Dīn Amīr-Shāh, took his place with the same duties, and at one time extended his authority over all the country from Sivas and Tokat to Kastamonu and Sinop. It goes without saying that by the mere fact of this regional power held directly from the Mongols, both father and son exercised considerable influence on the general politics of Asia Minor, and sometimes combined their Ilkhanid commission with that of *nā'ib* of the sultan in Rūm. Nevertheless at the end of his life Mujīr al-Dīn was exposed to the hostility of the magnates in Asia Minor and at the Ilkhanid court simultaneously, while at Sinop his power was practically reduced to nothing by that of the Pervane's descendants. He died in 701/1302 and, although money evidently continued to be sent from Rūm to Iran, it is doubtful whether his post was passed on to anyone. The direct administration of the country by Mongol governors had to some extent ended the reason for its existence.

For a precise understanding of the situation resulting in Asia Minor from this Mongol interference, a careful distinction must be drawn in the sources between what relates to the Ilkhanid Great Divan and what concerns the administration of Rūm proper. The money received by the Mongols was derived from *muqāṭa'āt*, which may be taken to signify (as does the classical Arabic term) arrangements for the farming of the taxes of certain districts or types of sources, also of the *balish*, the *injü* and the *dalay*. The *balish* meant in the Ilkhanate, especially at the beginning, tax or tribute in general, but its details cannot be precisely given. *Injü* meant the domain of the Ilkhanid state, some acquired in Rūm, and forming a source of revenue. In 676/1277–78 the Ilkhanid vezir Shams al-Dīn Juvaynī, for example, added to the *injü* new territory dependent on Erzincan. The word *dalay* is rarely found, and its meaning is not clear. To Osman Turan it means simply the domain of the Seljukid state administered by Mongol commissioners, his principal argument being that there was no *dalay* in the Ilkhanid state properly speaking. It seems difficult to be so positive. It can only be asserted that *injü* and *dalay* were two categories of revenue, at the same time related and distinct, which came under the Mongol treasury in Asia Minor. In 692/1293 each of them had its divan with two responsible heads, a *mustawfī* and a separate director subordinate to Mujīr al-Dīn. Apart perhaps from the enigmatic *balish*, which no longer appears at this date, the terms *injü* and *dalay* refer to the attribution of the taxes named, and do not imply that the taxation system had been modified.

There is no doubt however that there was modification, but it is difficult to see precisely where it lay. Aksarayi, who is the fundamental source here, says that on the accession of Kay Khusraw III (664/1265) it was decided to separate taxation into four named sectors, to be levied in four distinct operations. Apart from the first, of uncertain designation, the names of the other three (signifying cavalry, post and general superior) suggest a definition by attribution rather than assessment. Although Aksarayi adds that no other taxes were raised, apart from the frontier territories on which a modest lump sum was levied, this need not be conclusive. A passage already cited from Aksarayi indicates that the *jizya*, meaning no doubt a general tax on non-Muslim cultivators, continued to be the basic tax in Rūm under the Mongols as formerly. The methods used by some of those concerned were not directed to the modification of the system, but to the forcible exaction of irregular payments; Fakhr al-Dīn Qazwīnī made himself particularly unpopular in this way. A little later Kamāl al-Dīn Tiflisī became unpopular in his turn by arbitrarily levying the tax on grain before the harvest.

As the direct Mongol administration tightened its grasp, however, innovations were introduced. These consisted particularly in the introduction of usages found in the rest of the empire, e.g. in Ghazan's period of reorganization. Such was the establishment of the *tamgha*, a tax on commercial transactions, which was usual in Iran but had not existed in Rūm. In fact Asia Minor was above all a territory for public and private exploitation by the Mongols. Such governmental control by the Seljukids or Ilkhanids as existed was remote and irregular. The dominant impression is of disorder with brief fits and starts of gross abuses and efforts at sanctions or redress which were equally brief. This was of course before the break-up of the empire.

Ḥamdallāh *Mustawfī* Qazwīnī, writing his *Geography* in 1339, gives the amount of taxes due or levied for a fairly large number of provincial capitals of the Ilkhanate, and the Turkish scholar Zeki Veledi Togan has collated the manuscripts in order to improve the reading of the figures. For Asia Minor the total, given separately, may be accepted as 3,300,000 dinars, as against his total of 15 million dinars under the Seljukids, but it is difficult to see what reliance may be placed on the rest. Not only are the figures of varying degrees of uncertainty, and not only are some place names given without their taxes (and are omitted from Togan's table for this reason), but we do not know on what basis the tax is given, perhaps not always the same one (e.g. in vassal provinces where the taxes were farmed), nor the date of reference. It is true that for some budget data given elsewhere, Qazwīnī says he is speaking of the year 1336, but it must be admitted that this date (which is already doubtful for the Ilkhanate as a whole, then in anarchy after Abū Sa'īd's death) is hardly credible for Rūm, if looked at closely. If the list claims to include all Rūm, it is incomplete; and if it refers only to the provinces effectively taxed, it is certainly too extensive for 1336. It would be more normal to refer it to an earlier period inasmuch as it makes no allusion to the Turcoman principalities, were it not that the total is close to that of 3 million dinars given some years later by Ibn Kiyā Māzandarānī, also according to a theoretical list. In short, for the present it is prudent to record it without claiming to deduce anything.

CHAPTER TWENTY-THREE

The towns

The military interventions of the Mongols in Asia Minor do not seem to have ended in the ruin of towns as had happened in Iran and Central Asia, and indeed at Baghdad. Kayseri, pillaged in 1243, returned almost to what it had been, and perhaps only the small Turcoman towns on the periphery suffered from the campaign of Geikhatu at the end of the century. Mongol rule may have modified to some extent the order of importance of some cities by drawing the political chiefs towards the east; so Kayseri and Sivas gained a little importance, while Konya lost a little. Konya however was too clearly the traditional and cultural capital to lose this role in a day in the absence of total overthrow, inasmuch as the opponents of the Mongols found themselves more at ease there than in the chief towns of the east, and at the start it even increased its mosques, *madrasas* and other foundations from Karatay, Fakhr al-Dīn ʿAlī and others. It suffered from Karamanid action later, but in the fourteenth century it remained a noteworthy city. The fourteenth century is characterized rather by the multiplication of cities of medium rank than by the disappearance of any of the great ones.

But if the towns thus kept on their way, their internal organization was nevertheless modified in a fairly marked fashion. This appears in part in the foundation of public works; the great figures are no longer the rulers but the great ministers and officials, and indeed in the medium-sized cities the local notables, including the *ahi* chiefs. For a while it is Karatay, for rather longer it is the Pervane, above all it is the vezir Fakhr al-Dīn ʿAlī, called *Ṣāḥib ʿAṭā'*, the Lord of Giving, who filled Konya and almost all the cities of Asia Minor with their foundations. At the start of the Mongol period, Konya was still being enriched by numerous new foundations: the mosques of Lârende and Ince Minareli, i.e. the Slender Minaret, the *khānqāh* (i.e. dervish convent) and tomb of Fakhr al-Dīn 'Alī himself, the *khānqāh* and tomb of Jalāl al-Dīn Rūmī, and so forth. Karatay enriched Kayseri also. This fertile period came to an end with the century, when the petty Turcoman rulers undertook the nurture of their modest capitals. Previously even the Muslim ministers of the Mongols were obliged to display their generosity, in particular Shams al-Dīn Juvaynī at Sivas.

The weakening of the central authority not only increased the power of the Turcomans but also that of the *futuwwa* groups, sometimes because the lack of a sufficient coercive force encouraged them to manifest themselves more openly and readily in protest, sometimes because the government or some magnate would call on their strength to supplement or replace the ordinary military force against an adversary. There is particular information about this in Konya, but it was the same elsewhere.

The first episode in which the *ahi*s made a clear appearance took place shortly after the disaster of Kösedağ. *Rind*s of Akşehir and Abgurum, north-west of Konya, were then made use of by some of the magnates in the entourage of Kay Khusraw II to make a criminal attack on others; the *rind*s of Konya were sent by the vezir Shams al-Dīn Iṣfahānī to search the victims' houses, and at the same time to forestall other acts of this kind. Soon, however, when the vezir was accused to the Mongols of complicity in the crime, they aided in his arrest. In this case they can be seen as participating in the factional power struggle, but this was not normal.

For a comparable situation, a generation must be passed to arrive at the affair of Cimri. The information about the *ahi*s and *rind*s of Konya is provided by the anonymous citizen who wrote the *Tārīkh-i āl-i Saljūq*, who obviously had a special interest in them. According to him, the *ahi*s of the capital were directed by two chiefs, *Ahi* Aḥmad and *Ahi* Aḥmad-Shāh, mentioned also by Eflaki, the hagiographer of the Mevlevis. Eflaki takes a poor view of Aḥmad because he was insufficiently aristocratic and was an opponent of Jalāl al-Dīn Rūmī. Perhaps he was the author of a treatise on the *futuwwa*, written in the same period by a writer of the same name; in this case he would originate from Ardabīl in north-western Iran, the centre of the Safavids, who were helped by some *ahi*s. Eflaki takes a better view of Aḥmad-Shāh, whom he finds more respectable, and he calls him the chief of thousands of *rind*s. In 1291 he may have helped to dissuade Geikhatu from sacking the Seljukid capital. His successor, *Ahi* Ṣiddīq, had discussions with the Mevlevis, recalling them to their mysticism, while he himself was occupied with worldly affairs, and was capable of using force. It seems that this group maintained better relations with the Mevlevis, who watched over the remains of the dead after the massacres ordered by the Karamanids in 1312. If there was evidently a *futuwwa* in a general way, there was not necessarily complete unity either of organization or of spirit.

A third *ahi* named as influential in the contemporary sources is a certain *Ahi* Emir Mehmed, to whom the most famous *futuwwa* treatise, that of Nāṣirī, was probably dedicated. His example, as subsequently that of others, is evidence that there was no antithesis between membership of the *futuwwa* and membership of the social category of political and military chiefs, the emirs.

The role of the *ahi*s in the defence of Konya against the Karamanids and Cimri are not presented in the same way in the extant accounts, and may moreover not have been uniform. There is little doubt that they, like all the citizens, were hostile in principle to the Turcomans. The city governor was however mistrustful of them, and only made use of them in operations for lack of other sufficient troops, yet nothing indicates that they betrayed his trust. Their attitude was the same some years later, when the widow of Kay Khusraw III attempted to gain the support of the Karamanids in 1285. The *ahi*s opposed this policy, and the vezir's diplomacy together with formal guarantees by the Turcoman chiefs were necessary to appease the tumult.

The events of 1290–91 make it possible to give confirmation and precision to impressions. When the chief of the Eşref Turcomans laid hands on Siyāwush, the brother of Sultan Mas'ūd II, there were disorders in Konya, where the *rind*s do not seem to have been unanimous. One group was surrounded and burnt to death in their building in the suburb. No doubt they had hoped to misuse the situation, but normally the *rind*s were rather inclined to favour Mas'ūd. After his liberation he sought their support, particularly that of Aḥmad-Shāh, to resist the financial exigencies of the vezir Fakhr al-Dīn Qazwīnī, installed by the Mongols. However, the sultan left for Kayseri, leaving in Konya only his brother Siyāwush and the Mongol deputy, Qutluja. The *ahi*s succeeded in persuading Siyāwush to have the Mongol prince assassinated. Against the Karamanids, who appeared too much of a threat, the *ahi*s, like the sultan, apparently advocated a rapprochement with the Eşref. At a time when the fortunes of war turned against the Eşref, there was a bloody reaction against some *ahi*s at Konya. But a few months later the *ahi*s reappear, defending their city against the Germiyan. The power of Aḥmad-Shāh was unshaken (whereas Aḥmad had perhaps fallen victim to one of the previous repressions), and the *Tārīkh-i āl-i Saljūq* says that 15,000 persons followed his brother's funeral cortège in 1294. When he himself was assassinated in 697/1298, Sultan Kay Qubādh III explicitly authorized vengeance against the assassin, although he was one of his own officers; and in fact he was killed some months later. Shortly before his death, Aḥmad-Shāh brought about the expulsion of an insufferable representative of the Karamanids. Although the documentation becomes very defective at this point, it can be said that bad relations continued as long as the Karamanids could be combated since, when they occupied

Konya in 1292, they proceeded to massacre the *ahis*. For all that, the *ahis* were not favourable to the Mongols, but were rather local patriots; there was no question of Turkish solidarity.

In Ibn Baṭṭūṭa and elsewhere there are sufficient references to the *ahis* and their chiefs to make it possible to say that they existed in every city. Henceforward their character is particularly that of a professional association. Without dealing with individuals, one name must be mentioned: that of *Ahi* Evrân, since his reputation allowed pretenders to his succession to claim in later centuries a sort of control over *ahis* in general. As often, the historical personality of *Ahi* Evrân is surrounded by legend. It can be affirmed that he was a holy man, that he lived in the small town of Kırşehir, and that he died there around the year 1300. Legend connects him with the tanners' corporation, but this is not mentioned in the few old texts. Tanner or not, it was not as such that he became famous, but as a holy man, more or less connected with the other holy men of his period.

Ahi Evrân is a particularly illustrative example of the duality of manifestations throughout the *futuwwa* which has already been stressed. On the one hand the *ahis* act, and often with violence. One of their chiefs affirms to the Mevlevis the necessity for violence. While Ibn Baṭṭūṭa also appears to find it very normal, he himself says that there was no one like them for challenging the police. On the other hand they, or at least those who directed them, had a mystical ideal; and since it was only these leaders who wrote, the mystical and ritual aspect comes out in the *futuwwa* treatises, so that at first sight one might ask if they are talking about the same thing.

These treatises (T. *fütüvvetname*) multiplied. There are some from outside Asia Minor, but it was quite clearly there that this genre flourished most at that period, which also indicates the special development of the phenomenon itself. The works of Aḥmad of Ardabīl and Nāṣirī have already been mentioned, but without straying beyond the period there are also chapters on the subject in some encyclopaedias, which at that time were written only in Persian. It was in the same period that the *ahis*, who are known to have been much penetrated by Iranian influences, adopted the figure whom the Iranians had made into a hero of quasi-national romance, Abū Muslim.

However, the decline of Seljukid and Mongol authority, and reciprocally the evolution of the Turcoman rulers by the formation of principalities incorporating the towns, resulted in a degree of rapprochement between the two sole surviving authorities. Almost everywhere Ibn Baṭṭūṭa goes, he mentions their officially recognized power and the credit they enjoyed. He adds that in the cities where there was no resident prince, such as Ankara, the *ahi* chief was the city chief. Past Islamic history had known some comparable cases, but nowhere with the frequency and strength of Seljukid-Mongol Asia Minor. It must be added in order to prevent confusion that, if some cities fell for a while under the quasi-autonomous government of their *ahi*s, this was in no way parallel to the Italian cities of the same period.

CHAPTER TWENTY-FOUR

The non-Muslims

Mongol domination did not change the condition of the non-Muslims in Asia Minor as much as might be thought, partly because this was, as has been seen, fairly good, and furthermore because the protectorate did not fundamentally modify the autonomy of the Seljukid regime in this respect. In general the first generations of Mongols were indifferent in matters of religion. All faiths were respected, Islam among others – but just among others, that is to say no longer with the superiority over the others which it had previously held. Also the new masters found it to their political advantage to obtain support, when they could, from those who had been inferiors under the preceding regimes; hence often from the Christians or, in the framework of Islam, the Shīʿa.

In western Asia the most favoured group were the Armenians, who from the start had deliberately made themselves the Mongols' agents. The Greeks, however, to the lesser extent that there were dealings with them, were also well regarded since policy had drawn Michael Palaeologus and the *īlkhāns* together, and Trebizond, like the Armenians of Cilicia, had become their vasals. Contingents of Armenians from Cilicia sometimes appeared locally in the Mongol armies in Syria; but the Armenians of Armenia proper no longer served in arms since the conquests in which they had lost their political independence, and they remained excluded from military life in spite of an effort by the bishop of Erzincan. On the other hand, the Georgians, who had displayed military valour in the recent past, were on several occasions incorporated in the forces sent to the west by the Mongols. However, the advantages enjoyed by the various Christian sects, thanks to Mongol indifference, diminished as the *īlkhāns* and their people were converted to Islam. There were no persecutions, but there was on the other hand the restitution of its privileges to Islam, e.g. by the use of *waqf*s, and sometimes the introduction of more restrictive measures towards the non-Muslims than they had previously known. For another thing, the favour from which they had briefly profited increasingly aroused hostile reactions. Finally, the nomadization of some regions of cultivation contributed to the progress of Islam at the expense of the native faiths. On assessment, the Mongol domination was not totally favourable to the non-Muslims, yet progress of a temporary and specific nature may be discerned.

As regards the Greeks, the Acts of the Patriarchate (unfortunately only known for the fourteenth century) give the impression that with Mongol agreement the re-establishment of some lost bishoprics was permitted in law, and sometimes in fact. In spite of the difficulties connected with the period when the Mongols became Muslims, Christians and a bishop are to be found at Zile near Sivas, Amasya, Keltzine in Erzincan and Malatya, and communities at Kemah, Nazianzus, Comana near Tokat and others. In the second half of the fourteenth century the activity of a suspected heretic shows again that there were Christians throughout the whole of central Asia Minor, that the Patriarchate of Constantinople had some contact with the localities and that relative isolation did facilitate various forms of propaganda. Linguistically the isolated populations were becoming turcicized to the degree that in the fifteenth century they no longer understood Greek. In western Anatolia, from which the Greek aristocrats had fled, there were no more inter-confessional princely marriages.

As regards the Armenians, everything essential happened at Erzincan, which long remained the metropolis of those in Turkey. Bishop Sarkis (Sergius) did not only represent a local power, but was reputed to be a counsellor who had the ear of the *īlkhān*s. He had even sought, albeit in vain, to be granted his city in *iqṭā*ʿ in return for furnishing a contingent of 500 troops. In the troubles of 1276, some Kurds, who had been encouraged to intervene against the Mongols and their allies in eastern Anatolia, conspired to assassinate him. Erzincan nevertheless remained a great Armenian city. The Monophysites, at Malatya for example, also suffered at times from the freedom of action given to the Kurds, but Bar Hebraeus does not give the impression of a general decline.

In some particular cases the conversion of the Mongols to Islam brought about such dramatic episodes as the massacre of Christians in 708/1310 at Irbīl in Mesopotamia, or financial difficulties when someone tried to enforce the payment of forty years' arrears of the *jizya*. It does not seem that the structure of Asia Minor was generally open to this kind of problem. Temür-Tash tried to enforce sumptuary restrictions according to the Sharīʿa on the non-Muslims in some cities. In 1314 a Franciscan who was also honoured by the Armenians was martyred at Erzincan; the date was probably not a matter of chance. After the death of the *Ilkhān* Abū Saʿīd in 1335, European merchants almost ceased to visit Anatolia, but this was because of the troubled conditions, not religious intolerance.

CHAPTER TWENTY-FIVE

Administrative and political institutions

The organs of the government and the administration in the Mongol period remained the same as at the time of independence, except that they were headed or twinned by representatives of the Ilkhanid power, but for this very reason their conditions of action were profoundly transformed. It will be sufficient to recapitulate the observations arising from the narrative of events.

A first feature is that the sultan rapidly lost all real power, especially in the eastern half of his realm, which was of the chief importance to the new masters. Apart from the Mongol intervention, this decline was sometimes due to mistrust of the sultan, sometimes to his being a minor, perhaps through assassination. Of course even before the destruction of the caliphate, and all the more afterwards, the sultan was not theoretically invested by the caliph but nominated by the *īlkhān*, saving the inalienable rights of the Seljukid family. By contrast the ministers gained in importance, not because they were independent of the Mongol power, but because, unlike the sultan, who held his place by right, they only held theirs by more or less direct delegation from the Mongols. In the end the fiction of the sultanate silently disappeared, and the *īlkhān* himself appointed the great officers of Rūm.

A second characteristic of these ministers is that in order to provide for the expenses of the functions they exercised, they divided the state lands among themselves, and thus became the holders of genuine lordships. These were recognized by the Mongols, and were sheltered from their encroachments. At least two of them deserve to be stressed: those of the Pervane and of the vezir Fakhr al-Dīn ʿAlī. It has already been mentioned that neither of them had a Turkish military career as his background. The Pervane's father was a vezir of Iranian stock; Fakhr al-Dīn ʿAlī was also of Iranian origin, and made his first appearance as *amīr-dād*. Their rise was possible only because there had previously been no genuine feudalism. They had however no military force, failing a small army, except so far as they had agreements with the Turcomans. They gave each other support through intermarriage, as did also the *malik al-sawāḥil*, the Pervane's son-in-law.

A list of the holders of the various offices in the Mongol period must stop in general at the end of the thirteenth century for lack of further documentation. In fact the resulting gap is not very great in view of the increasing fragmentation of the territory, and consequently a reorganization of the administrative machinery in the narrower, and in some cases modified, framework of the new principalities.

Above or beside the Seljukid ministers there were various representatives of the Mongol power, who naturally interfered with their administration, even if neither they nor the *īlkhān* formally wished to do so. At the start it was the commanders of military contingents, the *noyans*, who had no official power apart from this command, but in fact assumed it, profiting from the distance which rendered them unaccountable, and because they had to feed their men as well as anticipate their own profits, while the Seljukid office-holders intrigued with them against one another. In the same period there were also and constantly Mongol ambassadors or representatives, who often stayed with Seljukid ministers or military commanders, or with the sultan or his spokesmen. As long as the Pervane lived there was not really anything more, apart however from the increasing number of Mongol troops and the permanence of their settlement, which grew in proportion to the power of their chiefs, particularly in the eastern part of the country. They were quartered there not only because of its proximity, but also because there they were ready for operations against the Mamluks. Consequently there were now often scions of the Ilkhanid house at their head, whom it was difficult to oppose, and who sought to enrich themselves.

Furthermore the loans to Kay Kāwūs II and Kılıc Arslan IV in 1258–60, for the repayment of which some categories of revenue had been designated as security, and no doubt other reasons and transactions, had led to the establishment in Rūm not merely of private estates by Mongol notables, but even of Mongol state domains conflicting with the domains of the Seljukid state. At the head of these Ilkhanid domains was a general permanent representative of the Mongol power, Taj al-Dīn Muʿtazz, whom the Seljukid officials could not ignore. When finally, after the Pervane's death, the Mongol protectorate turned into direct government, a personage appeared as the successor to the former military commander-in-chief. His title is not known, but his office had the Perso-Turkish style of *iyālat-i wilāyat* (*eyalet-i vilayet*). His powers are difficult to determine but were clearly of the nature of a governor-general's. Three holders of the post are known in the last decade of the seventh/thirteenth century; their names may be either of

Mongols or non-Mongols. At the same time the *imāra*, i.e. the post of supreme emir, was given to Mujīr al-Dīn Mehmed Amīr-Shāh, then to the *pervane* Mehmed (son of the great Pervane) in addition to their other titles, then to a third holder who had no other title. It is not known to what extent these titles corresponded in reality to similar titles found here and there in other provinces of the Mongol empire.

Several formularies or collections of documents were compiled in the Mongol period. The Arabic documents forming the basis for the calculation of taxes were translated into Persian for Fakhr al-Dīn ʿAlī. The Karamanid attempt to set up a Turkish-language chancery at Konya in Cimri's time bore no immediate fruit. Finally, to repeat, there was no longer an army or a military administration apart from some temporary private forces, as the Mongols took charge of everything.

CHAPTER TWENTY-SIX

Cultural life in Asia Minor in the Mongol period

It is a well-known fact that the cultural evolution of a society is always slower than its material and political development. If, of course, the occurrences which mark such material and political development must have their repercussion in the thoughts of the members of that society, it remains true that they were formed before these occurrences, and it will be their children of later formation who will be able to deduce the full consequences. So it is not surprising that in some respects the spiritual life of Asia Minor after 1243 was at first the expansion of that which had begun to flourish in the later times of Seljukid independence.

Moreover the effects of the Mongol conquest were not simple. Their actual direct influence was trifling, and some effect may perhaps be found at most in the realm of folklore and popular beliefs. But the indirect results were threefold: first, the unification of countries which had been separate. Second, the arrival of Iranian officials behind the Mongol warriors, and reciprocally the journeys of Anatolian notables to the Ilkhanid court in Iran, accentuated the Iranian influence which individual immigrants had begun to introduce in the twelfth century, followed in the two or three decades preceding Kösedağ by the far more numerous Iranians fleeing the Mongols themselves on the heels of the Khwarazmians. Finally, the movements among the Turcomans aroused by the Seljukid-Mongol regime, or in reaction to it, had spiritual as well as political and social aspects, and these were tinged by the influx of popular preachers from Central Asia. The disorganization which was to be on the whole the consequence of the Mongol regime was also significant in the realm of culture; more precisely, if Persian and in the second place Arabic remained the vehicle of culture among the aristocracy, their share diminished from the end of the thirteenth century, and the Turkish of the Turcomans acquired a growing place during the fourteenth.

In religion Asia Minor remained a Muslim country; that is to say, the inter-confessional neutrality of Ilkhanid Iran found no true extension there. At first the Christians did enjoy some favour, but were nowhere able to regain a dominant position. It was still necessary to recruit the administrative personnel in the Muslim Iranian circles which had held office for two or three generations. This was reinforced by the fact that in Iran itself the administration always remained almost without exception in Muslim hands, such as the great vezir Shams al-Dīn Juvainī. The case was even stronger when the *īlkhāns* and the Mongols generally were converted to Islam at the end of the thirteenth century. The confessional neutrality had at most allowed, in Asia Minor as in Iran, the resurgence of a Shī'ī current; this moreover at a time when the differences between Shi'ism and Sunnism were often perceived with difficulty, and when a man such as Naṣīr al-Dīn Ṭūsī was in touch with thinkers of both persuasions alike.

The strength of the iranizing current should not however conceal the fact that there was also to some degree the development of an arabizing current, which was favoured by relations, whether good or bad, with Syria. Since Arabic had never acquired the place of Persian even among the aristocracy, the importance of the arabizing movement would clearly remain inferior. Nevertheless it contributed, particularly in the disciplines connected with the Sharī'a, to the formation of the culture of Turkey. There seems also to have been no hostility between the two languages.

The great figure in arabophone Islam is Ṣadr al-Dīn Konevi, whose name has been mentioned in connection with the links between his father and Ibn 'Arabī at the beginning of the thirteenth century. They belonged to an Arab family of Malatya, but he himself passed almost the whole of his life at Konya, where he died in 673/1274–75. It was to this origin that he also owed his adherence to the Shāfi'ī law school; this was exceptional in Irano-Turkish circles, but in no way harmed his career. His writings, which are almost all in Arabic, bear witness to his solidly traditional culture, but his form of mysticism was learnt from Ibn 'Arabī through the intermediary of his father and other disciples of the master established in Asia Minor. At the end of his life his prestige was to shine well beyond Asia Minor. One should note beside him Sa'īd al-Farghānī, mentioned earlier for his commentary on 'Umar b. al-Farīd, and also Fakhr al-Dīn al-'Irāqī (actually an Iranian), whom the Pervane established near to himself at Tokat, and who was later to make Ṣadr al-Dīn known in India. It is interesting to note some similarities between Ṣadr al-Dīn and Naṣīr al-Dīn Ṭūsī.

A high reputation was also enjoyed by the great *qāḍī* and jurist Sirāj al-Dīn al-Urmawī, among whose disciples was Ṣafī al-Dīn al-Hindī, who was born in India and later established himself in the Yemen, living in Rūm during 674–85/1275–86. Quṭb al-Dīn Shīrāzī, formerly a pupil of

Naṣīr al-Dīn Ṭūsī in Khurāsān, passed some time in Rūm before dying at Tabrīz in 710/1310. He wrote astrological treatises in Arabic as well as a Persian encyclopaedia.

We make no pretension to list more extensively the Persian writings of Rūm. This would include the collections of *inshā'* (state papers) and treatises of *futuwwa* which have been mentioned elsewhere. It may only be noted that the reduction of the role of Konya and the emancipation of local powers multiplied the number of small patrons; written in Kayseri in 675/1276, for example, beside an astrological work which is dedicated to Kay Khusraw III, there is Shīrāzī's encyclopaedia and a treatise on heresiography, as well as a treatise on administration dedicated to some princes of Kastamonu. Another encyclopaedia written by a certain Muḥammad b. Ayyūb of Dunaysir in Diyār Bakr is addressed to an unidentified emir of Karahisar. Even one of the Eşref is the subject of the dedication in 1310 of an Arabic philosophical treatise by a certain Shams al-Dīn of Tustar in Khūzistān.

It was of course in the realm of mysticism that there continued to be the most important achievements. The author of one of the *futuwwa* treatises, which are themselves semi-mystical in nature, left a work of pure mysticism. Al-'Irāqī and al-Farghānī already mentioned wrote in Arabic and Persian. But they are all dominated by Jalāl al-Dīn Rūmī, his disciples and his descendants. In spite of the literary value of this great man's works, his powerful religious achievement must now be considered in itself.

According to pious legend, it was in 643/1245 that Jalāl al-Dīn Rūmī, whose youth has already been mentioned, met Shams al-Dīn Tabrīzī in Konya. This was a thunderbolt, the effect of which survived until the day in 1247 when Shams al-Dīn, who was regarded with envy by Jalāl al-Dīn's disciples, disappeared, probably assassinated. Thereafter the life of a mystic was all-important for Jalāl al-Dīn, who sought his ideal in Shams al-Dīn, and then found his reincarnation in one of his disciples, Ṣalāh al-Dīn Zarkūb the goldsmith. So many adepts of mysticism came to him that he had to organize them as a community, which was managed under Jalāl al-Dīn himself by disciples whom he designated, sometimes against the wishes of the others. In particular after the death of Zarkūb, the first chief, there was Ḥusām al-Dīn, one of the leading chief *ahi*s of Konya. Such was the birth of the order of the Mevlevis, taking its name from 'Our Master', *Mawlānā*, in Turkish *Mevlana*, Jalāl al-Dīn. In modern times it has become better known under the name of the Dancing Dervishes. On Jalāl al-Dīn's death, Ḥusām al-Dīn remained as his *khalīfa* (successor), but in 683/1284 the headship of the order passed to Jalāl al-Dīn's eldest son, Sulṭān Walad (Sultan Veled), whose sons retained the position until the mid-fourteenth century. It was Sultan Veled who, as well as being a poet, was the true organizer of the order.

It is as difficult to measure Jalāl al-Dīn's influence as to characterize his thought. Above all he is a poet, who in passionate verses, the sincerity and simplicity of which contrast with the over-frequent embellishments of Persian literature, expresses sentiments and convictions which are spontaneous and ardent rather than logical and original. He impressed by the apparent paradoxes of his statements, by the prescience seen in them and by the shrewdly calculated alternation of his periods of 'absence' and 'presence'. Those whom he did not convince called him and his followers crazy dervishes; but his prestige at Konya and elsewhere is indubitable among the aristocracy and in various urban circles, not all of which were Muslim. He was a Muslim, and on the whole more orthodox in rejecting any pantheist tendency than Ibn 'Arabī, for example, and the adherents he gained among non-Muslims signified in the first place their conversion. It is nevertheless true that from the height or the situation where he placed himself confessional differences were blurred, and he recognized a kind of common value in all faiths. The scattering of Greek and Turkish verses which occur in his Persian works also express this ecumenism, even though they are little more than a pastime. His principal works are the *Dīwān*, a collection of short poems; the *Mathnawī*, a didactic poem in couplets, the meaning of the title; *Fīhi mā fīhi*, i.e. 'There is what there is', a collection of various sayings; and correspondence with all his principal contemporaries in Rūm, and indeed occasionally in the rest of the Ilkhanid empire.

The practices of the Mevlevis were not codified until the fourteenth century. It is however certain that already for Jalāl al-Dīn their principal element was the 'spiritual concert' of music accompanied by dancing, which terminated in bringing the believer into a state close to mystical ecstasy. Although the idea was not entirely new, the importance conferred on it caused it to be seen by the unsympathetic as *bid'a*, innovation, a fact in itself reprehensible to those holding a certain concept of traditionalist Islam.

Some of Jalāl al-Dīn's disciples should be mentioned, such as Fakhr al-Dīn Ghaḍanfar of Tabrīz (630–92/1230–92), who lived at Konya. The letter of the *ispahsālār* Farīdūn b. Aḥmad about his master considerably improved knowledge of Jalāl al-Dīn. The verse and prose writings of Sultan Veled contain a remarkable number of Turkish and Greek phrases. Finally, and from a later generation, Eflaki in the mid-fourteenth century, the author of a considerable historical and hagiographical work, remains almost the sole source for the history of both the order and its founder.

As well as mysticism, another literary genre, this time in prose, makes its appearance in Rūm with three important Persian works: the chronicle of Ibn Bībī (finished in 1280), that of Aksarayi (finished about 1325), and the anonymous *Tārīkh-i āl-i Saljūq* (about 1294, apart from an arid continuation). The authors of the first two were high officials, the third was written by a citizen of Konya in a more straightforward and less florid style. The independent appearance of these three works evidently indicates the recognition of the distinctive value of the state of Rūm beside the rest of the Ilkhanid empire, its intellectual value being in no way inferior to Ilkhanid historiography.

However great Jalāl al-Dīn's influence may have been among the aristocracy and urban population of Rūm, it certainly lay completely outside Turcoman society. It was by contrast in the Mongol period that religious movements which were to have a wider development in the future established themselves in mainly Turcoman society. As always however at this stage of development, it is almost impossible to have direct and valid evidence of them, since almost everything written about them was by later hagiographers, who not only embellished the reality but also travestied it, whether or not intentionally.

Baba Isḥāq and the Babais will be remembered. Somehow or another links were established in the mid-thirteenth century between this group and a certain Hacı Bektaş from Khurāsān, the eponym in the following century of the Bektaşi order, where the name of Isḥāq is still remembered as that of a subordinate figure. Some have sought to identify or link Baba Isḥāq with a certain Baba Ilyās, also from Central Asia, the transmitter of the tradition of the great mystical poet, Aḥmad Yasawī (Yesevi) who wrote in Turkish, because both were roughly contemporaries and stood more or less at the origin of Turcoman movements. This is unsound: Baba Isḥāq was an Anatolian before the coming of the Mongols, and the name of Ilyās does not appear in the account of his troubles. The Turcomans who became attached to Ilyās through a certain Nure Sufi were to give rise a little later to the Karamanid dynasty, to which the Ilyāsīs were to remain attached for two or three centuries. The Bektaşis, who were to survive to our own times, were soon to link themselves to the Ottomans, the victorious enemies of the Karamanids. The Bektaşis did not follow the ritual practices of Islam from the thirteenth century; it is not known whether this is also true of the Ilyāsīs.

It was also in the Mongol period that orders from other eastern countries penetrated various popular circles in Rūm, such as the Rifāʿiyya originating in Egypt, and the Qalandariyya coming from India or Central Asia, half wandering monks, half charlatans. Too little is yet known of them to merit further discussion.

Although under the independent Seljukids the Turcomans had given unequivocal proofs of their self-awareness, those in Asia Minor, unlike their kinsmen in Central Asia, had felt no need to express themselves in a written literature. Perhaps for self-assertion confronting the Mongols, the sense of Turkishness asserted itself, sometimes among the townspeople but always resting on the Turcomans. It profited also from the influx of the new immigrants, or from contact with the descendants of the former Anatolian *gazis*, such as those who transmitted the knowledge of the saga of Sayyid Baṭṭāl. As regards specifically Turkish themes, it is hardly by chance that the oldest attested Turkish work, the *Danişmendname*, was composed for Kay Kāwūs II, who came to depend on the Turcomans in his strife with the Mongols or their partisans. In its present form dating from the fourteenth century, the story makes hardly any allusion to the Seljukids, but it is possible that there were however epic traditions dealing with them, to judge from the introductory lines and first pages of Aksarayi's chronicle. In contrast there are established links with the sagas of Baṭṭāl and the Iranian Abū Muslim.

It is not surprising that beside the epic, the principal primitive genre of Turkish literary achievement was that of mystical works. The few Turkish verses inserted in Jalāl al-Dīn Rūmī's *Dīwān* attest the possibility of henceforward writing Turkish in the Arabo-Persian alphabet, but it was not until the establishment of real principalities that there appeared authors of important works entirely in Turkish. Nothing is extant from Baba Isḥāq, and probably nothing ever existed. It has been seen that there are from his time some verses of the townsman and anchorite, Aḥmad-Faqīh, and a little later there is Shayyād Ḥamza's work, a Turkish adaptation of the story of Yūsuf and Zulaykhā, probably inspired by an earlier opuscule written in Central Asia. But some more important works come as the century ended. Yūnus Emre, who seems to have lived in north-western Anatolia, wrote a poem bearing the date (which may not be authentic) of 707/1307. He was a popular poet, but had read or heard the verses of Jalāl al-Dīn and the even older verses of the great Persian poet of Ādharbāyjān, Niẓāmī. Nearly contemporary, it would seem, was Gülşehri, the Turkish adapter of *Manṭiq al-ṭā'ir*, 'The speech of the birds', by the twelfth-century Iranian mystic, Farīd al-Dīn 'Aṭṭār. He also celebrated the contemporary holy man, *Ahi* Evrân.

All this should not be exaggerated, but the outcome is that henceforward there was a Turkish literary language, distinct from that which had established itself somewhat earlier in Central Asia.

Finally, it was probably in some popular circle of Mongol-Seljukid Asia Minor that there lived Nasreddin Hoca, who as the generations passed became the hero of a growing number of anecdotes, and has for several centuries been a typical figure of both simplicity and rude common sense, the amusement of the Turks and their neighbours to our own days.

In south-eastern Asia Minor similar movements may have been at work among the Kurds. Before the Mongol conquest the Sufi order of the 'Adawiyya, founded by Shaykh 'Adī and more or less linked to the ancient Yazīdī sect, was established there. In 1257 during the troubles of the Malatya region, a son or descendant of Shaykh 'Adī was a military chief. Furthermore the Germiyan, soon to be installed in western Anatolia but then in the region of Malatya, were considered to be Yazīdī Kurds by Ibn Baṭṭūṭa's informants in the fourteenth century. They were probably a mixture of Kurds and Turks. Whatever the detail and truth of these facts, they clearly suggest an extension of Yazīdī propaganda in Kurdish circles in the time leading up to the Mongol conquest.

It is in the realm of art that the Mongol conquest had the least perceptible immediate effects. Even in the long term, if the fragmentation of power evidently brought greater restraint into the achievements of the Turcoman period, it cannot be said that its general orientation was modified. Under the Mongol protectorate properly speaking, however paradoxical it may appear at first sight, there was rather an intensification of production. It was then that the effects of the cultural progress of the first half of the thirteenth century made themselves clear; and the emulation among the notables of the new regime to manifest their glory, their concern to safeguard their cultural values, the equally great concern of the Ilkhanid vezir Shams al-Dīn Juvaynī to evince to them the interest offered by the regime he represented – all these factors entailed both multiplication and decentralization alike in public works such as caravanserais, as already mentioned, and in more strictly religious foundations as mosques, *madrasas*, tombs and so forth. The nature of the art changed but little. Certainly, as might be expected, attentive study of the monuments might reveal an intensification of Iranian influence, especially in the eastern part of the country; but this influence could not occasion a breach, since it had already made itself felt and, when there is no explicit dating, it is not always easy to decide whether a monument belongs to the first or second half of the thirteenth century.

At the elementary technical level dealt with here, it would be useless to do more than mention several monuments. At Sivas, which was now a rival to Konya, the mosque called Çifte Minare (the Double Minaret) and the Gök Medrese (the Blue *Madrasa*) were both built in 1271, the first by Juvaynī, perhaps for the use of Iranian merchants passing through Anatolia, the second by Fakhr al-Dīn 'Alī *Ṣāḥib 'Aṭā'*. The latter, whose earlier foundations at Konya have already been mentioned, also built a *madrasa* at Kayseri, a mosque in his *iqṭā'* of Karahisar and so forth; he was perhaps the greatest patron of buildings in his time. However, the Pervane or his clients also multiplied the foundation of mosques and *madrasas* in their possessions of Tokat, Amasya, Kastamonu and Sinop, as well as caravanserais, as has been mentioned. From the same period date the tombs of the great men, Jalāl al-Dīn Rūmī, Ṣadr al-Dīn Konevi and Fakhr al-Dīn 'Alī himself, all three at Konya. Among the foundations of minor personages, the *madrasa* of Caca Bey at Kırşehir is particularly worth mention.

From the end of the thirteenth century however the movement slowed down. On the Ilkhanid side it seems that neither Ghazan, although a Muslim, nor his great minister, Rashīd al-Dīn, were greatly interested in building in their remoter dependencies; and there were no longer magnates in what remained of the Seljukid state. Insofar as there was still building going on, it was now initiated by the representatives of the new petty powers on the periphery at Beyşehir, Birgi in Aydın, Karaman (formerly Lârende) and Kastamonu, to give only some well-known examples. But there was nothing new in this field comparable to the dynamism of Turkish literature, and their modest activity as builders simply signifies that, as they were gradually assimilated to urban culture, they wished to prove to the townspeople that they were the valid successors of those who had preceded them.

CONCLUSION

In none of the countries dominated by the Turks in the Middle Ages did they form a majority; a fundamental distinction must however be made. In the Arab lands and part of Iran they were an army imposed upon the native population, detached from the society of which they originally formed part, and integrated to some small extent in that of the country where they settled. By contrast in Asia Minor as in north-western Iran, if there remained a native population of whatever proportion, there took place the immigration of a people with women, children, animals, traditions and organization brought from their home in Central Asia. As regards the native population on the other hand, there was not a single people but several distinct ones, each occupying a part of the territory, while the Turks were almost everywhere, thus forming a 'Turkey' above zones that were more or less Greek, Armenian and so on. A marked characteristic of this 'Turkey' was the utilization of the various peoples for the benefit of the dominant group, but it cannot be said that there was any fusion.

However, in this respect, a distinction must be made between two categories of peoples in this 'Turkey'. The Turkish aristocracy and the groups settled in the cities had been more or less iranized, and aspired to reproduce in Asia Minor models known in Iran, attracting or welcoming Iranians, and behaving, especially in the thirteenth century, linguistically and culturally as Iranians rather than Turks. The earlier Byzantine influence had yielded the preponderant place to Iranian influence, partly because of the religious barrier between Muslims and Christians. Among the little people of the countryside things went differently. At the outset the Turcomans and the Greek peasantry had got on badly together, but things changed fairly quickly. There were two peoples in the land who could profit mutually, and it might be thought that the native peasantry of the thirteenth century were not altogether worse off under the Turks than under the great Byzantine landowners. But there was no fusion, so that the Turcomans underwent neither iranization nor hellenization, but remained confronting the urban Iranian elements as a Turkish element which was gradually to carry the day.

The Ottoman Empire was later to be represented as a Graeco-Turkish empire; an over-simplified view, but one not wholly lacking in reality. The Seljukid state was not the Ottoman Empire; it did not entirely comprise the whole of Anatolia. There is however an unavoidable observation; paradoxical as it may seem to minds formed in the framework of the last two centuries, it is indisputable. The Byzantines called on the West for aid against the Turks, but also on the Turks against the West – and it cannot be said that they took a particularly favourable view of the Crusades. Marriages between Turks and Greeks were frequent, and do not seem to have met with disapproval on either side. No such symbiosis can be found either between Byzantines and Arabs, or between Turks and Arabs in spite of their common religion. It is true that in the Mongol period, and to a lesser extent already beforehand, the Iranian influence supplanted that of the enfeebled Byzantium; then with the rise of the Turcomans there developed a movement of turcicization. This balance characterizes the period studied here, before it reappears in other forms over a wider territory in the Ottoman Empire. It is ridiculous to begin the history of the Ottoman Empire with the petty principality of Osman, as if it had been born with no environment. It is also ridiculous to consider the Seljukid period as a preface to the Ottoman period. One can discover common characteristics, but they do not necessarily lead to the same ends. It is hoped that this book will have encouraged some reflections on this subject.

NOTES

1 Alexius Comnenus's principal auxiliary, called in the Greek sources Tatikios, was perhaps a Turk from Byzantine Europe. He appears in the anonymous *Gesta Francorum* as Tetigus.

2 The Damascene chronicler Ibn al-Qālanisī *sub anno* 493/1100 represents al-Dānishmand (i.e. Gümüştekin b. Danişmend) as the leader of Kılıc Arslan I's army.

3 The principal cause was the presence of Arab and Kurdish pastoralists and the unsuitability of the hotter climate of Syria and Upper Mesopotamia for the Turkish Bactrian camel.

4 The sources give various dates between August 1140 and October 1143 for Mehmed's death. It probably made possible John Comnenus's Cilician campaign in mid-1142.

5 In 1182 the traveller Ibn Jubayr met this princess on pilgrimage in Baghdad, where she died.

6 Kay Khusraw had at first intended to go to Constantinople to seek aid. Prevented by Süleyman's victory, and discouraged either from going by the hostility of the people of Lâdik (north-west of Konya), or from returning by Alexius III's non-intervention, he reached an agreement with his brother, and made his way by Lârende, Cilicia, Elbistan, Malatya, Āmid and Ahlat to Trebizond, whence he went to Constantinople by sea.

7 In the usage of the Muslims of Asia Minor, 'Turk' signifies particularly the Turcomans in contrast to the townspeople.

8 The Karamanlis of the province of Karaman, known from the end of the Middle Ages, were, it seems, an autochthonous group, Turkish-speaking but remaining Christian.

9 The gulf of Meğri (now Fethiye) is opposite Rhodes.

10 The importance of textiles was also a result of the development of the *qaysāriyya*s (organized assemblages of shops, warehouses and workshops in the great cities), which specialized in cloth, jewellery and other luxury goods.

11 The building of one caravanserai was even financed by a rich Armenian merchant. It has inscriptions in Arabic, Armenian and Syriac.

12 I cannot quite follow Osman Turan when he seems to think that there were some kinds of property dependent on taxes not on the landed basis, the eminent domain of the land remaining with the state. In those grants where (as in that to Kir Farīd) the amount of the expected revenue is specified in accordance with the official cadaster, it is merely a matter of stating explicitly the value of the grant in question. Only in the case of *iqṭā‘* is the land not really alienated, and this is explicitly distinguished in the texts from true property. It is likewise necessary to indicate the revenue of a *waqf*, but this does not imply the grant of the revenue alone.

13 Qazwīnī has a natural tendency to exaggerate the contrast; in any case the total in his time should certainly be understood as taking alienations into account.

14 The word *ikdīsh/ikdiş* corresponds to the Byzantine *Francopouli*, *Turcopouli* ('Turcopoli' of the *Gesta Francorum*), or the *basmules* of Frankish Greece.

15 The concept of the *ghāzī/gazi* is perhaps partly that of the Muslim historians rather than the Turcomans, who raided without any real religious ideology.

16 From his name it is possible that Theodore Lascaris was of Turkish descent.

17 Cahen has dealt with this aspect of the question elsewhere (cf. his article IḲṬĀ‘ in *The Encyclopaedia of Islam* (2nd edn), III, 1088–91), and has shown that the process of 'feudalization' (if one uses this word, which is anyhow somewhat inadequate) is always a process of disintegration, and does not correspond to the concept of the Seljukid state when it really possessed authority.

18 Two other inscriptions in Tokat, of 631/1233–34 and 648/1250–51 respectively, show a mausoleum which Abu'l-Qāsim 'Alī al-Ṭūsī was constructing for himself, and a bridge built by his son, the *amīr ispahsālār* Sayf al-Dīn Ḥamīd. Their family is elsewhere described as important in the city; however, the father also built at Kayseri, which he certainly did not hold, while at Tokat there was also building in 645/1247–48 by one Najm al-Dīn Yağıbasan (perhaps a junior Danişmendid) as well as others.

19 In the twelfth century Joscelin of Courtenay, the principal Frankish lord in the county of Edessa, was established in Tall Bāshir/Turbessel before becoming count of Edessa in 1119. After the loss of the city of Edessa in 1144, Turbessel was for several years the capital of the county. The fortress continued to play an important part under Muslim rule from 1151 until the Mongol invasion, and it was finally dismantled by Baybars.

20 Shihāb al-Dīn Yaḥyā al-Suhrawardī is styled *al-Maqtūl*, 'the Slain', because he was executed in Aleppo in 587/1191 by Saladin's order. He should not be confused with Shihāb al-Dīn 'Umar al-Suhrawardī (d. 632/1234), mentioned elsewhere in the book.

21 The death-date of Kay Khusraw is uncertain: Simon of St Quentin gives October 1145; *Tārīkh-i āl-i Saljūq*, mid-Rajab 643/early December 1245; the

Armenian chronicler Sempad, 1246. Inscriptions and coins of 644/1246–47 are divided between his name and that of his son, Kay Kāwūs, which suggests a date after the start of this year 19 May 1246, if one could be sure that his successor was proclaimed immediately.

22 The Hakkārī Yazīdīs normally lived in the mountains north-east of Mosul, but many of them served in the armies of the period. It is hard to believe that Sharaf al-Dīn was a son of Shaykh ʻAdī rather than a remoter descendant, if ʻAdī is indeed identical with the Sufi of this name, who died *c.* 557/1162.

23 For some years the coinage of Rūm continued to use the name of the Caliph al-Mustaʻṣim, killed by the Mongols in 656/1258; that of the ʻAbbasid caliph in Cairo is never used.

24 *Bitikçi*, a secretary and translator. Tuqu was the son of Ilge *noyan*, one of Hülegü's generals and the ancestor of the Jalayirids, a successor-dynasty to the *īlkhān*s.

25 ʻIzz al-Dīn Ibn Shaddād's account of this incident is translated in P.M. Holt, *Memoirs of a Syrian prince*, Wiesbaden, 1983, 92–3.

26 The embassy to Qalāwūn is the subject of an article by P.M. Holt, 'The Ilkhān Aḥmad's embassies to Qalāwūn: two contemporary accounts', *Bulletin of the School of Oriental and African Studies*, London, XLIX/1, 1986.

27 Shams al-Dīn Lākūshī was of unknown origin. He first appears in the entourage of the Sons of Kilavuz, a notable family of the emirs of Rūm, who were dependants of the *īlkhān*s. It seems that they were allotted the two parts of the realm of Rūm, which were tending to become traditional; but in fact they had little influence there, and did not long continue.

28 At Konya Geikhatu, although a pagan, was present at the usual Muslim Feast of Sacrifices.

29 This cannot mean the dynasty of the descendants of Çopan, as Aksarayi states that when Siyāwush seized the province, Ḥusām al-Dīn Alp Yürük fell fighting. Here he is in error as it is certain that Alp Yürük had been succeeded by his son Muẓaffar al-Dīn Yavlak Arslan at the latest when Masʻūd arrived, since it was Yavlak Arslan who greeted him. It is probable that Yavlak Arslan had also disappeared before 690/1291, and had been succeeded by Ḥusām al-Dīn Maḥmūd.

30 On the origins and early history of the Ottomans, see now Colin Imber, *The Ottoman Empire 1300–1481*, Istanbul, 1990.

31 Pegolotti also specifies that European textiles should be exported in a finished condition as the required dyestuffs were not available locally.

Appendices

APPENDIX 1: THE SELJUKID SULTANS OF RŪM

(a) List of the sultans

Note: After the first three rulers, each sultan has a double designation consisting of his honorific (Ar. *laqab*) ending in 'al-Dīn', i.e. 'of the Faith', and his personal name (Ar. *ism*). The *laqab* is always an Arabic phrase, while the *ism* may be Turkish (e.g. Kılıc Arslan), Persian (e.g. Kay Qubādh) or Arabic (e.g. Mas'ūd). Thus Kay Qubādh I bears the honorific 'Alā' al-Dīn, 'Loftiness of the Faith'.

	Accession
Süleyman I	473/1081
Kılıc Arslan I	485/1092
Shāhānshāh/Malik Shāh	502/1109
Rukn al-Dīn Mas'ūd I	510/1116
'Izz al-Dīn Kılıc Arslan II	551/1156
Ghiyāth al-Dīn Kay Khusraw I	588/1192 (first reign)
Rukn al-Dīn Süleyman II	593/1197
'Izz al-Dīn Kılıc Arslan III	600/1204
Ghiyāth al-Dīn Kay Khusraw I	601/1205 (second reign)
'Izz al-Dīn Kay Kāwūs I	608/1211
'Alā' al-Dīn Kay Qubādh I	616/1220
Ghiyāth al-Dīn Kay Khusraw II	634/1237
Battle of Kösedağ	*641/1243*
'Izz al-Dīn Kay Kāwūs II	644/1246
'Izz al-Dīn Kay Kāwūs II Rukn al-Dīn Kılıc Arslan IV	646/1248 (joint rulers)
'Izz al-Dīn Kay Kāwūs II Rukn al-Dīn Kılıc Arslan IV 'Alā' al-Dīn Kay Qubādh II	647/1249 (joint rulers)
Rukn al-Dīn Kılıc Arslan IV	655/1257
Ghiyāth al-Dīn Kay Khusraw III	663/1265
Ghiyāth al-Dīn Mas'ūd II	681/1282 (first reign)
'Alā' al-Dīn Kay Qubādh III	683/1284 (first reign)
Ghiyāth al-Dīn Mas'ūd II	683/1284 (second reign)
'Alā' al-Dīn Kay Qubādh III	692/1293 (second reign)
Ghiyāth al-Dīn Mas'ūd II	693/1294 (third reign)
'Alā' al-Dīn Kay Qubādh III	700/1301 (third reign)
Ghiyāth al-Dīn Mas'ūd II	702/1303 (fourth reign)
Ghiyāth al-Dīn Mas'ūd III	707/1307

(b) Genealogy of the Seljukid dynasty of Rūm

- Kutulmuş
  - Süleyman I
    - Kılıc Arslan I
      - Shāhānshāh/Malik-Shāh
      - Masʿūd I
        - Kılıc Arslan II
          - Kay Khusraw I
            - Kay Kāwūs I
            - Kay Qubādh I
              - Kay Khusraw II
                - Kay Kāwūs II
                  - Masʿūd II
                  - Farāmurz
                    - Kay Qubādh III
                      - Masʿūd III
                - Kılıc Arslan IV
                  - Kay Khusraw III
                - Kay Qubādh II
          - Süleyman II
            - Kılıc Arslan III

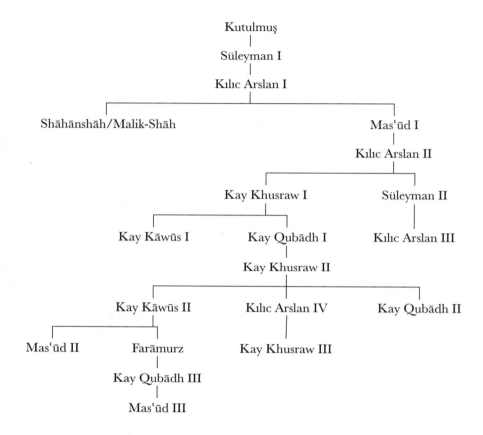

APPENDIX 2: THE BYZANTINE EMPERORS 1081–1328

	Accession
Alexius I Comnenus	1081
John II Comnenus	1118
Manuel I Comnenus	1143
Alexius II Comnenus	1180
Andronicus I Comnenus	1183
Isaac II Angelus	1185
Alexius III Angelus	1195
Isaac II Angelus / Alexius IV Angelus	1203 (joint rulers)
Alexius V Murtzuphlus	1204
Latin Empire of Constantinople 1204–61	
Byzantine Emperors of Nicaea to 1261; thereafter of Constantinople	
Theodore I Lascaris	1204
John III Ducas Vatatzes	1222
Theodore II Lascaris	1254
John IV Lascaris	1258 (nominal emperor)
Michael VIII Palaeologus	1259
Andronicus II Palaeologus	1282–1328

APPENDIX 3: THE ĪLKHĀNS

	Accession
Hülegü	1253 (start of western campaign)
Abaqa	1265
Tegüder (Aḥmad)	1282
Arghun	1284
Geikhatu	1291
Baidu	1295
Ghazan (Maḥmūd)	1295
Öljeitü	1304
Abū Saʿīd	1316–35

BIBLIOGRAPHICAL GUIDE

The following pages do not pretend to give a comprehensive bibliography of the reading material on Seljukid Anatolia. They are intended rather to indicate, first, the principal primary sources on the Seljukids of Rūm as noted by Cahen; second, modern works on various aspects of the subject.

Primary sources

The essential source for the fifth/eleventh century is *Mir'āt al-zamān* of Sibṭ Ibn al-Jawzī (d. 654/1256), which transmits earlier data for the years 448–79/1056–86; it is also valuable for the seventh/thirteenth century to 651/1253. The principal sources dating from the mid-sixth/twelfth century are a chronicle by al-ʿAẓīmī (d. after 556/1161), of which only an abridgement made in 538/1143–44 is extant; and the continuation of a chronicle of Damascus, *Dhayl Ta'rīkh Dimashq* by Ibn al-Qalānisī (d. 555/1160). Extracts from this covering the years from 490/1096–97 to 555/1160 were published in translation by H.A.R. Gibb, *The Damascus Chronicle of the Crusades*, London, 1967. Ibn al-Azraq al-Fāriqī (d. after 572/1176–77) was the author of a chronicle of Mayyāfāriqīn, *Ta'rīkh Mayyāfāriqīn wa-Āmid*. Material from lost Syrian local histories was used by Ibn Abī Ṭayyi' (d. between 625/1228 and 630/1233), extracts from whose universal chronicle were transmitted by Ibn al-ʿAdīm (d. 660/1262) in his history of Aleppo, *Zubdat al-ḥalab fī ta'rīkh Ḥalab* and his biographical dictionary, *Bughyat al-ṭalab fī ta'rīkh Ḥalab*. Arabic sources on the Zengid and Ayyubid periods are abundant. These include the universal chronicle, *al-Kāmil fī'l-ta'rīkh* of Ibn al-Athīr (d. 630/1233), a partisan of Nūr al-Dīn and the Zengids, and the biographies of Saladin by his advisers, *al-Nawādir al-sulṭāniyya* by Bahā' al-Dīn Ibn Shaddād (d. 632/1235), and *al-Fatḥ al-Qussī fī'l-fatḥ al-Qudsī* by al-Iṣfahānī (d. 597/1201). These are largely peripheral to the history of Rūm. Of more importance are the biographies of the last Khwarazm-Shāh by his secretary, Nasawī (d. 647/1249–50), *Sīrat al-Sulṭān Jalāl al-Dīn*; and of the Mamluk sultan, al-Ẓāhir Baybars. There are two of these, as well as a third giving a revisionist view of the sultan. The first is by his head of chancery, Muḥyī al-Dīn Ibn ʿAbd al-Ẓāhir (d. 692/1292), *al-Rawḍ al-zāhir fī sīrat al-Malik al-Ẓāhir*, the second by a more detached contemporary, ʿIzz al-Dīn Ibn Shaddād (d. 684/1285), the third by a writer of the next generation, Shāfiʿ b. ʿAlī. The travels of Ibn Baṭṭūṭa (d. 770/1368–69 or 779/1377), described in his *Riḥla* include a journey through Rūm some ninety years after Kösedağ, and he gives valuable information about the country in the age of the Turcoman principalities; the account appears in the second volume of H.A.R. Gibb's translation, *The travels of Ibn Baṭṭūṭa*, Cambridge, 1958. The encyclopaedic work compiled for the Egyptian chancery by Ibn Faḍlallāh al-'Umarī (d. 749/ 1349), *Masālik al-abṣār fī mamālik al-amṣār*, contains sections on Rūm and the Mongol states.

The sole important work in Persian which deals with the earlier seventh/ thirteenth century is that produced by Ibn Bībī (d. *c.* 683–84/1284–85), which covers the period 588–679/1192–1280. Besides the original form entitled *al-Awāmir al-'alā'iyya fī'l-umūr al-'Alā'iyya*, it exists in an anonymous epitome and a Turkish paraphrase. Later there are two Persian histories; one, known as *Tārīkh-i āl-i Saljūq* or *Saljūqnāma*, is by an anonymous citizen of Konya; the other, *Musāmarat al-akhbār wa-musāyarat al-akhyār*, was written by Aksarayi, a high official, in the early years of the eighth/fourteenth century. A seminal survey of the Anatolian sources is Mehmed Fuad Köprülü, *The Seljuks of Anatolia* (tr. and ed. Gary Leiser), Salt Lake City, 1992.

Byzantine sources for the eleventh century are the chronicles of John Scylitzes from 811 to 1057, and Michael Attaleiates, an eyewitness for the years 1034–79. On the period of the Comneni, there is the work of Nicephorus Bryennius, husband of Anna Comnena, herself the biographer and encomiast of her father, Alexius I Comnenus, in her *Alexiad* (translation by E.R.A. Sewter, *The Alexiad of Anna Comnena*, Harmondsworth, 1969). Further coverage of the twelfth century is provided by John Cinnamus and Nicetas Choniates; the latter's history ends in 1206, after the Latin conquest of Constantinople. The Empire of Nicaea is the subject of the contemporary George Acropolites (1217–82), who was followed chronologically by two other contemporary writers, George Pachymeres (1242–*c.* 1310), writing on the period 1255–1308, and Nicephorus Gregoras (1295–1359), the author of an encyclopaedic history running from 1204 to 1359.

Syriac historical writing of this period is important because the authors, although Christian, lived for the most part in Asia Minor. At the end of the twelfth century, the principal historian was Michael the Syrian, the Jacobite patriarch of Antioch. Approximately a century later, the Jacobite metropolitan of Aleppo, Abu'l-Faraj Ibn al-'Ibrī alias Bar Hebraeus, produced a Syriac universal history, which was published and translated by E.A. Wallis Budge, *The Chronography of Bar Hebraeus*, 2 vols, Oxford, 1932. An anonymous Syriac chronicle originating in Edessa was partially translated by A.S. Tritton and H.A.R. Gibb, 'The First and Second Crusades from an Anonymous Syriac Chronicle', *Journal of the Royal Asiatic Society*, 1933, 69–101.

Modern works

A number of Claude Cahen's other writings are relevant to the history of the Seljukids of Rūm. His earlier monumental study of the neighbouring Frankish principality of Antioch, *La Syrie du nord à l'époque des Croisades*, Paris, 1940, is valuable in this respect, not only for its occasional references to the Seljukids, but particularly for the detailed account of sources in the Introduction, and the geographical and topographical survey of the region, which overlaps the eastern territories of the Seljukid sultanate. Several of his numerous articles, including the important piece, 'La première pénétration turque en Asie-Mineure' (1946), are reprinted in his collection, *Turcobyzantina et Oriens Christianus*, London, 1974. The first two volumes of *A History of the Crusades* (General Editor, Kenneth M. Setton), Madison, Wirconsin, 1969, include several chapters written by him: I, v, 'The Turkish invasion: the Selchükids'; II, xix, 'The Turks in Iran and Anatolia before the Mongol invasions'; xxi, 'The Mongols and the Near East'. In addition to Cahen's work, one should mention a clear and useful survey by Osman Turan, 'Anatolia in the period of the Seljuks and the beyliks', *The Cambridge History of Islam*, I, Ch. 3. As well as outlining the background and political history of the Seljukids of Rūm, their culture and art history are examined by Tamara Talbot Rice in *The Seljuks in Asia Minor*, London, 1961.

A view of the history of the Turks in their homeland of Central Asia is provided by two important works: W. Barthold, *Turkestan down to the Mongol invasion* (2nd edn), London, 1958; and idem, *Histoire des Turcs d'Asie centrale*, Paris, 1945, published in the series *Initiation à l'Islam*, III. The Great Seljuks and the Mongols of the Ilkhanate, with necessarily some reference to the Seljukids of Rūm, are treated in *The Cambridge History of Iran*, vol. 5, Cambridge, 1958.

Mongol institutions and history are treated more widely by Bertold Spuler in *The Muslim World: A historical survey*, Part II: *The Mongol period*, Leiden, 1960; *The Mongols in history*, London, 1971; *History of the Mongols*, London, 1972. The last is a collection of source materials. To these should be added a more recent study, David Morgan, *The Mongols*, Oxford, 1986.

The neighbour and long-term adversary of the Rūm Seljukids was the Byzantine Empire. Its general history is covered in George Ostrogorsky, *History of the Byzantine state* (2nd edn), 1968. A valuable counterpart to Cahen's account of the Turkish conquest and settlement of Asia Minor is the examination of the Byzantine response is Speros Vryonis Jr, *The decline of medieval Hellenism in Asia Minor and the process of Islamization from the eleventh through the fifteenth century*, Berkeley, 1971. The standard collective work on the Byzantine Empire is *The Cambridge Medieval History*, vol. IV (2 Parts), Cambridge, 1966–67. The Mamluk Sultanate is treated in Robert Irwin, *The Middle East in the Middle Ages: The Early Mamluk Sultanate 1250–1382*, London, 1986 and P.M. Holt, *The Age of the Crusades*, London, 1986. Baybars's clash with the Mongols in Rūm is dealt with in Peter Thorau, *The Lion of Egypt*, London, 1987. The history of Cilician Armenia is outlined in *A History of the Crusades* (Setton), II, xviii, Sirarpie Der Nersessian, 'The kingdom of Cilician Armenia'; see also T.S.R. Boase (ed.), *The Cilician kingdom of Armenia*, Edinburgh and London, 1978.

Three very different works of reference should finally be mentioned. *The Encyclopaedia of Islam* (2nd edn), Leiden, 1960, contains numerous articles (by Cahen among others) on many of the principal persons, places and groups in Seljukid history. A convenient handbook of the tribal and other dynasties is provided by

C.E. Bosworth, *The new Islamic dynasties*, Edinburgh, 1996. Lastly, since so much concerning the history of the Seljukids has appeared in learned periodicals, recourse must be made to the essential guide to these, *Index Islamicus*. The first volume, compiled by the late J.D. Pearson, and covering the years 1906–55, was published at Cambridge in 1958. The latest pair of volumes in the series are *Index Islamicus 1981–1985* (ed. G.J. Roper), London 1991. The most helpful maps will be found in Donald Edgar Pitcher, *An historical geography of the Ottoman Empire*, Leiden, 1972, although the bulk of the work deals with a later period; the Index is useful for Byzantine/Turkish identification. William C. Brice, *An historical atlas of Islam*, Leiden, 1981, is also useful.

GLOSSARY

This glossary comprises chiefly important terms which are not explained on their first appearance. Numerous other terms with explanations appear in Parts Two and Four of the book.

Abbreviations: A Arabic   G Greek   M Mongolian   P Persian   T Turkish

Ağaceris (T. *ağac*, tree; *er*, man). A Turcoman group, perhaps particularly Turcomans of the forested regions.

Ahi T, *akhī* A. A member of an association, primarily of young men, linked to craft guilds, and influenced by the ideals of the *futuwwa* (below). The *ahi*s played at times a part in the urban politics of Anatolia. A popular synonym for *ahi* was *rind* (originally P) meaning rogue or debauchee.

Amīr A, *emir* T. Basically, a military commander but also part of the title of various offices, e.g. *amīr ākhūr*, master of the horse, constable (*kundestabl* is also found as a loan word from 'Frankish').

Amīr al-umarā', *amīr* of *amīrs*, i.e. commander-in-chief.

Beg. The Turkish equivalent of *amīr*; *beglerbegi* is the equivalent of *amīr al-umarā'*.

Atabeg T. (*ata*, father) means a *beg* acting as the guardian of an infant ruler.

Çaşnigir T, *chāshnīgīr* P. Taster; a high officer-holder of the royal household.

Catholicos G. The head of the (Georgian) Church.

Çift T from *juft* P. Literally, a yoke; in Turkish usage, an area of cultivable land forming a unit for taxation.

Dihqān P. A village headman.

Divan T, *dīwān* A. Among a range of meanings, the chief are a government office or department, and a literary anthology.

Faqīh A. A specialist in *fiqh*, Islamic jurisprudence.

Fatwā A. An authoritative opinion on a point of Islamic law, delivered by a *muftī*.

Futuwwa A, *fütüvvet* T. A popular movement linked with the craft guilds and the *ahi*s (above), and remotely descended from the courtly *futuwwa* originated by the Caliph al-Nāṣir (575–622/1180–1225).

Gazi T, *ghāzī* A. A fighter in the Holy War (see *jihād*); in practice, often a raider over the frontier of Islam.

Ḥājib A. A chamberlain, and as such a high (military) office-holder of the royal court. *Ḥājib al-ḥujjāb*, head chamberlain.

Han T. *khān* A. A caravanserai offering secure accommodation for merchants and other travellers.

Ikdiş T, *ikdīsh* A. Originally signifying a mule or other half-breed, in Anatolia the term came to mean a prosperous urban group, perhaps of mixed ethnic origin, who served as a militia under an *ikdişbaşı*.

Imām A. Basically the leader in prayer of a group of Muslims. Among the Shīʿa, the term has the specific meaning of the descendants of ʿAlī and Fāṭima, the Prophet's daughter, who were the divinely guided and infallible leaders of the Muslim community.

Iqṭāʿ, A. Often inaccurately translated 'fief', this was strictly a grant of revenue arising from land to a military or administrative office-holder, the *muqṭaʿ*, to whom quasi-feudal privileges over the land and its inhabitants tended to accrue.

Ispahsālār P. Commander-in-chief.

Jāndār P. The royal bodyguard.

Jihād A. Warfare for the expansion or defence of Islam. A participant on the *jihād* was styled a *mujāhid* or *gazi/ghāzī* (above).

Jizya A. Poll-tax paid by *dhimmīs* (Jews and Christians) living permanently in Muslim states.

Kharāj A from G. Primarily the land-tax paid by Muslims on some categories of land; sometimes used in a wider sense.

Khawāja P. A title implying respectable status.

Khuṭba A. The sermon given at Friday prayers in the mosque by the *khaṭīb*. It includes a mention of the ruler, and is thus an attribute of sovereignty.

Kōtwāl Hindi. The governor of a town or citadel.

Lâla T. The tutor in charge of a young prince.

Madrasa A. A school for higher Islamic learning, especially of law.

Malik A. Primarily a king. The root *mlk* signifies possession and hence primacy. Related terms are *malik al-umarāʾ* (variant of *amīr al-umarāʾ*), signifying commander-in-chief; *malik al-sawāḥil*, governor of the (southern Anatolian) coastlands; *milk*, freehold (allodial) tenure of land; *mamlūk*, literally something possessed, specifically a military slave.

Mardaites. Known in Arabic as *Jarājima*, the Mardaites were a Christian community in the Amanus mountains, north of Antioch, long a frontier region between the Muslims of Syria and Byzantine territory.

Mirî T from A. The sultan's personal treasury.

Muḥtasib A. An official theoretically responsible for the promotion of good and prohibition of evil – the duty known as *ḥisba*. In practice he was mainly responsible for the supervision of markets.

Muzāriʿ A. A peasant cultivator.

Nāʾib A. In general, a deputy; specifically the sultan's deputy, e.g. during his absence. His office is styled *niyābat al-salṭana*.

Noyan M. A Mongol general.

Pervane T from P *parwāna*, moth. The sultan's personal assistant, who conveyed the royal orders and instructions to ministers and officials.

Qāḍī A. An Islamic judge.

Qaṭīʿa (pl. *qaṭāʾiʿ*) A. In early Islam, land from the public domain assigned to individuals and subject to the payment of tithe (*ʿushr*). From the same root *qtʿ*,

signifying cutting, are derived *iqṭāʿ* (above) and *muqāṭaʿa*, the fixed sum paid by a tax-farmer.

Serleşker T, *sarlashkar* P (*sar*, head; *lashkar*, army). Commander-in-chief.

Tamgha M. A Mongol tax on commercial transactions.

Ṭashtdār P. The keeper of the (royal) washing basin; a high office-holder of the royal household.

Uc T. The debatable lands of the frontier regions between the Turks and the Byzantines.

Vezir T, *wazīr* A. The sultan's chief minister.

Waqf A. An endowment, usually of land, in perpetuity for pious causes. The deed of endowment is termed *waqfiyya*.

Zakāt A. Obligatory alms paid by Muslims and forming one of the bases ('pillars') of Islam. This came to be equated with the *ʿushr* or tithe payable on some categories of land which were not liable to *kharāj* (above).

Zāwiya A. A building, usually containing the tomb of a holy man, often the centre of religious and mystical (Ṣūfī) teaching.

INDEX OF PERSONS

INDEX OF PLACES

Note: Byzantine place names are generally followed by their Turkish equivalents; Turkish names with Byzantine equivalents prefixed by B.